UNITED STATES ARMY IN WORLD WAR II

The War in the Pacific

GUADALCANAL:
THE FIRST OFFENSIVE

by

John Miller, jr.

BARNES
&NOBLE
BOOKS
NEW YORK

This edition published by Barnes & Noble, Inc.
by arrangement with W. S. Konecky Associates, Inc.

1995 Barnes & Noble Books

First printed in 1949 by The Center of Military History
United States Army, Washington, DC

Printed and bound in the United States

ISBN: 1-56619-982-4

M 10 9 8 7 6 5 4 3 2 1

. . . to Those Who Served

UNITED STATES ARMY IN WORLD WAR II

Kent Roberts Greenfield, General Editor

Advisory Committee

James P. Baxter
President, Williams College

William T. Hutchinson
University of Chicago

Henry S. Commager
Columbia University

S. L. A. Marshall
Detroit News

Douglas S. Freeman
Richmond News Leader

E. Dwight Salmon
Amherst College

Pendleton Herring
Social Science Research Council

Col. Thomas D. Stamps
United States Military Academy

John D. Hicks
University of California

Charles H. Taylor
Harvard University

Walter L. Wright
Princeton University

Historical Division, SSUSA

Maj. Gen. Harry J. Malony, Chief

Chief Historian
Chief, World War II Group
Editor-in-Chief
Chief Cartographer

Kent Roberts Greenfield
Col. Allison R. Hartman
Hugh Corbett
Wsevolod Aglaimoff

Foreword

In publishing the history of combat operations the Department of the Army has three objectives. The first is to provide the Army itself with an accurate and timely account of its varied activities in directing, organizing, and employing its forces for the conduct of war—an account which will be available to the service schools and to individual members of the Armed Services who wish to extend their professional reading. The second objective is to offer the thoughtful citizen material for a better understanding of the basic problems of war and the manner in which these problems were met, thus augmenting his understanding of national security. The third objective is to accord a well-earned recognition to the devoted work and grim sacrifices of those who served.

No claim is made that the series constitutes a final history. Most of the material has been gathered from the observations and research of trained historians who, while in uniform, were attached to the headquarters of larger units engaged in the campaigns about which the histories are written. These historians made use of all official records, of interviews with both officers and enlisted men who took part in the action, and of captured enemy records. They have scrupulously weighed the evidence in accordance with the Chief of Staff's directive that Army histories must present a full and factual account, thoroughly documented and completely objective. The authors of the volumes in the series were carefully selected from among trained civilian historians; many of them were formerly historical officers in the wartime Army. They are under no restrictions in their work except those imposed by the requirements of national security and by the standards of historical scholarship.

The level on which the volumes are written necessarily varies. In accounts of campaigns during which many large units moved rapidly over extensive areas, detailed consideration of small-unit action is not practicable. Such a volume as *Guadalcanal,* on the other hand, recounts the activities of a comparatively small number of units operating in a restricted area; it has thus been possible to carry the narrative down to the level of companies, platoons, and even individuals. Since this is a field recognized as of great importance but one in which available literature is very meager, the present volume adds material which should prove of much value to prospective commanders of lower units.

The Department of the Army gratefully acknowledges the co-operation of the U. S. Navy, including the U. S. Marine Corps, and the U. S. Air Force in making available such of their records and research facilities as were pertinent to the preparation of this volume.

HARRY J. MALONY
Maj. Gen., U. S. A.
Chief, Historical Division

Washington, D. C.
3 August 1948

Preface

"The successes of the South Pacific Force," wrote Admiral Halsey in 1944, "were not the achievements of separate services or individuals but the result of whole-hearted subordination of self-interest by all in order that one successful 'fighting team' could be created."* The history of any South Pacific campaign must deal with this "fighting team," with all United States and Allied services. The victory on Guadalcanal can be understood only by an appreciation of the contribution of each service. No one service won the battle. The most decisive engagement of the campaign was the air and naval Battle of Guadalcanal in mid-November 1942, an engagement in which neither Army nor Marine Corps ground troops took any direct part.

This volume attempts to show the contribution of all services to the first victory on the long road to Tokyo. It does not describe all ground, air, and naval operations in detail but it does attempt, by summary when necessary, to show the relationship between air, ground, and surface forces in modern warfare.

Guadalcanal: The First Offensive rests upon somewhat different sources from most other volumes in the Pacific series of U. S. ARMY IN WORLD WAR II. The War Department's historical program had not yet been established in August 1942 when the Solomon Islands were invaded by the Allies. No historians accompanied the Marine or Army divisions to Guadalcanal with the mission of preparing thorough and detailed histories of the campaign. The interviews of whole companies and critiques of actions that were conducted by Army and Marine historians in later campaigns were never conducted on Guadalcanal. Interviews with individual officers and men were conducted by theater and War Department historians long after the fighting was over, but by that time memory was none too fresh. As a result it has not been possible to analyze the actions of small units on Guadalcanal as completely as in other volumes in the Pacific series.

* Admiral William F. Halsey, Jr., Narrative Account of the South Pacific Campaign (September 1944), p. 14.

The official records for the Guadalcanal campaign, upon which this volume is based, are often sparse and inadequate. The Army units which served on the island were usually sent there in piecemeal fashion, one regiment or battalion at a time. Army and Marine staff procedures on Guadalcanal were of necessity extremely simple and informal. Most staff business was conducted orally, for the area held by American troops was so small that all headquarters were in close proximity, obviating the immediate necessity for extensive records. Most staff officers, working in headquarters which were seriously undermanned, often held dual positions and carried a tremendous burden of work. They had neither the time nor the facilities to maintain extensive files. In consequence, full Army divisional records do not exist. Headquarters, U. S. Army Forces in the South Pacific Area (USAFISPA), which had just been activated when the first landings were made in Guadalcanal, also suffered from a chronic shortage of staff officers and clerks. Its own records for the period, therefore, are not complete, and it never received full records from the units on Guadalcanal.

Enemy records, though now fairly extensive, are by no means complete. It is expected that new information will continue to come to light.

A history of the Guadalcanal campaign was first begun in 1944, more than a year after its close, by Maj. Frederick P. Todd and Capt. Louis Morton, then members of the Historical Section, USAFISPA. A short manuscript dealing with ground, air, and surface action was prepared first. A more detailed study was begun later in 1944, but the lack of records, coupled with the necessity for preparing other operational histories and an administrative history of USAFISPA, prevented its completion. Both the short manuscript and the incomplete longer manuscript were forwarded to the Historical Division of the War Department.

Preparation of this volume was begun after the conclusion of hostilities. By 1946 virtually all the existing records of Army units had been filed in the Adjutant General's office; records of the Joint and Combined Chiefs of Staff, of the Operations Division, WDGS, and of the Navy had been opened to War Department historians. A wider range of sources was available to me than had been available to the South Pacific or earlier War Department historians.

My debts of gratitude are too numerous to make it possible for me to express my thanks publicly to every person who has assisted in the preparation of this volume. Some contributions, however, have been so important that they merit particular mention.

To Dr. Louis Morton, now Chief of the Pacific Section of the Historical Division, under whose immediate direction this book was written, are due my thanks for his careful reading of every chapter, and for his sound counsel on the many problems of organization and content presented by such a volume. Dr. Kent Roberts Greenfield, Chief Historian of the Department of the Army, was a strong support during the period of preparation of the volume and offered many valuable suggestions which were adopted. Maj. Gen. Harry J. Malony, Chief of the Historical Division, and Lt. Col. Allen F. Clark, Jr., Executive Officer, both showed a keen appreciation of the problems of the historian, and made it possible to utilize all the sources in the Department of National Defense bearing on the subject.

The manuscript was prepared for publication under the direction of Col. Allison R. Hartman, Chief of the World War II Group of the Historical Division, assisted by Miss Edith M. Poole and Miss Grace T. Waibel. Mr. Wsevolod Aglaimoff, Chief Cartographer of the Historical Division, drew the layouts for the excellent maps, all prepared under his supervision, which appear in this volume. Capt. Robert L. Bodell selected the photographs from Army, Navy, Marine Corps, and Air Force files. Mr. George R. Powell and Mrs. Miriam J. Meyer assisted in solving statistical problems, and prepared the strength table on page 219; Maj. Charles F. Byars prepared the list of Army units serving in the Guadalcanal campaign which appears in the Appendix. Mr. W. Brooks Phillips prepared the index. Final editing was the responsibility of Mr. Hugh Corbett, Editor-in-Chief of the Historical Division.

The documents in the files of the Army, Air Force, Navy, and Marine Corps bearing on the Guadalcanal campaign are numerous and widely diffused. The generous assistance of other historians and archivists in locating these documents made possible the completion of the volume in slightly over two years. The General Reference Section of the Historical Division, under the direction of Mr. Israel Wice, procured for me many documents from the files of all the armed forces. Miss Alice M. Miller, Maj. Darrie H. Richards, and Mr. Joseph B. Russell furnished me with the documents that explain the strategic direction of the Pacific War. Miss Thelma K. Yarborough, Miss Margaret Emerson, and Miss Clyde Hillyer provided the bulk of the sources of information on the operations of Army units on Guadalcanal. Capt. John W. McElroy, USNR, and Miss Loretta I. MacCrindle of the Office of Naval Records and Library guided me to the naval documents relating to the Guadalcanal campaign. Lt. Col.

Robert D. Heinl, Jr., USMC, Mr. John L. Zimmerman and Mr. Joel D. Thacker of the Historical Section, Division of Public Information, Headquarters, U. S. Marine Corps, furnished me with a great deal of information on Marine Corps operations and units, and made Marine Corps records available to me.

I wish also to express my gratitude to Whittlesey House for permission to quote from *Admiral Halsey's Story*.

To Miss Martha J. Daniel, Mrs. Wynona H. Haydon, Miss Ann Pasternack, and Mrs. Laura M. Whitmire are due my thanks for their careful typing of the manuscript.

Responsibility for the deficiencies of this book is entirely mine.

Washington, D. C.
3 August 1948   JOHN MILLER, JR.

Contents

Charts

Maps

Illustrations

xvi

GUADALCANAL:
THE FIRST OFFENSIVE

The Strategic Decision

On 2 July 1942 the U. S. Joint Chiefs of Staff ordered Allied forces in the Pacific to mount a limited offensive to halt the Japanese advance toward the line of communications from the United States to Australia and New Zealand. At the same time the United States was committed to a program for building up forces in Great Britain to launch an offensive in Europe in 1942 or 1943. There were then available so few warships, transports, and cargo ships, so few trained troops, so few weapons and supplies, that any offensive in the Pacific, for which the United States would have to provide most of the forces, would necessarily be limited in scale. Yet it was essential to halt the Japanese who were then moving ever nearer to the flank of the tenuous line of communications. The Joint Chiefs' decision of 2 July led to the long, grim struggle for the possession of Guadalcanal, an island in the remote British Solomon Islands Protectorate which was not specifically named in the orders dispatched by the Joint Chiefs.

Allied Organization and Missions in the Pacific Theater

The decision to mount a limited offensive in the Pacific was a logical corollary to earlier strategic decisions. The highest political and military authorities of the United States and Great Britain had decided to defeat Germany before concentrating on Japan. The world had been divided into spheres of primary military responsibility, and the United States assumed responsibility for directing the war in the Pacific. Subject to decisions of the U. S.–British Combined Chiefs of Staff on global strategy, the strategic direction of the war in the Pacific was assigned to the U. S. Joint Chiefs of Staff. In March 1942 they had agreed to assemble forces in Britain during that year to mount an offensive in Europe at the earliest possible moment. For the time being, Allied strategy in the Pacific was to be limited to containing the Japanese with the forces then committed or allotted.[1] Concentration against Germany, it was believed, would give the most effective support to the Soviet Union and keep the forces in the British Isles

[1] See JCS 23, Strategic Deployment of Land, Sea, and Air Forces of the United States, 14 Mar 42.

from being inactive, while containment of the Japanese would save Australia and New Zealand from enemy conquest. The two dominions, important to the Allies as sources of supply, as essential economic and political units of the British Commonwealth of Nations, and in the future to become bases for offensive operations, would have to be held.[2] The implications of this decision were clear. If Australia and New Zealand were to be held, then the line of communications from the United States to those dominions would have to be held. Forces to defend the Allied bases along the line, including New Caledonia, the Fijis, and Samoa, had already been sent overseas. There were not enough ships, troops, weapons, or supplies, however, to develop each base into an impregnable fortress. The bases were designed to be mutually supporting, and each island had been allotted forces sufficient to hold off an attacking enemy long enough to permit air and naval striking forces to reach the threatened position from adjacent bases, including the Hawaiian Islands and Australia.[3]

For the conduct of operations in the Pacific, two separate commands, the Southwest Pacific Area and the Pacific Ocean Areas, embracing almost the entire ocean and its land areas, were designated by the Joint Chiefs of Staff with the approval of the President on 30 March. (*Map I*)* The Southwest Pacific Area (SWPA) included the Philippine Islands, the South China Sea, the Gulf of Siam, the Netherlands East Indies (except Sumatra), the Solomon Islands, Australia, and the waters to the south. The post of Supreme Commander of Allied forces in this vast area was given to Gen. Douglas MacArthur (CINCSWPA), who had just reached Australia from the Philippines.

The even vaster Pacific Ocean Areas included the remainder of the Pacific Ocean west of the North American Continent except for one area—the Southeast Pacific Area, the western boundary of which ran from the western Mexican–Guatemalan boundary southwest to the 11th parallel of north latitude, to longitude 110 degrees West, and thence due south along the 110th meridian. The Pacific Ocean Areas (POA) included three subordinate Areas— the North, Central, and South Pacific Areas. The North Pacific Area included all the Pacific north of latitude 42 degrees North. The Central Pacific Area, embracing the Hawaiian Islands, Christmas, Palmyra, Johnston, most of the Japanese-held Gilberts, and the Japanese-held Marshalls, Carolines, Marianas, Formosa, in addition to most of the Japanese home islands, lay between the

*Maps numbered in Roman are placed in inverse order inside the back cover.
[2] JCS Minutes, 6th Meeting, 16 Mar 42.
[3] See JPS 21/7, Defense Island Bases along the Line of Communications between Hawaii and Australia, 18 April 42. (JCS 48 has the same title.)

equator and latitude 42 degrees North. South of the equator, west of longitude 110 degrees West, and east of the Southwest Pacific was the South Pacific Area, which included thousands of islands and more than one million square miles of ocean. New Zealand, New Caledonia, and the New Hebrides, Santa Cruz, Fiji, Samoan, Tongan, Cook, and Society Islands all lay in the South Pacific.

Admiral Chester W. Nimitz, Commander in Chief, U. S. Pacific Fleet (CINCPAC), was appointed Commander in Chief of all Allied forces in the Pacific Ocean Areas (CINCPOA) except those forces responsible for the land defense of New Zealand, which were controlled by the New Zealand Chiefs of Staff. Admiral Nimitz, with headquarters at Pearl Harbor, was to command the Central and North Pacific Areas directly, but was ordered to appoint a subordinate who would command the South Pacific Area.

Both General MacArthur and Admiral Nimitz were responsible to the Joint Chiefs of Staff in Washington. Gen. George C. Marshall, Chief of Staff of the U. S. Army, acted as executive for the Joint Chiefs of Staff for the Southwest Pacific Area. Admiral Ernest J. King, Commander in Chief, U. S. Fleet, was executive for the Joint Chiefs of Staff for the Pacific Ocean Areas.

The missions assigned to MacArthur and Nimitz were virtually the same. They were to hold those island positions between the United States and Australia which were essential to the security of the line of communications and to the support of air, surface, and amphibious operations against the Japanese; to contain the Japanese within the Pacific; to support the defense of North America; to protect essential sea and air communications; and to prepare major amphibious offensives, the first of which were to be delivered from the South and Southwest Pacific Areas. Each area was to support its neighbor's operations. When task forces from the Pacific Ocean Areas operated beyond their boundaries, either the Combined or the Joint Chiefs of Staff would co-ordinate their operations with those of other forces.[4]

Japanese Advances

The speed and breadth of the Japanese offensive which opened on 7 December 1941 had rendered ineffective the Allied organization of the Pacific which preceded the establishment of the Pacific Ocean and Southwest Pacific Areas. From December 1941 until May of the following year, the Japanese had been

[4] JCS, Directive to General MacArthur and Admiral Nimitz, 30 Mar 42. The correct title of POA was actually Pacific Ocean Area, but because the POA included three Areas, the plural will be used.

expanding their empire; they defeated the scanty Allied forces opposing them and established a perimeter of bases to guard their newly-won gains. When Rabaul, a small town on Gazelle Peninsula on New Britain in the Bismarck Archipelago, fell on 23 January 1942, the Japanese had gained a major objective. (*Map II*) Rabaul lay just 1,170 nautical miles southeast of the Japanese bases in the Palau Islands, and 640 miles south of Truk in the Carolines. Easily defended, Rabaul possessed the best harbor in the entire archipelago as well as excellent sites for airfields. A key base for the Japanese effort to dominate both eastern New Guinea and the Solomon Islands, it was to be the focus of the Allied war effort in that area for two years. The coast of New Guinea lies 440 nautical miles southwest of Rabaul, and the center of the north coast of Guadalcanal Island in the British Solomon Islands Protectorate is only 565 nautical miles southeast of Rabaul. Since Japanese bombers from Rabaul could easily attack both areas, the Japanese were well situated for a push to the south. They could cover their advance by constructing forward fighter plane bases as they advanced. No island in the New Guinea–New Britain–New Ireland–Solomons area lies beyond fighter plane range of its nearest neighbor. The Japanese could advance step by step along the island bases covered by aircraft throughout their entire advance. Even if the Japanese commanders had ventured to seize bases beyond the range of their aircraft, they probably could have done so easily, for only a handful of aircraft and Australian soldiers were defending the New Guinea–Bismarck–Solomons area. The Japanese, fortunately, elected to move southward cautiously and deliberately.

After capturing Rabaul the Japanese garrisoned the Duke of York Islands in Saint George's Channel between New Britain and New Ireland. They also moved to New Ireland itself and built an air base at Kavieng, 130 nautical miles northwest of Rabaul. Having covered their rear, they began to move south in a series of amphibious advances which, had they succeeded completely, would have encircled the Coral Sea. The first efforts were directed against New Guinea. The Japanese did not move into the Solomons until later. The Allied base at Port Moresby on the south coast of the Papuan Peninsula of New Guinea was their main objective. Instead of taking it at one blow in early 1942 and developing it before the Allies could retaliate, the Japanese moved gradually. They occupied Gasmata off the south coast of New Britain in February 1942, then crossed to New Guinea and took Lae and Salamaua in March.[5]

---

[5] U.S. Strategic Bombing Survey, *The Allied Campaign Against Rabaul* (Washington, D.C., 1946), p. 7. U. S. Strategic Bombing Survey will be cited hereafter as USSBS.

They first moved into the Solomons in March 1942.(*Map III*)On 13 March naval landing and construction forces took Buka, the northernmost island in the Solomons, 170 nautical miles southeast of Rabaul, and built a fighter strip there. Additional forces began building fighter strips at Buin and near-by Kahili on the south coast of Bougainville, 270 nautical miles from Rabaul. Others were begun at Kieta on the east coast and in the Shortland Islands.

The Japanese also assembled a carrier task force and an amphibious force at Truk to attack Port Moresby. A detachment of the amphibious force landed on Tulagi in the Solomons on 3 May. The main body of the Japanese force, however, failed to capture Port Moresby. Intercepted by Allied naval and air forces in the Coral Sea in May, the Japanese lost one aircraft carrier and were forced to withdraw. Allied forces also struck at Tulagi during the Coral Sea engagement.

The Japanese then turned their attention to Midway and the Aleutian Islands. Orders issued by *Imperial General Headquarters* during the opening phases of the Coral Sea battle had directed the Commander in Chief of the *Combined Fleet* to "cooperate" with the Army in invading Midway and the Aleutians.[6] These attacks were to be followed by invasions, in co-operation with the *17th Army,* of "strategic points around the NEW CALEDONIA, FIJI, and SAMOA Islands" and the destruction of "important enemy bases," to effect the isolation of Australia.[7]

In June the Japanese obtained a foothold in the Aleutians, but their main effort at the same time against Midway did not succeed. Four of their aircraft carriers were sunk off Midway and the Japanese withdrew without attempting to land on the island. This engagement, so disastrous for the enemy, did much to restore the naval balance in the Pacific and enabled the Allies to take the initiative.

On 11 July *Imperial General Headquarters* canceled the orders which had called for invasions of Midway, New Caledonia, Fiji, and Samoa.[8] But at Tulagi the Japanese had already built a seaplane base which had originally been designed to support the attack on Port Moresby. The tiny island of Tulagi, seat of government of the British Solomon Islands Protectorate, dominates Tulagi Harbor, the best ship anchorage in the southern Solomons, and lies 560 nautical

---

[6] *Imperial General Headquarters,* Navy Stf Sec, Ord No. 18, 5 May 42, in ATIS, SCAP, Doc No. 14016 B.

[7] *Ibid.,* Ord. No. 19, 18 May 42; Japanese Studies in World War II, XXXIX., *17th Army* Opns, I, (n.p.). A copy is filed with the Hist Div, SSUSA.

[8] ATIS, SCAP, Doc No. 14016 B, Ord. No. 20, 11 Jul 42.

BUKA ISLAND AIRFIELD *was built by the Japanese in the spring of 1942 as one of a chain of fighter strips permitting their aircraft to "island hop" in the drive to the south.*

miles from Espiritu Santo in the British–French condominium of the New Hebrides. Noumea in New Caledonia is 800 miles southeast of Tulagi, and the Fijis are 1,000 miles away.

Even before the Japanese orders directing the attacks against New Caledonia, the Fijis, and Samoa were canceled, the Japanese commander at Tulagi had reconnoitered the island of Guadalcanal, twenty miles away. Perhaps on his own initiative he decided to build an airfield near the mouth of the Lunga River in the center of the north coast.[9] This airfield, which was intended to provide a base for sixty naval planes, was to have been completed by 15 August.[10] If the Japanese intended to continue their advance,[11] the next logical step would certainly have been a series of moves through the New Hebrides toward the Fijis, Samoa, and New Caledonia.[12] The seaplane base at Tulagi and the airfield under construction on Guadalcanal did not yet directly threaten the Allied South Pacific air route, but they portended a serious threat.

There was no unified Japanese command controlling operations in the eastern New Guinea–Bismarck–Solomons area. Rabaul was to become the site of separate Army and Navy commands, each of which was responsible to separate higher headquarters. The initial landings in the Solomons had been effected under naval command, but ground operations in the Solomons and eastern New Guinea later came under control of the *17th Army,* headquarters of which were established at Rabaul in July 1942. Later in July the headquarters of the *Southeastern Fleet* was also established at Rabaul. This fleet controlled the *8th Fleet,* the *11th Air Fleet,* and the *8th, 14th, 1st,* and *7th Base Forces* at Rabaul, New Ireland, Buin, and Lae, respectively.[13]

The Japanese advances into the Bismarcks, New Guinea, and the Solomons had generally not been strongly opposed, and the few Australian troops had been killed or driven out of the Bismarcks and Solomons. The Allies, fortunately, had been able to keep watch on the enemy's movements. The Australian Government, long before World War II, had created the Coastwatching Service as an integral part of the Directorate of Naval Intelligence of the Royal

[9] USSBS, *Interrogations of Japanese Officials* (OPNAV–P–03–100, 2 vols.), I, 68.

[10] GHQ, SCAP, ATIS, MIS: Hist Rpts, Naval Opns: Rpt Battle Savo, 8 Aug 42 (Doc No. 15685, 15 Mar 46). ATIS reports and translations are in the MIS Library, Dept of the Army.

[11] See USSBS, *Interrogations,* I, 70; II, 474, 524; *Allied Campaign Against Rabaul,* pp. 46, 87.

[12] Maj Gen Shuicho Miyazaki (former CofS, *17th Army*) Personal Account of His Experience during the Solomons Campaign, p. 5. Miyazaki and other *17th Army* officers were interrogated, at the author's request, by G–3 AFPAC historians and ATIS, SCAP, in Tokyo in 1946. Miyazaki also proffered his personal account which, together with the interrogations, is in the files of the Hist Div, SSUSA.

[13] *Allied Campaign Against Rabaul,* pp. 43, 87; *17th Army* Opns, I.

Australian Navy. The coastwatchers, most of whom were former planters and civil servants who had lived in the islands for years, remained behind the Japanese lines after the invasions, and radioed reports on the enemy's troop, ship, and plane movement to the Directorate of Naval Intelligence at Townsville, Australia.[14]

When the Japanese moved to Guadalcanal, coastwatchers hidden in the mountains reported the fact to Allied headquarters in Australia. This information was transmitted to the Joint Chiefs of Staff in Washington on 6 July 1942.[15] But even before the Japanese were known to have begun their airstrip on Guadalcanal, and before *Imperial General Headquarters* canceled the orders to invade New Caledonia, Samoa, and the Fijis, the Joint Chiefs of Staff had issued orders for the limited offensive in the area to protect the line of communications to Australia.

The Problem of Command and Strategy

With the Japanese threatening to cut the line of communications to Australia, or to attack Australia directly, the American officers responsible for the conduct of the Pacific war had agreed that an offensive should be mounted to end the threat. Before the Joint Chiefs of Staff could issue orders for the attack, they had to settle serious problems regarding command and the employment of forces.

The Army's Plan

As early as 8 May, after the Japanese defeat in the Coral Sea, General MacArthur was preparing plans for an offensive. He pointed out that the Japanese victories in the Philippines and Burma would free at least two infantry divisions and additional aircraft, and that the enemy forces in Malaya and the Netherlands East Indies might also be moved forward. Still able to move unhindered along interior lines of communication, the enemy could attack New Guinea and the line of communications between the United States and Australia. To prevent these attacks, MacArthur wished to take the offensive, but he desired that his naval forces first be strengthened by aircraft carriers, and that more planes and troops be added to his air and ground forces.[16]

---

[14] See Commander Eric A. Feldt, RAN, *The Coastwatchers* (Melbourne, 1946).

[15] Rad, CINC SWPA to WDCSA, CM–IN–2068, 6 Jul 42. All times and dates given in this volume are local time except those in citations in the South Pacific War Diary. The latter bear Greenwich Civil Time.

[16] Rad, CINC SWPA to WDCSA, CM–IN–2333, 8 May 42.

At the same time Admiral Nimitz was contemplating the possibility of attacking Tulagi in the Solomons, a project which found favor with Admiral King. Admiral Nimitz first suggested using a Marine raider battalion for the attack, but Admiral King and Generals Marshall and MacArthur all agreed, on 1 June, that one raider battalion would be too small a landing force.[17] General MacArthur's plans envisaged a larger operation than a raid. Believing that one Japanese regiment was then holding Tulagi but was not thoroughly dug in, and that one division was stationed at Rabaul, he desired to mount a large-scale offensive against the Solomons and New Britain. He suggested that as more troops became available, the South Pacific forces might profitably move farther forward into the Loyalty, Santa Cruz, and New Hebrides Islands.[18]

After the great Japanese defeat off Midway on 3–4 June 1942, General MacArthur, on 8 June, again suggested taking the offensive at an early date, with the New Britain–New Ireland area as the objective. Available trained troops in the Southwest Pacific Area then included the 32d and 41st U. S. Infantry Divisions and the 7th Australian Division. These divisions, however, were not equipped or trained for amphibious operations. They could support an amphibious attack by moving ashore once a beachhead had been taken, but they could not take a beachhead themselves. The objectives of the offensive lay beyond range of U. S. fighter aircraft. Close air support would have to be provided by aircraft carriers, but none were assigned to the Southwest Pacific Area. General MacArthur therefore requested that one trained amphibious division and a suitable naval task force be made available at the earliest possible date. If these forces seized the New Britain–New Ireland area, the Japanese would be forced back to Truk.[19]

At the same time the Joint Chiefs of Staff were considering the possibility of persuading the British to use the Eastern Fleet against Timor, or against the Andaman and Nicobar Islands in the Bay of Bengal, in co-ordination with the offensive effort of the United States.[20]

General Marshall, who favored placing the prospective offensive under General MacArthur's command, explained his views to Admiral King on 12 June. He believed that an attack designed to retake eastern New Guinea and

[17] Rad, GHQ SWPA to OPD, 1 Jun 42. OPD 381 PTO Sec. II (5–28–42); Rad, WDCSA to CINC SWPA, CM–OUT–0095, 1 Jun 42.

[18] Memo, WDCSA for COMINCH, 6 Jun 42, sub: Early Attack on Japanese Adv Bases. OPD 381 SWPA Sec. II.

[19] Rad, GHQ SWPA to WDCSA, CM–IN–2264, 8 Jun 42.

[20] COMINCH to COMNAVEU, 0046 of 10 Jun 42. OPD 381 SWPA Sec. I.

New Britain could be mounted in early July. If the attack succeeded, it might be followed by a raid on Truk. The 1st Marine Division, part of which was soon to land at Wellington, New Zealand, could make an initial amphibious assault against the Japanese positions. This division, plus twelve transports and four destroyer-transports, could be assembled at Brisbane by 5 July. The three trained divisions in Australia could support and eventually relieve the Marine division after adequate beachheads had been established and normal land warfare had begun. One hundred and six heavy bombers, 138 medium bombers, 48 light bombers, and 371 fighters, to be assembled in Australia by 1 July, would provide land-based air support. Additional bombers could be dispatched from Hawaii. Army fighters and bombers could support attacks against Lae and Salamaua. Bombers could reach Rabaul, but the fighters, from their present basis in Australia and Port Moresby, could not fly that far. Aircraft carriers would therefore be required to provide fighter support, and other naval surface vessels would naturally be needed. Unity of command would be absolutely essential to make the operation a complete success.[21]

General Marshall had also directed General MacArthur to prepare tentative plans along these lines.[22] The War Department and General MacArthur both believed that the operation, since it would take place in his area, should be conducted under General MacArthur's control. As the forces involved would be largely naval, the War Department suggested that a naval officer, under General MacArthur, be placed in command of the task force which would execute the operation.[23]

The Navy's View

The Navy's ideas differed from those of the Army. Admiral King presented his views to General Marshall on 25 June. Regretting that the United States had not been able to attack the Japanese immediately after Midway, he thought that the offensive should be launched about 1 August by a task force under the control of Admiral Nimitz. The immediate objectives would be positions in the Solomons in the Southwest Pacific Area and in the Santa Cruz Islands in the South Pacific Area, 335 nautical miles east-southeast of Guadalcanal. The ultimate objectives would be the New Guinea–New Britain area.

[21] Memo, WDCSA for COMINCH, 12 Jun 42, sub: Opns in SWPA. OPD 381 SWPA Sec. I Case 73; rad, GHQ SWPA to WDCSA, CM–IN–7976, 24 Jun 42.

[22] Rad, WDCSA to CINC SWPA CM–OUT–2319, 10 Jun 42.

[23] Memo, ACofS USA for WDCSA, 24 Jun 42, sub: Opns in SWPA. OPD 381 SWPA Sec. II Case 76; Rad, GHQ SWPA to WDCSA, CM–IN–7976, 24 Jun 42.

THE BATTLE OF MIDWAY *did much to restore naval balance in the Pacific. At 1945 hours 6 June 1942, dive-bombers from the U.S.S.* Hornet *attacked a Japanese heavy cruiser of the* Mogami *class leaving it gutted and abandoned.*

Admiral King believed that the force should include at least two aircraft carriers with accompanying cruisers and destroyers, the 1st Marine Division and transports of the South Pacific Amphibious Force, five Marine air squadrons, and the land-based planes from the South Pacific. The Southwest Pacific would furnish the task force with land-based aircraft, surface ships, and submarines. The permanent occupation of the Santa Cruz and other islands in the South Pacific Area would be effected by the commander of that area with forces to be designated later. The captured islands in the Solomons–New Guinea area would be permanently occupied under General MacArthur's direction by troops moved forward from Australia on shipping provided by Admiral Nimitz.

Admiral King wished General MacArthur's forces and elements of the British Eastern Fleet to conduct diversionary attacks against Timor in the Netherlands East Indies at the same time that Admiral Nimitz' task force struck the Solomon and Santa Cruz Islands.[24] He informed General MacArthur, Admiral Nimitz, and the South Pacific Area Headquarters of his ideas.[25]

Army–Navy Discussions

Admiral King's plans did not find favor in the War Department. Navy planners had been discussing the projected offensive with members of the Operations Division (OPD) of the War Department General Staff who were General Marshall's strategic advisers. The Army planners estimated that the Japanese ground forces in the target area included two brigades around Rabaul, about 1,000 *Special Naval Landing Force* troops at Lae and Salamaua, two companies on New Ireland, one battalion in the Admiralties, a small garrison on Bougainville, and a regiment in the Tulagi area. One hundred and twenty-six aircraft, including bombers, fighters, and reconnaissance planes, were believed to be located in New Britain, New Ireland, New Guinea, and the Solomons. It was considered possible that thirty-three bombers on Timor would be used to reinforce Rabaul. Japanese naval strength in the target area included only small units, but strong forces were believed to be based at Truk. The Operations Division concluded that these forces were capable of attacking Port Moresby, the east coast of Australia, or New Caledonia, and could be expected

---

[24] Memo, COMINCH for WDCSA, 25 Jun 42, sub: Offensive Opns in SO and SOWESPAC Areas, copy of FF/1/A16–3 (1) Ser 00544. OPD 381 SWPA Sec. II Case 80.

[25] *Ibid.;* CINCPAC to COMSOPAC, 0017 of 23 Jun 42, in War Diary, South Pacific Area and South Pacific Force, 1 May 42–31 Dec 42 (hereafter cited as SOPAC War Diary); COMINCH to COMSOWESPAC-FOR, 1255 of 23 Jun 42; COMINCH to CINCPAC, 2306 of 24 Jun 42. SOPAC War Diary. A copy of the SOPAC War Diary is in the Office of Naval Records and Library, Dept of the Navy.

to try to take Port Moresby, which was necessary as a base for operations against northern Australia. Loss of Port Moresby would deprive the Allies of the only advanced base from which they could strike Lae, Salamaua, and Rabaul. If the Allies were to attack the Japanese at Rabaul, the enemy would be able to move troops from Tulagi and the Admiralties to Rabaul in four days, although no strong reinforcements could be sent to Rabaul in less than three weeks. Unless the Japanese air installations at Rabaul could be reduced by preparatory bombardment, the projected offensive would meet strong resistance from land-based planes.

The seizure of Rabaul, followed by the seizure of eastern New Guinea, New Ireland, New Britain, and the Solomons, would deprive the Japanese of bases from which they could attack Australia and the Allied-held islands in the South Pacific, and advance the radius of Allied reconnaissance and air attack as far as Truk. Such a plan would require the three available infantry divisions and aircraft in Australia as well as the five cruisers, twelve destroyers, and thirty submarines in the Southwest Pacific, in addition to the 1st Marine Division, twelve transports and cargo ships, and at least two aircraft carriers from the Pacific Ocean Areas. The Navy's plan to attack and occupy Tulagi first and then move progressively against Rabaul would require a naval task force, an Army garrison force, and additional land-based aircraft from Australia and Port Moresby, all under naval command. Neither plan could be executed before August, as the necessary shipping could not be assembled in time.

The Operations Division concluded that a plan to take Rabaul first offered the greater promise of success, since it would provide for the maximum use of available forces and would strike directly at the primary objective. A quick stroke at Rabaul, the key Japanese base in the entire area, could be supported by land-based bombers although aircraft carriers would have to provide fighter support. Once Rabaul fell, the Operations Division believed, the remaining Japanese positions in the area, isolated beyond their supply lines, would be rendered impotent. The Navy plan, on the other hand, involved a gradual move from Tulagi to Rabaul. The capture of Tulagi, an operation in which the Allied forces could be supported by long-range bombers, would not be difficult, but two factors would militate against the success of the Navy plan. First, further advances northward toward Rabaul would be subjected to continuous aerial bombardment, and, second, a step-by-step advance would warn the Japanese and permit them to reinforce Rabaul with air and ground forces before enough Allied strength could be mustered to strike directly at Rabaul.

On the basis of these conclusions, the Operations Division recommended that Rabaul be attacked first, that the Navy provide the marine division and twelve transports and at least two carriers and supporting vessels, that the attack be launched as early as possible, and that the operation be under General Mac-Arthur's command.[26]

The Army and Navy plans differed considerably, but the greatest obstacle to agreement between the services was the selection of a commander. Army planners reported to General Marshall that they would be able to resolve all differences with the Navy planners except that of command. According to the Army point of view, unity of command would be essential since the offensive would involve not only the amphibious assault force and land-based aircraft but also the movement and supply of the garrison forces and co-ordination with the Allies. Since the offensive would take place in General MacArthur's area he should control it, and the tactical command of the attacking force should be in the hands of a naval officer.

The Navy agreed that unity of command was essential but feared that, if the high command were given to General MacArthur, he might dangerously expose the aircraft carriers by placing them in the waters between the Solomons and New Guinea within range of land-based aircraft. Tulagi would have to be reduced first to lessen the hazard to the carriers. Command of the attacking force, the Navy planners concluded, should go to Admiral Nimitz' subordinate, Vice Adm. Robert L. Ghormley, the commander of the South Pacific Area and South Pacific Force. The Army planners recommended to General Marshall that he and Admiral King personally choose a commander for the invasion.[27]

Informed by General Marshall of the Navy's opposition to his plan,[28] General MacArthur responded vigorously. The Navy, he asserted, had misunderstood his proposals. Rabaul was the ultimate objective, but direct assault upon it would be rendered impossible by the limited amount of land-based air support which could be brought to bear from present bases. His plans involved a progressive advance against the Solomons and New Guinea's north coast to obtain airfields from which to support the final attacks against Rabaul and to cover the naval surface forces. He felt that only confusion would result if

---

[26] OPD Estimate, in memo of Col W. L. Ritchie (Chief, SWPA Theater Gp), OPD, for Brig Gen St. Clair Streett (Ch Theater Gp, OPD), 23 Jun 42, sub: Offensive Opns in SWPA. OPD 381 SWPA Sec. II Case 80.

[27] Memo ACofS OPD (Brig Gen T.C. Handy) for WDCSA, 24 Jun 42, sub: Opns in SWPA. OPD 381 SWPA Sec. II Case 76; rad, WDCSA to GHQ SWPA, CM–OUT–5704, 23 Jun 42.

[28] Ibid.

ground forces from the Pacific Ocean Areas were employed inside the Southwest Pacific Area under a naval command exercised from a distant headquarters, as the Navy had suggested. The Southwest Pacific Headquarters was the logical agency to direct the offensive, for the necessary intelligence, reconnaissance, and planning agencies were all in its area, and General MacArthur believed that he should command any large operation through his air, ground, and surface commanders. Finally, he opposed the idea of trying to retake Timor at that time, on the ground that there were not enough air or naval forces in the area to support such an effort.[29]

An exchange of memoranda between General Marshall and Admiral King on 26 June failed to produce agreement. General Marshall opposed the plan to place the invading force under Admiral Nimitz' control. He sought to allay the Navy's fear for the safety of the aircraft carriers by suggesting that the Joint Chiefs of Staff could pass on the arrangements for the employment of naval forces, and he reiterated the argument that, since the ultimate objectives lay in General MacArthur's area, he should command.[30] Admiral King, still unconvinced, felt that Admiral Nimitz should command. At the conclusion of the amphibious phase, King suggested, General MacArthur could control further movements into the target area; the movements would be supported by the Pacific Fleet. South Pacific operations would be primarily amphibious and naval in character. As the nearest bomber base in Australia lay nearly 1,000 miles away from Tulagi, the Southwest Pacific Area would be able to render little support at first. Admiral King therefore insisted on a naval commander, and he suggested that the Navy would begin operations immediately even if Army forces in the Southwest Pacific Area gave no support.[31]

At the same time Admiral King, believing that the Army might delay its participation in the attack, directed Admiral Nimitz to proceed with preparations for an offensive in the Solomon and Santa Cruz Islands and to make recommendations regarding both the movement of Army aircraft from Hawaii and support by Southwest Pacific Forces.[32] Admiral Nimitz immediately began

[29] Rad, GHQ SWPA to WDCSA, CM–IN–7976, 24 Jun 42. Apparently OPD had also misunderstood General MacArthur's plans. Complete details on General MacArthur's plans during this period will be given in a forthcoming volume of U.S. ARMY IN WORLD WAR II.

[30] Memo, WDCSA for COMINCH, 26 Jun 42, sub: Offensive Opns in SO and SOWESPAC Areas. OPD 381 SWPA Sec. II Case 80.

[31] Memo, COMINCH for WDCSA, 26 Jun 42, sub: Offensive Opns in SO and SOWESPAC Areas. OPD 381 SWPA Sec. II Case 80.

[32] COMINCH to CINCPAC, 1415 of 27 Jun 42. SOPAC War Diary.

preparations, as did Admiral Ghormley in the South Pacific. The commanding general of the 1st Marine Division, a part of which had just landed in Wellington, was ordered to prepare plans and load ships for an attack against the Solomon and Santa Cruz Islands. Admiral Nimitz requested of the Joint Chiefs that eight Army B–17's and thirteen Army B–26's be moved from Hawaii to New Caledonia, and the same number from Hawaii to the Fijis, to be under his control. He also asked that the surface ships and all available submarines of the Southwest Pacific naval forces be made available to Admiral Ghormley, and that long-range aircraft from the Southwest Pacific lend whatever support Ghormley should recommend.[33]

The implications in Admiral King's belief that the Army might not fully participate disturbed General Marshall, for he believed that all available support should be given to the offensive regardless of the outcome of the command dispute, and he sent orders to that effect to General MacArthur.[34] He decided to settle the disagreement by personal conferences with Admiral King.[35] The two officers negotiated, in person and in writing, from 29 June until 2 July. Admiral King suggested that Admiral Ghormley command the offensive until the Tulagi operation was over, and that thereafter General MacArthur should control the advance toward Rabaul.[36] The Army had some objections, but opposed even more strongly an alternative proposal by Admiral King that Ghormley command the operation directly under the Joint Chiefs of Staff. Admiral King's first compromise proposal was adopted. To prevent depleting General MacArthur's area of trained troops, General Marshall insisted that occupation forces for Tulagi be drawn from the South Pacific instead of from the Southwest Pacific Area. By 2 July it seemed possible that three aircraft carriers instead of two could be provided, although the serious German threat to the British in the Middle East made the raid on Timor seem unlikely.[37]

The Decision

On 2 July 1942 General Marshall and Admiral King, having reached agreement on all questions at issue, signed the "Joint Directive for Offensive Opera-

---

[33] Memo, COMINCH for WDCSA, 29 Jun 42, sub: Amph Opns in SO and SOWESPAC. OPD 381 SWPA Sec. II Case 80.

[34] Rad, WDCSA to CINC SWPA, CM–OUT–7356, 28 Jun 42.

[35] Memo, WDCSA for COMINCH, 29 Jun 42 (no sub). OPD 381 SWPA Sec. II Case 80.

[36] Rad, WDCSA to CINC SWPA, CM–OUT–7501, 29 Jun 42.

[37] Rad, WDCSA to CINC SWPA, CM–OUT–0677, 3 Jul 42.

tions in the Southwest Pacific Area Agreed on by the United States Chiefs of Staff." This directive ordered that an offensive be mounted at once. The ultimate object was the seizure of the New Britain–New Ireland–New Guinea area. The operation was divided into three tasks. Task One was the seizure and occupation of the Santa Cruz Islands, Tulagi, and "adjacent positions," and would be under the command of an officer designated by Admiral Nimitz. General MacArthur was to attach the necessary naval reinforcements and land-based aircraft to the South Pacific forces, and to interdict enemy air and naval activity west of the target area. The target date of Task One for planning purposes would be 1 August.

Task Two, the seizure and occupation of the remainder of the Solomons, of Lae, Salamaua, and of the northwest coast of New Guinea, would be under General MacArthur's command, as would Task Three, the seizure and occupation of Rabaul and adjacent positions in the New Britain–New Ireland area. The composition of forces, the timing of the tasks, and the passage of command would be determined by the Joint Chiefs of Staff.

The boundary between the Southwest Pacific and the South Pacific Areas was to be moved west to longitude 159 degrees East on 1 August, a change which placed the entire Task One target area—Tulagi, Guadalcanal, and Florida, as well as the Russells, Malaita, and San Cristobal—in the South Pacific under Ghormley but left the remainder of the Solomons in the Southwest Pacific under MacArthur.

Forces for all three tasks were to be drawn from the ground, air, and naval forces then under General MacArthur, and from Marine air squadrons and land-based aircraft in the South Pacific, plus at least two aircraft carriers with accompanying cruisers and destroyers to support the South Pacific Amphibious Force (which included transports, cargo ships, and the 1st Marine Division). Army forces from the South Pacific were to be used to garrison Tulagi and the adjacent positions, while troops from General MacArthur's command would provide other necessary garrisons.

Naval task force commanders would exercise direct command of the amphibious forces throughout the conduct of all three tasks. The Joint Chiefs of Staff reserved the power to withdraw U. S. Fleet units upon the completion of any phase of the operation if the aircraft carriers were jeopardized or if an emergency arose elsewhere in the Pacific.[38]

---

[38] Joint Directive for Offensive Opns in SWPA Agreed on by U.S. CofS, 2 Jul 42. OPD 381 Sec. II Case 83.

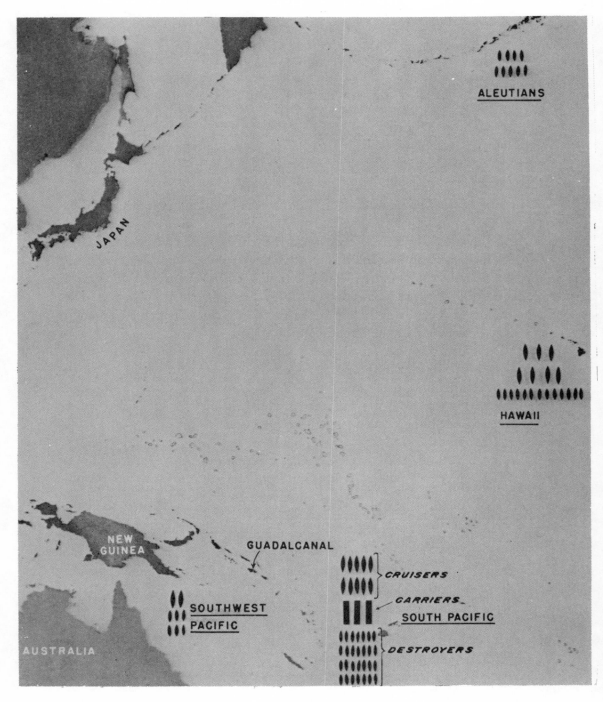

DISTRIBUTION OF U.S. NAVAL FORCES IN THE PACIFIC *at the time of planning for the Guadalcanal operation.*

Admiral King dispatched orders to Pearl Harbor[39] embodying the provisions of the directive and went to San Francisco to confer with Admiral Nimitz. General Marshall informed General MacArthur of the plan and told him that Admiral Ghormley, who would command during Task One, would visit Melbourne for conferences.[40] Admiral King's orders of 2 July did not actually initiate naval preparation for the offensive, for both Nimitz and Ghormley had begun their preparations in June when Admiral King had contemplated making the offensive an all-Navy operation.

By the first week in July Admiral Nimitz' plans were approaching completion. He decided that Admiral Ghormley should exercise strategic control over the forces in the Task One operation. Vice Adm. Frank J. Fletcher would command, under Admiral Ghormley, the entire seaborne invasion force. Designated as the Expeditionary Force, it was to be made up of aircraft carriers and other warships organized as the Air Support Force. and the Amphibious Force consisting of warships, transports, and the troops who would make the landing. Rear Adm. Richmond K. Turner was to command the Amphibious Force of the Expeditionary Force. Fletcher and Turner were present at Pearl Harbor during the first days of July. Turner, by a previous appointment, was then on his way to the South Pacific to take command, under Admiral Ghormley, of the South Pacific Amphibious Force. Nimitz, Fletcher, Turner and their staffs discussed the forthcoming invasion at this time. The Japanese were known to be building the airstrip on Guadalcanal, and at these conferences it was suggested that Guadalcanal be specified as an objective. This possibility was made known to Admiral Ghormley on 7 July.[41]

Admiral Ghormley had formally assumed his duties as Commander of the South Pacific Area and South Pacific Force (COMSOPAC) on 19 June, with headquarters at Auckland, New Zealand. He flew from Auckland to Melbourne on 7 July to confer with General MacArthur, as the Joint Chiefs had directed. The general and admiral discussed the directive and agreed on the obvious necessity for invading Guadalcanal as well as Tulagi. Their plans and recommendations, subject to change after Fletcher and Turner arrived in the South Pacific, were immediately radioed to the Joint Chiefs of Staff. MacArthur and Ghormley strongly objected to the immediate launching of Task One, which they defined as an orthodox landing in the Guadalcanal–Tulagi area.

[39] COMINCH to CINCPAC, 2100 of 2 Jul 42. SOPAC War Diary.
[40] Rad, WDCSA to CINC SWPA, CM–OUT–0677, 3 Jul 42.
[41] CINCPAC to COMSOPAC, 0125 of 7 Jul 42. SOPAC War Diary.

There were enough forces available for Task One, they believed, but only one amphibious division had been assigned, and heavy casualties might render it incapable of engaging in all the subsequent invasions which were needed to carry out the remaining two tasks. Not enough ships to move all the necessary troops were available. A third major difficulty arose from the fact that the successful execution of Task One would require that the ships of the South Pacific Amphibious Force remain for perhaps two days in the Guadalcanal–Tulagi area, beyond range of Allied land-based aircraft and exposed to attacks by Japanese warships. Southwest Pacific aircraft were too few in number to prevent enemy air and surface forces from attacking the invasion force, and the aircraft carriers would be exposed to attacks by land-based aircraft.

It would be difficult, they believed, for the attacking forces to surprise the enemy, whose patrol planes could cover the approaches to the target. In addition, the Japanese were known to have been increasing their efforts to develop the airdromes at Rabaul, Lae, Salamaua, and Buka as well as on Guadalcanal. To begin Task One without the assurance of sufficient aircraft for complete support of each succeeding operation would be dangerous, as the Japanese had discovered in the Coral Sea and Midway battles. They believed that once Task One had been started it would be necessary for Tasks Two and Three to follow it quickly. If Rabaul, which could be strengthened by forces from Truk, were to remain in enemy hands throughout Task One, the attacking Allied forces might be destroyed.

General MacArthur and Admiral Ghormley therefore recommended that the Allied forces continue to move into the New Hebrides and the Santa Cruz Islands, but that Task One be postponed until the South and Southwest Pacific forces were strengthened to such an extent that Tasks One, Two, and Three could be executed in one continuous movement.[42]

The Joint Chiefs of Staff rejected this recommendation on 10 July. The Japanese development of positions in the Solomons and their southward advance had to be halted immediately, regardless of the disadvantages. The British Eastern Fleet would not be able to take part, the Joint Chiefs explained, but Admiral Nimitz was sending more naval forces than had been planned originally and Army B–17's of the 11th Bombardment Group would be sent from Hawaii to Ghormley's area. In addition, the Army had decided to speed the movement of replacement aircraft to the Pacific, and would do its best to follow

---

[42] Disp, CINC SWPA and COMSOPAC to WDCSA, COMINCH, CINCPAC, 1012 of 8 Jul 42, CCR 82 S, in ABC 370.26 Sec I (7–8–42), in Plans and Opns Div, GSUSA.

up Task One with appropriate measures.[43] Guadalcanal and Tulagi were to be invaded at once.

It is clear that the Joint Chiefs and the Pacific commanders knew precisely the strategic advantages that would be gained for the Allies by the seizure of Guadalcanal and Tulagi. An immediate invasion, which would halt the advancing Japanese and secure for the Allies an advanced base from which part of the offensive operations against Rabaul could be mounted, would enable the Allies to capitalize on the victory at Midway by wresting the initiative from the Japanese.[44] Equally clear is the fact that the Joint Chiefs realized that invading Guadalcanal and Tulagi before sufficient forces could be mustered for the advance against Rabaul would be an operation in which the margin for error would be perilously small.

[43] WDCSA and COMINCH to CINC SWPA and COMSOPAC, 2100 of 10 Jul 42. SOPAC War Diary.

[44] On 12 July, the Joint Chiefs of Staff suggested the possibility that the offensive against Rabaul might be followed by an advance northward from the ". . . TRUK–GUAM–SAIPAN line, and/or northwestward through the Malay barrier and Borneo to the Philippines." Memo, Gen Marshall, Admiral King, Gen Arnold for the Pres, 12 Jul 42, sub: Pacific Opns. ASF docs in Special Collections subsection, Hist Rec Br, DRB, AGO.

CHAPTER II

Plans for Invasion

As Admiral King has written, "Because of the urgency of seizing and occupying Guadalcanal, planning was not up to the usual thorough standard."[1] Admirals Nimitz and Ghormley had begun planning in June, but the planes and men which were to make the attack were scattered from the South Pacific to California.

General MacArthur's and Admiral Ghormley's assertion that there were few troops available for beginning the attack was well founded. Besides the three divisions in Australia and the elements of the 1st Marine Division in New Zealand, there were several units in the South Pacific assigned to the defense of bases along the line of communications. Two Army divisions were in the area; the 37th Division was in the Fijis, the Americal Division in New Caledonia. The 7th Marines, a regiment detached from the 1st Marine Division, was in Samoa. Army infantry and artillery units were at Bora Bora; the 147th Infantry, formerly of the 37th Division, was at Tongatabu. Some Army, Navy, and Marine Corps troops were holding Efate in the New Hebrides and part of the Efate force was building an airfield at Espiritu Santo in the New Hebrides.

The majority of the Army troops in the South Pacific had been dispatched prior to the establishment of the South Pacific Area; they had been administered directly by the War Department and supplied directly by the San Francisco Port of Embarkation. The organization of the South Pacific Area, the commitment of more Army Air Forces units, and the imminence of the forthcoming campaign led the War Department to organize these forces into a single comand—the U. S. Army Forces in the South Pacific Area (USAFISPA). On 14 July Maj. Gen. Millard F. Harmon was appointed its commanding general (COMGENSOPAC) with the concurrence of the Navy.[2]

[1] Admiral E. J. King, *Our Navy at War: A Report to the Secretary of the Navy Covering Our Peacetime Navy and Our Wartime Navy and including Combat Operations up to March 1, 1944 (U.S. News*, March 1944), p. 34.

[2] History of the United States Army Forces in the South Pacific Area during World War II: 30 March 1942–1 August 1944 (4 vols.), Pt. I, I, Ch. I, *passim*. Hereafter cited as Hist USAFISPA. A copy of the manuscript is filed in the Hist Div, SSUSA.

CHART NO. 1

Organization of South Pacific Forces at the Inception of Task One

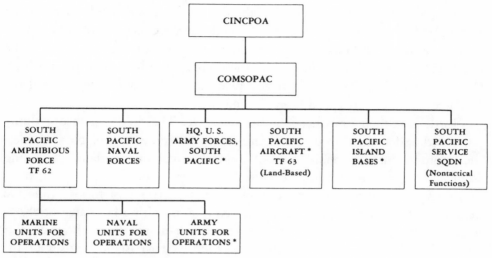

*Hq, U. S. Army Forces, South Pacific, exercised administrative control over Army units.

Prior to his appointment as Commanding General of U. S. Army Forces in the South Pacific, Harmon, who was one of the senior officers of the Army Air Forces and a pioneer in military aviation, had been Chief of the Air Staff. Born in 1888, he was graduated from the U. S. Military Academy in 1912, and entered the Aviation Section of the Army Signal Corps while in the Philippines. After active service in France during World War I, he attended the Army Command and General Staff School and the Army War College, taught Military science and tactics at the University of Washington in Seattle, and served with various training and tactical air units until the end of 1940. In January 1941 he was sent to Britain as an air observer. Returning to the United States four months later, he was made a major general in July and in January 1942 he became Chief of the Air Staff.

General Harmon, under Ghormley's command, was to be responsible for the administration and supply of Army units in the South Pacific. His letter of appointment directed him to advise the Area Commander, but gave him no operational or tactical authority. On 26 July he assumed his duties, with headquarters first at Auckland and later, adjacent to Ghormley's, at Noumea, New

Caledonia. His services proved so valuable that both Admiral Ghormley and his successor consulted him in the planning and execution of the Guadalcanal and subsequent South Pacific campaigns.

Despite the fact that there were about 32,000 Army ground troops in the South Pacific,[3] they could not be freely used for reinforcement of the marines in the attack against Guadalcanal. There was not enough shipping space in the South Pacific for free movement, and the divisions holding the Fijis and New Caledonia could not be moved until replacements were available, or until the Japanese offensive threat had been eliminated.[4]

Little was then known about the objective. The Solomons are a thinly populated and undeveloped area. Lying about 800 miles east of New Guinea, the Solomons form a double chain of tropical, mountainous islands extending from latitude 5 degrees South to latitude 12 degrees 30 minutes South, from northwest to southeast, and from longitude 155 degrees East to longitude 170 degrees East. They include several hundred islands, with a land area of 18,670 square miles. The largest in the northeastern chain are Buka, Bougainville, Choiseul, Santa Isabel, and Malaita. The southwestern islands consist of the Shortland, Treasury, and New Georgia groups, the Russells, Guadalcanal, Florida, San Cristobal, and Rennell.

The Solomon Islands chain was divided politically. Bougainville and Buka were part of the Australian Mandated Territory of New Guinea. The rest of the islands formed the British Solomon Islands Protectorate. A British district officer, responsible to the Resident Commissioner at Tulagi, administered civil affairs on each island in the protectorate. The Resident Commissioner reported to the High Commissioner for the Western Pacific in the Fijis, who in turn was responsible to the Colonial Office in London. Economic development had been slight. Lever Brothers, with local headquarters at Gavutu, had been operating fairly extensive coconut plantations since before the war, and the Burns-Philp South Seas Company, Ltd., controlled island shipping. The few white residents before the war were government officials, planters, missionaries, and their families. Some, including the Resident Commissioner and several district officers, missionaries, and nuns, had remained in the Solomons during the Japanese occupation. The government officials, like the coastwatchers, had withdrawn to the hills. The missionaries and nuns, with some exceptions, had not been molested, but had continued to operate their stations under surveillance.

[3] *Ibid.,* Pt. III, I, 441.
[4] COMSOPAC to CINCPAC, 0414 of 13 July 42. SOPAC War Diary.

The native inhabitants are Melanesians of primitive culture. Noted in former years for their ferocity, they remained generally loyal to the Allied cause and throughout the Solomons campaign assisted the coastwatchers, rescued fliers and sailors, and acted as guides, scouts, and laborers.[5]

The Solomons are one of the world's wettest areas. Rainfall in some places exceeds 200 inches per year; from 1922 to 1942, annual rainfall at Tulagi averaged 164 inches.[6] The tropical temperatures are enervating, ranging daily from 73 to 93 degrees Fahrenheit at sea level. Humidity is high. There are only two seasons, the wet and the dry. Northwest monsoons bring almost daily rain during the wet season from November to March. The term dry is relative, for southeast trade winds bring frequent rains during the dry season.

There are few good harbors, but the narrow, restricted channels between the islands are usually calm. In the southern Solomons the best anchorage is Tulagi Harbor between Tulagi and Florida Islands. Tulagi, Gavutu, and Tanambogo Island, near Gavutu in Tulagi Harbor, all possessed some docks, jetties, and machine shops. There are few clear, flat areas suitable for airfields except on Malaita, Bougainville, New Georgia, and the grassy plain on Guadalcanal's north coast. (*Map IV*)

Between Guadalcanal and Malaita lies the smaller island of Florida (Nggela), which is separated from Guadalcanal by Sealark Channel. Reefs jut above the water to make the channel north of the center of Guadalcanal very narrow. The waters between the southern reefs and Guadalcanal are called Lengo Channel; those between the northern reefs and Florida are Nggela Channel.[7] Between the southeast part of Guadalcanal and Malaita is Indispensable Strait, and at the northern end of Sealark Channel, between Guadalcanal and Florida, lies the small symmetrical island of Savo.

Air and Naval Plans

Admiral Nimitz' Plan

By late June Admiral Nimitz had decided to send five Marine air squadrons to the South Pacific to take part in the campaign. Airfield construction

---

[5] See (British) Central Office of Information, *Among Those Present: The Official Story of the Pacific Islands at War* (London, 1946).

[6] R. W. Robson (ed.), *The Pacific Islands Year Book,* (4th ed., Sydney, 1942), p. 131.

[7] For simplicity, Sealark Channel will be used throughout this volume to refer to all the waters between Tulagi and Guadalcanal.

MAJ. GEN. MILLARD F. HARMON, *appointed to command the Army forces in the South Pacific Area, discusses a phase of the Guadalcanal campaign with Brig. Gen. Nathan F. Twining in New Caledonia.*

in the South Pacific was, therefore, to be given a high priority.[8] As the five squadrons, all consisting of short-range aircraft, would have to be ferried across the Pacific on an aircraft carrier, the pilots would first have to train for carrier operations.[9] Following Admiral Nimitz' request that more Army bombers be sent to the South Pacific, General Marshall authorized the creation of two Mobile Air Forces for the Pacific Theater—one in the Southwest Pacific Area and one in the Pacific Ocean Areas. Each was composed of one B–17 heavy bombardment group.[10] The Pacific Ocean Areas Mobile Air Force might be used anywhere within the Pacific Ocean Areas at the Joint Chiefs' discretion. The 11th Heavy Bombardment Group, then in Hawaii, was selected as the Pacific Ocean Areas Mobile Air Force on 16 July, and within four days its four squadrons had taken off for New Caledonia.[11]

To provide more troops for the landings, Admiral King had suggested that the reinforced 2d Marines (of the 2d Marine Division), then in California, be shipped to the South Pacific immediately; Admiral Ghormley agreed, and he requested that the 2d Marines be combat-loaded and ready for landing operations on arrival.[12] Admiral Nimitz ordered the 2d Marines to be ready to sail from San Diego aboard five ships on 1 July.[13] Admiral Nimitz also decided to send the 3d (Marine) Defense Battalion from Pearl Harbor to the South Pacific to provide antiaircraft and seacoast defense of the target areas. Three aircraft carriers, one battleship, and accompanying cruisers and destroyers would be available to constitute the naval supporting forces to which would be added warships from the Southwest Pacific Area.

Admiral Nimitz issued his final plan for the attack on 8 July. He ordered the South Pacific Force, under Admiral Ghormley, to capture the Santa Cruz Islands and the Tulagi–Guadalcanal area in the Solomons. As the Joint Chiefs had planned, marines were to capture the areas. Army forces, under Admiral Ghormley's direction, would then relieve the marines. Naval forces would support these operations and construct and operate the air bases for both land-based planes and seaplanes, and Army aircraft were to operate from the bases as di-

---

[8] CINCPAC to COMINCH, 0251 of 27 Jun 42. SOPAC War Diary.

[9] Disp, CINCPAC to COMINCH, 2251 of 27 Jun 42. OPD 381 SWPA Sec. II Case 80.

[10] Rad, WDCSA to CINC SWPA, CM–OUT–2222, 3 Jul 42.

[11] ACofS for Intelligence, Air Staff, Hist Div, AAF Hist Studies No. 35: Guadalcanal and the Origins of the Thirteenth Air Force, p. 2.

[12] COMINCH to CINCPAC, 1415 of 27 Jun 42; COMSOPAC to CINCPAC, 0607 of 28 June 42. SOPAC War Diary.

[13] 2301 of 27 Jun 42 (no addressee). SOPAC War Diary.

rected. A seaplane base, providing for thirty planes, was to be built at Tulagi. Air bases, each large enough to support four air squadrons, were to be built both at Guadalcanal and at Ndeni in the Santa Cruz Islands. The Navy was to be responsible for maintaining radio stations, harbor facilities, inshore patrol, port control, hospitals, underwater defenses, and roads and bridges at the bases. A 60-day level of subsistence supplies and ammunition and a 90-day supply of building materials were to be maintained. The Navy was to furnish materials for the construction of airfields, bases, and harbors.[14]

Admiral Ghormley's Plan

The problems facing the South Pacific commanders in preparing for the invasion were tremendous, and time was short. Admiral Ghormley, acting on the first orders from Admiral King before the issuance of the Joint Chiefs' directive and Admiral Nimitz' final plan, had called the commanding general of the 1st Marine Division from Wellington to his headquarters at Auckland on 26 June. The 1st Division commander and part of his staff began conferring with Admiral Ghormley on that date, and were joined the next day by Rear Adm. John S. McCain, the commander of all Allied land-based aircraft in the South Pacific (COMAIRSOPAC).[15] Not all the commanders who were to take part in the operation were present. Vice Adm. Frank J. Fletcher and Rear Adm. Richmond K. Turner, who were to command the Expeditionary and Amphibious Forces, had not then reached the South Pacific. Admiral Ghormley informed the Marine officers of the plan to invade the Solomon and Santa Cruz Islands, and ordered them to prepare plans and load ships in Wellington for the invasion. Detailed planning in the South Pacific had thus been initiated prior to the issuance of the directive on 2 July; the directive did not necessitate any basic changes in Ghormley's or the marines' concepts of the operation.

Admiral Ghormley issued his Operation Plan No. 1–42 on 16 July 1942. It was to govern the execution of Task One which was to be divided into three phases. The first would be a rehearsal in the Fiji Islands; the second would be the seizure and occupation of Tulagi and Guadalcanal. The projected occupation of Ndeni in the Santa Cruz Islands would be the third and final phase.

Operation Plan No. 1–42 organized two forces, Task Forces 61 and 63. The Expeditionary Force of eighty-two ships (designated as Task Force 61), was

---

[14] CINCPAC, File A4–3/FF 12/A16 (6) Ser 01994, Basic Supporting Plan for Advanced Air Bases at Santa Cruz Island and Tulagi–Guadalcanal, 8 Jul 42, in Plans and Opns Div, GSUSA.

[15] Rear Adm. Aubrey W. Fitch replaced McCain as COMAIRSOPAC on 21 September 1942.

CHART NO. 2
Organization of Forces for Task One

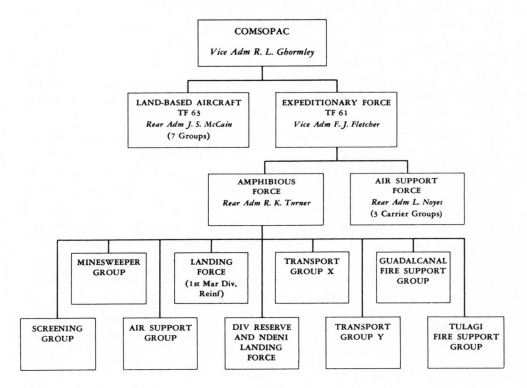

placed under the command of Admiral Fletcher. The main body of warships of Task Force 61 came from the Pacific and Atlantic Fleets, while a second came from the naval forces of the Southwest Pacific. The third component assigned to Task Force 61 was the amphibious force, which included the marines who were to make the landings. Admiral Turner was to assume command of the South Pacific Amphibious Force on 18 July.[16] The second force, Task Force 63, consisted of all the Allied land-based aircraft in the South Pacific under Admiral McCain.

Analyzing the strength and capabilities of the enemy forces which Task Forces 61 and 63 were to attack, Admiral Ghormley anticipated that the Japa-

[16] Commander, Amphibious Force, South Pacific Force, Pacific Fleet (TF62), War Diary, Aug 42–30 Sep 42, 18 Jul 42. A copy of this diary, hereafter cited as COMAMPHIBFORSOPAC War Diary, is in the Office of Naval Records and Library.

nese garrisons in the Solomons and Bismarcks might soon be reinforced. The Japanese could shuttle their aircraft between the Marshall Islands, New Britain, and the East Indies. Elements of the *4th Fleet* had already been operating in the vicinity of the Solomons and Bismarcks, and the addition of a submarine division might be expected. Rabaul was known to be a major air base, and seaplane bases were known to be in use at Gizo, Rekata Bay, Faisi, Kieta, Buka, and Gavutu. Two planes had been based at Tulagi, thirteen at Gavutu. The runway under construction at Lunga Point was not thought to have been completed.

Ghormley estimated that about 3,100 Japanese troops were in the Tulagi–Guadalcanal area. He believed that, of these, one thousand *Special Naval Landing Forces* and pioneers were stationed on Guadalcanal at Cape Esperance, the Segilau River, Lunga Point, Tenaru, and Taivu Point on the north coast. It was assumed that there were at least six antiaircraft guns at both Lunga Point and Kukum, with more at Taivu Point to the east. Ghormley considered, correctly, that the south coast was not held in any strength.

After assembling and rehearsing in the Fijis, the Expeditionary Force (Task Force 61) was to capture and occupy Tulagi and near-by areas, including that part of Guadalcanal most suitable for the construction of airfields. The tentative date for D Day set by the Joint Chiefs of Staff—1 August—could not be met. On 16 July Ghormley notified Admiral Nimitz that the late arrival of the 1st Marine Division's second echelon at Wellington, New Zealand, coupled with the delay in loading caused by bad weather in Wellington, would necessitate postponing the target date until 7 August.[17] The date could not be postponed further, however, lest the Japanese complete their airstrip for use against the Allied forces.[18]

Once Tulagi and the landing field on Guadalcanal had been taken, the Expeditionary Force would occupy Ndeni, and troops were to be ready to work on airfields on Guadalcanal and Ndeni immediately. Airfield construction materiel and troops would be sent forward as soon as possible. To free the Amphibious Force for further offensive action, occupation troops were to be dispatched to relieve the marines. Operation Plan No. 1–42 did not specifically designate the forces to effect the relief and occupation but stated that orders would be issued at a later date.

The land-based aircraft of Task Force 63 were to support and cover the

[17] COMSOPAC to CINCPAC, 0612 of 16 Jul 42. SOPAC War Diary.
[18] COMINCH to COMSOPAC, 1830 of 28 Jul 42. SOPAC War Diary.

movements of the Expeditionary Force, arrange special missions at the request of Task Force 61, and carry out their regular scouting missions. Task Force 63 was to cover the Amphibious Force's approach to Tulagi and Guadalcanal and the landing there, as well as to execute air attacks by arrangement with Task Force 61. Amphibious patrol bombers were to patrol temporarily from Ndeni, which had not been occupied by the Japanese, by D minus 1, and additional patrol planes would scout from the east coast of Malaita on D plus 1.[19] After the conclusion of the Guadalcanal phase, Task Force 63 would cover the occupation of Ndeni by the landing force.

Admiral Ghormley, announcing his intention to proceed from Auckland to Noumea aboard his flagship *Argonne* about D minus 5, stated that he would arrange a conference between representatives of the commanders of the Expeditionary and Amphibious Forces and of the South Pacific land-based aircraft to settle the final details of air support and to co-ordinate the various air efforts. The commander of Task Force 63 was also ordered to arrange for air scouting by Southwest Pacific Air Forces.

Logistical plans for the operation took into account the lack of good bases in the South Pacific Area. During the rehearsal, all vessels were to take on fuel as the tactical situation permitted from tankers at Noumea and the Fijis, and from tanks on shore in the Fijis and Espiritu Santo and Efate in the New Hebrides. Fleet units were to take on full loads of ammunition after the rehearsal. Only minor ship repairs could be effected in the South Pacific. Auckland had a dockyard and a drydock, and a floating drydock at Wellington could accommodate a heavy cruiser. In addition the repair ship *Whitney* was stationed at Tongatabu, and a salvage tug was to be stationed initially at Espiritu Santo. For major repairs, heavy fleet units would have to go to Pearl Harbor.

Fleet units would carry sufficient provisions to be self-sustaining, while the Amphibious Force would embark sixty days' supply and ten units of fire for the marines. Fresh foods would be supplied to the Amphibious Force if enough ships were available.

Once they were unloaded, ships of the Amphibious Force were to leave the Solomon and Santa Cruz Islands and return to Noumea unless directed elsewhere, and would be escorted by warships assigned by Admiral Fletcher. Returning ships would carry American wounded to the hospital ship *Solace* at

---

[19] COMSOPAC to COMAIRSOPAC, 1300 of 20 Jul 42 in SOPAC War Diary, altered the plan. The original had been D minus 2 for Ndeni and D Day for Malaita.

Noumea, which would either retain the wounded on board or distribute them among the Army hospitals at Noumea and the Fijis, or take them to the naval base hospital at Auckland.[20]

Admiral McCain's Plan

Toward the end of July, when Admiral McCain's tactical plan for Task Force 63 was completed, South Pacific air strength had increased and the air bases had been improved. Two companies of the 182d Infantry and one engineer company of the American Division had occupied Efate in the New Hebrides on 18 March to build an airfield. Marine Corps and naval personnel followed these forces, until by May there were 7,500 on the island. On 28 May 500 men of the Efate garrison had occupied Espiritu Santo, 145 miles to the north. Admiral Ghormley had ordered the construction of a bomber strip on Espiritu Santo, to be completed by 28 July, in time to support the invasion of the Solomons.[21] B–17's of the 11th Heavy Bombardment Group arrived in the area during July. The 98th Squadron landed in New Caledonia on 22 July, followed by the 42d the next day. The 431st Squadron landed in the Fijis on 24 July, and the 26th landed at Efate on 25 July.[22]

By the end of July Task Force 63 consisted of 291 aircraft of various types, based on New Caledonia, the Fijis, Tongatabu, Samoa, and Efate, and assigned to the defense of those islands. Of the 291 planes, 31 Navy patrol bombers (PBY's) were based on New Caledonia and the Fijis. Ninety-three naval fighters were based on Efate, New Caledonia, the Fijis, Tongatabu, and Samoa. Twenty-five naval observation planes were operating from Efate, New Caledonia, Tongatabu, and Samoa, and seventeen Navy scout bombers (SBD's) were based in Samoa.

Ninety-five Army planes were in Task Force 63. Thirty-five Army B–17's and twenty-two B–26's were stationed at New Caledonia and the Fijis. Thirty-eight Army P–400's were also operating from New Caledonia. Nine Vincents, eighteen Hudsons, and three Singapores of the Royal New Zealand Air Force were based on New Caledonia and the Fijis.[23]

---

[20] COMSOPAC, Opn Plan No. 1–42, A4–3/A 16–3, Ser 0017, 16 Jul 42. Copy No. 120 of Operation Plan 1–42 is in the Office of Naval Records and Library. Code names assigned were as follows: Task One, PESTILENCE; rehearsal, DOVETAIL; Guadalcanal–Tulagi invasion, WATCHTOWER; Ndeni occupation, HUDDLE. The code name of Guadalcanal was CACTUS; that of Tulagi, RINGBOLT.

[21] COMSOPAC to COMAIRSOPAC, 2314 of 2 Jul 42; COMSOPAC to CG Efate, 2538 of 5 Jul 42, SOPAC War Diary.

[22] 11th Bomb Gp (H), Hist, p. 4, in Archives, AF Hist Off.

[23] COMAIRSOPAC, Opn Plan No. 1–42, A4–3/A16–3, Ser 0016, 25 Jul 42. A photostatic copy of this plan is in the Office of Naval Records and Library.

Admiral McCain issued his orders on 25 July. He divided Task Force 63 into seven task groups. One group, consisting of the 69th (Army) Bombardment Squadron, the 67th (Army) Fighter Squadron, a New Zealand Air Force Hudson Squadron, and two PBY's, was to scout over 400-mile sectors from New Caledonia. A second group, consisting of the 11th (Army) Heavy Bombardment Group, to be based on New Caledonia, Efate, Espiritu Santo, and the Fijis, was to scout between New Caledonia and the Solomons and over and west of the Solomons. It was this group which carried out bombing attacks on Guadalcanal and Tulagi prior to D Day. The third group, consisting of the seaplane tender *Curtiss* and attached patrol planes, was to move part of its patrol planes to Espiritu Santo. Beginning on D minus 2 the planes based in Espiritu Santo were to search both east and west of the Solomons, while the remaining patrol planes moved from Noumea to Ndeni and Espiritu Santo. The fourth group, composed of the seaplane tender *MacFarland* and attached patrol bombers, was to move to Ndeni to inaugurate the air searches northeast of the Solomons on D minus 1. The fifth, composed of the seaplane tender *Mackinac* and attached patrol planes, was to proceed to the east coast of Malaita on D minus 3. The sixth group, consisting of Marine Fighting Squadron 212 and Scouting Squadron D–14, was to send three scouts to Espiritu Santo, and to aid the bombardment effort from Efate. The final group, consisting of Marine Observation Squadron 251, was to assist the bombardment effort from Espiritu Santo.

The air searches of Task Force 63 would thus cover the general area between New Caledonia and the Solomons, over the Solomons, east to Ndeni, and south to the Fijis. General MacArthur agreed to have Southwest Pacific air forces patrol the northern and western approaches to the Solomons during Task One. Prior to D minus 5, Southwest Pacific air forces were to reconnoiter over eastern New Guinea, Lorengau, Kavieng, Buka, Ontong Java, and Tulagi. Thereafter no Southwest Pacific planes were to fly east of longitude 158 degrees 15 minutes East (a line just west of Guadalcanal and east of New Georgia, Choiseul, and Bougainville, in the Solomons group), and latitude 15 degrees South unless requested by Ghormley. From D minus 5 to D plus 4, Southwest Pacific aircraft were to conduct daily reconnaissance flights over eastern New Guinea, Kavieng, and the easternmost point of New Georgia, and combat aircraft were to be ready to strike any Japanese naval vessels within a 550-mile radius of Port Moresby. From D Day to D plus 4, when the transports and cargo ships of the Amphibious Force would be unloading at Guadalcanal and Tulagi, Allied aircraft would thus be interdicting Japanese aerial operations in the Rabaul–Kavieng area. At the same time Buka was to be attacked to prevent the Japanese from refueling there. During this critical period, short-range aircraft were to attack Lae and Salamaua periodically to prevent those bases from sending aircraft to reinforce Rabaul.[24]

Admiral Fletcher's Plan

The Expeditionary Force Commander, Admiral Fletcher, issued his Operation Order No. 1–42 to Task Force 61 on 28 July. Task Force 61 was divided into two groups, the Air Support Force and the Amphibious Force. The Air Support Force, under the command of Rear Adm. Leigh Noyes, consisted of twenty-six warships and five tankers. This group was subdivided into three units, each built around an aircraft carrier. The first included the *Saratoga*, two heavy cruisers, and five destroyers. The carrier *Enterprise*, the battleship *North Carolina*, one heavy cruiser, one light antiaircraft cruiser, and five destroyers constituted another unit. The third unit was composed of the carrier *Wasp*, two heavy cruisers, six destroyers, and five tankers.[25]

The Amphibious Force, under the command of Admiral Turner, consisted of twenty-three transports and twenty-eight warships. Turner's force was composed of the South Pacific Amphibious Force, the naval forces from the Southwest Pacific, and three heavy cruisers, one light antiaircraft cruiser, and six destroyers from the Central Pacific.

The Amphibious Force was to sail from the Fijis to a point about 400 nautical miles south of the west tip of Guadalcanal, and then to sail north at 12 knots toward the objectives. This course would keep the force well away from Japanese-held islands until time for the assault.

As the Amphibious Force would be landing its troops on islands which lay beyond range of fighter planes from the nearest Allied bases, it was to receive tactical air support directly from the Air Support Force which would also execute necessary aerial reconnaissance. It was apparently Fletcher's intention to withdraw the carriers prior to D plus 3, somewhat short of the time required for the Amphibious Force to unload its ships completely. Admiral Ghormley was aware of this intention. Emphasizing the need for continuous air cover over the target area, he stated that if the airfield at Guadalcanal was operational he intended to base there squadrons from the carriers. These squadrons

[24] COMSOWESPAC (CINC SWPA) to COMSOPAC, 1034 of 19 Jul 42. SOPAC War Diary.

[25] See also ONI, USN, Combat Narratives: Solomon Islands Campaign, I, The Landing in the Solomons, 7–8 August 1942 (Washington, 1943).

would then be relieved by land-based fighters sent in from Efate with extra gasoline tanks.[26] But Admiral McCain pointed out that ten days would be required to fit the extra tanks to the Navy F4F fighters.[27]

The advancing Amphibious Force was to be further protected by submarines operating in the vicinity of major Japanese bases. Five submarines of the Pacific Fleet were to cover the Truk area from 22 July to 20 August, while submarines from the Southwest Pacific were to patrol the waters near Rabaul.[28]

Admiral Ghormley's plan provided that, on the withdrawal of the Air Support Force, the Amphibious Force was to secure air support from Task Force 63. It should be noted, however, that the distances separating Espiritu Santo and Efate from Guadalcanal would prevent Task Force 63 from providing fighter cover for the marines on Guadalcanal until the airfield there could be developed enough to serve as a base. The Amphibious Force was to furnish escorts for its transports returning to Noumea after unloading. Damaged ships were authorized to return either to Noumea or to put in to other convenient friendly ports.[29]

Admiral Turner's Plan

Like General Harmon, the officer assigned to command the Amphibious Force, Rear Adm. Richmond K. Turner, was also an aviator, but he had taken up flying at a comparatively late date. In 1908 when Turner was graduated from the U. S. Naval Academy as a passed midshipman, he held fifth place in a class of 201. Commissioned an ensign in 1910, he studied naval ordnance and engineering in the years prior to World War I. During the war he was a gunnery officer aboard several battleships, and in 1925 and 1926 he was on duty with the Navy Bureau of Ordnance. He completed naval aviation pilot training at Pensacola in August 1927, and commanded air squadrons for nearly two years. From 1929 to 1931 he served in the Plans Division of the Bureau of Aeronautics, and in 1932 he was a technical adviser to the United States delegation at the General Disarmament Conference at Geneva. He then served aboard the carrier *Saratoga,* and after graduation from the Naval War College in 1936 he served on the

---

[26] COMSOPAC to CTF 61, 0240 of 2 Aug 42. SOPAC War Diary.

[27] COMAIRSOPAC to COMSOPAC, 1436 of 4 Aug 42. SOPAC War Diary.

[28] COMSOPAC Opn Plan No. 1–42.

[29] CTF 61, Opn Ord No. 1–42, Opn WATCHTOWER, Ser 0032 N, 28 Jul 42. A photostatic copy of this order is in the Office of Naval Records and Library. The numerical designations assigned to the component units may be confusing. What had been task forces of the Pacific Fleet became task units of one group of TF 61. The amphibious force, made up of two task forces, was given a task group number.

staff there for two years. In 1939 he commanded the cruiser *Astoria* when she carried the remains of Ambassador Hirosi Saito to Japan. In 1940 Turner became Director of the War Plans Division of the Office of the Chief of Naval Operations, and in early 1942, a change in the organization of the Office of Naval Operations gave him the title of Assistant Chief of Staff to the Commander in Chief of the U. S. Fleet. He held that post, which was also concerned with war plans, until he was ordered to the Pacific in the summer of 1942, at the age of fifty-seven.

Admiral Turner, who after conferring with Admiral Nimitz at Pearl Harbor had reached Wellington on 15 July, issued Operation Plan No. A3–42 to the Amphibious Force on 30 July. He divided his force into eight groups: Transport Group X, Transport Group Y, the Guadalcanal Fire Support Group, the Tulagi Fire Support Group, the Minesweeper Group, the Screening Group, the Air Support Group, and the Landing Force Group, which consisted of the 1st Marine Division, Reinforced (less the 7th Marines).

Transport Group X, assigned to the Guadalcanal landing, consisted of four transport divisions. Two of the divisions were each composed of three transports and one cargo ship; the third, of two transports and one cargo ship; and the fourth, of one transport and three cargo ships. Transport Group Y, assigned to the landings in the Tulagi area, consisted of two transport divisions—one made up of four transports and the other of four destroyers previously converted to troop carriers (APD's). Four more ships, the *Zeilin* and the *Betelgeuse* and their escorting destroyers, were to transport the 3d Defense Battalion from Pearl Harbor.

The Guadalcanal Fire Support Group consisted of three fire sections composed of one heavy cruiser and two observation planes each, and of two fire sections of two destroyers each. The Tulagi Fire Support Group consisted of one light antiaircraft cruiser and two destroyers. There were five minesweepers in the Minesweeping Group.

The Amphibious Force's second-in-command, Rear Adm. V. A. C. Crutchley, R.N., commanded the Screening Group. It consisted of three Australian cruisers, one U. S. heavy cruiser, nine destroyers, two fighter squadrons based on the aircraft carriers, but detached to the Screening Group on D Day, and eight observation seaplanes from the cruisers. The Air Support Group was made up of one fighter and one dive bomber squadron, plus one additional fighter and one additional dive bomber squadron for the initial mission, all drawn from the carriers.

The Landing Force was led by the commanding general of the 1st Marine Division. It was divided into two groups—the Guadalcanal Group directly under the division commander, and the Northern Group under the assistant division commander. Six observation planes from the cruisers *Astoria* and *Quincy* were assigned to the Guadalcanal Group, and two planes from the cruiser *Vincennes* were assigned to the Northern Group.

Admiral Turner, in his analysis of enemy strength against which the Amphibious Force would have to contend, estimated that at least 150 Japanese planes were based in the Bismarck–New Guinea area, and that 11 Japanese cruisers, 13 destroyers, 15 submarines, 12 patrol bombers, 15 or 17 transports, and a number of motor torpedo boats were available. The Amphibious Force was to expect attacks by the planes based at fields from Rabaul to Salamaua. Admiral Turner warned his force that submarines, motor torpedo boats, cruisers, destroyers, and transports might be met around Tulagi. The Guadalcanal–Tulagi garrison was estimated to total 7,125, a figure more than double Ghormley's. It was believed that 1,850 men constituted Tulagi's garrison, whose armament included antiaircraft and coast defense guns, seaplanes, and picket boats. The rest of the troops were supposed to be in the Lunga area on Guadalcanal, which was protected by antiaircraft and coast defense guns.

The Amphibious Force was to assume attack dispositions on D minus 1 and to arrive in the transport areas off Guadalcanal and Tulagi before sunrise of D Day. The main landings were to be made on the center of the south coast of Tulagi, and on a 1,600-yard-long sandy beach between the Tenaru and Tenavatu Rivers on the north coast of Guadalcanal, about 6,000 yards east of Lunga Point. H Hour, the time of the Tulagi landing, was set for 0800 for planning purposes. Zero Hour, the time of the Guadalcanal landing, was originally set for 0830. Admiral Turner's flagship, the cargo ship *McCawley,* was the site of the 1st Marine Division's floating command post. Admiral Crutchley flew his flag aboard the *Australia.*

The majority of the Amphibious Force—Transport Group X, the Guadalcanal Fire Support Group, one fighter squadron and one dive bomber squadron, and about two regimental combat teams of the 1st Marine Division—was assigned to the assault on Guadalcanal. Transport Group Y, the Tulagi Fire Support Group, one fighter squadron, one dive bomber squadron, and the balance of the Marine division, except the reserve, were assigned to the northern attack.

Air attacks by the planes directly supporting the Amphibious Force were to inaugurate operations on D Day. Communication and control between the

Amphibious Force and the air squadrons were to be effected through an air support director group from the carrier force stationed aboard the *McCawley*. An alternate director group was to be aboard the *Neville*.

Fifteen minutes before sunrise of D Day, while the transports were approaching their unloading areas, one fighter squadron was to destroy any aircraft at Lunga or Koli Points on Guadalcanal, and any seaplanes, motor torpedo boats, or submarines operating near the island's north coast. At the same time a second fighter squadron would strike similar targets near Tulagi. Two dive bomber squadrons, assisted by the fighters, were to hit antiaircraft and coast defense guns on Guadalcanal, Tulagi, and Gavutu. Dive bombers were also to cover the assaulting landing craft as they moved toward the beaches. Beginning one hour after sunrise on D Day, fighters and dive bombers were to maintain stations overhead to protect the transports.

Admiral Turner ordered the fire support warships to fire at all antiaircraft and coast defense guns, to cover the minesweepers, and to be on the alert against torpedo boats and submarines. Warships were to take care to avoid interfering with landing craft formations, and for the safety of the American troops were to use percussion instead of time fuzes against shore targets. The warships were to provide naval gunfire liaison teams, equipped with radios, to go ashore with the troops.

The naval gunfire support problem in the Tulagi area was more complicated than that for Guadalcanal. Numerous near-by islets and promontories of Florida Island lie within artillery and even small-arms range of Tulagi. The ships' gunfire plan called for supporting fires to be placed, prior to the landings, on all the islets as well as on parts of Florida and on Tulagi. The ships were also to put fire on the radio station on the southeastern part of Tulagi, and on Tulagi's antiaircraft positions. Starting at H plus 30 minutes the party on shore was to designate targets. The Tulagi Fire Support Group and the air squadrons were also to bombard the southeast portion of Tulagi when the troops, advancing southeast from the landing beach, had reached the first phase line, about two-thirds of the way down the island. The signal from the troops for this bombardment would be a green star cluster flare.

The cruisers of the Guadalcanal Fire Support Group were to cover the area between Lunga and Koli Points with fire starting at daylight of D Day. The four destroyers were to take stations at Zero minus 30 minutes to serve as control and salvage vessels by the landing beach; they were to mark the line of departure for the initial boat waves 5,000 yards north of the beach. All ships of the group were to close in by Zero minus 10 minutes to give direct support to the landing. From Zero minus 10 to Zero minus 5 minutes, they were to put fire to a depth of 200 yards on an area extending 800 yards on either side of the beach, using 135 8-inch and 1,400 5-inch rounds. Starting at Zero plus 5 minutes, the ships were to put fire ashore to assist the advance of the combat teams from the landing beach west to the Lunga airfield.

The liaison planes assigned to the landing forces were to mark the flanks of the beaches with smoke at H minus 20 and Zero minus 20 minutes, respectively. Starting at H plus 1 hour, one plane was to assume station over Guadalcanal for observation duty for the field artillery. If ground-to-air radio communication failed, communications between the ground forces and the liaison planes were to be maintained by message drops and ground panel codes.

Transport Groups X and Y were to land the troops, equipment, and supplies of the 1st Marine Division on Tulagi and Guadalcanal in accordance with that division's plans. The destroyer-transports of Group X would act as control and salvage vessels for the boats landing at Tulagi.

The minesweepers were to sweep the shallows south of Tulagi from H to H plus 1½ hours. Three minesweepers were then to sweep the waters from the Guadalcanal landing beach east to Taivu Point, while two cleared the area off the beach itself. The Transport Group commanders were authorized to move their ships in close to the landing beaches once the waters were proved safe. On D plus 1, the minesweepers would clear the Kukum Beach area just west of Lunga Point.

The Screening Group would guard the Amphibious Force against surface, air, and submarine attacks. One fighter squadron was to cover the transport areas during daylight while the ships were unloading. Control would be exercised through a fighter director group from the carrier forces aboard the *Chicago*. During enemy air attacks the fire support warships would come under Admiral Crutchley's control to screen the transports with antiaircraft fire, and, in the event of surface attack, would also support the Screening Group. On the completion of their shore fire missions the fire support warships were to pass to Admiral Crutchley's command. During the amphibious phase, one observation plane from the *Vincennes* was to conduct antisubmarine patrols, reporting results to the Screening Group.

Admiral Turner intended to establish Amphibious Force headquarters ashore once the objectives had been captured and the amphibious phase ended. Communications with the area commander would be maintained through the

1st Marine Division's radio. A small naval force, including a boat repair section, boat crews, and twelve LCM's (landing craft, mechanized), twenty LCP(L)'s (landing craft, personnel) and thirty LCV's (landing craft, vehicle), was to be established at Guadalcanal and Tulagi.

It was estimated that the transports would be unloaded and could withdraw from the forward area by the night of D plus 1. They were to retire under the command of Rear Adm. Norman Scott, the commander of the Tulagi Fire Support Group. The cargo ships were to be unloaded by D plus 4, and were to retire under command of Admiral Crutchley.

The force for the Santa Cruz operation, consisting of one cruiser, four destroyers, four transports, one cargo ship, and the 2d Marines, Reinforced, having formed an integral part of the Amphibious Force for the Guadalcanal–Tulagi invasion, was to depart from the Guadalcanal area about D Day to occupy and defend Ndeni.

On completion of the entire operation the air squadrons were to revert to Task Force 61. The Amphibious Force organized for the invasions was to be dissolved on orders from Admiral Fletcher, but the South Pacific Amphibious Force proper would remain in existence.[30]

Landing Force Plans

The 1st Marine Division, which was to make the landings, had been moving overseas while the Joint Chiefs of Staff were discussing the attack against the Solomons. Brought to war strength at New River, N.C., between 7 December 1941 and 1 May 1942, it had then been organized around two infantry regiments, the 1st Marines and 5th Marines, and one artillery regiment, the 11th Marines. The 7th Marines, the third infantry regiment, had been detached for service with the 1st Provisional Marine Brigade in Samoa. The division had engaged in field exercises and combat firing at New River, and during March and April each battalion landing team of the 5th Marines and one of the 1st Marines engaged in 10-day landing exercises at Solomon's Island, Md.

The division was commanded by a 55-year-old veteran of Caribbean and Chinese expeditions, Maj. Gen. Alexander A. Vandegrift. After attending the University of Virginia for two years, Vandegrift had been commissioned a 2d lieutenant in the Marine Corps in 1909. He served in Nicaragua, Mexico, and

---

[30] CTF 62, Opn Plan No. A3–42, Opn WATCHTOWER, Ser 0010, 30 Jul 42. A copy of this plan is in the Office of Naval Records and Library. Admirals Fletcher and Turner, who prepared their plans separately, used different numbers to designate the amphibious force. Fletcher used 61.2, Turner, 62.

Haiti, and in 1916 began two years' service with the Haitian Constabulary. After a brief tour of duty in the United States, he served again in Haiti from 1919 to 1923. Upon completing the Field Officers' Course at Quantico, Va., in 1926, he became Assistant Chief of Staff at the Marine Base at San Diego, Calif. Vandegrift then served for over a year as Operations and Training Officer on the staff of the 3d Marine Brigade in China. Returning to the United States in 1928, he held various staff positions, including one with the newly-founded Fleet Marine Force, until 1935. He served in Peiping, China, for two years, and from 1937 to 1941 was at Marine Corps Headquarters in Washington. Ordered to the 1st Marine Division in 1941 as a brigadier general, he was promoted to major general and took command of the division in March 1942 with Brig. Gen. William H. Rupertus as his assistant division commander.

Vandegrift had not believed that his division was sufficiently well trained for combat when he was notified in April that it was to be sent to New Zealand as part of the South Pacific Amphibious Force to establish bases and train for "minor landing offensives and counter-attacks to be designated at a later date".[31] He had not expected that any combat missions would be assigned before January 1943.[32] Division headquarters and the 5th Marines reached Wellington, the capital city of New Zealand, on 14 June, but the second echelon did not arrive until 11 July.

The second echelon was still at sea when Admiral Ghormley called Vandegrift to Auckland on 26 June to announce the plan to use the 1st Marine Division (less 7th Marines), reinforced by the 2d Marines, the 1st Raider Battalion, and the 3d Defense Battalion, in the Solomons about 1 August 1942. The division's plans had to be prepared semi-independently, for Admirals Fletcher and Turner had not yet arrived in the South Pacific. According to Vandegrift, "there was no time for a deliberate planning phase, and in many instances irrevocable decisions had to be made even before the essential features of the naval plan of operations could be ascertained"; there was "an absence of meeting of minds of commanders concerned." General Vandegrift's plans were based upon the assumption that the Allies would firmly control the air and sea routes to the Solomons.[33]

[31] COMINCH, F F 1/A3–1/A16–3(5) Basic Supporting Plan for the Establishment of the SOPAC AMPHFOR (Lone Wolf Plan), Ser 00322, 29 Apr 42. Copies of this plan are in Plans and Opns Div, GSUSA.

[32] 1st Mar Div, Final Rpt Guadalcanal Opn, I, 2. Copy in the files of the Hist Div, SSUSA.

[33] Ltr, CG 1st Mar Div to Comdt Mar Corps, 1 Jul 43, sub: Final Rpt Guadalcanal Opn, in 1st Mar Div Rpt, V.

GUADALCANAL'S NORTH COAST CORRIDOR *between the sea and high ground to the south (left) was the scene of the major portion of the island battle. West of the Lunga River (narrow gorge just beyond the first lateral range of hills) the land is covered by dense forest broken by open, grassy ridges and ravines running at right angles to the coast line. The tip of land near the upper right corner of the picture is Point Cruz, with the village of Kokumbona at the turn of land beyond. The mountain range on the horizon ends in Cape Esperance just right of the highest hill point and some 25 miles from Lunga Point.*

In a little over one month the division, hiding its preparations under the guise of preliminaries for amphibious training, had to prepare tactical and logistical plans, unload part of its ships, reload for combat, sail from Wellington to the Fijis, rehearse, and sail to the Solomons, in addition to gathering data on the islands and on Japanese strength and dispositions there.

Terrain and Intelligence

The 1st Marine Division's intelligence section, on receiving Ghormley's orders, immediately began to gather data on terrain, landing beaches, climate, and the natives, from U. S. Army and Navy monographs, extracts from the *Pacific Islands Year Book,* and reports of the British Navy and Colonial Office. There was no opportunity for ground patrols to reconnoiter the islands prior to the invasion. Col. Frank B. Goettge, the intelligence officer of the 1st Marine Division, and his section interviewed former Solomons residents, civil servants, and merchant ships' officers in New Zealand. On 1 July Colonel Goettge flew to General MacArthur's headquarters to collect information. Spending one week in Melbourne and several days in Sydney, he interviewed former residents of the Solomons in those cities. Eight of these men were given commissions or warrants by the Australian forces and were attached to the 1st Marine Division as guides, advisers, and pilots. They reported to division headquarters on 15 July to interpret maps and aerial photographs.

The Solomons, with their green mountains, forested shores, low-hanging clouds, and coral reefs, are beautiful when viewed from the air or from the calm interisland channels, but they present difficult terrain for military operations. They are covered by heavy, tropical rain forests. Mountains, deep rivers, swamps, heat, humidity, heavy rains, and mud, combined with the jungle, make all movements extremely difficult. Except along the sandy beaches vehicles cannot move until roads have been built. At the opening of the campaign there were few vehicular roads. Tulagi had some trails, and a trail had been built through the coconut groves on the north coast of Guadalcanal, but the only inland passages were native footpaths. There were no bridges suitable for artillery and heavy equipment.

The islands are unhealthful; malaria as well as dengue fever is common. The malarial (Anopheles) mosquito breeds in swamps, lagoons, sluggish streams, and puddles, and has seeded the natives heavily. In addition, fungus infections and sores were to plague all the troops. Only the utmost efforts at the prevention of disease would keep troops healthy, but living and combat conditions on Guadalcanal were to make systematic malaria control difficult.

Guadalcanal, which is shaped like a Paramecium, is ninety miles long and averages over twenty-five miles in width. A backbone of forested mountains and quiescent volcanoes, rising in some places as high as 7,000 feet, runs the length of the island. Coral reefs and sharply rising mountains make the south coast inhospitable for ships. The north coast has no harbors, but Sealark Channel is calm. Many sandy beaches on the north coast are free of reefs and provide suitable landing areas for amphibious operations. From Aola Bay to the Matanikau River, between the mountains and Sealark Channel, there is a flat, narrow, grassy plain. Coconut plantations line most of the beach, and there are some stretches of high, tough kunai grass. The plain is cut by many rivers and streams. They are generally deep and swift, and are frequently flooded by rains. Stagnant pools have formed at most of the river mouths through the accumulation of silt which, massing cones and sand bars, blocks the flow of water.

The coastal plain ends east of the Matanikau River; between the river and Cape Esperance at the northwest tip of the island a narrow corridor lies between the coastline and the high ground on the south. Steep ravines and abruptly rising ridges cut laterally across the corridor. Lunga Point, where the Japanese were building their airstrip in July and August of 1942, is dominated by Mount Austen, a 1,514-foot-high series of ridges and knolls about six miles southwest of the point.

Colonel Goettge returned from General MacArthur's headquarters with its intelligence estimate of enemy strength and dispositions in the Solomon Islands, New Guinea, and the Bismarck Archipelago. This estimate, supplemented by aerial reconnaissance and reports from coastwatchers, was the basis of the division's estimate of enemy strength and dispositions in the Solomons. On 20 July division headquarters believed that 8,400 Japanese were on Guadalcanal and Tulagi, a figure which, like Admiral Turner's, much exceeded Admiral Ghormley's.[34] However, by 30 July, Admiral Turner had reduced the Marines' estimate to 7,125.

The 1st Marine Division continued to receive radio reports from the coastwatchers, which were monitored and transmitted by the American radio at Efate, even after the division's departure from Wellington. During the week preceding D Day, the Solomons coastwatching net broadcast reports three times daily in a special code. The reports were to have been relayed directly from Efate to Admiral Turner's flagship at sea, but as the code had not been

---

[34] 1st Mar Div Opn Ord No. 7-42, 20 Jul 42, Annex A, included in CTF 62, Opn Plan No. A3-42 as App. D.

properly intercepted they had to be relayed through Australia and New Zealand, a process which sometimes delayed them for three days.[35]

On 17 July two officers of the Marine division were taken by a B–17 on a reconnaissance flight from Port Moresby over Guadalcanal and Tulagi. They saw no evidence of any airfields, except for burned-off areas at Lunga Point and Tetere, nor any extensive beach defenses on the north coast of Guadalcanal. Returning to Wellington by way of Townsville, Australia, they brought back aerial photographs of Tulagi and a strip map of the Guadalcanal coast between Koli Point and the Matanikau River.

There were no good maps of Guadalcanal, a deficiency that was, in fact, never remedied throughout the campaign. During the planning phase the division's intelligence section never received what it considered an adequate number of aerial photographs of Guadalcanal, although it received a large number of the Tulagi area. The intelligence section used two U. S. Navy Hydrographic Charts as the bases for its maps. Chart No. 2658 of Tulagi and Gavutu, on a scale of 1/12,000, was fair, showing approximate elevations. Chart No. 2916 of Guadalcanal and Florida was enlarged to a scale of 1/108,643 but was inaccurate and lacked recent corrections. A crude sketch which had been prepared by colonial officials before the war aided in locating some trails and buildings but lacked contour lines and elevations. The division's base map for the Guadalcanal landing was a 9-sheet strip drawn and reproduced by the photolithographic section from aerial photographs which Colonel Goettge had brought from Australia. The map, based on photographs taken in late June, covered a narrow coastal strip on Guadalcanal from Lunga Point east to Aola. A rough, uncontrolled sketch showing rivers, plains, plantations, and forests, it was reproduced before the Amphibious Force's sortie from Wellington. No more photographs reached the division until 2 August, when Admiral McCain forwarded photographs which had been taken by a B–17 and had been developed aboard the *Enterprise*. These pictures of Tulagi and Lunga Point showed that the airstrip was nearly complete.

Logistics

The problems of logistics proved as serious as had those of procuring information about enemy strength and dispositions. Preparations began before the intelligence section had completed its work and before the final tactical plans were prepared. The logistical plans were based upon General Vandegrift's or-

---

[35] 1st Mar Div Rpt, I, Int Annex E.

MARINE COMMANDERS ON GUADALCANAL, *photographed 11 August 1942, in-cluded almost all the ranking Marine Corps officers who led the landing operations and early fighting of the campaign. Left to right, first row: Col. George R. Rowan, Col. Pedro A. del Valle, Col. William C. James, Maj. Gen. Alexander A. Vandegrift, Col. Gerald C. Thomas, Col. Clifton B. Cates, Col. Randolph McC. Pate and Commander Warwick T. Brown, USN. Second row: Col. William J. Whaling, Col. Frank B. Goettge, Col. LeRoy P. Hunt, Lt. Col. Frederick C. Biebush, Lt. Col. Edwin A. Pollock, Lt. Col. Edmund J. Buckley, Lt. Col. Walter W. Barr, and Lt. Col. Raymond P. Coffman. Third row: Lt. Col. Francis R. Geraci, Lt. Col. William E. Maxwell, Col. Edward G. Hagen, Lt. Col. William N. McKelvy, Lt. Col. Julian N. Frisbee, Maj. Milton V. O'Connell, Maj. William Chalfont, III, Capt. Horace W. Fuller, and Maj. Forest C. Thompson. Fourth row: Maj. Robert G. Ballance, Maj. Henry W. Bues, Jr., Maj. James G. Frazer, Maj. Richard H. Crockett, Lt. Col. Leonard B. Cresswell, Maj. Robert O. Bowen, Lt. Col. John A. Bemis, Maj. Robert B. Luckey, Lt. Col. Samuel G. Taxis, and Lt. Col. Eugene H. Price. Last row: Lt. Col. Merrill B. Twining, Lt. Col. Walker A. Reeves, Lt. Col. John DeW. Macklin, Lt. Col. Hanley C. Waterman, and Maj. James C. Murray.*

ganization of the division for combat. On 29 June he organized the division into two regimental combat groups each of about 4,500 men. Each group was organized into a headquarters and support group and three battalion combat teams.[36] Every combat group consisted of one infantry regiment, one artillery battalion, one company each from the tank, engineer, pioneer, amphibian tractor, and medical battalions, and scout, special weapons, and transport platoons. Each combat team was originally composed of one infantry battalion, one field artillery battery, and platoons of engineer, pioneer, and amphibian tractor personnel. Scouts, signal, medical, and other service personnel were added to the combat teams prior to the invasion.

Combat Group A, commanded by Col. Le Roy P. Hunt, was composed of the 5th Marines and supporting troops. Combat Teams Nos. 1, 2, and 3 of Combat Group A consisted of the reinforced 1st, 2d, and 3d Battalions, respectively, of the 5th Marines. Combat Group B, Col. Clifton B. Cates commanding, was made up of the 1st Marines and supporting troops. Combat Teams Nos. 4, 5, and 6 of Combat Group B consisted of the reinforced 1st, 2d, and 3d Battalions, respectively, of the 1st Marines. On 9 July the division support group was organized.[37] It consisted of about 3,500 men under Col. Pedro A. del Valle organized into four subgroups made up of headquarters, communications, medical, artillery, special weapons, pioneer, engineer, and amphibian tractor personnel and the 1st Parachute Battalion. The parachutists, fighting as infantry, were later assigned to the assault on Gavutu. The rear echelon, 1,729 men from all divisional units, including the 4th Battalion, 11th Marines (155–mm. howitzers), was to remain in Wellington when the division departed.

As each combat group was to be embarked in a transport division consisting of three transports and one cargo ship, every transport in each division was assigned to carry one combat team, three units of fire, thirty days' rations, and quartermaster, ordnance, engineer, chemical, signal, and medical supplies. Supporting troops, heavy equipment, seven units of fire, thirty days' rations and other supplies, and clothing stocks were assigned to each cargo ship.[38]

The logistical difficulties did not stem from shortages of materiel, for the division had come overseas with nearly all its equipment and supplies. The

[36] 1st Mar Div Opn Ord No. 5–42, 29 Jun 42, in 1st Mar Div Rpt, I, Annex B. The terms in the operation order differ from present day usage. The combat groups would now be regimental combat teams. The combat teams would be battalion landing teams.

[37] 1st Mar Div Opn Ord No. 6–42, 9 Jul 42, in 1st Mar Div Rpt, I, Annex D.

[38] Airmailgram, CG 1st Mar Div to CO, Combat Gp A, 29 Jun 42, in 1st Mar Div Rpt, I, Annex C.

shortages were in dock space, time, and shipping. In late June there were just seven ships of the Amphibious Force in Wellington Harbor—five transports and two cargo ships.[39] More vessels had been assigned, but it was apparent that there would not be enough cargo space to combat-load all the division with its supplies and equipment. To embark the maximum number of troops, General Vandegrift ordered that "all units . . . reduce their equipment and supplies to those items that are actually required to live and fight."[40] The division was ordered to embark bulk supplies, including rations and fuel, for sixty days instead of the ninety days then considered necessary.[41] The ammunition allowance was reduced by one-half. Office equipment, cut to a minimum, included no more than two typewriters per battalion headquarters and four per regimental headquarters. Mess equipment was limited to water bags, vacuum food carriers, camp kettles, coffee mills, and stoves. The order directed that all the division's motor transport would be embarked; all sandbags, rubber boats, outboard motors, camouflage and chemical warfare equipment, all engineering materiel,[42] water purification equipment, sixty days' clothing replenishment (shoes, socks, and green utility suits), and thirty days' post exchange supplies (tobacco, matches, soap, and razor blades only) were to be embarked. Officers and enlisted men were ordered to take with them all their individual equipment but to reduce their baggage to a minimum. Each officer was allowed one bedding roll, clothing roll, or handbag, while enlisted men were limited to what they could carry in their packs.

Loading the division's weapons and supplies on board the ships was a difficult matter. Aotea Quay in Wellington was small and could berth only five ships at the same time. Combat Group A had already landed, unloaded, and been established inland in base camps prior to 29 June. To clear the quay for the second echelon, it was decided to begin the embarkation of Combat Group A and its equipment and supplies on 2 July. The division supply officer organized the embarkation and combat loading, exercising control through transport quartermasters on the ships and through field officers in charge of the 300-man working parties assigned to each ship. Organized into three reliefs, the working parties labored around the clock in 8-hour shifts. Except for a few skilled

---

[39] SOPAC War Diary, 19 Jun 42.

[40] 1st Mar Div Admin Ord No. 1a–42, 29 Jun 42, in 1st Mar Div Rpt, I, Annex J.

[41] 1st Mar Div Rpt, I, 6; Ltr, CG 1st Mar Div to Comdt Mar Corps, 1 Jul 43, sub: Final Rpt Guadalcanal Opn.

[42] The first orders stated that the temporary pier would not be loaded. They were apparently changed, for the engineers brought the pier to Guadalcanal. No subsequent orders regarding the pier are in 1st Mar Div Rpt, I.

civilian operators of loading machines, cranes, hoists, carriers, and stacking machines, marines performed all dockside labor. All divisional motor transport plus eighteen 10-wheeled trucks of the 1st Base Depot and thirty flat-bedded New Zealand Army lorries moved supplies, equipment, and ammunition from their depots to the dockside. By 13 July Combat Group A and its gear had been embarked. A few shortages were made up by local purchases in Wellington, and others were alleviated by materiel carried by the second echelon. After embarkation Combat Group A practiced landings in Wellington Harbor.

The second echelon—largely troops of Combat Group B and the Support Group—encountered much greater difficulty. It arrived at Aotea Quay on 11 July, while Combat Group A was completing its embarkation. As it had not been anticipated that the division would be tactically employed after its arrival in New Zealand, the ships had not been combat-loaded before leaving the United States. Most of the troops had been carried across the Pacific aboard passenger vessels, while cargo ships carried their supplies and equipment. The second echelon was forced to unload, sort, and classify stores and equipment on the limited dock space, and to reload for combat by 22 July. The weather had been clear while the first group had embarked, but, during the entire period of the second echelon's unloading and reembarkation, cold, driving rains typical of a New Zealand winter made the task miserable. The morale of the troops, working in the rain, was low.[43] Many of the supplies had been packed in cardboard cartons, which, becoming soggy from the rains, burst and strewed their contents over the docks. Other cardboard cartons, stacked inside the warehouse, were crushed.

Lack of cargo space prevented the division from loading all its motor transport aboard the twelve available ships. Nearly all the quarter-ton and one-ton trucks were put aboard, but 75 percent of the heavier vehicles were left behind in Wellington with the rear echelon. The engineers expected that the Lunga Point airfield would perhaps be almost complete by D Day, but put earth-moving equipment, in addition to bridging equipment and a portable dock, aboard the cargo ship *Fomalhaut*.

Medical preparations for the campaign had not been difficult. Those medically unfit for foreign service had been left behind in the United States. The standard of health remained fairly high, except for troops on board one transport of the second echelon. Among those marines rotten food on the voyage to

---

[43] 1st Mar Div Rpt, I, Logistics Annex L.

New Zealand had caused a loss of weight varying from sixteen to twenty pounds per man, as well as a diarrhea epidemic. Exposure while loading in Wellington had resulted in some cases of colds and influenza, and a few sporadic cases of mumps broke out en route to the target area. The medical plans provided for medical care, under combat conditions, of 18,134 men for ninety days.[44]

By 22 July reloading had been completed, and the division was ready to sail from Wellington.

Tactical Plans

On 20 July, when logistical preparations had been almost completed in Wellington, General Vandegrift issued tactical orders for the landings. The grouping of forces for Tulagi and Guadalcanal was based upon the premise that of the 8,400 Japanese which the intelligence section believed to be defending the objectives 1,400 troops, including one infantry and one antiaircraft battalion, were in the Tulagi area. One reinforced infantry regiment, one antiaircraft battalion, one engineer battalion, pioneers, and others—7,000 in all—were thought to be on Guadalcanal.[45] The major part of these were expected to be at Lunga Point, with a smaller force at Koli Point. These estimates greatly exaggerated enemy strength. In early August there were about 780 Japanese in the Tulagi–Gavutu–Tanambogo area, and 2,230 on Guadalcanal.[46] Admiral Ghormley's original estimate of 3,100 had been correct.

As it was anticipated that the invasion of the Tulagi area, involving direct assaults against small islands, would be the most difficult, the most experienced battalions were assigned to this attack. To protect the flanks of the units landing on Tulagi and other islets, small forces were to land first on near-by Florida. One battalion would then land on Tulagi, followed quickly by a second. A third battalion would land on Gavutu at H plus 4 hours to seize Gavutu and Tanambogo.

The Guadalcanal landing presented a simpler tactical problem than did the landing on Tulagi. The large number of undefended beaches on the north coast would make it possible for the remainder of the division to land unopposed at some distance from the Japanese. The area selected for the landing lies between

---

[44] 1st Mar Div Rpt, I, Med Annex M does not mention malaria.

[45] Ist Mar Div Opn Ord No. 7–42, Annex A.

[46] AFPAC G–3 Hist Sec, and ATIS, interrog of Lt Gen Harukichi Hyakutake (former CG, *17th Army*), Maj Gen Shuicho Miyazaki (former CofS, *17th Army*), and Lt Gen Masao Maruyama (former CG, *2d Div*), 31 Aug 46; *17th Army* Opns, I, gives even lower figures—1,850 on Guadalcanal, 1 company on Tulagi, and 1 platoon on Gavutu.

CHART NO. 3
Organization of Landing Force for Task One

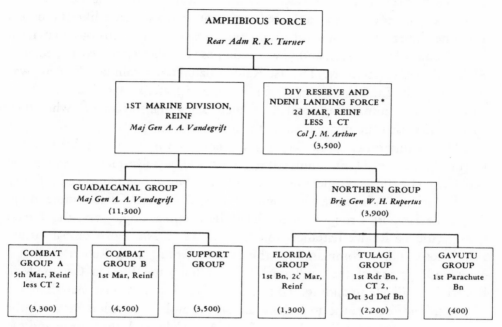

* Division reserve was released to Vandegrift 7–9 August.

the Tenaru[47] and Tenavatu Rivers, about 6,000 yards east of the Lunga airstrip, well away from both Lunga and Koli Points. Having landed and established a beachhead, the Guadalcanal Group of the division under General Vandegrift could then attack west to capture the airfield. This maneuver would require the troops to cross both the Tenaru and the Ilu Rivers, but the Tenaru and the Tenavatu Rivers, on either flank of the beach, would help to protect the beachhead if the Japanese counterattacked while men and supplies were coming ashore.

The orders issued on 20 July utilized the previous organization of the division into combat groups, combat teams, and the support group. The orders also organized the reinforcing units—the reinforced 2d Marines, the 1st Raider Battalion, and 3d Defense Battalion—which had not then joined the division. The

[47] In the early maps, the names of the Tenaru and the Ilu Rivers were transposed. The Ilu lies about 2¾ miles east of the Lunga. The wide part of the river is also known as Alligator Creek.

2d Marines, Reinforced, commanded by Col. John M. Arthur, included the 2d Marines, the 3d Battalion of the 10th Marines (75-mm. pack howitzers), and engineer, pioneer, amphibian tractor, tank, medical, and other service troops— a total of 4,840 men. This reinforced regiment was organized like the others into a headquarters and support group and three combat teams of about 1,300 each. Combat Teams A, B, and C were composed of the reinforced 1st, 2d, and 3d Battalions, respectively. The 1st Raider Battalion, totaling 828 men, was commanded by Lt. Col. Merritt A. Edson. The 3d Defense Battalion, Col. Robert H. Pepper commanding, totaled 872 men. These reinforcements, when they arrived, increased the division strength to over 19,000.[48]

The 20 July orders prescribed eight groups of varying strengths: Combat Group A, Colonel Hunt commanding, 4,398 (to be subsequently reduced by about 1,100 by the assignment of Combat Team No. 2, one reinforced infantry battalion, to the Tulagi attack); Combat Group B, Colonel Cates commanding, 4,531; the Support Group, Colonel del Valle commanding, 3,537; the Tulagi Group (the 1st Raider Battalion and Combat Team No. 2 of Combat Group A), Colonel Edson commanding; the Gavutu Group, Maj. Robert Williams commanding, 395 of the 1st Parachute Battalion; the Florida Group, Maj. Robert E. Hill commanding, 1,295 of Combat Team A (1st Battalion, 2d Marines, Reinforced); the 3d Defense Battalion; and the Division Reserve—the 2d Marines, Reinforced (less Combat Team A)—Colonel Arthur commanding, 3,545.

These forces were to attack and destroy the hostile garrisons on Guadalcanal, Tulagi, Gavutu, Tanambogo, and Makambo by landings on D Day, and then to organize the defense of those islands. There were not enough landing craft, however, to execute all landings simultaneously. At H minus 20 minutes, one rifle company and one machine gun platoon of Combat Team A (1st Battalion, 2d Marines, Reinforced) were to land at Haleta on Florida, just west of Tulagi, to cover the Tulagi landing. At H plus 30 minutes the remainder of Combat Team A would seize Halavo, the peninsula on Florida just east of Gavutu, and support the Gavutu assault by fire.

The Tulagi Group, led by the 1st Raider Battalion, would land on a 500-yard front on Tulagi at H Hour and seize the northwest part of the island. Having reached the first phase line about 1,500 yards northwest of the southeast shore, the assault troops would signal for a 5-minute air and naval bombard-

---

[48] 1st Mar Div Rpt, I, 9, gives 19,546; Annex K gives 19,105; V, Personnel Annex W, gives 19,360 effectives.

ment upon the defense positions in the hills and ravines around Government House, the cricket field, the hospital, the prison, and the radio station, then attack and capture that area. Once taken, the island was to pass to the control of the commander of Combat Team No. 2 (2d Battalion, 5th Marines, Reinforced, less E Battery, 11th Marines) of Combat Group A. The 1st Raider Battalion would then prepare to re-embark for further operations. Combat Team No. 2 was to embark enough troops to seize Makambo, northeast of Tulagi, and also was to relieve the 1st Parachute Battalion after it had captured Gavutu and Tanambogo. The 3d Defense Battalion was to land one-third of its antiaircraft strength on Tulagi.

The 1st Parachute Battalion was to land on the east coast of Gavutu at H plus 4 hours, seize it, and then take Tanambogo, the small island connected with Gavutu by a concrete causeway. The firing of a green star cluster would be the signal for five minutes of naval gunfire on Tanambogo from the Tulagi Fire Support Group. After the capture of the islets the battalion was to be prepared to re-embark for employment elsewhere.

While operations were being conducted against the northern islets by air squadrons, the Tulagi Fire Support Group, Transport Group Y, and the Marine units under General Rupertus' command, the rest of the force—air squadrons, the Guadalcanal Fire Support Group, Transport Group X, and the majority of the Marine division under General Vandegrift—would be operating against Guadalcanal. Combat Group A (5th Marines, Reinforced), less Combat Team No. 2 (2d Battalion, Reinforced, less E Battery, 11th Marines), was to land at Zero Hour on a 1,600-yard front with combat teams abreast to take the beachhead. Combat Group B (1st Marines, Reinforced) was to land in column of battalions at Zero plus 50 minutes, pass through Group A, and attack westward toward the "grassy knoll" (Mount Austen) which was erroneously believed to be only four instead of six miles southwest of Lunga Point. This course, it was hoped, would prevent the Japanese from escaping southward into the mountains. The 1st Marines was to maintain contact with the units advancing on its right. The formation would be a column of battalions echeloned to the left and rear to protect the left flank. Group A, after Group B had passed through, was to send Combat Team No. 1 (1st Battalion, 5th Marines) west along the shore to seize the Ilu River line. In the order the Ilu was mistakenly called the Tenaru. Combat Team No. 3 (3d Battalion, 5th Marines) was to seize the line of woods running southeast from the Tenavatu River, thus covering the east line of the beachhead. The division's light tanks, landing with the combat groups, were also to cover the east flank of the beachhead but were not to be committed to action except on orders from General Vandegrift. Platoons of A Battery of the 1st Special Weapons Battalion were to land on the flanks of the beach to provide antiaircraft defense with automatic weapons. They were to revert to control of the 1st Special Weapons Battalion of the Support Group upon the landing of that battalion's headquarters.

The artillery battalions of the combat groups were to land with their groups, but to pass to control of the headquarters of the 11th Marines of the Support Group upon the landing of that headquarters. The Support Group, including elements of the artillery, engineer, special weapons, and pioneer battalions was to land on orders from division headquarters, and to co-ordinate the artillery support for the attacks of the Combat Groups as well as the antiaircraft defense of the beachhead. The 3d Defense Battalion (less one-third of its antiaircraft units) was to land on divisional order, pass to control of the Support Group, and assist in the defense of the beachhead.

Combat Team A of the division reserve (2d Marines, Reinforced) had been released to General Vandegrift for the Florida landing, but the remainder of the reserve was to remain under Admiral Turner's control for the occupation of Ndeni if it was not required for Guadalcanal and Tulagi. General Vandegrift ordered the reserve, however, to be prepared to land Combat Team B less its reinforcing elements at H plus 4 hours, and to be ready to attach Combat Team C minus its reinforcing units to the Tulagi Group.[49]

Final Preparations

While the division was making ready for combat, the other units which were to make up the invading force were sailing toward their respective rendezvous areas. The carrier *Wasp* came from the Atlantic Ocean through the Panama Canal. On 1 July she sailed from San Diego, escorting the five ships bearing the 2d Marines, Reinforced, across the Pacific. On 7 July the carrier *Saratoga,* with Admiral Fletcher on board, and her supporting warships departed from Pearl Harbor, followed by the carrier *Enterprise* and her supporting ships. The destroyer-transports, which had helped to escort the *Enterprise,* left the carrier at sea and sailed to New Caledonia to embark the 1st Raider Battalion. The ships from the Southwest Pacific left Brisbane, Australia, on 14

[49] 1st Mar Div Opn Ord No. 7–42, 20 Jul 42, in 1st Mar Div Rpt, I, Annex F, and in CTF 62, Opn Plan No. A3–42, App. D.

July and arrived at New Zealand five days later to come under Admiral Turner's control. On 21 July Admiral Fletcher, commanding Task Force 61, ordered all units to rendezvous southeast of the Fiji Islands at 1400, 26 July. The 3d Defense Battalion, on board the *Zeilin* and *Betelgeuse,* escorted by two destroyers, did not leave Pearl Harbor until 22 July and did not join the task force until 3 August.[50]

The twelve transports and cargo ships of the Amphibious Force, carrying the 1st Marine Division together with their escorts, sailed from Wellington on 22 July under Admiral Turner's command. On 26 July the entire Expeditionary Force (Task Force 61), except the *Zeilin* and *Betelgeuse* and their escorts, assembled southeast of the Fijis, and on the next day sailed to Koro for the rehearsal.

From 28 through 31 July the Expeditionary Force rehearsed with carrier air groups participating. The rehearsal was far from being a success. One of the most serious handicaps was the necessity for maintaining radio silence which made ground-to-air communication impossible and impeded the co-ordination of ground force attacks with close air support.[51] Two complete landing exercises simulating the scheme of maneuver had been planned, but coral reefs made the beaches impracticable for landings. General Vandegrift, who firmly believed in the necessity for complete rehearsals, later wrote that the advantages gained from the Koro rehearsal were "dubious" when compared with the loss of "priceless time."[52] The rehearsal had some value, however, for the force received practice in debarkation procedure and in the conduct and timing of boat waves. The forces supporting the ground troops had an opportunity for firing and bombing practice. Since McCain, Fletcher, Turner, and Vandegrift all attended the rehearsal, they seized this first opportunity for close personal conferences during which they discussed their plans in detail.[53]

Since the performance of landing craft at the rehearsal led the commanders to expect numerous mechanical break-downs, a boat pool was organized. It was at Koro that the decision was made to land first at Tulagi and later at Guadalcanal on D Day. The transport *Heywood,* carrying both the 1st Parachute Battalion and elements of the Guadalcanal Support Group, would have

[50] See Landing in the Solomons, pp. 9–13.

[51] *Ibid.,* p. 21.

[52] Ltr, CG 1st Mar Div to Comdt Mar Corps, 1 Jul 43, sub: Final Rpt Guadalcanal Opn.

[53] 1st Mar Div Rpt, I, 7; Landing in the Solomons, pp. 21–22; COMAMPHIBFORSOPAC War Diary, 29 Jul 42.

OLD-TYPE LANDING CRAFT *used in the Guadalcanal operation included the fixed-bow LCP(L)'s shown above being hand-unloaded at Red Beach by newly arrived Americal Division troops, and the unarmored amphibian tractor (LVT) which was protected by machine guns.*

to unload the Parachute Battalion in the Tulagi area and then cross the channel to land tanks on Guadalcanal.

The landing craft carried by the ships of the Amphibious Force amounted to 480 1942-model boats of various types,[54] in addition to the vehicles of the 1st Amphibian Tractor Battalion of the 1st Marine Division. There were 8 30-foot landing craft, 308 36-foot LCP(L)'s and LCP(R)'s, 116 36-foot LCV's, and 48 45-foot LCM's.[55] The 30-foot boats and the LCP(L)'s were the old fixed-bow type without ramps. The LCP(R)'s, the LCM's and the LCV's were equipped with movable bow ramps. The LCV's, each with a 10,000-pound cargo capacity, could carry 75-mm. and 105-mm. howitzers or 1-ton trucks, but heavier equipment (90-mm. and 5-inch guns and heavy trucks) would have to be carried in the LCM's. The LCP(L)'s could carry troops and portable supplies, but all supplies brought ashore by the LCP(L)'s would have to be lifted over the gunwales by hand at a considerable expense of time and manpower. The amphibian tractors (LVT's), about to make their first appearance in action, were an early, unarmored type mounting two machine guns.

The final details of organization of the boat pool, including all boats from the ships of the Amphibious Force, were completed during the rehearsal. Ten boat groups, varying in size from sixteen to sixty-four boats of various types, were organized. Nearly every group included one craft assigned as a repair boat. Four groups, including 103 craft, were assigned to the Tulagi area to unload Transport Group Y, and the remaining six groups were assigned to unload Transport Group X at Guadalcanal. The assaulting combat teams would be brought ashore by ninety-one craft—sixty-three carrying Combat Team No. 1 and Headquarters and supporting troops of Combat Group A, and twenty-eight carrying Combat Team No. 3. Combat Group A's tanks would be brought in by sixteen LCM's. Forty-one boats would carry the next waves—Combat Team No. 4 and Headquarters, Combat Group B. Following the landing of the first elements of Combat Group B the forty-one boats would join an additional fifty-one to carry Combat Team No. 5. Combat Team No. 6 would be borne ashore by fifty-seven craft.

After the landing of the assault troops, the LCM's of the boat groups, in

[54] 1st Mar Div Opn Ord No. 7–42, Annex F, in App. D, CTF 62, Opn Plan No. A3–42; Landing in the Solomons, p. 34, gives 467.

[55] Marine Corps designations for landing craft have been changed since August 1942. These craft were then designated as follows: 30-foot boats, X; LCP(L)'s, T Boats; LCP(R)'s, TP Boats; LCV's, TR Boats, and LCM's, YL's.

general, were to continue unloading heavy equipment from certain specified ships, while the other boats returned to their mother ships to unload them, bringing in supporting troops and supplies on the second, third, and succeeding trips to shore. General Vandegrift also ordered that amphibian tractors be used wherever possible to haul supplies. Although not a tactical vehicle, the unarmored amphibian tractor could sail from ship to shore, surmount the beach, and carry supplies overland directly to regimental and battalion dumps, with a resulting economy in both time and labor.

Those troop commanders who were to be responsible for the complete unloading of the ships were to assign enough men to work all ships' holds twenty-four hours per day, for all ships were to be unloaded in the shortest possible time. Supplies were to move over the beaches in accordance with the following priority: ammunition, water, combat transport, rations, medical supplies, gasoline, other transport, and lastly, miscellaneous supplies.

All men, as originally planned, were to wear green utility suits and to carry head nets and cot nets for protection against mosquitoes. Each man was to carry two canteens of water if enough canteens were available.

The men of the task and landing forces were to initiate the first Allied offensive in the Pacific, one of the largest amphibious operations in the history of the United States up to that time. The tactical plans were hastily prepared, but they had a broad and well-established base in the doctrines governing landings on hostile shores which had been developed during the years preceding the outbreak of war.[56] It is significant to note that whereas plans for the landing operations proper were detailed and comprehensive, there was no reference to systematic re-supply of the 1st Marine Division which carried sufficient supplies for sixty days. Although on 14 July Admiral Ghormley had directed the 7th Marines in Samoa to be ready to embark on four days' notice with ninety days' supply and ten units of fire, no Army units for reinforcing or relieving the division were alerted.[57]

---

[56] For a complete exposition of doctrine on landing operations, see Division of Fleet Training, Office of Naval Operations: Landing Operations Doctrine, United States Navy, (FTP 167), 1938, and subsequent revisions.

[57] COMSOPAC to CG Samoa, 0245 of 14 Jul 42. SOPAC War Diary.

CHAPTER III

The Invasion

While the invasion force was assembling and rehearsing, Army B–17's of the 26th Squadron of the 11th Bombardment Group, which were part of Task Force 63, had been executing daily bombardments of Guadalcanal and Tulagi to "soften" them before the invasion. The 26th Squadron was then based at Efate and Espiritu Santo. The air strips at both islands were each 5,000 feet long and 150 feet wide by the end of July,[1] but facilities were primitive. The runways were soft and were frequently covered by water from the many rains. For night take-offs, the ends of the runways were marked by truck headlights, and the sides by rags stuck in bottles of gasoline and set ablaze.[2] Beginning on 31 July, the B–17's bombed Guadalcanal and Tulagi for seven days. One B–17 was lost, but the 26th Squadron shot down three Japanese fighters. Since the airfield on Guadalcanal had no planes, the principal targets were the runways and suspected supply depots and antiaircraft positions on both Guadalcanal and Tulagi.[3]

The Approach

The Amphibious Force, covered by the Air Support Force and by Task Force 63, had left Koro in the Fijis on a southwesterly course on 31 July. Four days later the *Betelgeuse* and *Zeilin* with their escorts joined Transport Groups X and Y, respectively, to bring the total number of ships in the Expeditionary Force to 82, and the number of men in the landing force to over 19,000. Sailing in three great concentric circles—the transports in the middle, the cruisers around them, and the screening destroyers in the outer circle—the Amphibious Force reached a point south of Rennell, then swung north and set its course for Savo Island, while the carriers sailed for a point southwest of Guadalcanal. On

[1] Hist USAFISPA, Pt. I, I, 85.
[2] 11th Bomb Gp (H) Hist, p. 6.
[3] Rads, COMGENSOPAC to WDCSA, CM–IN–3200, 4 Aug, and CM -IN–5391, 14 Aug 42.

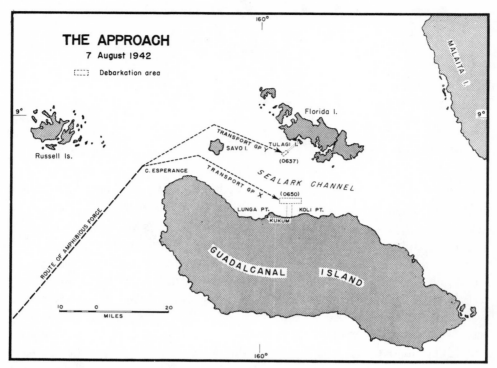

THE APPROACH

7 August 1942

☐☐☐☐ Debarkation area

Russell Is.

Florida I.

SAVO I.

TULAGI I.

(0637)

C. ESPERANCE

SEALARK CHANNEL

(0650)

LUNGA PT.   KOLI PT.

KUKUM

GUADALCANAL   ISLAND

ROUTE OF AMPHIBIOUS FORCE

TRANSPORT GP Y

TRANSPORT GP X

MALAITA I.

10   0   20

MILES

MAP NO. 1

5 and 6 August, during the Amphibious Force's northward run west of Guadalcanal, overcast skies and a heavy haze reduced visibility to four miles and limited air operations.[4] Intermittent rain squalls helped to cover the ships, which
were maintaining radio silence. There were no contacts with the enemy.[5]

The weather cleared for the approaching American ships on the night of
6–7 August, and the Amphibious Force, still undetected, raised Savo Island at
0200.[6] Clear skies and a moon in the last quarter provided good visibility as the
force passed into the calm, narrow waters between Savo, Guadalcanal, and
Florida. The transport groups separated at 0240, 7 August. (*Map 1*) The four
transports and four destroyer-transports of one group sailed around Savo to enter
Sealark Channel between Savo and Florida. The fifteen transports of the Guadalcanal Group entered the channel between Savo and Cape Esperance on

[4] COMAMPHIBFORSOPAC War Diary, 6–7 Aug 42.
[5] *Ibid.*
[6] 1st Mar Div Rpt, I, 9.

Guadalcanal.[7] As daylight broke, the islands lay quiet. The Japanese were taken by surprise; not one shot had been fired at the Amphibious Force.

The supporting warships took station, while their observation planes flew over the target areas. The three cruisers and four destroyers of the Guadalcanal Fire Support Group opened fire on their targets between Kukum and Koli Point on Guadalcanal at 0614. Two minutes later the cruiser and two destroyers comprising the Tulagi Fire Support Group opened fire on Tulagi.[8] The minesweepers covered their assigned areas but found no mines. By 0651 the transport groups had reached their areas, 9,000 yards off the landing beaches, and lowered landing craft into the water. A calm sea permitted the troops to descend via cargo-net gangways on both sides of all transports into the landing craft. H Hour, the time for the Tulagi landing, was set for 0800. Zero Hour, the time for the landing on Guadalcanal, was finally set at 0910.[9]

Ships' gunfire and strafing by fighter planes quickly sank a small gasoline schooner, the only visible enemy vessel in Sealark Channel. Dive bombers and fighters from the carriers, then maneuvering seventy-five miles to the south in open waters, bombed and strafed the target areas, but encountered only feeble antiaircraft fire. Forty-four planes struck at Guadalcanal, and forty-one attacked Tulagi. Eighteen Japanese seaplanes were destroyed.[10]

The Northern Attack

Tulagi

The initial Allied landing in the Solomon Islands, which preceded those on Tulagi, Gavutu, and Tanambogo, was made by a covering force. (*Map 2*) Supported by fire from the cruiser and destroyers of the Tulagi Fire Support Group and the minesweepers, landing boats put B Company of the 2d Marines ashore near Haleta, a village adjoining a promontory on Florida Island which commands Beach Blue on Tulagi.[11] The remainder of the 1st Battalion of the 2d Marines landed at Halavo on Florida to cover the landings. No enemy forces opposed either landing, and the battalion was later withdrawn.

Covered by fire from the supporting cruiser and destroyers, the first wave

[7] CTG 62.1 SOPACFOR: Rpt Action Guadalcanal–Tulagi Area, Solomon Islands, Aug 7–8 and 9, 1942, Ser 0027, 23 Sep 43, p. 3. This report is filed in the Office of Naval Records and Library.

[8] COMAMPHIBFORSOPAC War Diary, 7 Aug 42.

[9] 1st Mar Div Rpt, II, Annex N (1st Mar Div D–3 Journal), 1.

[10] Landing in the Solomons, p. 10.

[11] Hist Sec, Hq, USMC: The Guadalcanal Campaign: August 1942 to February 1943 (June 1945), p. 14.

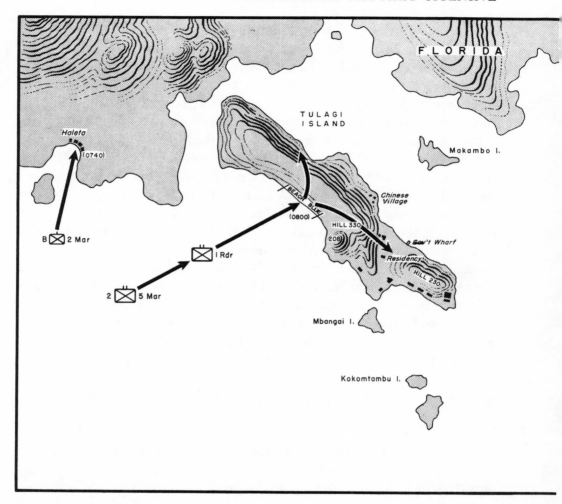

MAP NO. 2

of landing craft carrying B and D Companies of the 1st Raider Battalion sailed to Beach Blue on Tulagi, a small, hilly island about three miles long. The enemy was not defending Beach Blue but had retired to caves and dugouts in the hills and ravines on the southeast part of the island. The only casualty in landing was one raider killed by rifle fire. The second wave, A and C Companies, quickly followed B and D Companies which then advanced north across the island. The 2d Battalion, 5th Marines, then came ashore and pushed north-

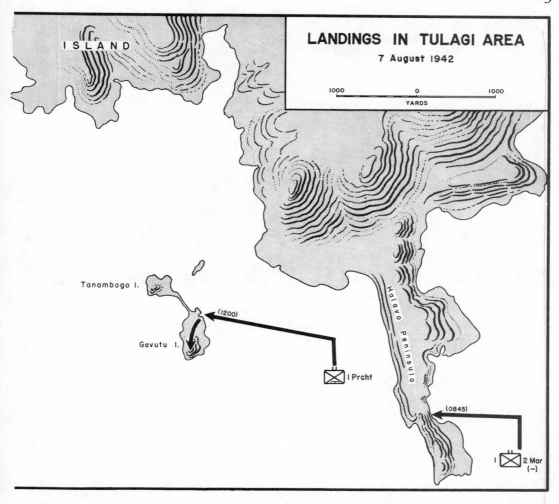

LANDINGS IN TULAGI AREA
7 August 1942

1000   0   1000
YARDS

west to clear out the enemy in the northwest part of the island. The raider companies turned right and advanced to the southeast, supported by E Company,
the raiders' heavy weapons company. There was no hard fighting until the
afternoon when fire from Japanese caves and dugouts halted the raiders about
one mile short of Tulagi's southeast tip. The marines discovered that the ships'
gunfire and dive bombing had not destroyed the caves and dugouts, most of
which would withstand everything but a direct hit. Machine-gun fire was rela-

TULAGI ISLAND, *photographed 7 August during a pre-invasion bombardment. Florida Island is in the background across Tulagi anchorage.*

LANDINGS ON FLORIDA ISLAND *were made by 2d Marines without opposition.*

tively ineffective against the tunnels and caves, which were not constructed along straight lines. The most efficient means for destroying the enemy positions were grenades and high explosive charges placed by hand.[12]

The Japanese sailors and laborers fought from foxholes, pillboxes, slit trenches, and caves. They refused to surrender and fought until they were shot or blown up. Machine gunners fired their weapons until they were killed. When one gunner fell, another would take his place, a process that continued until all in the position were dead.

By late afternoon it had become obvious that the raiders could not complete the capture of Tulagi on 7 August, and the battalion established a defensive line about 1,000 yards from the southeast tip of the island. The five raider companies and G Company of the 5th Marines occupied these positions, which the enemy attacked repeatedly but unsuccessfully throughout the night of 7–8 August.

The first reports estimated that the raiders had suffered casualties amounting to 22 percent of their total strength on Tulagi; the 1st Parachute Battalion was reported to have lost from 50 to 60 percent on Gavutu. General Vandegrift requested Admiral Turner at 0135, 8 August, to release the remaining battalions of the 2d Marines from division reserve for the Tulagi–Gavutu operation. Admiral Turner assented.[13]

On the morning of 8 August F and E Companies of the 5th Marines, having cleared the northwest part of Tulagi, joined G Company and the five companies of the 1st Raider Battalion. The combined force pressed its attack, reduced the enemy positions, and by 1500 had completed the occupation of Tulagi. Only three of the original Japanese garrison surrendered; an estimated forty escaped to Florida by swimming. The remainder, about 200 men, were killed. The Marine casualties on Tulagi, Gavutu, and Tanambogo, which had been exaggerated in the first reports, were lighter than those of the Japanese. On Tulagi thirty-six were killed and fifty-four wounded.[14] Captured materiel included trucks, motorcycles, ammunition, gasoline, radio supplies, two 13-mm. antiaircraft guns, one 3-inch gun, and ten machine guns.

Gavutu and Tanambogo

While the 1st Raider Battalion and the 2d Battalion of the 5th Marines were

---

[12] Flame throwers were not then in use. General Vandegrift wrote that they would have been "practical and effective," and recommended dive bombing with depth charges. 1st Mar Div Rpt, II, 8.

[13] COMAMPHIBFORSOPAC War Diary, 8 Aug 42.

[14] 1st Mar Div Rpt, II, 4.

GAVUTU and TANAMBOGO, *photographed on the afternoon of 7 August from the northeast, were taken after heavy fighting. Fires in a warehouse area on Tanambogo were started by bombardment before the unsuccessful first attempt to capture the small island.*

THE SOUTHEAST END OF TULAGI *was heavily defended by the enemy dug into the steep hillsides and ravines. On the hill, center, are two antiaircraft positions and at right, the prison. Marines' attack came from the left of the picture.*

reducing Tulagi, the islets of Gavutu and Tanambogo, lying 3,000 yards to the east, also saw hard fighting. Gavutu is 250 by 500 yards in size and Tanambogo, a slightly smaller island, is joined to Gavutu by a 300-yard-long concrete causeway.

Dive bombers (SBD's) attacked Gavutu from 1145 to 1155 on 7 August. The Tulagi Fire Support Group shelled Gavutu from 1155 to 1200 to cover the 7-mile approach of the thirteen landing craft bearing the 1st Parachute Battalion to the seaplane slips and jetties on Gavutu's northeast corner. The bombardment had knocked several large concrete blocks from the ramps into the water, and the parachutists were forced to land at the docks and mount them in face of enemy small-arms fire. The first wave reached shore safely, but succeeding waves were hit hard, about one man in ten becoming a casualty. By 1400 the parachutists were advancing inland under fire from the Japanese emplaced on the island's single hill and on near-by Tanambogo. By 1800 the battalion had secured the hill and raised the national colors there. The Japanese retained possession of several dugouts until the afternoon of 8 August, when they were reduced by the parachutists and two companies of the 2d Marines.

In spite of air bombardment and naval shelling, the Japanese on Tanambogo continued active on 7 August. After being withdrawn from Haleta, B Company of the 2d Marines attempted to land on Tanambogo's north coast after a 5-minute naval bombardment, but the attack failed. About 1130 the next day, the 3d Battalion of the 2d Marines and two light tanks attacked Tanambogo from the beach and the causeway and secured most of the island by late afternoon. By nightfall all the Japanese were dead. Marine casualties in the Tanambogo–Gavutu attacks had been relatively heavy; 108 were dead or missing, 140 wounded. The marines later estimated that nearly 1,000 Japanese had held Gavutu and Tanambogo, but the actual figure was about 500.

On 8 and 9 August the 2d Marines completed the northern attack by seizing the adjacent islets of Mbangai, Makambo, and Kokomtambu.[15]

The Invasion of Guadalcanal

The Landings

Beach Red, which lies about 6,000 yards east of Lunga Point, between the Tenaru and Tenavatu Rivers, had been selected for the Guadalcanal landings.

[15] Rpt, Asst Div Comdr 1st Mar Div to CG 1st Mar Div, 1714, 8 Aug 42, in 1st Mar Div Rpt, II, Annex B; Ltr, Col John M. Arthur to Hist Sec, Hq, USMC, 11 Oct 45, in files of USMC Hist Sec.

MARINE LANDINGS ON GUADALCANAL *were made from transports anchored 9,000 yards off Red Beach. Smoke from preliminary shelling still obscured the beach.*

BRIDGING THE TENARU RIVER, *amphibian tractors were used to support the flooring as the Marines moved to expand the beachhead 7 August.*

(*Map V*) The transports of Group X initially anchored 9,000 yards off Beach Red on the morning of 7 August. The destroyers of the Guadalcanal Fire Support Group took their stations 5,000 yards north of the beach at 0840 to mark the line of departure for the landing craft. The assigned liaison planes made eight runs at low altitudes to mark the extremities of the beaches with smoke.[16] The three cruisers and four destroyers of the Guadalcanal Fire Support Group began firing at 0900, to cover a 3,200-yard-long area from a point extending 800 yards on either side of Beach Red to a depth of 200 yards.

The first wave of landing craft, carrying troops of the reinforced 5th Marines (less the 2d Battalion), crossed the line of departure 5,000 yards off Beach Red. As the landing craft drew to within 1,300 yards of the beach, the warships ceased firing. There were no Japanese on the beach. The marines went ashore at 0910 on a 1,600-yard front, the reinforced 1st Battalion on the right (west), the reinforced 3d Battalion on the left. Regimental headquarters followed at 0938, and by 0940 heavy weapons troops had come ashore to act as regimental reserve.[17] All boat formations had crossed the line of departure promptly and in good order, and had reached their assigned beach areas.[18] The assault battalions of the 5th Marines then advanced inland about 600 yards to establish a beachhead perimeter bounded on the west by the Tenaru River, on the east by the Tenavatu River, on the south by an east-west branch of the Tenaru, and to cover the landings of successive units.

Landing of the reinforced 1st Marines in column of battalions had begun at 0930. The 2d Battalion led, followed by the 3d and 1st Battalions. By 1100 the entire reinforced regiment had come ashore. Meanwhile, in the absence of enemy mines and shore defenses, the transports had moved 7,000 yards closer to the shore.[19]

To provide direct support, the 75-mm. pack howitzers of the 2d and 3d Battalions of the 11th Marines came ashore with the assault battalions of the 5th and 1st Marines. The 105-mm. howitzers of the 5th Battalion, 11th Marines, had been assigned to general support but were not ready for action until the afternoon. The howitzers were landed separately from their prime movers, which had been held on board ship because there were not enough ramp boats

[16] The 1st Marine Division had objected to this use for liaison planes on the ground that they might easily have been shot down, and because smoke is not good for marking beaches. 1st Mar Div Rpt, II, 15, and Avn Annex K.

[17] 1st Mar Div Rpt, II, Annex L (5th Mar Record of Events, 7 Aug 42), 1.

[18] 1st Mar Div Rpt, II, 1.

[19] CTG 62.1, Rpt Guadalcanal–Tulagi.

to bring them ashore promptly. When the 105's reached shore, there were no prime movers immediately available to pull them up the beach. Whenever amphibian tractors were available at the beach, they were used to pull the 105's until the prime movers (1-ton trucks, instead of the authorized 2½-ton 6-wheel-drive trucks) came ashore in the afternoon.[20] The artillery battalions reverted to control of Headquarters, 11th Marines, when that headquarters landed. All battalions upon landing registered their fire by air observation.[21]

The Advance

When the assaulting regiments and their supporting pack howitzers were ashore, the advance toward the airfield was ready to begin. The 1st Battalion of the 5th Marines was to advance west along the beach toward the Lunga River while the 1st Marines attacked southwest toward Mount Austen. The 3d Battalion of the 5th Marines, the artillery, engineer, pioneer, and special weapons and defense battalions were to hold the beach during the advance.

At 1115 the 1st Marines passed through the 5th Marines' lines. Engineers put a temporary bridge upstream on the Tenaru, using amphibian tractors as pontons. The 1st Marines crossed the river and turned southwest toward Mount Austen. On the beach the 1st Battalion of the 5th Marines crossed the mouth of the Tenaru at 1330 and marched toward the Ilu. Neither regiment met any Japanese.

The 1st Marines, advancing inland with battalions echeloned to the left and rear, progressed slowly. The only map which the regiment had to guide it was vague; the angle of declination between grid and true north was not shown. The regimental historian stated later that, had commanders been able to study aerial photographs before the landing, they might have picked easy, natural routes instead of a straight compass course through the jungle.[22]

The troops were heavily loaded with ammunition, packs, mortars, and heavy machine guns as they struggled through the thick, fetid jungle. The humid heat exhausted the men, whose strength had already been sapped by weeks aboard crowded transports. Salt tablets were insufficient in number. Troops in the Solomons needed two canteens of water per day per man, but the number of canteens available had permitted the issue of but one to each man. All these factors served to slow the advance of both regiments.

---

[20] 1st Mar Div Rpt, II, Arty Annex I, 1.

[21] Interv, AGF Mil Obs, SWPA, with CG 11th Mar and ExO 11th Mar, 19 Dec 42, included as App to Rpt, Mil Obs, SWPA, to CG AGF, 20 Sep–Dec 42, 2 Jan 43. OPD 381 SWPA Sec. II Case 108.

[22] 1st Mar Div Rpt, II, Annex M (1st Mar Hist), 2.

By dusk the regiments had each advanced about one mile. General Vandegrift, who had come ashore at 1601, ordered them to halt in order to reorient and establish contact. The 1st Battalion of the 5th Marines established a perimeter defense at the mouth of the Ilu River, while the three battalions of the 1st Marines dug in for the night in the jungle about 3,500 yards to the south.

Considering the division's state of training and the inexperience of the junior officers and noncommissioned officers, tactical operations were satisfactory, but General Vandegrift criticized the "uniform and lamentable" failure of all units to patrol their fronts and flanks properly.[23] Organization for landing and the ship-to-shore movement of troops had been very good. As the Japanese were not opposing the advance, the operation did not involve a thorough test of methods of controlling ships' gunfire by shore-based fire control parties, but nothing had indicated the need for fundamental changes in doctrine.[24] Co-ordination between ground forces on the one hand, and naval and air units on the other, had been unsatisfactory, for the naval forces were not using the same map as the 1st Marine Division.[25] In view of the relatively few air support missions requested by the ground troops, the centralized control of supporting aircraft had been satisfactory. Had the division met heavy resistance on Guadalcanal, a more direct means of air-to-ground communication would probably have been necessary. The problem had been recognized in advance, but there had not been time to organize and train air control groups for liaison duty with regiments and battalions. The liaison planes furnished little information to division headquarters, for the pilots were not able to observe very much in the jungle, and some of the messages they transmitted were vague.[26]

The Capture of the Airfield

At 2000, when 10,000 troops had come ashore,[27] General Vandegrift ordered the 1st Marines to attack toward the Lunga the next morning instead of taking Mount Austen. He recognized that Mount Austen commanded Lunga Point, but because it was too large and too far away for his relatively small force to hold he decided not to take it immediately.

Supported by tanks, the 1st Battalion of the 5th Marines crossed the Ilu at 0930 on 8 August. Progress was slow at first as the battalion advanced on a wide

---

[23] 1st Mar Div Rpt, II, 10.

[24] Ltr, CG 1st Mar Div to Comdt Mar Corps, 1 Jul 43, sub: Final Rpt Guadalcanal Opn.

[25] 1st Mar Div Rpt, II, 18; Int Annex G, 2.

[26] 1st Mar Div Rpt, II, Avn Annex K.

[27] COMSOPAC to COMINCH, 1400 of 13 Aug 42. SOPAC War Diary.

THE LUNGA POINT AIRFIELD *and Mount Austen photographed from the air over the
mouth of the Ilu River west of the Red Beach landing area two weeks after the initial invasion.*

front. General Vandegrift, then convinced that his division was not faced by a sizable organized force on Guadalcanal, ordered the battalion to contract its front, cross the Lunga River, and seize Kukum village before nightfall. By 1500 the advance guard had traveled almost 6,000 yards to overrun a small party of Japanese firing rifles and machine guns from knolls on the outskirts of Kukum. Kukum, containing one 3-inch antiaircraft gun, one 1-inch antiaircraft gun, two 37-mm. antitank guns, and heavy machine guns, was otherwise undefended.

Meanwhile the 1st Battalion of the 1st Marines had covered 4,500 yards to capture the airfield by 1600. The enemy garrison, composed of 430 sailors and 1,700 laborers, had fled westward without attempting to defend or destroy their installations, including the nearly completed runway. General Vandegrift wrote:

> The extent to which the enemy had been able to develop their Lunga Point positions was remarkable in view of the short time of occupation. Since 4 July they had succeeded in constructing large semi-permanent camps, finger wharves, bridges, machine shops, two large radio stations, ice plants, two large and permanent electric power plants, an elaborate air compressor plant for torpedoes, and a nearly completed airdrome with hangars, blast pens, and a . . . runway.[28]

Besides the runway and the weapons in Kukum, the Japanese had abandoned a store of .25-caliber rifles, .25- and .303-caliber machine guns, two 70-mm. and two 75-mm. guns, ammunition, gasoline, oil, individual equipment, machinery, Ford and Chevrolet-type trucks, and two radars. They left stocks of rice, tea, hardtack, dried kelp, noodles, canned goods, and large quantities of beer and sake behind.[29] The marines took over the abandoned weapons and used them to bolster their defenses. The 100-pound bags of rice and other food in the commissary dumps were added to the marines' limited stores. The Japanese left among their personal belongings many diaries which were valuable sources of information for Allied intelligence.

About thirty-five of the Japanese trucks were serviceable. Lighter than American military transport, they proved less efficient. Without powered front axles, they stuck easily, but were a valuable addition to the 1st Marine Division's limited motor transport, and were used as long as they held together. The division engineers also used the Japanese rollers, mixers, surveying equipment, gasoline locomotives, and hopper cars in the subsequent completion of the airfield.

---

[28] 1st Mar Div Rpt, II, 12.
[29] *Ibid.,* Int Annex G, 8.

JAPANESE EQUIPMENT *found in the Lunga Point area included many trucks such as the one above. The 70-mm. gun shown below was one of many weapons abandoned as the enemy retreated westward to new positions.*

Tactical operations had proceeded favorably. The Guadalcanal forces had landed unopposed and captured the airfield without casualties. In the Tulagi–Gavutu–Tanambogo area, all objectives had been taken at the cost of 144 killed and 194 wounded, while the defending garrisons had been destroyed. By 9 August, 10,900 troops had landed on Guadalcanal, and 6,075 on Tulagi.[30] To support the infantry, 3 field artillery battalions, with 3 units of fire, plus special weapons, tanks, tank destroyers, and part of the 3d Defense Battalion, had landed on Guadalcanal, while the 3d Battalion, 10th Marines (75-mm. pack howitzers), and part of the 3d Defense Battalion had landed on Tulagi.

Unloading

Logistical operations, in contrast with tactical developments, had seriously bogged down. The 1st Pioneer Battalion had been charged with the duty of unloading supplies from the landing craft as they touched at Beach Red, while a navy beachmaster and shore party directed the boat movements at the beach. Of the 596 men (including naval medical personnel) of the Pioneer Battalion, one platoon of 52 went to Tulagi with the 2d Battalion, 5th Marines, and another remained on board one of the cargo ships. About 490 men on Beach Red were to handle supplies for the Guadalcanal force of the 1st Marine Division. By 1043 of 7 August the beachmaster's party was operating on Beach Red.[31]

Unloading the landing boats proved to be an exhausting and almost impossible job, for so many of them lacked movable bow ramps which could be let down to speed the removal of supplies from the boats. The pioneers had to lift the supplies up and over the gunwales to unload them. On the other hand, the unarmored amphibian tractors "demonstrated a usefulness exceeding all expectations."[32] Used as an ambulance, a prime mover, and an ammunition carrier, the amphibian tractor, later to play such an important tactical role in the Pacific, was able to move directly from ship's side to inland dump, easily traversing the sea, reefs, beaches, and swamps without halting. But there were only a few amphibian tractors.

Too few troops had been provided to unload boats and move materiel off the beach. While loaded landing craft hovered off Beach Red, which was

[30] COMAMPHIBFORSOPAC War Diary, 9 Aug 42.
[31] *Ibid.*, 7 Aug 42.
[32] 1st Mar Div Rpt, II, 16.

SUPPLIES ACCUMULATING AT RED BEACH *presented this scene of confusion the morning of 8 August. Stacks of ammunition were dangerously piled with other supplies and gear under the palms to clear the beach for further unloading operations.*

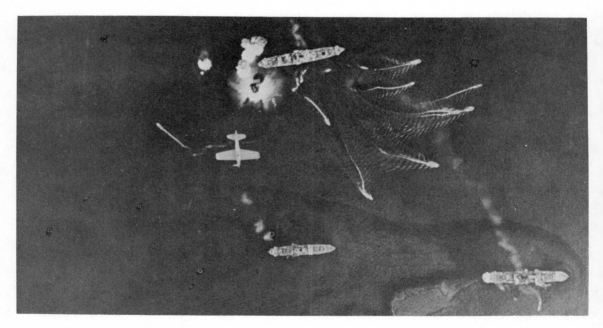

ENEMY AIR ATTACKS ON THE TRANSPORTS *forced a delay in unloading operations, but caused only light damage 7 August. This Japanese* Mitsubishi "Hap" *was flying fighter cover for the aircraft whose bombs are seen exploding off the stern of the transport. White streaks are wakes of landing craft scattering for safety.*

already cluttered with unsorted gear, hundreds of marines who were waiting to move forward were in the vicinity, but did not assist on the beach.[33] General Vandegrift later stated that the unloading party had been too small; he pointed out that he had anticipated that his division would have to fight a major engagement before capturing the airfield and he had therefore expected to use most of his troops tactically. At that time, too, the 2d Marines (less one battalion) had not been released by Admiral Turner.[34]

When supplies began to pile up on the beach, sailors from the transports joined the shore party to try to get the boats unloaded and the supplies moved farther inland. Pioneers and sailors worked to the point of exhaustion; the extreme heat caused many to suffer from nausea and severe headaches. But the beach remained cluttered.

Enemy air attacks also delayed unloading operations. Twenty-five twin-engined Japanese bombers from Rabaul attacked the ships in the early afternoon of 7 August. Several planes were shot down by the covering fighters and gunfire from the transports and screening warships. The Bougainville coastwatcher had warned the Allied ships in time so that none were hit,[35] but the transports had been obliged to cease unloading and get underway. About one hour later, a second wave of Japanese bombers drove the transports off again and damaged the destroyer *Mugford*. The Japanese aircraft fortunately did not attack the gear which crowded the beach, but three hours of unloading time had been lost.

By nightfall on 7 August 100 landing craft were beached, waiting to be unloaded, while an additional 50, unable to find landing room on the beach, stood offshore. Unloading was continued into the night, but the tired shore party could not cope with its task and operations broke down completely. At 2330 the shore party commander, stating that unloading was "entirely out of hand," requested that the ships cease discharging cargo until 1000, 8 August, when he estimated the beach would be cleared. Admiral Turner and General Vandegrift assented.

To provide more room for incoming supplies, General Vandegrift doubled the length of the beach by extending Beach Red's boundary west to the Block Four River on 8 August. But the situation did not improve. Forty more enemy bombers flew over Florida about noon to disperse the ships again, this time setting the *George F. Elliott* afire and damaging the destroyer *Jarvis*. The *El-*

[33] CTG 62.1, Rpt Guadalcanal–Tulagi.
[34] Ist Mar Div Rpt, II, 11. General Vandergrift suggested using 1,500 in a division unloading party.
[35] Feldt, *op. cit.*, pp. 88–89.

liott burned until she was a total loss. The *Jarvis* left for Noumea but was never heard from again. A false air alarm later in the afternoon forced the ships to get underway once more.

The Enemy Strikes Back

The Japanese garrisons on Guadalcanal and in the Tulagi area had not been able to resist the American attack effectively, although an enemy report claimed that ten transports and the greater part of the escorting naval forces had been destroyed.[36] The air attacks on 7–8 August had not seriously damaged the Amphibious Force, but they had caused serious delays in unloading.

These were only preliminaries, however, to the heavy blow the Japanese were preparing to deliver. Five heavy and two light cruisers and one destroyer assembled in St. George's Channel off Rabaul on the morning of 8 August with orders to attack the American transports in Sealark Channel.[37] This force sailed south along the east coast of Bougainville until sighted by an Allied patrol plane from the Southwest Pacific Area, which radioed a warning to Melbourne. The Japanese ships then reversed their course for a time, but after the plane departed, turned west through Bougainville Strait and then south through the narrow waters (the "Slot") between the two chains of the Solomons.

At 1800 on 8 August, Admiral Turner received word that the Japanese force was approaching.[38] The Screening Force, augmented by the fire support warships, was then covering the northern approaches to Sealark Channel. Two destroyers, the *Ralph Talbot* and the *Blue,* were posted northwest of Savo Island on either side of the channel to maintain watch by radar. Three cruisers, the *Australia, Canberra,* and *Chicago,* and the destroyers *Bagley* and *Patterson,* were patrolling the waters between Savo and Cape Esperance. The cruisers *Vincennes, Astoria,* and *Quincy* and the destroyers *Helm* and *Wilson* patrolled between Savo and Florida. Two cruisers, screened by destroyers, covered the transports.

Aircraft from the American carrier force southwest of Guadalcanal had been supporting the Amphibious Force during daylight hours, but this protec-

---

[36] ATIS, SWPA: Int Rpts, *Yazawa Butai Hq* and *Oki Shudan (17th Army) Gp Hq,* 8 Mar–30 Sep 42: Enemy Publication No. 28, 21 Jul 43, p. 50.

[37] USSBS, *The Campaigns of the Pacific War* (GPO, Washington, 1946), p. 106; *Interrogations,* I, 255–56.

[38] COMAMPHIBFORSOPAC War Diary, 8 Aug 42. The warning stated that three cruisers, two destroyers, and two gunboats or seaplane tenders were approaching.

tion was about to be withdrawn. Two days of enemy air action and operational losses had reduced fighter strength from ninety-nine to seventy-eight planes. Fuel was running low. Admiral Fletcher, commanding Task Force 61, was worried by the numbers of enemy bombers operating in the area. At 1807, 8 August, he asked Admiral Ghormley for permission to withdraw his carriers.[39] Admiral Ghormley consented. The force would be withdrawn, he announced, until enough land-based aircraft to protect the line of communications to Guadalcanal could be assembled, and until sufficient stocks of aviation fuel could be maintained at Guadalcanal to support fighter and bomber operations.[40] The carrier forces retired southward early the next morning.

When informed that the carrier forces were to be withdrawn, Admiral Turner called General Vandegrift and Admiral Crutchley aboard the flagship *McCawley*.[41] General Vandegrift left his command post at the mouth of the Ilu River to board the *McCawley* about 2325, 8 August. Admiral Crutchley took the flagship *Australia* out of the Screening Force and sailed aboard her to the *McCawley* to attend the conference. Turner informed them that the imminent retirement of the carriers would leave the Amphibious Force without effective air protection and that he had decided to withdraw the ships of the Amphibious Force at 0600 the next morning.

General Vandegrift was seriously disturbed by this news. The retirement of the ships, he felt, would place his division in a "most alarming" position.[42] Unloading of supplies at Tulagi had not even started at 7 August because the Japanese had held so much of the island.[43] The 1st Marine Division's plans were based on the assumption that the transports would remain offshore until 11 August, and by the night of 8–9 August more than half the supplies embarked by the division still remained in the ships' holds.

Meanwhile the Japanese cruisers and destroyers which had earlier been discovered had now approached Savo Island undetected. Shortly before reaching Savo, the cruisers catapulted seaplanes which flew over Sealark Channel to

---

[39] CTF 61 to COMSOPAC, 0707 of 8 Aug 42. SOPAC War Diary. For fuller accounts of the naval aspects of these operations, see ONI, USN, Combat Narratives: Solomon Islands Campaign. I, The landing in the Solomons, and II, The Battle of Savo Island, 9 August 1942 (Washington, 1943) relate to the operations described in this chapter.

[40] COMSOPAC to CINCPAC, 0834 of 9 Aug 42. SOPAC War Diary.

[41] COMAMPHIBFORSOPAC War Diary, 8 Aug 42.

[42] 1st Mar Div Rpt, II, 13.

[43] CTF 62.6 (Rear Adm V. A. C. Crutchley), Rpt Battle Savo Island, 8–9 Aug 42, Ser 231, 6 Apr 43, 16. A photostatic copy of this report is in the Office of Naval Records and Library.

search for the American and Australian ships.[44] About midnight of 8 August the Allied ships in the channel reported that unidentified aircraft were overhead. About 0145, 9 August, a seaplane from the Japanese cruiser *Chokai* dropped flares over the transports, while the Japanese warships slipped unobserved past the *Ralph Talbot* and the *Blue.*

After passing the destroyers, the Japanese sighted the Allied ships between Savo and Cape Esperance. Still undetected, they fired torpedoes which struck the *Chicago* and the *Canberra.* After this attack the Japanese left to strike the American ships between Savo and Florida. They illuminated their targets briefly with searchlights, then put heavy fire into the American cruisers. Unwilling to risk further action with the Allied cruisers and fearful that American aircraft might attack his ships at daylight, the Japanese commander then led his force northward away from Savo. On the morning of 9 August the Japanese force reached Rabaul. The next day, off New Ireland, the cruiser *Kako* was sunk by torpedoes from an American submarine.

The Battle of Savo Island was one of the worst defeats ever suffered by ships of the U. S. Navy. The enemy had taken them by surprise and defeated in detail the two forces on either side of Savo. The only enemy ship damaged was the *Chokai,* whose operations room was destroyed. The *Vincennes* and *Quincy* sank within one hour after being attacked. The badly hit *Canberra* burned all night and was torpedoed by American destroyers the next morning to sink her prior to the departure of the Amphibious Force. The severely battered cruiser *Astoria* sank about midday on 9 August. The *Chicago* and the *Ralph Talbot* had both been damaged. Fortunately the Japanese commander had lacked sufficient daring to execute his orders to attack the weakly defended transports in Sealark Channel.[45] Had he done so, he could have effectively halted Allied operations in the South Pacific and completely cut off the 1st Marine Division from reinforcement and supply, for all the transports and cargo ships of the South Pacific Force were present in Sealark Channel.

The damage which the Japanese inflicted upon the warships delayed the departure of Admiral Turner's ships, which remained in Sealark Channel until the afternoon of 9 August. But at 1500 ten transports, one cruiser, four destroyers and the minesweepers sailed toward Noumea, followed at 1830 by the remaining ships. Admiral Turner accompanied the latter force.[46]

[44] USSBS, *Interrogations,* II, 472.

[45] *Ibid.,* pp. 361–62.

[46] CTF 62 to CTF 61, COMSOPAC, COMAIRSOPAC, 0508 and 0725 of 9 Aug 42. SOPAC War Diary.

Of the original marine landing force of over 19,000 men, nearly all were ashore before the departure of the ships, but a few detachments of the 1st Marine Division remained on board. Most of the men of the 2d Marines, Reinforced, had landed, but 1,390 men of the regiment, including regimental headquarters, companies from the 2nd Amphibian Tractor and 2d Service Battalions, and part of the 3d Battalion, 10th Marines (75-mm. pack howitzers), were subsequently landed at Espiritu Santo by the retiring Amphibious Force.[47] Almost 17,000 marines and naval personnel had landed on Guadalcanal and Tulagi.[48]

Supplies for these men were limited. Of the sixty days' supplies and ten units of fire with which the division had embarked, less than half had been unloaded. There were about four units of fire available on Guadalcanal and Tulagi. Guadalcanal had 6,000,000 rounds of .30-caliber ammunition, and 800 90-mm. shells.[49] Food stocks were low. When an inventory was completed about 15 August, it was found that food for only thirty days was on hand—B rations for seventeen days, C rations for three days, and Japanese rations for ten days. Troop rations were reduced to two daily meals.

None of the 3d Defense Battalion's 5-inch coast defense guns, nor any long-range warning or fire control radar sets had been landed. Only eighteen spools of barbed wire had been brought ashore. Heavy construction equipment was still in the ships' holds. Since the liaison planes assigned to the division had been destroyed on board their cruisers in the Battle of Savo Island, air reconnaissance of Guadalcanal would not be possible.[50]

The departure of the Air Support and Amphibious Forces left the 1st Marine Division alone in the Guadalcanal–Tulagi area exposed to Japanese attacks, without air cover or naval surface support. The nearest Allied outpost was the primitive base at Espiritu Santo. The enemy posts at Buka and the Shortlands were only 363 and 285 nautical miles away, respectively, and Rabaul itself lay only 565 nautical miles to the northwest. The 1st Marine Division was virtually a besieged garrison.[51]

---

[47] CO 2d Mar to COMSOPAC, CINCPAC, CTF 62, and COMSOWESPAC, 1400 of 12 Aug 42. SOPAC War Diary.

[48] COMAMPHIBFORSOPAC War Diary, 9 Aug 42; 1st Marine Division Report does not give exact figures.

[49] Rad Noumea to rad Tulagi, 0640 of 14 Aug 42. SOPAC War Diary.

[50] 1st Mar Div Rpt, II, Annex K, 1.

[51] Messages from commanding general of the 1st Marine Division in SOPAC War Diary in August, September, and October 1942 report enemy air raids and naval bombardments almost daily.

CHAPTER IV

Consolidating the Beachhead

In a letter to General Marshall on 11 August, General Harmon, the commander of U. S. Army Forces in the South Pacific, expressed serious doubts about the possible success of the invasion: "The thing that impresses me more than anything else in connection with the Solomon action is that we are not prepared to 'follow up' . . . . We have seized a strategic position from which future operations in the Bismarcks can be strongly supported. Can the Marines hold it? There is considerable room for doubt."[1] A week later he pointed out that two lines of action lay open to the Japanese. They might deliver an amphibious assault, with strong air and surface support, against Guadalcanal and Tulagi, or they might move into New Georgia and infiltrate into Guadalcanal. They probably would not occupy Malaita or San Cristobal, for these would be within fighter range of the newly won Allied base at Guadalcanal, where, to achieve significant results, the Japanese would need to land strong forces. A rapid development of Allied air power at Guadalcanal would render New Georgia untenable for the Japanese. It was Harmon's view that American forces should mount intensive air and surface operations to destroy Japanese surface forces; base fighters, dive bombers, and heavy bombers on Guadalcanal; replenish Guadalcanal's supplies; and as General Vandegrift desired, send more troops to Guadalcanal at the earliest possible time.[2]

Admiral Ghormley also stressed the precariousness of the Allied situation in the South Pacific. He warned Admirals King and Nimitz that there could be no further advances until more troops and planes arrived, or until the new positions could be consolidated. If the three aircraft carriers then assigned to the South Pacific were to be withdrawn, or if no reinforcements were to be made available, Guadalcanal and other South Pacific positions might fall to the Japanese. Yet using the carriers to support the Guadalcanal garrison, he observed, would be dangerous. Expenditure of carrier-based aircraft and of de-

---

[1] Ltr, COMGENSOPAC to WDCSA, 11 Aug 42. OPD 381 PTO Sec. II.
[2] COMGENSOPAC, Summary of Situation, 20 Aug 42. OPD 381 PTO Sec. III.

stroyers in supporting Guadalcanal would jeopardize the carriers, which were then the principal defense of the line of communications between the United States and New Zealand and Australia. Sending supplies by ship to Guadalcanal would be dangerous until planes could be based there.[3]

Construction and Defense of the Airfield

The rapid completion of the airfield on Guadalcanal was a project of the utmost importance, for planes were needed there immediately to protect supply ships and the newly captured position, and to carry on the offensive against the Japanese. On Guadalcanal work on the uncompleted airstrip had begun on 9 August, when the 1st Engineer Battalion had moved to Lunga Point from Beach Red. The battalion's equipment was inadequate, for the ships had withdrawn before power shovels, bulldozers, or dump trucks had been unloaded. Using abandoned Japanese equipment, the engineers put forth their best efforts and added 1,178 feet to the 2,600 feet of runway completed by the Japanese. To fill a 196-foot gap in the center of the runway, they moved 100,000 cubic feet of earth with hand shovels, trucks, and captured dump cars. At first there were no steel mats to surface the field, which in consequence was covered with sticky mud after every hard rainfall.

On 10 August General Vandegrift announced that the field, named Henderson Field after Maj. Lofton Henderson, a Marine hero of the Midway battle,[4] might be used by thirty-six fighters and nine scout bombers.[5] No ground crews were then present, but there were 400 drums of aviation gasoline, and some oil and machine gun ammunition.[6] The first plane to use Henderson Field was a Navy patrol bomber (PBY) which landed for a short time on 12 August. On 17 August the radio station at Tulagi reported that the field was ready for operation.[7]

On 12 August Admiral Ghormley ordered Admiral McCain, commanding Task Force 63, to load all available destroyer-transports with aviation gasoline and lubricants, bombs, ammunition, and ground crews and dispatch them from Espiritu Santo to Guadalcanal. Sending these speedy ships to Guadalcanal bore

---

[3] COMSOPAC to CINCPAC, COMINCH, 0230 of 17 Aug 42, and 1156 of 16 Aug 42. SOPAC War Diary.

[4] 1st Mar Div Rpt, III, Annex E, 6.

[5] CG 1st Mar Div to CTF 62, 0915 of 10 Aug 42; CG 1st Mar Div to COMAIRSOPAC, 1140 of 11 Aug 42. SOPAC War Diary.

[6] CTF 62 to rad Noumea, 1220 of 10 Aug 42. SOPAC War Diary.

[7] Rad Tulagi to rad Noumea, 1000 of 17 Aug 42. SOPAC War Diary.

IMPROVING THE LUNGA AIRFIELD. *Engineers used this Japanese roller to complete the half finished runway shown in the lower photo, taken shortly after the Marines landed on Guadalcanal. Note the profusion of bomb holes.*

a close resemblance to blockade-running. To avoid being attacked by Japanese planes while lying offshore during daylight, they were to leave Espiritu Santo in time to reach Guadalcanal in the late afternoon, and to depart from there early in the morning. Aircraft of Task Force 63 were to cover them.[8]

Admiral Ghormley ordered the South Pacific carrier forces to operate generally south of Guadalcanal against Japanese carriers, transports, battleships, cruisers, destroyers, and other shipping, in that order of priority. He ordered the carriers not to venture north of latitude 10 degrees South unless they were pursuing a promising target within striking distance. In addition Admiral Ghormley directed the carrier forces to protect the line of communications between Noumea and Espiritu Santo, and to cover the shipborne movement of ground crews and equipment to Guadalcanal.[9] South Pacific land-based aircraft under Admiral McCain were to serve as a scouting and attack force, sharing with the surface forces the responsibility for defending and supplying Guadalcanal. Admiral McCain was to be responsible for the movement of all airborne supplies and reinforcements to Guadalcanal.

The immediate effects of the completion of Henderson Field were disappointing. Air operations were severely limited by lack of equipment. General Harmon believed that this shortcoming stemmed from the fact that the campaign "... had been viewed by its planners as [an] amphibious operation supported by air, not as a means of establishing strong land based air action." The marines on Guadalcanal could not obtain gasoline, airfield matting, or bulldozers, General Harmon wrote, because "... the plan did not have as its first and immediate objective the seizure and development of Cactus [Guadalcanal] *as an air base.*"[10] "... Airdrome construction ... is going to be disappointingly slow ... ," the Army commander reported on 28 August after an inspection trip, for the marines lacked enough "worthwhile equipment."[11]

The primitive conditions obtaining at Henderson Field limited the use of heavy bombers. There were no bomb-handling trucks, no carts, bomb hoists, or gas trucks. All planes had to be fueled from gasoline drums by hand pumps. Further, pending the arrival of sufficient fighters and antiaircraft guns to defend the field, General Harmon felt that it would be too risky to base B–17's

[8] COMSOPAC to CTF 63, 0216 of 12 Aug 42. SOPAC War Diary.

[9] COMSOPAC to CTF's 61, 62, 63, 1026 of 27 Aug 42; COMSOPAC to CTF 61, 0206 of 11 Sep 42. SOPAC War Diary.

[10] Ltr, COMGENSOPAC to CG AAF, 15 Sep 42, cited in Hist USAFISPA, Pt. II, p. 309.

[11] Ltr, COMGENSOPAC to CG AAF, 28 Aug 42, cited in *ibid.*, Pt. I, I, 44.

permanently on Guadalcanal. Suggesting to General Marshall that Army P–38 fighters be made available to the South Pacific, he also warned that fighters at Henderson Field would experience intensive action and a high attrition rate.[12]

Until heavy Army bombers could be based permanently on Guadalcanal, General Harmon suggested staging them from rear bases through Henderson Field to their targets. The B–17's could not carry profitable bomb loads from the New Hebrides directly to Faisi, Gizo, Tonolei, Kieta, Rekata Bay, Buka, and other targets in the northern Solomons, but they could reach and strike those areas from the New Hebrides by refueling at Guadalcanal, and continuing northward.[13]

Even with improved defenses at Henderson Field, it would be difficult to stage the B–17's through. A round-trip flight from the New Hebrides to Buka was over 1,800 nautical miles by the shortest route. Henderson Field lay about 560 nautical miles from Espiritu Santo and about 400 nautical miles from Buka. To send twenty B–17's, each carrying one ton of bombs, from Espiritu Santo through Henderson Field to Buka required that 35,800 gallons of gasoline be pumped into the B–17's at Henderson Field by hand,[14] and Henderson's fuel stocks could rarely support such an operation.

The first planes arrived for duty at Henderson Field on 20 August. Marine Fighting Squadron 223 (VMF 223) and Marine Scout Bombing Squadron 232 (VMSB 232) had reached Noumea from Pearl Harbor on the escort carrier *Long Island*. From Noumea they flew to the New Hebrides, refueled, and continued their way to Henderson Field. These squadrons, the forward echelon of Marine Air Group 23 of Brig. Gen. Roy S. Geiger's 1st Marine Air Wing, included nineteen Grumman fighters (F4F–4's) and twelve Douglas dive bombers (SBD–3's).

Eleven dive bombers of Flight 300 from the carrier *Enterprise* landed at Henderson Field on 24 August, to remain there for three months. The first Army Air Force planes—five P–400's of the 67th Fighter Squadron—came on 22 August, and were followed on 27 August by nine more.[15]

---

[12] COMGENSOPAC, Summary of Situation, 20 Aug 42.

[13] Ltr, COMGENSOPAC to WDCSA, 9 Sep 42. OPD 381 PTO Sec. III.

[14] 11th Bomb Gp (H), Plan Attack Buka Airdrome, in 11th Bomb Gp Hist.

[15] Other naval squadrons which served at Henderson Field in October and November 1942 were torpedo and fighter squadrons from the *Saratoga*, a composite squadron from the *Hornet*, and a few planes from the *Wasp*. Admiral William F. Halsey, Jr., Narrative Account of the South Pacific Campaign, 20 Apr 42–15 Jun 44, distributed 3 Sep 44 (Third Flt, Pac Flt A 16–3/(000) Ser 021), p. 3. A copy is in the files of the Hist Div, SSUSA.

The 67th Fighter Squadron had debarked at Noumea, New Caledonia, on 15 March 1942, and had trucked its crated aircraft over the mountains along the narrow twisting trail (the "Little Burma Road") which led to the squadron's base. When the squadron's mechanics uncrated the planes, they discovered forty-five P–400's, a converted model of the P–39 designed for export to the British, and two P–39F's. None of the pilots had ever flown a P–400 before, and only two had flown a P–39. None of the mechanics had ever worked on a P–400, and no instruction books for this type had been included in the shipment. However, they successfully assembled the planes, and the pilots learned to fly them.[16] To get from New Caledonia to Henderson Field, the P–400's flew the 277 nautical miles from New Caledonia to Efate, then the 153 nautical miles from Efate to Espiritu Santo, and, using extra gasoline tanks and guided by a B–17, flew the 560 nautical miles to Henderson Field.

Operations of the P–400's were disappointing at first. They could not fly higher than 12,000 feet, and thus were no match for high-flying Japanese aircraft. It was standard practice, when Henderson Field was warned of air attack, for the Army P–400's and Marine SBD's to take off from the field before the raid to prevent these vulnerable craft from being destroyed on the ground. During the raids they strafed and bombed Japanese positions. The P–400's armor, its 20-mm. cannon and two .50- and four .30-caliber machine guns, and its ability to carry one 500-pound bomb made this plane extremely effective in close support of ground troops.[17]

On 20 August, when Henderson Field began operating, supply and evacuation by air were inaugurated by the twin-engined R4D's (C–47's) of Marine Air Group 25. These planes made daily flights from Espiritu Santo to Guadalcanal, usually bringing in 3,000-pound cargo loads, and evacuating sixteen litter patients per trip.

The combat troops on Guadalcanal began to construct defenses for the airfield immediately after its capture. Since they lacked enough tools, sandbags, or barbed wire, the work was difficult. A small quantity of wire was salvaged from the coconut plantations and added to the original eighteen spools. Captured rice bags served in place of sandbags. By the afternoon of 9 August hasty positions had been established. Considering that an enemy amphibious attack against the shore line was the most immediate danger, General Vandegrift concentrated the bulk of his strength to hold the beaches. The marines built a defense

[16] 67th Fighter Sq Hist, Mar–Oct 42, pp. 3–4, in AF Hist Sec Archives.
[17] Guadalcanal and the Thirteenth Air Force, pp. 9–10; and n. 12, p. 194.

FIRE SUPPORT *for the Marines moving west from Lunga Point was provided by these P-400 fighter aircraft of the 67th Fighter Squadron (AAF), as well as by 75-mm. pack howitzers firing on Japanese positions along the Matanikau River.*

along 9,600 yards of shore line from the mouth of the Ilu River to the village of Kukum. The right (east) flank was refused inland 600 yards along the west bank of the Ilu, where the river line would give the defending forces a tactical advantage. The left (west) flank line at Kukum was refused inland over the flat ground between the beach and the jungle to the first hills. Caliber .30 and .50 machine guns and 37-mm. guns, supported by riflemen, defended the beach front. The 5th Marines (less one battalion) held the left sector, from the Lunga to Kukum; the 1st Marines held the right, from the Lunga to the Ilu.

Except for troops required to cover the beach defense weapons, the infantry battalions were concentrated inland to be in position to launch counterattacks, or to contain any forces which might penetrate the beach line. In the south (inland), a 9,000-yard-long stretch of jungle running from the Ilu across the Lunga to Kukum posed a grave problem. The northern line along the shore of Lunga Point ran across ground which was generally flat and covered with even rows of coconut trees. But the inland line ran up and down steep, heavily jungled ridges and hills where visibility was extremely limited. There were not enough troops to hold a continuous line in the south sector, and the rough, tangled terrain increased the difficulty of maintaining contact between separated units. Local security detachments from the artillery, pioneer, engineer, and amphibian tractor battalions first held separated strong points in the southern sector until continual nocturnal enemy infiltration made necessary an outpost line between the Ilu and the Lunga. However, large-scale enemy operations in the south sector at first seemed unlikely because of the difficult terrain.

Mortars, 60-mm. and 81-mm., were placed in supporting positions for normal fire missions. The 1st Special Weapons Battalion dug in its 75-mm. tank destroyers in positions inland, but were ready to move to firing positions on the beach in the event of an attack.

The troops dug foxholes, slit trenches, and dugouts to protect themselves from enemy rifle, artillery, and naval gun fire, and from the frequent bombing raids. On the outpost and beach lines the troops built two-man foxholes fitted with fire slits; deep pits to catch rolling hand grenades were dug in front of these emplacements.

There was not enough artillery. The 2d, 3d, and 5th Battalions of the 11th Marines had landed their howitzers and set them up in central positions from which they could put fire in front of all sectors. The 2d and 3d Battalions had 75-mm. pack howitzers, the 5th Battalion, 105-mm. howitzers. There were no 155-mm. howitzers or guns for effective counterbattery fire, nor any sound-and-

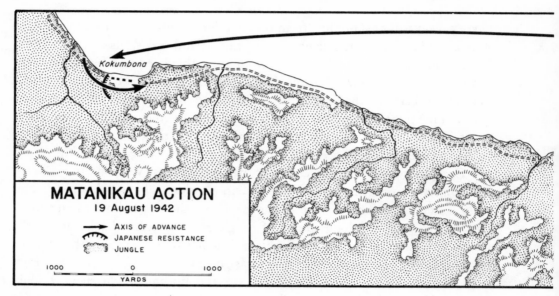

MATANIKAU ACTION
19 August 1942

→ AXIS OF ADVANCE
⊲⊲⊲⊲ JAPANESE RESISTANCE
JUNGLE

1000   0   1000
YARDS

MAP NO. 3

flash units for locating enemy artillery pieces, a deficiency that was to prove costly.[18] The defenses against air and surface attack were to be inadequate for many weeks. The radars and 5-inch seacoast guns of the 3d Defense Battalion had not been brought ashore prior to the hasty departure of the Amphibious Force. Automatic antiaircraft weapons, 90-mm. guns, and searchlights, however, had been landed on both Guadalcanal and Tulagi. An air warning system was obviously necessary, and one was established on 9 August in the "Pagoda," a tower which the Japanese had built on the airfield. From the Pagoda, observers could alert the Lunga garrison before an air attack by sounding a siren which the Japanese had abandoned. The adequacy of the defenses against Japanese ground attacks was soon to be tested.

Action on the Ilu River

The Japanese forces on Guadalcanal in August 1942 were believed to be concentrated near Lunga Point between the Matanikau River, approximately 7,000 yards beyond Lunga Point, and the native village of Kokumbona, about

[18] See Brig Gen Pedro A. del Valle, "Marine Field Artillery on Guadalcanal," *Field Artillery Journal* (October 1943), XXXIII, No. 1.

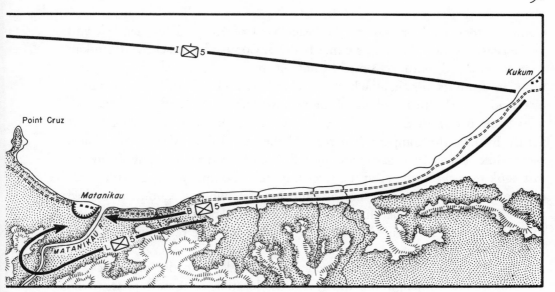

7,500 yards west of the Matanikau. A prisoner captured on 12 August confirmed this belief, and intimated that some of the Japanese garrison, many of whom were believed to be wandering aimlessly without food, might be willing to surrender. 1st Sgt. Stephen A. Custer of the division intelligence section prepared a plan to take a patrol by boat from Kukum to the Matanikau area to make contact with the Japanese and give them an opportunity to surrender. Col. Frank Goettge, the division intelligence officer, decided to lead the patrol himself. The patrol embarked from Kukum about dusk on 12 August. Colonel Goettge had planned to land between the Matanikau River and Point Cruz, about 1,200 yards west of the river, but in the darkness he landed at an unknown spot somewhere west of the river. The Japanese, instead of surrendering, attacked the patrol and killed all but three men who escaped by swimming. Colonel Goettge, three other officers, and Sergeant Custer were among the casualties. Subsequent patrols never found any traces of Colonel Goettge's party.[19]

A vigorous effort one week later to clear Matanikau and Kokumbona villages west of the river mouth met with greater success when B, L, and I Companies of the 5th Marines attacked the villages from three sides. (*Map 3*) I

[19] 1st Mar Div Rpt, III, 4.

Company took landing craft to the beach west of Kokumbona, landed, and pushed east through the village while B and L Companies attacked Matanikau from the east and south. L Company, having crossed the river about 1,000 yards upstream from its mouth, attacked northward after a brief artillery preparation by the 2d, 3d, and 5th Battalions of the 11th Marines. As L Company advanced, it met rifle fire from enemy emplacements on the ridges to its front and left flanks. By 1400 the company had reached the outskirts of Matanikau village. Meanwhile, enemy fire had prevented B Company from crossing from the east bank over the sand bar at the river mouth. B Company engaged the Japanese in the village with rifle and machine-gun fire while L Company pushed through the village. The three companies killed about sixty-five Japanese, themselves losing four killed and eleven wounded, before returning to Lunga Point.

As the division commander wrote later, this skirmish did not affect the outcome of the campaign, but did reveal the location of those Japanese who had retreated from the Lunga area. The Matanikau River, flowing through a deep valley, was to prove an important terrain feature. Deep, swift, and about 160 feet wide, it could not be forded in the coastal area.[20] In the absence of bridges the alluvial sand bar across the mouth was the only means by which vehicles and artillery could cross the river. To protect Henderson Field from artillery fire it was essential that the marines hold the easily defended east bank, but not until the addition of more troops to the Lunga garrison would enough men be available to extend the lines from Kukum to the Matanikau.

During the first weeks on Guadalcanal the white coastwatchers and friendly natives were proving their value. The coastwatchers were performing an invaluable service for the Allied cause by giving warning of approaching enemy aircraft almost three hours before their arrival over the Lunga. In August, coastwatchers were stationed on the south coast of Guadalcanal, and on Buka, Bougainville, New Georgia, Santa Isabel, and Malaita, to radio reports on Japanese aircraft and ship movements to the intelligence section of the division. Since most enemy bomber flights from Rabaul passed over New Georgia, the coastwatcher on that island was especially valuable, and his reports usually enabled the U. S. fighter planes on Guadalcanal to take to the air in time to meet the oncoming enemy. Other sources of intelligence were reports from higher headquarters, observation posts, regimental and battalion patrols,

---

[20] ATIS, SWPA, Trans, Int Rpts, *Yazawa Butai* and *Oki Gp Hq*, 8 Mar–30 Sep 42, Enemy Pub No. 28, 21 Jul 43, *Oki Gp* Rpt No. 39, p. 99.

and air reconnaissance. The few Japanese captured during the campaign usually poured out information voluminously. Also useful to the Allied cause was the Japanese habit of carrying orders, diaries, and other documents to the front lines. A vast quantity of such papers was captured on Guadalcanal and sent to Noumea.[21]

Shortly after the 1st Division had landed, Capt. Martin Clemens of the British Solomon Islands Defense Force, who was also British District Officer for Guadalcanal in the Protectorate Government, left Vungana, his hiding place in the hills south of Aola Bay. With his sixty native scouts he entered the marine lines to offer their services to General Vandegrift who accepted.[22]

On 19 August came the first evidence that Japanese ground forces were planning to attack the Lunga airfield. Patrols had already informed division headquarters that the Japanese were operating a radio station about thirty-five miles east of Lunga Point. Ordered to patrol the coast eastward to locate the enemy, A Company of the 1st Marines surprised a Japanese party of four officers and thirty enlisted men walking openly along the beach near Taivu Point, about twenty-two statute air miles east of Lunga Point. The company killed all the Japanese but two who escaped into the jungle. Examination of the dead men's effects revealed that these were enemy soldiers who had recently landed. Their helmets bore the *Army* star instead of the anchor-and-chrysanthemum insignia of the *Special Naval Landing Forces*. Among the documents which A Company captured was a code for ship-to-shore communication during landing operations. That an enemy force might attack by land against the 1st Marine Division's east flank, or force a landing against the Lunga shore defenses in an effort to recapture the airfield, or to attempt both, was an inescapable conclusion.

Headquarters of the Japanese *17th Army* at Rabaul, acting on orders issued from Tokyo on 13 August, had just assumed responsibility for directing ground operations on Guadalcanal,[23] but its intelligence estimates were extremely inaccurate. The landing on 7 August had taken the Japanese by surprise. They had retaliated with surface and air attacks, but there were not enough troops under *17th Army* command to permit the immediate dispatch of strong forces to Guadalcanal. The Japanese thought that a small force had been landed on 7 August. Some estimated that only 1,000 American troops had come ashore. The Japanese

[21] 1st Mar Div Rpt, III, Annex B, 2; IV, Int Annex A, 3–5.
[22] *Among Those Present*, p. 26.
[23] *17th Army* Opns, I.

CAPTAIN MARTIN CLEMENS *and a group of his native scouts.*

AN IMPROVISED FERRY *carried Marines across the Matanikau River. Cables prevented the raft from drifting down the swift stream.*

Army apparently based its estimates of the forces needed to destroy the American beachhead upon its experiences in China and Malaya.[24] The officer who was later to become Chief of Staff of the *17th Army*, Maj. Gen. Shuicho Miyazaki, was then in Tokyo. He wrote later that "at that time we had no means of ascertaining actual facts regarding the extent of the enemy counter-offensive."[25]

The *17th Army*, commanded by Lt. Gen. Harukichi Hyakutake, had decided to retake the Lunga area. Hyakutake planned to use initially a force composed of part of the *28th Infantry* of the *7th Division* and the *Yokosuka Special Naval Landing Forces*, and later the *35th Brigade*—about 6,000 troops in all.[26] *The 2d Battalion, 28th Infantry,* had been formed into a 2,000-man combat team of infantry, artillery, and engineers known as the *Ichiki Force,* after its commander, Col. Kiyono Ichiki. This force had been attached to the *Navy* to make the projected landing on Midway. When the Japanese carrier fleet was defeated, the *Ichiki Force* had sailed for Guam. On 7 August, when the force was at sea bound for Japan, it received orders to reverse its course. Landing at Truk on 12 August, it was attached to the *35th Brigade,* which was then in the Palau Islands. This brigade, commanded by Maj. Gen. Kiyotake Kawaguchi, was usually called the *Kawaguchi Force.*[27] The first echelon, about 1,000 men of the *Ichiki Force,* including Colonel Ichiki, sailed for Guadalcanal via Rabaul. They made the trip from Rabaul to Guadalcanal on the "Tokyo Express," the Japanese destroyers and cruisers which operated at night among the islands. This echelon landed at Taivu Point about 18 August, at approximately the same time that 500 men of the *Yokosuka 5th Special Naval Landing Force* landed at Kokumbona.[28] The soldiers whom A Company of the 1st Marines had killed on 19 August were from Ichiki's first echelon. Ichiki apparently decided to attack immediately because his forces had been discovered, for he did not wait for his second echelon to land before advancing west against the airfield.

The 1st Marine Division was then holding Lunga Point with four infantry battalions in line, one in reserve, and three field artillery battalions in support. As division headquarters was not sure of the size of the enemy force to the east,

---

[24] USSBS, *Interrogations,* II, 468.

[25] Miyazaki, Personal Account, p. 2.

[26] *17th Army Opns,* I; ACofS, G–2, XIV Corps, Enemy Opns on Guadalcanal, 24 Apr 43: *17th Army* Hist, p. 1. Hyakutake's first name is variously given as Fusayasu, Seikichi, and Harukichi.

[27] ACofS, G–2, USAFISPA, Japanese Campaign in the Guadalcanal Area, 7 Aug 43, p. 4. Hyakutake had originally planned to send the *Kawaguchi Force* to Guadalcanal first, but was prevented from so doing by a shortage of ships.

[28] *17th Army* Opns, I; XIV Corps, Enemy Opns, p. 1; see also ATIS SWPA's Int Rpts of *Yazawa Butai Hq* and *Oki Shudan Gp Hq, Oki Gp* Int Summary No. 6, pp. 58ff. Some translations render Ichiki's name as Ikki.

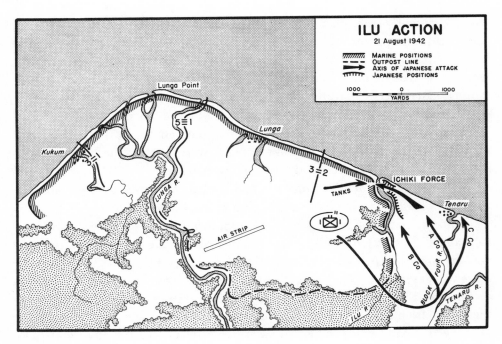

MAP NO. 4

nor even certain that one had been landed, it could not risk sending troops beyond the front lines to attack the enemy. The marines continued to work on the defenses and extended the eastern line farther inland along the west bank of the Ilu.

The first important ground action on Guadalcanal, after the landing, opened on the evening of 20 August when marines in listening posts on the east bank of the Ilu opened fire at some enemy troops hidden in the jungle. They then fell back to the west bank to report that enemy forces were moving up from the east. Some rifle fire followed, then subsided.

The Ilu front lay quiet until about 0310, 21 August, when about 200 infantrymen of the *Ichiki Force* tried to cross the sand bar at the mouth of the Ilu in a bayonet assault designed to overrun the positions occupied by the 2d Battalion, 1st Marines. (*Map 4*) The defending battalion had emplaced a 37-mm. gun, protected by machine guns and rifles, to cover the 45-yard-wide sand bar. As the Japanese drew near, the 2d Battalion opened fire with rifles, machine guns, and the 37-mm. gun which was firing canister. A few of the *Ichiki Force* succeeded in crossing the bar to overrun some of the 2d Battalion's positions which were not protected by barbed wire. The majority were killed or wounded by the defenders' fire. The few who had crossed were prevented from reorganizing or extending their foothold by fire from the positions which the 2d Battalion had been able to hold. G Company of the 2d Battalion then counterattacked and drove the enemy survivors back across the river. The *Ichiki Force* installed itself along the beach east of the river mouth.

At 0403 the 3d Battalion, 11th Marines, which had previously registered on the area, put howitzer fire on the narrow triangle of beach from which the *Ichiki Force* had begun the attack, and repeated the concentrations at 0515, 0722, 0742, and 0851. When the initial rush failed, the *Ichiki Force* concentrated artillery, mortar, and machine-gun fire on the marine positions at the end of the sand bar. All available marine weapons replied immediately. From their positions on the west bank the marines enfiladed the enemy on the sand bar and beach, and by morning the sluggish river mouth was filled with enemy corpses.

By daybreak it was apparent that the 2d Battalion, aided by artillery support and the tactical advantages of its position, could hold the west bank of the Ilu. The 1st Battalion of the 1st Marines was ordered out of division reserve to cross the Ilu upstream to attack the enemy left flank and rear. The 1st Battalion crossed the river in column and posted one heavy weapons platoon to cover the Japanese escape route. By 1230, 21 August, C and A Companies had advanced over 2,000 yards, and C Company, on the right, had reached the mouth of the Block Four River in the rear of the Japanese. When the enemy was surrounded, at 1400, the battalion delivered its assault. Some Japanese ran into the sea in an effort to escape, and D Company stopped some who were attempting to retreat inland. Others fleeing to the east were attacked by fighter planes.

To conclude the engagement before dark and to destroy some obdurate enemy machine gunners at the west end of the beach, a platoon of light tanks, supported by infantry, crossed the sand bar at 1500 and with 37-mm. canister and machine-gun fire attacked the *Ichiki Force* survivors and destroyed them. Two tanks suffered light damage, but by 1700 the engagement had ended. The attacking Japanese force had been destroyed, and Ichiki committed suicide. Japanese casualties numbered almost 800; only 130 survived.[29] Thirty-five marines had been killed, seventy-five wounded. Captured Japanese materiel included 10 heavy and 20 light machine guns, 20 grenade dischargers, 700

[29] *17th Army* Opns, I.

AFTER THE ILU RIVER BATTLE *bodies of enemy soldiers littered the sand bar which they had attempted to cross against heavy fire from the 1st Marines. Only a few Japanese escaped; Colonel Ichiki committed suicide. Below, testing an unused flame-thrower abandoned at the Ilu by the Japanese.*

rifles, 20 pistols, an assortment of sabers and grenades, 3 70-mm. guns, 12 flame throwers (which were not used in the engagement), and demolition equipment. One Japanese had surrendered, and fourteen, of whom twelve were wounded, had been taken prisoner.[30]

At no time had the *Ichiki Force* seriously threatened the airfield. The amazingly small force which attacked the marines indicated either defective intelligence work, or sublime confidence on the part of the enemy. If by 20 August Ichiki had become aware of the numerical strength of the Americans he was attacking, he must have had complete contempt for the military prowess of the marines.

The Battle of the Eastern Solomons

Before the *Ichiki Force* had launched its hopeless attack, the Japanese had attempted to send a second force to Guadalcanal. An impressive amount of naval strength had been concentrated near Rabaul. By 23 August Allied air reconnaissance reports led to the estimate that there were 3 or 4 aircraft carriers, 1 or 2 battleships, from 7 to 15 light and heavy cruisers, from 10 to 20 destroyers, 15 or more transports, cargo ships, and oilers, and 160 land-based aircraft at Rabaul.[31] The increase in enemy naval strength since early August led to the conclusion that the Japanese were preparing to put a major force ashore on Guadalcanal.

Admiral Ghormley's naval forces were weaker than those of the Japanese. Total American naval strength in the South Pacific included three aircraft carriers, one battleship, six cruisers, and eighteen destroyers, organized into three carrier task forces under Admiral Fletcher's command. A fourth force, built around the *Hornet,* had left Pearl Harbor on 17 August and reached the South Pacific on 29 August after the Battle of the Eastern Solomons had ended. Thirty-nine PBY's and thirty B–17's, plus the Guadalcanal aircraft, were also available in the South Pacific.

Four Japanese transports carrying about 1,500 men of the second echelons of the *Ichiki Force* and the *Yokosuka 5th Special Naval Landing Force,* screened by four destroyers, had left Rabaul on 19 August to attempt to land

---

[30] Lt Gen Millard F. Harmon, The Army in the South Pacific (6 Jun 44), p. 14, asserts that Army planes killed some of the Japanese, but no Army planes were then on Guadalcanal.

[31] ONI, USN, Combat Narratives: Solomon Islands Campaign, III, Battle of the Eastern Solomons, 23–25 October 1942 (Washington, 1943), 43–44.

the troops on Guadalcanal on 24 August. Two screening units were sailing south about a hundred miles to the east. The total enemy force included three aircraft carriers, eight battleships, four heavy cruisers, two light cruisers, and twenty-one destroyers as well as the four transports. The *25th Air Flotilla* at Rabaul provided land-based air cover.[32]

The three U. S. carrier task forces under Fletcher were then operating about one hundred miles southeast of Guadalcanal. When erroneous intelligence reports on 23 August led to the belief that the Japanese naval forces had retired north of Truk, the *Wasp* force departed from the main body to refuel, leaving only two carrier forces under Fletcher's command, including the carriers *Saratoga* and *Enterprise*, one battleship, four cruisers, and ten destroyers.

That the Japanese had not retired but intended to attack became clear on 23 August after the *Wasp's* departure, when American patrol planes sighted the four transports about 350 miles north of Guadalcanal. The next day, 24 August, American carrier planes discovered the enemy screening forces about the same time that Japanese pilots located Admiral Fletcher's ships. The ensuing engagement, the Battle of the Eastern Solomons, was fought well to the east of Guadalcanal. Like that at Midway, it was a battle of aircraft against ships. Surface craft did not exchange a single shot. American land-based aircraft joined the carrier planes to attack the enemy ships, and some Japanese planes bombed the Lunga area on 25 and 26 August.[33] The Japanese lost the carrier *Ryujo,* one destroyer, one light cruiser sunk, ninety planes shot down, and the seaplane carrier *Chitose* and one cruiser damaged. The *Enterprise* suffered damage, and twenty American planes were lost.[34]

Late on 24 August Admiral Fletcher retired southward expecting to return and resume the fight next day. But the Japanese force also withdrew and by next morning, 25 August, was out of range. Marine dive bombers and Army B–17's attacked the enemy transport force on 25 August, and search planes located other scattered enemy ships converging toward Guadalcanal. By noon the Japanese ships everywhere in the southern Solomons had reversed their courses to follow the carriers northward. The Battle of the Eastern Solomons did not prevent the Japanese from landing troops on Guadalcanal, but it did postpone their landing for a few days. The postponement gave the 1st Marine Division more time to strengthen its defenses.

[32] USSBS, *Campaigns of Pacific War*, pp. 110–11, and App. 40, p. 112.
[33] 3d Def Bn, Rpt Air Action.
[34] USSBS, *Campaigns of Pacific War*, App. 40, p. 113.

After the victory in the Eastern Solomons, the naval force of the South Pacific, already weakened by the return of nine cruisers and destroyers to the Southwest Pacific,[35] lost several more ships in action, but did not inflict serious damage upon the enemy.[36]

On 31 August the *Saratoga*, patrolling west of the Santa Cruz Islands, was hit by an enemy torpedo. The crippled carrier reached Tongatabu safely, made emergency repairs, and on 12 September sailed for Pearl Harbor where she remained incapacitated until November. The *Wasp*, patrolling south and east of the Solomons, sank on 15 September after being struck by three torpedoes from enemy submarines. The battleship *North Carolina*, escorting the *Wasp*, was torpedoed on the same day and forced to return to Pearl Harbor. The South Pacific thus lost the services of four major fleet units. Its carrier strength was reduced to one—the *Hornet*.

Supply

The lack of provision for re-supply and reinforcement of the 1st Marine Division, the withdrawal of the supporting naval forces from Guadalcanal, the cruiser losses at Savo Island, and the failure to complete the unloading of the transports of the Amphibious Force had placed the division in a precarious situation. Having embarked sixty days' supplies to obtain freedom of action, General Vandegrift had been able to bring less than one-half that amount ashore. The lack of shipping, combined with air and surface weakness, would have prevented a free and rapid flow of Allied forces and supplies to Guadalcanal even if unlimited troops and materiel had been available to the South Pacific. To complicate matters further, the fact that the Japanese were free to land strong forces on Guadalcanal protracted the campaign for six months and required the commitment of many more American troops than had been originally planned.

After landing on Guadalcanal, the marines had begun to move the supplies from Beach Red to Lunga Point immediately. Fortunately the Japanese aircraft had not bombed or strafed Beach Red during the crucial period when a tangle of rations, ammunition, spare parts, and other materiel lay exposed. But the supplies had to be moved quickly lest the Japanese exploit the oppor-

[35] COMSOPAC to CTF's 61, 17, 18, 44 (ntg), 30 Aug 42. SOPAC War Diary.

[36] See ONI, USN, Combat Narratives: Miscellaneous Actions in the South Pacific, 8 August 1942–22 January 1943 (Washington, 1943).

HENDERSON FIELD *was operational when these pictures were taken about a month after the invasion. Though constantly busy filling bomb craters at the field, the Marines had found time to dig in a number of antiaircraft positions. Below, a jeep speeds a maintenance crew to duty along the runway improved and extended by the Americans.*

tunity they had hitherto missed. The division, which had landed only 30 percent of its authorized 2½-ton trucks, put to use every available vehicle, including artillery prime movers, amphibian tractors, and captured Japanese trucks. The pioneers repaired a Japanese-built bridge over the Lunga and improved the coast road. Beach Red was cleared in five days of hauling.[37] The supplies were segregated and dispersed throughout Lunga Point. Observation of the results of the naval bombardment and air attacks on D Day showed the marines that "the probability of damage to supplies varied directly in proportion to the vertical height of the dump."[38] The dumps were therefore kept at the lowest possible heights.

The 1st Marine Division, expecting that its sixty days' supplies would prove ample, had naturally not made provision for immediate re-supply. When advanced supply depots were established at Noumea and Espiritu Santo on 20 August by order of Admiral Turner, they were not under divisional control.[39] On Guadalcanal the movement of supplies brought in by ships proved difficult. Once the beachhead was secured, the handling of supplies from the beach to supply dumps was theoretically a naval responsibility. The nucleus of a Naval Operating Base had been formed on 9 August by landing craft and crews from the Amphibious Force, but there were not enough men for effective operation. The division pioneers, later supplemented by hired native labor, continued to unload ships until October when enough sailors to perform this duty had arrived. All supplies had to be lightered from the ships to the beaches, unloaded, placed aboard trucks, and hauled inland. But there were never enough trucks. The arrival of reinforcing units did not alleviate the shortage of 2½-ton trucks, for, to save cargo space, only 1½-ton trucks were now being shipped.[40]

No major reinforcements were sent in during the first month. Before Admiral Turner's departure on 9 August, Vandegrift had recommended that the 2d Marines remain with the division instead of occupying Ndeni, and most of the 2d Marines landed before Admiral Turner's departure. Admiral Ghormley agreed to Vandegrift's proposal, and on 9 August he directed the 2d Marines to remain in the Guadalcanal–Tulagi area if they had already landed.[41] The remainder of the regiment, 1,390 men, debarked at Espiritu Santo on 12 August.

[37] 1st Mar Div Rpt, II, Annex J, 2.

[38] *Ibid.*, III, 4.

[39] COMAMPHIBFORSOPAC War Diary, 20 Aug 42; ltr, CG 1st Mar Div to Comdt Mar Corps, 1 Jul 43, sub: Final Rpt Guadalcanal Opn.

[40] 1st Mar Div Rpt, V, Logistics Annex Z, 1, 11–12.

[41] COMSOPAC to all ships, 1000 of 9 Aug 42. SOPAC War Diary.

Colonel Arthur, commanding the 2d Marines, and his staff remained at Espiritu Santo for a few days, and on 22 August landed at Tulagi from the *Alhena*.[42]

The first ships to reach Guadalcanal after the landing were destroyer-transports which on 15 August put ashore aviation ground crews and supplies. By 20 August, when the bulk of Task Force 62 was operating out of Noumea, six destroyer-transports had been assembled to run between Espiritu Santo and Guadalcanal. The next day the destroyer-transports *Colhoun. Gregory,* and *Little* brought 120 tons of rations, enough for 3½ days, to Guadalcanal, and the seaplane tender *MacFarland* landed more aviation materiel.

The original plan of 12 August for the destroyer-transports to operate under McCain was changed on 17 August, when Admiral Ghormley charged Turner's force (Task Force 62) with the responsibility of establishing the line of communications to Guadalcanal. Task Force 62 was to defend and strengthen the Marine garrison there. Turner would plan and control all surface movements to Guadalcanal, including that of aviation personnel and materiel. Admiral McCain was to notify Turner whenever such personnel and supplies were available for shipment by water.[43]

The arrival of fighter planes at Henderson Field permitted large ships to enter Sealark Channel in daylight with some degree of safety. The cargo ships *Alhena* and *Fomalhaut,* escorted by destroyers, succeeded in landing some supplies and weapons during daylight on 22 and 23 August, although one of the destroyers was torpedoed and sunk. Seven destroyer-transports and destroyers brought supplies to Guadalcanal and Tulagi on 29 August. The small amounts involved in these shipments may be illustrated by the fact that the *Colhoun* was carrying only seventeen tons of stores when she was sunk in the afternoon of 30 August during an attack on the ships by eighteen enemy bombers.[44]

By the end of August the 1st Marine Division was in a slightly stronger position than had been the case on 9 August. The defenses of the airfield had been established, the field was in operation, the *Ichiki Force* had been defeated, and a tenuous line of communications between Espiritu Santo and Guadalcanal had been established. But the Americans were not yet firmly established on Guadalcanal.

[42] COMAMPHIBFORSOPAC War Diary, 22 Aug 42.

[43] CTF 62 to CTF 63, 2136 of 16 Aug 42, SOPAC War Diary; COMAMPHIBFORSOPAC War Diary, 17 Aug 42.

[44] COMAMPHIBFORSOPAC, Action Rpt, Ser 00486, 13 Dec 42: Annex A, ltr, Lt Comdr G. B. Madden to SEC NAV, 3 Sep 42, sub: Loss of *Colhoun*, Ser 45401. Copy in the Office of Naval Records and Library.

CHAPTER V

Increasing Air and Ground Action

Insufficiency of troops and weapons imposed severe limitations on the Marine garrison at Lunga Point. The number of troops available to General Vandegrift in late August and early September was too small to permit a sufficient extension of his defenses for the protection of Henderson Field from infantry attacks and artillery bombardments. He believed that to prevent enemy landings and protect the field, a 45-mile-long stretch of Guadalcanal's north coast should be held. But with less than 20,000 troops on Lunga Point, only a small area could be securely defended. Not until more troops arrived could offensive action be undertaken to keep the Japanese beyond artillery range of Henderson Field. In late August and early September the Japanese forces on Guadalcanal were not able to mount sustained attacks against the Lunga defenses, but aircraft and warships exerted almost continuous pressure by repeated bombardments. Almost daily, Japanese bombers from Rabaul attacked Henderson Field at noon during August, September, and October; a few warships and submarines sailed into Sealark Channel nearly every night to shell the airfield. General Vandegrift, forced to remain on the defensive within a restricted area, concentrated on the improvement of his air defenses, while awaiting the arrival of more troops and supplies.

Air Power and Supply

Radars and 5-inch guns of the 3d Defense Battalion had been added to the Lunga defenses in late August.[1] The 5-inch guns of the battalion's two coastal batteries were equipped with permanent mounts. These guns, landed without their trailers and sleds, were manhandled into positions on the beach east and west of the Lunga River, a task requiring ten days of hard labor. Set up on the beach to cover the channel, the 5-inch guns were frequently in action against Japanese warships but lacked enough hitting power to be completely effective.

[1] Memo, Brig Gen Robert H. Pepper, USMC (former CO, 3d Def Bn), for author, 23 Jun 47.

BOMBER STRIKES ON THE AIRFIELD *took a heavy toll of Marine aircraft. A hanger and supplies in several revetments (above) were fired in the same Japanese air attack during which a direct hit was scored on the Marine dive bomber seen below.*

Three automatic weapons and two 90-mm. antiaircraft batteries were assigned to the defense of the airfield before the end of August, and in early September, following the landing of antiaircraft guns of a detachment of the 5th Defense Battalion on Tulagi, one more 90-mm. battery of the 3d Defense Battalion was transferred from Tulagi to Guadalcanal. But the battalion could not provide a complete defense.

The Lunga beachhead was too restricted to permit the posting of pick-up searchlights where they could illuminate attacking aircraft soon enough for the gun batteries to fire with complete effectiveness. To catch a plane early in its bombing run would have necessitated placing the lights at points 6,000 to 10,000 yards from the batteries. In September, however, the beachhead was less than 10,000 yards east to west and less than 5,000 yards north to south.

The radar sets supplied to the 3d Defense Battalion were not uniformly good. The long-range warning set, SCR (Signal Corps Radio) 270, worked well, but the SCR 268, a primitive set originally designed for searchlight control, was not accurate enough for controlling 90-mm. gunfire at night. The guns of only one of the three 90-mm. batteries were equipped with remote control systems by means of which they could be automatically trained by the gun-laying fire control directors. In the other two batteries, the guns had to be trained by hand, a much less accurate method.[2]

During daylight fighter aircraft could usually afford Henderson Field reasonably adequate protection against enemy planes, but at night antiaircraft guns provided the main defense. The effectiveness of Henderson Field's aircraft was demonstrated on 24 August when Marine fighters intercepted the regular noon Japanese bombing attack and destroyed five twin-engined and five single-engined bombers and eleven fighters. The marines lost three fighters and their pilots.[3] But the accuracy of General Harmon's prediction that the attrition rate would be heavy was proved the next day when General Vandegrift reported to Admiral Turner that of the thirty-one Marine aircraft which had arrived on 20 August only twenty remained serviceable. One fighter had crashed on the field, four had been lost in action and three were being repaired; one bomber had crashed and two were being repaired.

General Vandegrift requested more planes; and on 29 August he repeated his request. Just eight Grumman fighters, the only planes with the ability to

---

[2] Ltr, CO 3d Def Bn to Comdt Mar Corps, 7 Mar 43, sub: Rpt 3d Def Bn Opns at Guadalcanal with recommendations concerning equipment and personnel changes.

[3] Rad Guadalcanal to COMSOPAC, 0730 of 24 Aug 42. SOPAC War Diary.

attain enough altitude to intercept the Japanese, remained in commission, although all fourteen of the P–400's were operational. The next day the P–400's fought with the Japanese and destroyed five planes but lost four of their own number. By 30 August only five of the original Grumman fighters would fly, but twenty-nine more fighters and dive bombers had reached Henderson Field. Admiral McCain suggested that two more F4F or P–38 squadrons be used at Henderson Field; if this were done, he believed, Allied air strength would turn Guadalcanal into a "sinkhole" for Japanese air power. Admiral Ghormley, asserting that Guadalcanal could not be defended without more fighters, concurred with McCain. When Admiral Ghormley asked General MacArthur for P–38's, the Southwest Pacific commander replied that he had in his theater only six operational P–38's which he needed badly, but he promised P–39's at a later date.[4]

Throughout September the lack of adequate fighter strength continued to be serious, and the lack of sufficient air supplies and ground crews prevented the field from being used as a permanent base for heavy bombers.[5] The inability of the P–400's to fight at high altitudes required that all aircraft which could be spared from the *Enterprise* and the *Saratoga* be used at Henderson Field. Admiral Nimitz and General Harmon also asked the Joint Chiefs of Staff for high-altitude Army fighters, but none were immediately available.[6]

Yet fighters were absolutely essential for the security of Lunga Point which was being raided almost daily by Japanese bomber forces. On 10 September eleven Grumman fighters rose to meet a flight of twenty-seven twin-engined bombers, escorted by thirty Zeroes, that attacked at 1225. Four bombers were destroyed for the loss of one Grumman. Despite their limited numbers, the effectiveness of American planes and tactics was being constantly demonstrated against the Japanese. One patrolling B–17 destroyed four attacking fighters on 12 September; the next day another shot down two more. On the same day six Grumman torpedo bombers (TBF's) and twelve more dive bombers arrived at Guadalcanal to strengthen the meager air forces, and twenty F4F's intercepted a flight of twenty-eight escorted twin-engined bombers fourteen miles north of

[4] CG 1st Mar Div to CTF 62, 0735 of 25 Aug 42; CG 1st Mar Div to COMSOPAC, 0905 of 29 Aug 42, 0519 of 30 Aug 42; COMAIRSOPAC to CINCPAC, COMINCH, 0402 of 31 Aug 42; COMSOWESPAC to COMSOPAC, 1330 of 2 Sep 42. SOPAC War Diary.

[5] Ltr, COMGENSOPAC to WDCSA, 9 Sep 42. OPD 381 PTO Sec. III (9–9–42).

[6] CINCPAC to COMINCH, 2331 of 1 Sep 42; COMGENSOPAC to WDCSA, 0800 of 8 Sep 42; COMINCH to CINCPAC, COMSOPAC, 2237 of 8 Sep 42. SOPAC War Diary.

Henderson Field. The Marine fighters attacked, shot down four bombers and four fighters, and forced the rest of the bombers to jettison their bombs and retire.[7]

The Japanese, pressing their attacks in spite of these losses, sorely tested the endurance of the defenders of Henderson Field. The feelings of the men who suffered the bombardments are expressed by the historian of the 67th Fighter Squadron:

Almost daily, and almost always at the same time—noon, "Tojo Time"—the bombers came. There would be 18 to 24 of them, high in the sun and in their perfect V–of–V's formation. They would be accompanied by 20 or more Zeroes, cavorting in batches of 3, nearby. Their bombing was accurate, and they would stay in formation and make their bombing run even as they knew the deadly fire from the Grummans would hit any minute.

There was a routine of noises at Tojo Time. First the red and white flag (a captured Japanese rising sun) would go up at the pagoda. That meant scramble. Every airplane that would fly would start up immediately and all would rush for the runway, dodging bomb craters. Often through the swirling dust the ground crews would see a wing drop. That meant another plane had taxied [into] a dud hole or a small crater, indistinct in the tall grass. The first planes to the runway took off first, and two at a time, whether . . . Grummans, dive-bombers or P–400's.

The formations would join later in the air. The P–400's and dive-bombers would fly away to work over the Jap territory. The Grummans would climb for altitude, test-firing their guns on the way. The whining of engines at high r.p.m., the chatter of machine guns, and settling dust.

On the ground the men would put in a few more minutes' work, watching the pagoda all the while. Then the black flag would go up. It was amazing how fast the tired and hungry men could sprint. . . . In a moment the field would be deserted.

Then the high, sing-song whine of the bombers would intrude as a new sound, separate from the noise of the climbing Grummans. Only a few moments now. The sing-song would grow louder. Then: swish, swish, swish. And the men would pull the chin straps of their helmets tighter and tense their muscles and press harder against the earth in their foxholes. And pray.

Then: WHAM! (the first one hit) WHAM! (closer) WHAM! (walking right up to your foxhole) . . . WHAAA MM! (Oh Christ!) WHAM! (Thank God, they missed us!) WHAM! (the bombs were walking away) WHAM! (they still shook the earth, and dirt trickled in). WHAM!

It was over. The men jumped out to see if their buddies in the surrounding fox holes had been hit. The anti-aircraft still made a deafening racket. Grass fires were blazing. There was the pop–pop–pop of exploding ammunition in the burning airplanes on the ground. The reek of cordite. Overhead the Grummans dived with piercing screams. And the Jap bombers left smoke trails as they plummeted into [the] sea.

[7] Msgs of 10–14 Sep 42. SOPAC War Diary.

In a little while the airplanes would return. The ground crews would count them as they landed. The ambulance would stand, engine running, ready for those who crashed, landed dead stick, or hit the bomb craters in the runway. Then the work of patching and repairing the battered fighters would start again.[8]

But naval shellings were much worse:

. . . a bombing is bad, because as the big planes drone overhead the whole field seems to shrink up to the size of your foxhole and when the bombs start to swish–swish–swish in their fall they seem to be aimed right at that tiny spot. But a bombing is over in a minute.

A shelling, however, is unmitigated, indescribable hell. It can go on for a few minutes or four hours. When the shells scream overhead you cringe expecting a hit and when there is a let-up you tremble knowing that they are getting their range and the next one will be a hit.[9]

During early September the flow of supplies to the beleaguered garrison on Lunga Point increased slightly, for the American victory in the Battle of the Eastern Solomons effected a greater measure of security for the line of communications between Espiritu Santo and Guadalcanal. The destroyer *Helm* towed three harbor patrol boats to Tulagi on 31 August. The transport *Betelgeuse* put 200 men of the 6th Naval Construction Battalion ashore on 1 September.[10] The *Fomalhaut* and three destroyer-transports landed more supplies on 3 September. The destroyer-transports *Little* and *Gregory* followed on the next day, when the *Gregory* took the 1st Raider Battalion on a patrol to Savo Island. No Japanese were found there, and the battalion withdrew. But on the night of 4–5 September, a superior force of enemy warships sank both the *Little* and *Gregory* in Sealark Channel.

The cargo ships *Bellatrix* and *Fuller* sailed into Sealark Channel on 7 September, but before they could discharge all their cargo the threat of enemy attack forced them to retire. Escorted by two destroyers, they returned one week later, arriving at 0730, 14 September. General Vandegrift ordered the *Bellatrix* to unload her gasoline at Tulagi because the Lunga area was under attack. During the day the *Bellatrix* also transferred the 3d Battalion, 2d Marines, from Tulagi to Guadalcanal, and at 1915 the four ships departed.

The Counteroffensive, 12–14 September

After the Ilu engagement on 20–21 August, the marines fought no major engagements until mid-September. An attempt in late August by the 1st Bat-

---

[8] 67th Fighter Sq Hist, Mar–Oct 42, pp. 15–16.
[9] *Ibid.*, p. 19.
[10] COMAMPHIBFORSOPAC War Diary, 1 Sep 42.

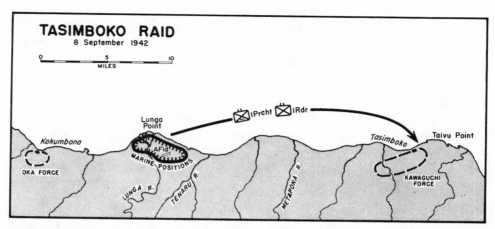

MAP NO. 5

talion of the 5th Marines to clear the enemy out of the Kokumbona area had failed to accomplish substantial results. Japanese forces were again gathering east of the Ilu. Native scouts had reported in late August that about two or three hundred well-equipped Japanese were building defensive works at the village of Tasimboko, some eighteen miles east of Lunga Point. In early September the native scouts reported that the enemy force at Tasimboko numbered several thousand troops, instead of two or three hundred. Division headquarters discounted this information but determined to destroy the force at Tasimboko by a hit-and-run raid. The force selected for the raid consisted of a provisional battalion composed of the 1st Raider and 1st Parachute Battalions under Colonel Edson's command. The two understrength units, rested after their hard fighting on 7–8 August, had been brought to Guadalcanal from Tulagi, Gavutu, and Tanambogo and formed, with their companies intact, into a provisional battalion.

The raiders and parachutists were to sail from Lunga to a point east of Tasimboko on destroyer-transports, and land in the rear of the enemy. (*Map 5*) Because there were not enough ships, the destroyer-transports carried the raider companies to Tasimboko first, then returned to Lunga Point for the parachutists.

The raider companies landed east of Tasimboko at dawn on 8 September, followed by the parachute companies. Advancing west, the raiders met a weak enemy force shortly after daybreak. They overran a Japanese outpost unit and captured one battery of light artillery. Supported by P–400's and SBD's from Henderson Field, they pushed west to the outskirts of Tasimboko where enemy resistance grew stronger. But the raiders pressed their attack, and forced the Japanese to evacuate the village. During the raid, the marines destroyed large stores of medical equipment, ammunition, radios, landing craft, four 75-mm. guns, and one 37-mm. gun.[11] At a cost to themselves of two killed and six wounded, they killed twenty-seven Japanese. Contact with the enemy was lost at 1230, and the marines returned east to board the transports.

The raiders had set out expecting to find a few exhausted and poorly armed Japanese.[12] Instead they had met elements of a strong force with artillery support, which General Vandegrift subsequently estimated to number between 3,000 and 4,000 men. The enemy had avoided action with the small raiding force which had engaged only the outposts. The fact that the Japanese main body did not attack the raiders is surprising, for the natives' reports had been correct.[13] A strong enemy force had been landed near Taivu Point.

The units which the raiders had met were part of the recently landed *Kawaguchi Force.* This *Force,* the nucleus of which was Col. Akinosuka Oka's *124th Infantry,* had originally been the *35th Brigade,* a part of the *18th Division* in China, until that division was triangularized in December 1941 and sent to Burma. On 6 December 1941, the *Kawaguchi Force* sailed from China for Borneo and landed there on 16 December. In March 1942 it arrived at Cebu in the Philippines, then proceeded to Mindanao in April. In June 1942 the *Kawaguchi Force* left for the Palau Islands, where it received 1,000 replacements.[14] It was then alerted for New Guinea.[15] The *Force* stayed in the Palaus until late August, when it departed to stage through Truk and sail in successive echelons for Guadalcanal.

The *Kawaguchi Force* echelons arrived at Guadalcanal between 29 August and 11 September; they landed at night from destroyer-transports and trans-

---

[11] CG 1st Mar Div to COMSOPAC, 1150 of 8 Sep 42. SOPAC War Diary. In the early years of the war the Americans often erroneously reported capturing 77-mm. pieces from the Japanese, who had no weapon of that caliber. In this volume, 75-mm. has been substituted for 77-mm. when the latter caliber is given in the sources. In the message cited, "75-mm. guns" is rendered correctly.

[12] Interv, USAFISPA Hist Off with Maj James G. Kelly, USMC (former CO, C Co, 1st Prcht Bn), 19 Jun 44.

[13] The Japanese appear to have thought that Edson's troops which landed at Tasimboko were a fresh body of reinforcements. *17th Army* Opns, I. At the time of the raid, some Allied supply ships were sailing westward through the channel.

[14] XIV Corps, Enemy Opns, *18th Div* Hist, p. 1.

[15] ATIS, SWPA: Int Rpts, *Yazawa Butai* and *Oki Shudan Gp Hq,* 8 Mar–30 Sep 42, p. 30.

BLOODY RIDGE, *with Henderson Field just beyond, appears scarred white along its crest in the picture above. A marine, below, surveys foxholes along the ridge where Colonel Edson's raider-parachute battalion fought off the* Kawaguchi Force.

ports.[16] The *Force* was composed of the *Ichiki Force* rear echelon (a part of the reinforced *2d Battalion, 28th Infantry*); the *124th Infantry,* and the *2d Battalion, 4th Infantry,* plus antitank, signal, engineer, and artillery elements. It included over 6,000 men.[17]

The 1st Marine Division's report subsequently estimated that total enemy strength on Guadalcanal at this time amounted to 7,000 men.[18] The majority of the *Kawaguchi Force*—the *1st* and *3d Battalions, 124th Infantry,* and the Ichiki rear echelon—had landed with General Kawaguchi near Taivu in late August and early September. Colonel Oka, with his regimental headquarters and the *2d Battalion, 124th Infantry,* landed at Kokumbona west of Lunga Point on 6 September.[19] The *2d Battalion, 4th Infantry,* was normally a part of the *2d Division* but was attached temporarily to General Kawaguchi's command. By the time the last units had landed, General Kawaguchi had assembled over 6,000 men, but they were divided between two widely separated points. On 8 September the main body was in the vicinity of Taivu Point, while Colonel Oka with a smaller force was in the vicinity of Kokumbona, more than thirty miles west of Kawaguchi's position.

Kawaguchi had been ordered to reconnoiter and decide whether his men were capable of seizing the airfield at once, or if they should first be reinforced. Confidently believing that reinforcements were unnecessary, he determined to attack immediately.[20]

About 2 September Kawaguchi's engineers, using hand tools, started to cut a trail from Tasimboko through the jungle toward a point south of Henderson Field. Tough vines, heavy undergrowth, dense forest, and steep ravines and ridges along the route of approach made all movement difficult in that area. As the trail progressed, infantry and artillery units followed the engineers. Documents captured later indicated that the Japanese had planned a co-ordinated attack, with strong air and naval surface support against three separate sectors.[21] The plan involved moving against the Lunga defenses from the west, south, and east. The western force was out of physical contact with Kawa-

---

[16] *Ibid.,* Int Summaries Nos. 14, 17, 19, 22, pp. 68–79; Amer Div, Int Annex to Combat Experience Rpt, Tab A; XIV Corps, Enemy Opns, OB, p. 4; *18th Div* Hist, p. 2; USAFISPA, Japanese Campaign in the Guadalcanal Area, p. 6.

[17] *17th Army* Opns, I.

[18] 1st Mar Div Rpt, V, Annex Y, 1–2.

[19] Amer Div Int Rpt, Tab A; XIV Corps, Enemy Opns, p. 3.

[20] *17th Army* Opns, I.

[21] 1st Mar Div Rpt, IV, 12.

guchi's main body, which was then proceeding through the jungle toward the 1st Marine Division's south and east flanks.

The 1st Marine Division headquarters was well aware that an attack was impending. Land patrols, observation posts, and patrolling aircraft were furnishing data on the enemy to the intelligence section. South and southeast of the Lunga defenses patrols of marines and native scouts clashed regularly with the Japanese. Accumulated evidence demonstrated that Kawaguchi's column was advancing toward the Lunga, but division headquarters did not know Kawaguchi's exact location until he attacked.[22]

The marines, meanwhile, had improved their defenses. The Lunga garrison, strengthened by the raiders and parachutists, was also augmented by the 2d Battalion of the 5th Marines, which was brought over from Tulagi on 21 August and assigned for a time as regimental reserve in the 5th Marines' sector west of the Lunga River. In preparation for an attack from the east the 1st Marines completed the extension of the east flank line to a point about 4,000 yards inland from the mouth of the Ilu. The right (south) flank of the line was unprotected. In the west sector a 4,000-yard gap between the Lunga River and the 5th Marines' lines southwest of Kukum lay open in the inland area. The pioneers held one strong point in this gap on a small ridge west of the river, and amphibian tractor drivers held a second separate strong point on a large open ridge northwest of the pioneers. General Vandegrift realized that a co-ordinated attack could penetrate these defenses, but he expected that the reserve would be able to contain any force attacking there before it reached the airfield.

East of the Lunga in the 1st Marines' sector the southern line was almost as weak. An outpost line extended across 4,000 yards of rough jungle between the east flank and the Lunga River. This line was held by the 1st Marines, and by artillerymen, engineers, and pioneers. The outpost line ran north of the low ridge, later called Bloody or Edson's Ridge, which lies about 800 yards east of the Lunga River. The dense growth and the rough ridges limited fields of fire; there were not enough troops to hold a continuous line in force. At the edge of the jungle at the north end of the ridge was the division command post.

General Vandegrift ordered the Raider-Parachute Battalion out of division reserve to develop a defense position along Bloody Ridge south of the outpost line. He believed that if it was undefended, the ridge would provide the enemy with a good route of approach to the airfield. The 1st Pioneer Battalion had

[22] See *ibid.*, 5–6.

already bivouacked northwest of the ridge along the east bank of the Lunga, and the 1st Engineer Battalion had bivouacked northeast of the ridge to help prevent the Japanese from advancing north along the Lunga or through the jungle east of the ridge.

Action on Bloody Ridge

On 12 September the Raider-Parachute Battalion attempted to patrol south along the ridge but met enemy rifle fire. (*Map VI*) The battalion dug in for the night on the southernmost knoll. During the night of 12–13 September there was continuous firing along the ridge. That the enemy had penetrated to the jungles around the ridge was obvious, but the dense growth and the blackness of the night limited visibility from Bloody Ridge. At one time during the night some Japanese actually broke through the sketchy positions of the Raider-Parachute Battalion, but apparently failed to realize it for they made no effort to exploit their advantage.

The Raider-Parachute Battalion attempted a further advance after daybreak on 13 September, but failed to gain. Exhausted by fighting in the heat, it halted in the afternoon to establish a slightly stronger, higher position about 250 yards north of its bivouac of 12–13 August. On the right the raiders had made a tenuous connection with the pioneers, but the left flank was open. The 2d Battalion of the 5th Marines, then in division reserve, moved to the south edge of the airfield on the afternoon of 13 September to effect the relief of the Raider-Parachute Battalion the next morning. One battery of the 5th Battalion, 11th Marines (105-mm. howitzers), had been assigned to provide direct support to the ridge area. Men from the 11th Marines Special Weapons Battery maintained an observation post on the ridge. In the afternoon the battery had registered on areas in the south but accurate plotting was impossible because there were no reliable maps.

On the ridge itself two companies of parachutists were holding the eastern spur of the center knoll, with their left flank uncovered; B Company of the Raiders held the center of the knoll on the parachutists' right. Posted on the right between the ridge and the Lunga River was A Company, and C Company was the battalion reserve. During the last hours of daylight on 13 September the troops dug in and extended their fields of fire.

Enemy aircraft attacked Lunga Point repeatedly during the day. American fighter planes forced one wave of bombers to turn back, but at 1020, 1320, and 1750 Japanese bombers protected by fighter escort came over to attack Henderson Field and positions adjacent to the ridge.

Shortly after nightfall on 13 September rocket flares over Bloody Ridge announced the opening of an attack by at least two battalions of the *Kawaguchi Force*. Without any artillery preparation, the main body attacked north against the center of the ridge while one force cut through the jungle west of the ridge and isolated the right platoon of B Company of the raiders and cut off A Company. Though surrounded, the platoon from B Company fought its way about 250 yards to the rear to join the battalion reserve on the northernmost knoll. The Japanese exploited the gap between the raider companies and the pioneer companies by moving strong parties in, while at other points small groups infiltrated through to cut telephone wires. B Company of the raiders, in danger of envelopment, refused its right flank along the western slopes of the ridge.

The registered battery of the 5th Battalion, 11th Marines, opened fire on the enemy at 2100, joined shortly thereafter by a second and then a third battery. All batteries fired over the heads of the marines on the ridge. As the enemy attack grew in intensity the 5th Battalion began firing heavy concentrations. Communications between the fire direction center and the forward observers were broken for about two hours, but the artillery continued to fire without observation.

While continuing the attack against B Company on the center of the ridge, the Japanese put heavy mortar fire on the parachutists' positions on B Company's left. At 2230, shouting loudly, the Japanese infantry stormed the parachutists' lines and drove them back off their eastern spur. This exposed B Company to attack from three sides. Colonel Edson, commanding the Raider-Parachute Battalion, decided to withdraw B Company from its dangerous position and to rally his forces on the northern knoll of Bloody Ridge, the battalion reserve line. Using C Company of the raiders as a nucleus, Colonel Edson and Maj. Kenneth Bailey, the executive officer, successfully re-established the lines on the last knoll in front of Henderson Field and the division command post.

The Japanese, continuing their attacks, advanced uphill against artillery, mortar, machine-gun, and rifle fire and grenades. As at the Ilu, these assaults failed to break the last lines. Kawaguchi's forces attacked Bloody Ridge about twelve times during the night. The direction and objective of every attack was preceded by a rocket flare, each of which served as a point of reference for the fire of the 5th Battalion, 11th Marines. From 2100, 13 September, until dawn the next day, the 105-mm. howitzer batteries fired 1,992 rounds in support of the Raider-Parachute Battalion at ranges as short as 1,600 yards. They sometimes put shells within 200 yards of the front lines, which was generally considered to be an unusually short distance in the early days of the war. By 0230 Colonel Edson had concluded that his troops could hold out, although they were still under attack. As morning drew near the vigor of the Japanese assaults declined.

By dawn of 14 September the Raider-Parachute Battalion was still holding the last knoll on Bloody Ridge. The Japanese attacks had ceased. After aircraft took off from Henderson Field and drove the remaining enemy from Bloody Ridge, the *Kawaguchi Force* began to retreat.

Action on the Flanks

While the main enemy body was attacking Bloody Ridge, a second unit of the *Kawaguchi Force* had attacked west about midnight against the right flank of the 3d Battalion, 1st Marines, on the Ilu. Here the line lay along the edge of the jungle in front of a 700-yard-deep flat, grassy plain to the east. The front was wired in; fields of fire had been prepared by burning and trampling the grass. The right end of the line was without flank protection and thus was open to envelopment.

About two companies of Japanese attacked against the front of the right flank unit, but failed to penetrate the line.[23] A fire fight developed which lasted throughout the night, but the 1st Marines' positions were never seriously endangered.

During the day division headquarters, believing that the force still facing the 1st Marines on the east flank was composed of one infantry battalion supported by artillery, sent six light tanks across the plain to destroy the enemy. When they made repeated sorties over the same routes of approach, three tanks were hit by antitank gunfire and one overturned in a creek. The Japanese did not attack the 1st Marines again but engaged the right flank of the east line with desultory fire until 16 September.

A third Japanese force, probably under Colonel Oka's command, struck on the afternoon of 14 September in the west sector. Part of the 3d Battalion of the 5th Marines was holding the sector from the coast inland to a ridge which commanded the coastal road. The Japanese, debouching from the jungles, struck suddenly at the ridge but failed to take it and were driven back down the slopes by infantry counterattacks and artillery fire.

The Cost

The exact composition of the three Japanese attacking forces is not clear. The *1st* and *3d Battalions* of the *124th Infantry* and the *2d Battalion* of the

---

[23] Interv, USAFISPA Hist Off with Capt Gerald W. Gates, USMC (former Bn-3, 3d Bn, 1st Mar), 17 Jun 44.

4th Infantry probably delivered the assault against Bloody Ridge while the *Ichiki Force* rear echelon may have attacked the 1st Marines. The *2d Battalion, 124th Infantry,* probably delivered the weak attack against the 5th Marines on 14 September.

Marine casualties on Bloody Ridge were about 20 percent of the total force engaged. Thirty-one were killed, 103 wounded, and 9 missing. The Japanese casualties were much higher. Of an estimated 2,000 who attacked Bloody Ridge, about 600 were killed on the ridge itself.[24] After its repulse, the *Kawaguchi Force* began to retreat, carrying its wounded in litters. The Japanese had entered the action with only a few days' rations, and these seem to have been quickly exhausted. About 400 men of the *2d Battalion, 28th Infantry* (Ichiki's rear echelon) made their way east to Koli Point. Some troops of the *2d Battalion, 4th Infantry,* were also reported to have gone to Koli Point.[25] The remainder of the *Kawaguchi Force* retreated to the west by cutting a trail around the rough southern slopes of Mount Austen to Kokumbona. Many of the wounded died, and the weakened survivors buried dead soldiers, heavy equipment, and artillery pieces along the way. The journey took over a week.[26] The Japanese reported that 633 men were killed in action, and 505 wounded.[27]

That the *Kawaguchi Force* could offer no immediate threat to Henderson Field was indicated in the week following the Bloody Ridge action. Marine patrols fought a series of successful engagements with Japanese units along the upper reaches of the Lunga River. They found stocks of the equipment, ammunition, small arms, and guns of two field artillery batteries which the *Kawaguchi Force* had abandoned. The second and more formidable threat to Henderson Field had been successfully averted.

Reinforcements

By mid-September the Marines, besides capturing the airfield, had fought two successful defensive actions and conducted minor offensive actions in the Matanikau area. Neither combat reinforcements nor additional ammunition had yet been sent to Guadalcanal. When Vandegrift had persuaded Turner in

[24] 1st Mar Div Rpt, IV, 11.

[25] XIV Corps, Enemy Opns, *18th Div* Hist, p. 3.

[26] XIV Corps, Enemy Opns, gives two figures: p. 2 estimates 12–14 days, and *18th Div* Hist, p. 2, estimates 7–10 days.

[27] *17th Army* Opns, I. XIV Corps, Enemy Opns, *18th Div* Hist, p. 3, estimates 2,000 killed in action or DW.

August that the 2d Marines should remain with the 1st Division, he had also asked Turner to consider sending the 7th Marines from Samoa to rejoin the division on Guadalcanal.[28]

Allied aerial reconnaissance in September showed that the Japanese were building up their strength at Rabaul, and Admiral Ghormley concluded that the Japanese could be expected to continue their ground operations in New Guinea and to mount a large-scale counteroffensive to retake the Lunga airfield.[29] Turner believed that until the Allies could muster sufficient strength to keep the Japanese air and surface forces away from Guadalcanal, additional positions there should be established outside the Lunga defenses. These additional positions should be strong enough to withstand direct enemy attack. From these new positions patrols could destroy enemy forces which succeeded in landing elsewhere along the coast. On 9 September Turner recommended to Ghormley that the reinforced 7th Marines establish the first additional position at Taivu Point, about twenty-five statute miles east of Lunga Point. Admiral Ghormley decided to withhold his final decision until Turner visited Guadalcanal to decide whether the 7th Marines could be used more advantageously at Taivu or at Lunga Point.

The 7th Marines and part of the 5th Defense Battalion had embarked on seven ships at Samoa on 2 September with equipment and vehicles. The ships had sailed under escort for Espiritu Santo, where they arrived on 12 September. While en route, the commanders of the transport division, the 7th Marines, and the 5th Defense Battalion detachment had been ordered to prepare landing plans for both Ndeni and Taivu Point.

In the meantime Admiral Turner had flown to Guadalcanal to confer with General Vandegrift, who wished the 7th Marines to reinforce the Lunga defenses. They agreed that while a wide deployment along the coast would be essential for ultimate security, the most pressing need was the reinforcement of the Lunga area by the 7th Marines. Admiral Turner presented these recommendations to Admiral Ghormley on 12 September, and the next day Ghormley ordered the 7th Marines to reinforce the Guadalcanal garrison as soon as possible.[30] The 5th Defense Battalion detachment remained at Espiritu Santo for

[28] COMAMPHIBFORSOPAC, Rpt Opn for Reinf Guadalcanal by 7th Mar (Reinf), Ser 00195, 27 Sep 42, p. 2. A copy of this report is in the Office of Naval Records and Library.

[29] *Ibid.*, p. 3.

[30] COMAMPHIBFORSOPAC to COMSOPAC, 0530 of 12 Sep 42. SOPAC War Diary; COMAMPHIB-FORSOPAC, Rpt Opn for Reinf Guadalcanal by 7th Mar, p. 4.

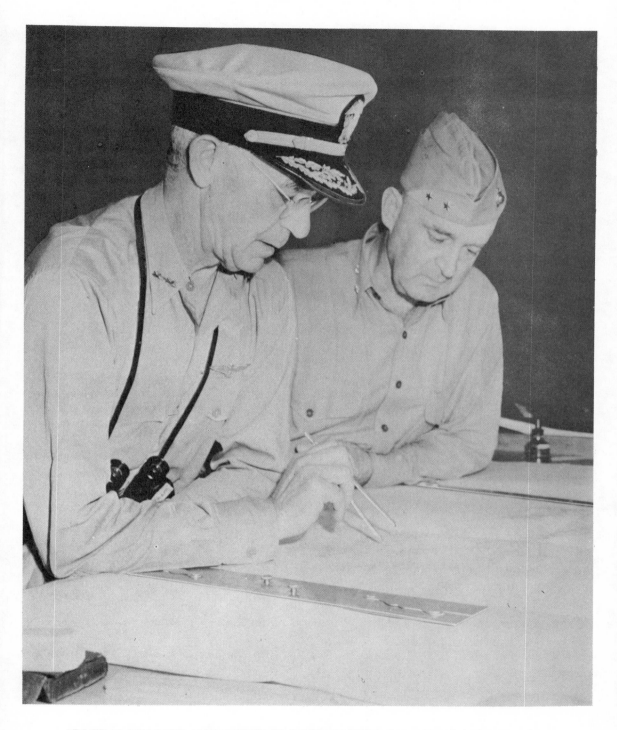

ADMIRAL TURNER AND GENERAL VANDEGRIFT *photographed during a conference on Guadalcanal plans.*

a time, and on 2 October occupied the island of Funafuti in the Ellice Group, about 1,250 miles to the east of Guadalcanal.[31]

For the movement of the 7th Marines to Guadalcanal, Admiral Turner organized a new task force—Task Force 65. The transport group of the force consisted of two transport divisions of three ships each. The 7th Marines, Reinforced, including the 1st Battalion of the 11th Marines (75-mm. pack howitzers), comprised the landing force. Three cruisers, including the New Zealand cruiser *Leander,* plus destroyers and minesweepers were to screen the transports.

Task Force 65, under Turner's command, sailed from Espiritu Santo at 0515, 14 September. The situation was delicate. The remaining Allied naval forces in the South Pacific were supporting Turner's force but were inferior in strength to the Japanese. Many enemy ships were present in the Solomons waters. On 15 September Turner decided not to continue toward Guadalcanal, for some Japanese warships had been reported to be operating near Santa Cruz and the Shortlands, and warships were shelling the Lunga area almost nightly. He did not wish to risk being attacked by the Japanese during debarkation. At 1500, 15 September, his force retired to a point southeast of San Cristobal to await more favorable conditions. Twenty-four hours later the force turned north toward the east end of San Cristobal to be in position to land the 7th Marines on Guadalcanal on 18 September. As the Japanese did not attack, Admiral Turner decided on 17 September to proceed with the landing plans.

General Vandegrift had wished to extend the east flank of the Lunga position one mile beyond the Ilu, and the 7th Marines were to have landed at Beach Red. After the night battle of 13–14 September he decided not to extend his flank, and suggested that the 7th Marines land between the Lunga and the Ilu Rivers. As heavy weather and rolling seas made this area unusable, Admiral Turner decided to land at Kukum where the beach was more sheltered. He planned to spend no more than twelve hours unloading off Kukum as his force would have to clear Sealark Channel before nightfall to avoid enemy warships. He desired to put ashore within that time all troops, weapons, and essential equipment, three units of fire, forty days' rations, and the vehicles carried on board the six transports.

The force anchored off Kukum on the morning of 18 September and by 0550 had begun unloading. As Japanese aircraft did not attack during the day, unloading operations proceeded without interruption until 1800. The *MacFar-*

---

[31] 5th AAA Bn (formerly 5th Def Bn) Rpt of Opns, 1 Dec 40–30 Apr 44.

land and the *Tracy* also sailed into the channel about 1000, followed by the *Bellatrix* at 1300, and all three ships, which were not part of Task Force 65, began unloading an emergency shipment of aviation gasoline.[32]

The results of the day's operations, according to Turner, actually exceeded his expectations. Four thousand, one hundred and eighty men of the reinforced 7th Marines came safely ashore.[33] One hundred forty-seven vehicles were landed, together with 90 percent of the engineering equipment, 82.5 percent of the organizational equipment, nearly all the ammunition, 82 tons of B rations, 930 tons of C and D rations, nearly all quartermaster stores, and 60 percent of the tentage. The *McCawley, Bellatrix, MacFarland,* and *Tracy* put 3,823 drums of fuel ashore. Still on board were 13 officers and 244 enlisted men; 15 tanks; 8,825 tons of B, C, and D rations, and 73 vehicles.[34] The ammunition landed at this time was the first shipment which the 1st Marine Division had received in response to its request for 10,000 rounds of 37-mm. canister and 10,000 hand grenades on 22 August.

Turner's force, having taken on board the 1st Parachute Battalion, 162 American wounded, and 8 Japanese prisoners, sailed for Espiritu Santo at 1800, 18 September, followed by the gasoline ships. Enemy warships entered Sealark Channel from the north on the night of 18–19 September but did not pursue the retiring task force.

Because Japanese warships regularly operated in Sealark Channel at night, Admiral Turner specified on 24 September that any vessels carrying supplies to Lunga Point were to unload only during daylight. If not fully unloaded they were to retire eastward out of the channel at night and return to the Point at dawn.[35] Following these orders, the *Betelgeuse,* escorted by one destroyer, unloaded off Lunga Point from 0628 to 1830, 24 September, and then retired eastward. The ships returned at 0530 the next morning to discharge cargo, and withdrew again for the night. They anchored once more off Lunga Point at 0630, 26 September, to resume unloading. During the same morning the *Alhena,* escorted by one destroyer, sailed into Sealark Channel to unload. The *Betelgeuse* and her escort retired, completely unloaded, at 1500. The *Alhena* sailed out of the channel at 2045, returned the next morning, and continued the process until 1200, 29 September, when she had discharged all her cargo.

[32] COMAMPHIBFORSOPAC War Diary, 16, 18 Sep 42.
[33] 1st Mar Div Rpt, V, Personnel Annex W, 1–2, lists 215 officers and 3,450 enlisted men, a total of 3,665.
[34] COMAMPHIBFORSOPAC, Rpt Opn for Reinf Guadalcanal by 7th Mar, Incl F.
[35] COMAMPHIBFORSOPAC War Diary, 24 Sep 42.

SUPPLIES AND REINFORCEMENTS *were landed during a lull in the incessant enemy air attacks on American shipping. An LCVP (above) is unloading an emergency gasoline supply and below, a Marine weapons carrier debarks from an LCM(2).*

Admiral Turner's orders on 29 September defined ships' operations more explicitly. Thereafter, ships of the Amphibious Force were to load cargo specifically either for Guadalcanal or Tulagi. Unless otherwise ordered they were to load no more than 3,000 tons, a quantity which could be unloaded in twenty-four hours. Ships discharging cargo off Guadalcanal, standing in the open channel, were to unload only during daylight, but ships unloading in the greater security of Tulagi Harbor could unload continuously.[36]

By about 18 September logistic support of the 1st Marine Division had improved sufficiently to restore full rations to all combat troops. By the end of the month, the Guadalcanal garrison's troop strength was still low; 19,251 men were on Guadalcanal, 3,260 on Tulagi.[37]

Actions on the Matanikau

The addition of the 7th Marines to the Lunga garrison and the arrival of more aircraft at Henderson Field made possible an improvement of the Lunga Point defenses. For the first time, General Vandegrift was able to establish a complete perimeter defense. On 19 September he divided the Lunga area into ten sectors. Defenses of the seven inland sectors on the west, east, and south were strengthened by the addition of infantry battalions. Two battalions constituted the division reserve. Each infantry regiment was to maintain one battalion in reserve, under regimental control but available for commitment by division headquarters if necessary. The 3d Defense Battalion, commanded by Colonel Pepper, with the 1st Special Weapons Battalion attached, continued to be responsible for providing beach and antiaircraft .defense. Each night the three beach sectors were to be strengthened by men of the pioneer, engineer, and amphibian tractor battalions who performed their regular duties during the day and helped to man the beach lines after dark.

The defense thus established was generally circular. Though some areas could not be strongly held, there were no exposed flanks and no large gaps. The southern (inland) area still posed problems which could not be completely solved. Positions on open ridges could be organized in depth, but on the low ground the dense vegetation prevented the establishment of completely mutually supporting positions. There were not enough men to carry out the enor-

[36] COMAMPHIBFORSOPAC, FE 25/4, 29 Sep 42, Ser 00206, sub: Instructions for ships furnishing logistic support to Cactus and Ringbolt. This order is in the Office of Naval Records and Library.
[37] 1st Mar Div Rpt, V, Personnel Annex W.

mous task of clearing fields of fire for a line which ran through 14,000 yards of jungle. Whenever possible the main line of resistance followed the hills and ridges. The field fortifications included foxholes and splinter-proof machine gun emplacements of logs and sandbags. Sufficient barbed wire had been brought to the marines to enable them to begin to wire in the whole front behind two bands of double apron fence with trip wires between the bands. The 11th Marines, strengthened by the 75-mm. pack howitzers of the 1st Battalion, remained grouped inside the perimeter to provide fire support to all sectors.

Although this cordon defense was far from ideal, it provided strong fire power and presented a continuous line to prevent enemy infiltration. It was vulnerable to intensive artillery fire, but as General Vandegrift observed, the Japanese demonstrated "a lack of efficiency and a low order of professional technique" in the use of artillery.[38]

The division was now ready to take the offensive. After the Bloody Ridge engagement, division headquarters knew that a sizable enemy force was operating from Matanikau village west of the river, in Kokumbona, and was occasionally patrolling Mount Austen. These troops were from the *4th Infantry* of the *2d Division* and the *Kawaguchi Force*. The rest of the *4th Infantry* had landed west of the Matanikau in mid-September to join forces with its *2d Battalion*.[39] Reasonably sure that the Japanese could offer no immediate threat to the south and east sectors, the 1st Division planned to clear the enemy out of the areas to the west by a series of offensives in regimental strength. Once those in the Matanikau area had been driven out or destroyed, the division would be able to establish defense positions to keep the Japanese beyond striking distance of Lunga Point.

The first plan called for operations by the newly arrived 1st Battalion, 7th Marines, and the 1st Raider Battalion. Lt. Col. Lewis B. Puller commanded the 1st Battalion of the 7th Marines; the raiders were then commanded by Lt. Col. Samuel B. Griffith, II. Colonel Edson, recently promoted to full colonel's rank, had taken command of the 5th Marines on 21 September after Colonel Hunt's departure for the United States.

On 23 September Colonel Puller's battalion was to proceed southwest to Mount Austen, advance west along its northern slopes, and cross the Matanikau inland to patrol the area between the river and Kokumbona. This patrol action was to be concluded by 26 September. On that day the raiders were to advance

[38] 1st Mar Div Rpt, V, 4.
[39] Amer Div Int Rpt, Tab A; USAFISPA, Japanese Campaign in the Guadalcanal Area, p. 9.

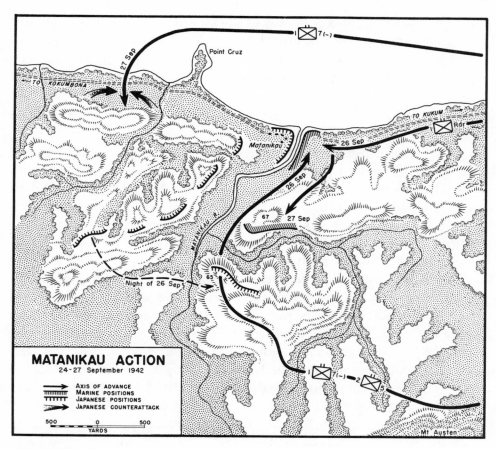

MAP NO. 6

west along the coast road to establish a temporary patrol base at Kokumbona where several inland trails intersected the coast road. Control of Kokumbona would not only deny a good landing beach to the Japanese, but would also prevent them from using the trails to advance inland.

The 1st Battalion, 7th Marines, passed through the perimeter defense line on 23 September. (*Map 6*) Upon reaching the Mount Austen area, it surprised and scattered a Japanese force shortly after sunset on 24 September. The battalion was reinforced by the 2d Battalion of the 5th Marines the next morning. Two companies of the 1st Battalion were detached to escort the marine wounded back to the perimeter. The main body of Puller's force moved slowly toward the Matanikau, and reached the river the next day, 25 September. As

Colonel Puller had been ordered to conclude his patrol on 26 September, he did not cross the Matanikau, but turned north and patrolled along the east bank to the river mouth, where he intended to cross the river. When the force reached the mouth it started across the sand bar, but was forced back by heavy Japanese mortar fire from the west bank. The colonel called for and received artillery support, but the fire failed to dislodge the Japanese, who were strongly entrenched in carefully prepared positions.

The 1st Raider Battalion had meanwhile reached the river mouth en route to Kokumbona. Division headquarters ordered the raiders to join forces with Colonel Puller's force to attack west the next day, 27 September. Colonel Edson was assigned to command the combined forces, with Puller as second-in-command. Edson ordered the 2d Battalion, 5th Marines, to attack west across the river mouth, while the raiders moved upstream to cross the river at a stream junction about 2,000 yards from the mouth.

Both battalions moved to the attack in the morning, but failed to gain ground. The 2d Battalion was unable to establish itself on the west bank. The raiders meanwhile had advanced to the high ground (Hill 67) on the east bank about 1,500 yards south of the beach where they were halted by unexpected enemy fire. During the previous night a Japanese force had crossed upstream to the east bank and occupied Hill 65, about 850 yards south of Hill 67. In the raiders' attempt to advance Colonel Griffith was wounded and Major Bailey, the battalion executive officer, was killed.

Unable to move farther, the raider battalion sent a message to Colonel Edson to explain the situation, but in the haste and excitement of battle it was badly phrased. Colonel Edson concluded from the message that the raiders had crossed the river and were meeting resistance in the village of Matanikau itself.[40] He decided on a new plan of attack which was based on the erroneous assumption that the raiders had reached Matanikau. The raiders were to resume the advance at 1330, while the 2d Battalion, 5th, attacked across the river mouth. Colonel Puller's 1st Battalion, 7th Marines, was to embark in landing craft at Kukum, land west of Point Cruz, and attack the Japanese in Matanikau from the rear. The 1st Battalion, supported by fire from the destroyer *Ballard,* landed west of Point Cruz as ordered, and advanced toward the first ridge about 350 yards inland. No

---

[40] 1st Mar Div Rpt, V, 6. Efforts to find this message have failed. 1st Marine Division staff and command procedures were simple, stressing verbal communication and direct contact between staffs and commanders. Field operations were handled orally, and written messages were usually destroyed on the spot. Col Raye P. Gerfen, Rpt to Hq AGF. OPD 381 Sec. IV PTO (3-15-43).

sooner had it gained the ridge than a Japanese force attacked it from both flanks and cut it off from the shore.[41] The acting battalion commander was killed.

Before the battalion could be withdrawn from its dangerous position, division headquarters lost control of the situation. Just as the battalion was being surrounded twenty-six Japanese bombers attacked the positions in the Lunga area, including the division command post. "Resultant damage included the complete disruption of all communication facilities at the division headquarters at a time when reliable communication was imperative." [42] The arrangements for withdrawal of the 1st Battalion were completed by Colonel Edson, while division headquarters re-established contact with Edson over the artillery telephone line to the forward observers. Fortunately, the *Ballard,* which had withdrawn during the air raid, had been notified of the 1st Battalion's plight. Colonel Puller, who was also aware of the situation, was taken aboard the destroyer which sailed in close to the beach west of Point Cruz. Receiving firing data from a 1st Battalion sergeant using signal flags, the *Ballard* laid down a barrage. Puller ordered his battalion to fight its way to the beach at all costs. The battalion successfully cut through the enemy, reached the beach, and boarded landing craft which had come up from Lunga Point. All the wounded men were brought out safely, and by nightfall the battalion had returned to the Lunga perimeter. Once Puller's battalion was safe, the raiders and the 2d Battalion, 5th Marines, also withdrew. In this hastily planned, unsuccessful action, the marines lost 60 killed and 100 wounded.

The next offensive came ten days later. Its object was to establish a line far enough to the west to keep the Japanese beyond artillery range of Henderson Field. Information from higher headquarters, coastwatchers, aerial reconnaissance, and ground patrols indicated that the Japanese were building up strength in the west in preparation for offensive action. Opposing patrols were clashing daily on the east bank of the Matanikau. Japanese 150-mm. guns capable of interdicting Henderson Field from Kokumbona were landed in late September. The 1st Marine Division therefore determined to trap and destroy the enemy near Point Cruz, and drive any survivors west beyond the Poha River, about 9,000 yards west of Point Cruz. If this operation succeeded a patrol base could be established at Kokumbona, and the airfield would be safe from artillery fire.

The division's plan of attack called for the 5th Marines (less one battalion) to execute a holding attack at the mouth of the Matanikau River, crossing the

[41] See ltr, Col Samuel B. Griffith, II, USMC, to Hist Sec, Hq, USMC, 6 Oct 45, in USMC HIST Sec files.
[42] 1st Mar Div Rpt, V, 7.

MARINE MISSION TO THE MATANIKAU. *Leaving its bivouac area in the defense perimeter, a Marine patrol crosses the Lunga River near its mouth, en route to the 7 October line of departure on Matanikau.*

POSITIONS ON HILL 67 *marked the farthest point of advance of the 1st Raider Battalion in the 27 September attempt to drive the Japanese out of the Point Cruz area. Two fingers of Hill 67 (left foreground and right) stretch toward the Matanikau River in the ravine and Hill 75 beyond. Point Cruz is seen on the left horizon.*

river on divisional order, while the 7th Marines (less one battalion) and one reinforced battalion enveloped Point Cruz. The reinforced battalion, commanded by Col. William J. Whaling, was composed of the 3d Battalion of the 2d Marines and the Division Scout–Sniper Detachment, a detachment which Colonel Whaling had personally trained on Guadalcanal in an effort to improve the quality of patrolling. The Whaling Group was to follow the 5th Marines along the coast road, then turn southwest and advance inland to a point about 2,000 yards southwest of the river mouth where the Matanikau is narrow. The group was to cross the river on a bridge made of logs thrown across the stream and then turn right (north) to attack. The ridges west of the Matanikau, from 200 to 300 feet in height, run from north to south. The Whaling Group was to attack north along the first ridge west of the river. The 7th Marines (less one battalion) was to follow the Whaling Group across the river, advance beyond the first ridge, and attack northward with battalions abreast on the left of the Whaling Group. If these attacks succeeded in reaching the beach and destroying the Japanese, the 5th Marines would pass through the Whaling Group and the 7th Marines to attack west toward Kokumbona. The 3d Battalion, 1st Marines, was in reserve.

The 1st Marine Air Wing was to support the offensive with dive bombing and strafing. Officers of the attacking infantry forces were assigned as air forward observers to radio target data to the supporting aircraft. The wing was also to provide liaison planes for the infantry and spotting planes for the artillery. The 1st Battalion, 11th Marines, was to provide direct artillery support to the 7th Marines; the 2d Battalion, to the 5th Marines; the 5th Battalion, to the Whaling Group. The 3d Battalion was to cover the perimeter while the other three were engaged.[43]

The Japanese had also prepared a plan of attack which was markedly similar to that of the Marines. In preparation for the counteroffensive against Lunga Point the *17th Army* and the *2d Division* had ordered the *4th Infantry,* commanded by Col. Tadamasu Nakaguma,[44] to seize positions east of the Matanikau about 8 October for use by the artillery.[45] The *1st Battalion* of the *4th Infantry* was to occupy the Point Cruz area and cross the Matanikau at its mouth while the *3d Battalion* made a crossing farther inland.[46] Should the *4th Infantry's* attack succeed, the Japanese would be able to deny to the marines the Matanikau River,

---

[43] 1st Mar Div Opn Plan No. 2–42, 6 Oct 42, in 1st Mar Div Rpt, V, Annex D.

[44] XIV Corps, Enemy Opns, *2d Div* Org, p. 1.

[45] 1st Mar Div Rpt, V, 13.

[46] USAFISPA, Japanese Campaign in the Guadalcanal Area, pp. 13–14.

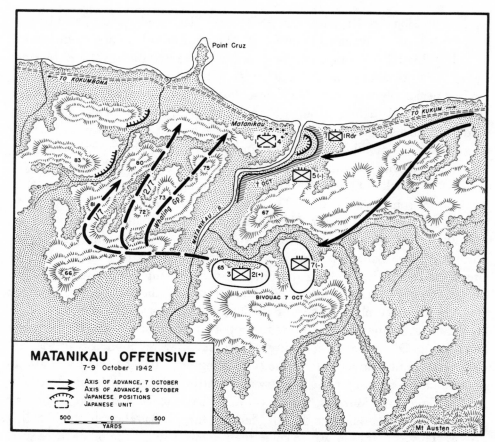

MAP NO. 7

one of the best defense lines west of the Lunga. Fortunately the marines struck before the enemy could execute his entire plan.

The attacking marines passed through the perimeter defense line near Kukum at 0700, 7 October, en route to the line of departure on the Matanikau. (*Map 7*) About 1005 the advance guard of the 3d Battalion of the 5th Marines, marching along the coast road, met enemy fire several hundred yards east of the river. The 3d Battalion deployed and forced the enemy slowly back toward the river, while the 2d Battalion moved to the left around the 3d. Meeting no opposition, the 2d Battalion reached the river by 1148. The Whaling Group and the 7th Marines, having turned southwest in column, advanced about 3,000 yards toward

Hill 65. They met light rifle fire but reached Hill 65 safely and bivouacked there for the night.

Some Japanese had escaped over the river, but others had meanwhile halted part of the 3d Battalion, 5th Marines, just short of the east bank of the river, and retained a small bridgehead about 400 yards south of the river mouth. One company of the 1st Raider Battalion, then at about one-half its authorized strength, moved up to reinforce the 5th Marines' right flank.

During the night of 7–8 October the 5th Marines and the raider company held a 1,500-yard front extending inland from the river mouth, and bowed to the east around the Japanese bridgehead. The Whaling Group and the 7th Marines occupied bivouac areas on high ground overlooking the river about 800 yards southeast of the 5th Marines' left flank. To divert the Japanese from the enveloping force, the 5th Marines noisily simulated preparations for an immediate river crossing. Amphibian tractors rumbled up and down the coastal area behind the lines to convince the Japanese that they were threatened by a tank attack across the river mouth. Otherwise the night was uneventful.

The attack across the river had originally been set for 8 October, but as heavy rains on that day turned the ground into mud, made the coral ridges slippery, and impeded air operations, the attack was postponed until the next day.[47] The 5th Marines and the raiders continued to reduce the Japanese bridgehead on the east bank. At 1800 some of the Japanese, climbing out of their standing-type foxholes, attempted to break out through the right of the line which was lightly held. In mass formation they struck against the raiders' right flank. Running abreast, the front ranks fired small arms while the rear ranks threw grenades over the heads of the first rank. In the gathering dusk a sharp hand-to-hand fight ensued between the Japanese and a small group of raiders. Casualties on both sides were heavy. Some of the surviving Japanese broke out, but were trapped and killed against the barbed wire barricade which the marines had erected over the sand bar.[48] Elsewhere the night of 8–9 October was quiet except for intermittent rifle and machine-gun fire.

At this point the nature of the offensive had to be changed. Division headquarters, warned on 8 October that the impending Japanese counteroffensive would employ strong reinforcements, canceled its plans to attack toward Kokumbona and the Poha and turned the operation into a large-scale raid against the

[47] CG 1st Mar Div to COMSOPAC, 2245 of 8 Oct 42. SOPAC War Diary.

[48] 1st Mar Div Rpt, V, 11; Annex P (5th Mar Record of Events), 5; Lt Col Russel P. Reeder, Fighting on Guadalcanal (OPD, WDGS, 1943), pp. 21–22.

Point Cruz area. With the enemy threatening to attack in strength, it was necessary to hold the Lunga perimeter with all available forces, then amounting to 19,000 men. To send troops more than one day's march from the Lunga perimeter involved a greater risk than General Vandegrift felt was feasible.

By 9 October the remaining Japanese east of the Matanikau had been killed. The weather had cleared; the troops were rested. The Whaling Group, followed by the 7th Marines, left its bivouac, crossed the Matanikau, climbed the first ridge, and rapidly attacked north along Hills 73 and 75 to the coastal area. The 2d Battalion of the 7th Marines, commanded by Lt. Col. H. H. Hanneken, advanced about 800 yards west of the river and turned right to attack over Hill 72 to Point Cruz. Hanneken's battalion met only light enemy fire. Colonel Puller's 1st Battalion, 7th Marines, advanced about 1,200 yards beyond the Matanikau and attacked north along a 2,000-yard ridge (Hills 66–81–80). The 1st Battalion met stronger Japanese resistance. One group of Japanese held positions in a deep ravine on the 1st Battalion's left between Hills 81–80 and the hill mass on the west, Hill 83. Calling on the 11th Marines for artillery fire to cover his front; the battalion commander directed the battalion mortars to fire into the ravine. When their positions were hit by this mortar fire, the Japanese attempted to escape from the ravine by climbing the steep, open, eastern slopes of Hill 83, where they were easy targets for rifle and machine-gun fire. Some returned to the ravine, which was still under mortar fire.

When his mortar ammunition ran out, Colonel Puller withdrew his battalion according to instructions, and by 1400 the whole enveloping force—the Whaling Group and the 2d and 1st Battalions of the 7th Marines—had crossed east over the mouth of the Matanikau to return to Lunga Point. The withdrawal was covered by the 5th Marines. The 11th Marines had fired 2,188 75-mm. rounds and 1,063 105-mm. rounds in support of the three-day operation.[49] A marine patrol later found a Japanese officer's diary which indicated that the *4th Infantry* had lost nearly 700 men during the three days.[50] The Marines lost 65 killed, 125 wounded.

Thus far during the campaign the ground engagements that had been fought were hot, sharp actions involving relatively small forces. But the Japanese were preparing for a much larger operation.

[49] 1st Mar Div Rpt, V, Arty Annex R.
[50] 1st Mar Div Rpt, V, 12.

CHAPTER VI

The October Counteroffensive

The Japanese, who had been planning for a full-scale counteroffensive ever since August, had completed their preparations by October, and were ready to strike. The first attempts by the inadequate *Ichiki* and *Kawaguchi Forces* had failed to dislodge the marines from their defenses around the airfield. The early Japanese estimates of American strength had proved to be disastrously low. Maj. Gen. Shuicho Miyazaki wrote later that, while in Tokyo prior to becoming Chief of Staff of the *17th Army,* he had lacked exact knowledge of American strength. "Does the American force which landed on Guadalcanal on August 7th," he had asked himself, "represent the entire enemy force committed to this campaign, or is it only the spearhead of a large counter-offensive? If it is the former, our operations will most certainly be successful. But if it is the latter, victory or defeat hangs in the balance." [1]

When the Japanese planned their operation in the spring of 1942, Miyazaki wrote, they hoped to sever the line of communications between the United States and Australia with two separate thrusts. One had as its goal Port Moresby in New Guinea, while the other, an advance through the Solomons, was aimed at the Fijis, Samoa, and New Caledonia. The Allied offensive in August, however, had turned these two thrusts into a single campaign.[2] Operations against Port Moresby, which had been repulsed in May at the Battle of the Coral Sea, had meanwhile been resumed by one small force moving overland across the Papuan Peninsula of New Guinea.

After August, *17th Army Headquarters* at Rabaul raised its estimates of American strength on Guadalcanal but still made serious miscalculations. It believed that 7,500 American troops were holding Lunga Point on 19 September.[3] Actually, U. S. strength on Guadalcanal at the end of September was above 19,000 and rose to over 23,000 on 13 October.

---

[1] Miyazaki, Personal Account, p. 1.

[2] *Ibid.,* p. 5.

[3] ATIS, SCAP: Int Rpts, *Yazawa Butai* and *Oki Shudan Gp Hq,* Int Rec No. 33, p. 93; see also ATIS SCAP, trans, interrog of Hyakutake, Maruyama, Miyazaki, Konuma, and Tajima.

REINFORCEMENTS LANDED AT LUNGA POINT *did not appear numerically great and, possibly, deceived the Japanese into underestimating American strength. These craft (above) came in at Lunga Lagoon, just east of the point. Henderson Field is seen beyond the smoke of cooking fires.*

Japanese Strategy

On the basis of erroneous estimates, General Hyakutake had been preparing elaborate plans for the recapture of Lunga Point even before the *Kawaguchi Force* had reached Guadalcanal. The first plan, issued on 28 August and altered several times afterward, established the basic concept for the Japanese counteroffensive which was to begin in October. General Hyakutake intended to command the operation on Guadalcanal personally. The *Kawaguchi Force* was to secure positions east and west of the Matanikau to cover a projected landing by a fresh division, to secure a line of departure, and to harass the Lunga defenses while a strong artillery force prepared to neutralize Henderson Field. The *17th Army* was to arrange for the transport of the necessary troops from Rabaul. Once the troops reached Guadalcanal and completed their preparations for the attack, they were to "... capture the enemy positions, especially the airfield and artillery positions in one blow." General Hyakutake also considered sending one force in an amphibious assault "behind the enemy." [4] "The operation to surround and recapture Guadalcanal," he grandiloquently announced, "will truly decide the fate of the control of the entire Pacific area...." [5]

Once Lunga Point was retaken, the Japanese planned to seize Rennell, Tulagi, and San Cristobal. During this phase, *17th Army* reserve forces and the *Imperial Navy* were to intensify the attacks against General MacArthur's force in New Guinea. Port Moresby was to be taken by the end of November. [6] Because the importance of Guadalcanal prevented planes, warships, and troop transports from being sent from the Solomons to New Guinea, the Japanese were forced to finish the Guadalcanal campaign before attempting to reinforce New Guinea. [7]

The Japanese offensive against Guadalcanal was to be a joint operation. In September *17th Army* representatives met at Truk with the commanders of the *Combined* and the *Southeastern Fleets* to plan the attack, which was tentatively set for 21 October. [8] Japanese warships were to co-operate fully until two weeks after the fresh division had landed.

Drawing troops for the projected operation from China, the East Indies, the Philippines, and Truk on orders from *Imperial General Headquarters,* the Japan-

[4] Interrog of Maruyama, Miyazaki, Konuma, and Tajima, 31 Aug 46, App. by *1st Demob Bureau,* Summary of *17th Army* Plan.
[5] USAFISPA, Japanese Campaign in the Guadalcanal Area, p. 8.
[6] Amer Div Int Rpt, Tab C, App. 12: *17th Army* Opn Ord, 5 Oct 42.
[7] Miyazaki, Personal Account, p. 2.
[8] USSBS, *Interrogations,* II, 468.

ese assembled, by October, a strong force in Rabaul and the Solomons under the *17th Army's* command. The infantry units consisted of two divisions, one brigade, and one reinforced battalion. Supporting them were three independent antiaircraft artillery battalions, three field antiaircraft artillery battalions, one field antiaircraft artillery battery, one heavy field artillery regiment plus extra batteries, one tank regiment and one tank company, one independent mountain artillery regiment and one independent mountain artillery battalion, one engineer regiment, one trench mortar battalion, and a reconnaissance plane unit.[9] Of these, the brigade and the reinforced battalion (*Kawaguchi* and *Ichiki Forces*) and additional battalions of the *4th Infantry* had already met defeat on Guadalcanal.

The *2d* and *38th Divisions,* forming the bulk of the main infantry force which had been assembled, had formerly belonged to the *16th Army*. In March 1942 the *2d Division,* which had been recruited in Sendai in the Miyagi Prefecture of Honshu, had moved from Manchuria to Java as a garrison force. In July 1942 the *4th Infantry* was detached for service in the Philippines, while the *16th* and *29th Regiments* remained in Java. In August 1942 the entire division was transferred to Rabaul and the Shortland Islands.[10]

The *38th Division* had been organized in September 1939 in Nagoya in the Aichi Prefecture of Honshu. A triangular division, it consisted of the *228th, 229th,* and *230th Infantry Regiments*. In 1941, it took part in the siege of Hong Kong, after which its regiments were detached. One detachment, the reinforced *228th Infantry* under Maj. Gen. Takeo Ito, assisted in the capture of Amboina and Timor. One battalion of the *229th Infantry* also helped to take Timor, while the remainder of the regiment campaigned in Sumatra. The *230th Infantry* had served in the Java campaign. The division then reassembled at Rabaul in late September 1942.[11] The *4th Heavy Field Artillery Regiment* (150-mm. howitzers) was dispatched from China in September 1942, arriving at Rabaul in early October.[12]

Although the *17th Army* was composed of veteran regiments, it had seldom operated as one unit. Likewise, the infantry divisions had seldom seen action as divisions. Individual regiments and battalions had campaigned actively, but had never fought against a foe who possessed superior numbers, equipment, or strong defensive positions.

[9] ATIS, SCAP: trans, *1st Demob Bureau,* OB of *17th Army.*

[10] XIV Corps, Enemy Opns, *2d Div Inf,* p. 1.

[11] *Ibid., 38th Div* Hist, p. 1.

[12] *Ibid., 17th Army* OB, p. 5.

The movement of Japanese forces from Rabaul and the northern Solomons to Guadalcanal, already begun in August, increased rapidly during September and October. By destroyer, by landing craft, by cargo ship and transport the enemy soldiers sailed down the inter-island channels to land on the beaches west of the Matanikau River under cover of darkness, while destroyers covered the landings by bombarding Lunga Point. The Allied forces which might have opposed them were too few in number to be risked in action north of Guadalcanal, and at night the darkness and clouds helped to hide the Japanese ships from Henderson Field aircraft.

By mid-October General Hyakutake had assembled a sizable portion of his army, except the main body of the *38th Division,* on Guadalcanal. The *2d Division* and two battalions of the *38th Division* were ready to fight beside the survivors of the *Ichiki* and *Kawaguchi Forces.* In addition there were present one regiment and three batteries of heavy field artillery, two battalions and one battery of field antiaircraft artillery, one battalion and one battery of mountain artillery, one mortar battalion, one tank company, and three rapid-fire gun battalions. Engineer, transport, and medical troops, and a few *Special Naval Landing Force* troops were also on the island. These forces, about 20,000 men, though below full strength, represented the largest concentration of Japanese troops on Guadalcanal up to that time.[18]

The U. S. Situation

The Americans on Guadalcanal thus faced a serious enemy threat. Yet as late as 5 October South Pacific Headquarters had not definitely decided to send additional reinforcements to the 1st Marine Division. Though deferred, the plans for occupying Ndeni in the Santa Cruz Islands had not been canceled. The purpose of holding Ndeni, 335 nautical miles east-southeast of Henderson Field and about 300 nautical miles north-northwest of Espiritu Santo, was threefold: to deny it to the Japanese; to protect the right flank of the Allied line of communications to Guadalcanal; and to provide an intermediate airfield for short range aircraft to stage through while en route from Espiritu Santo to Guadalcanal.[14] Admiral Nimitz had recommended early in September that Ndeni be occupied sometime

---

[18] The figure is derived from a graph in *17th Army* Opns, II. USAFISPA, Japanese Campaign in the Guadalcanal Area, pp. 16–17, estimates 22,000; XIV Corps, Enemy Opns, *17th Army* Hist, p. 2, estimates 25–28,000.

[14] Harmon, The Army in the South Pacific, Ref D.

later at a date to be determined by Admiral Ghormley.[15] Dispatches between Admirals King and Ghormley in late September discussed the possibility of using the 8th Marines of the 2d Marine Division for the Santa Cruz operation. On 29 September Admiral Ghormley announced that he was planning to occupy Ndeni with a part of that regiment, which was then in need of more training. On the same day he rejected Admiral Turner's suggestion that one battalion of the 2d Marines be withdrawn from the Guadalcanal–Tulagi area for Ndeni.[16] Admiral Turner then suggested transporting one Army infantry battalion, some Army field artillery, a detachment of the 5th (Marine) Defense Battalion, and naval construction forces to Ndeni in two transports and one cargo ship. These forces were to be followed by a second Army infantry battalion, one Army antiaircraft artillery regiment, and one Army coast artillery battery, transported in five ships.[17]

General Harmon, the Army commander in the South Pacific, regarded the entire Ndeni project as unsound and unnecessary. When Admiral Ghormley tentatively agreed to Admiral Turner's proposal, General Harmon, in a letter to Admiral Ghormley dated 6 October 1942, reviewed the reasons for the Ndeni operation in the light of the situation on Guadalcanal. (Appendix A) Ndeni, he wrote, would yield sparse results for two or three months, and was not vital to the security of the South Pacific. As long as Allied forces could operate from Espiritu Santo, the Japanese could not operate in strength from Ndeni. Since nearly all Allied aircraft could fly directly from Espiritu Santo to Guadalcanal, Ndeni was not needed as a staging base.

Occupation of Ndeni, General Harmon pointed out, would divert strength from the main effort. The situation on Guadalcanal was exceedingly grave, for if the Japanese were to use artillery against the airfield they could cause serious damage. If the beachhead on Guadalcanal fell, then the Ndeni operation would be a complete waste. The main effort must be in the Solomons. If the beachhead on Guadalcanal did not hold, the Japanese would have an outpost to protect the Bismarcks and to cover New Guinea, as well as a point of departure for advances to the south. "It is my personal conviction," he wrote, "that the Jap is capable of retaking Cactus–Ringbolt [Guadalcanal–Tulagi] and that he will do so in the near future unless it is materially strengthened." But if Guadalcanal was strengthened, the airfield improved for heavy bombers, and naval surface operations intensified, the enemy would not make the costly attempt to retake Lunga Point.

[15] CINCPAC to COMINCH, 2013 of 3 Sep 42. SOPAC War Diary.
[16] COMSOPAC to COMAMPHIBFORSOPAC, 0206 of 29 Sep 42. SOPAC War Diary.
[17] COMAMPHIBFORSOPAC to COMSOPAC, 0430 of 1 Oct 42. SOPAC War Diary.

General Harmon therefore recommended: (1) that the Ndeni operation be deferred until the southern Solomons were secure, (2) that Guadalcanal be reinforced by at least one more regimental combat team, (3) that naval surface operations in the Solomons be increased, and (4) that sufficient airdrome construction personnel and equipment be sent to Guadalcanal. What was needed at Henderson Field, he stated, was two all-weather runways, improved dispersal facilities and fueling systems, a standing fuel supply of at least 250,000 gallons, and intensive air operations from Guadalcanal against the northern Solomons.[18]

After Admiral Ghormley received this letter he conferred with Admiral Turner and General Harmon on the evening of 6 October.[19] After the conference Admiral Ghormley announced his intention to proceed with the plan to occupy Ndeni and build a landing strip. As it seemed likely that the Japanese would try to recapture the Lunga airfield, he accepted General Harmon's recommendations that Guadalcanal be reinforced by one Army regiment and that the island's airdrome facilities be improved.[20]

Reinforcements would prove valuable, for General Vandegrift could then safely enlarge the defense perimeter around Henderson Field to protect it from enemy fire. Although casualties from enemy action had not been prohibitive—by 18 September 848 wounded had been evacuated[21]—the 1st Marine Division was beginning to suffer heavily from tropical diseases. The enervating, humid heat, skin infections caused by fungi, and inadequate diet had weakened the troops. A mild form of gastro-enteritis had appeared in August. Although it caused only one death, this disorder made many temporarily unfit for duty and lowered their resistance to other diseases. During the third week in August malaria had first appeared among the troops. Suppressive atabrine treatment had been inaugurated on 10 September, but the disease had gained such a foothold that it was to become the most serious medical problem of the campaign. It sent 1,960 men of the division into the hospital during October.[22]

The force selected for the reinforcement of Guadalcanal was the 164th Infantry Regiment of the Americal Division, which was then in New Caledonia. The regiment was immediately alerted for movement, and began loading the

[18] Army in the South Pacific, Ref D.
[19] Rpt, COMAMPHIBFORSOPAC to COMSOPAC, Reinf Guadalcanal by 164th Inf, in COMAMPHIB-FORSOPAC War Diary, 17 Oct 42.
[20] Memo, COMGENSOPAC for WDCSA, 7 Oct 42. OPD 381 PTO Sec. III (10-7-42); Army in the South Pacific, p. 3.
[21] USMC, Guadalcanal Campaign, p. 52.
[22] 1st Mar Div Rpt, V, Med Annex X.

Zeilin and the *McCawley,* the flagship of the South Pacific Amphibious Force, at 0800, 8 October, at Noumea. The 147th Infantry (less two battalions), Col. W. B. Tuttle commanding, which was then at Tongatabu, was selected for Ndeni. The *McCawley* and *Zeilin,* loaded on 8 October, sailed from Noumea the next morning with the troops, weapons, and supplies of the 164th Infantry, 210 men of the 1st Marine Air Wing, 85 Marine casuals, and cargo for the 1st Marine Division.[23] Three destroyers and three mine layers escorted the transports, while four cruisers and five destroyers under Rear Adm. Norman Scott covered their left flank.[24]

The *McCawley* and the *Zeilin* sailed safely from Noumea to Guadalcanal, and arrived off Lunga Point to discharge troops and cargo at 0547, 13 October. Though interrupted twice during the day by Japanese bombing raids, the ships landed 2,852 men of the 164th Infantry, 210 of the 1st Marine Air Wing, and 85 casuals, plus forty-four ¼-ton trucks (jeeps), twenty ½-ton trucks, seventeen 1½-ton trucks, sixteen British Bren gun carriers, twelve 37-mm. guns,[25] five units of fire, seventy days' rations, sixty days' supplies, complete tentage, and 1,000 ships' tons of cargo for the 1st Marine Division and the naval units. The 164th Infantry supplies which were landed totaled over 3,200 ships' tons.[26] The *Mc-Cawley* and *Zeilin,* completely unloaded, embarked the 1st Raider Battalion and sailed out of Sealark Channel before nightfall to return to Noumea.

The first naval craft to be permanently based at Tulagi, aside from harbor patrol boats, were four boats of Motor Torpedo Boat Squadron 3, which the destroyers *Southard* and *Hovey* had towed in on 12 October. The *Jamestown,* arriving at Tulagi on 22 October, stayed there as a service ship for the torpedo boat squadron, which was brought to full strength on 25 October by the arrival of four more boats.

Before the Japanese counteroffensive in late October, therefore, the 1st Marine Division had been materially strengthened. With these reinforcements, troop strength on Guadalcanal and Tulagi totaled 27,727 of all services: 23,088 men were on Guadalcanal, the remainder on Tulagi.[27]

[23] Rpt, COMAMPHIBFORSOPAC to COMSOPAC, Reinf Guadalcanal by 164th Inf.

[24] COMSOPAC to CTF 63, CTG 17.8, 1402 of 8 Oct 42. SOPAC War Diary; see also ONI, USN, Combat Narratives: Solomon Islands Campaign, IV, Battle of Cape Esperance, 11 October 1942 (Washington, 1943), for a fuller account of naval operations.

[25] COMAMPHIBFORSOPAC War Diary, 13 Oct 42.

[26] Rpt, COMAMPHIBFORSOPAC to COMSOPAC, Reinf Guadalcanal by 164th Inf; 1st Mar Div Rpt, V, Personnel Annex W, states that 2,837 of the 164th were landed.

[27] 1st Mar Div Rpt, V, Personnel Annex W, 2.

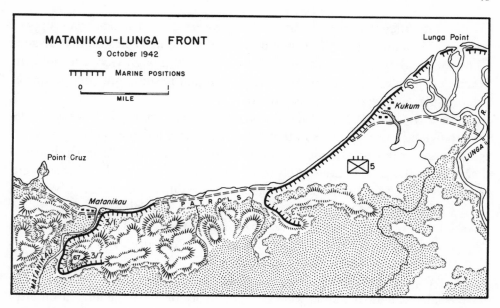

MAP NO. 8

When Admiral Ghormley ordered the 164th Infantry to Guadalcanal, General Vandegrift decided to establish permanent positions on the east bank of the Matanikau River, occupied in the offensive of 7–9 October. (*Map 8*) Domination of the mouth of the Matanikau was essential to the defense of Henderson Field. The rough terrain and thick jungles on the Matanikau effectively prevented heavy equipment from crossing the unbridged river at any point except over the sand bar at the mouth. Since tanks, trucks, and artillery pieces could cross the river over the bar, the Japanese, had they been able to dominate the position, could have put their tanks across it to deploy for attack against the perimeter defense. Had they been able to emplace artillery on the east bank, they might have damaged the Lunga positions and the airfield even more heavily than they did in October.

Two infantry battalions and elements of the 1st Special Weapons Battalion were assigned to hold the Matanikau. They established a horseshoe-shaped position, running from the mouth along the east bank to a point about 2,000 yards inland. They refused the right flank along the beach and the left flank east along the ridge line of Hill 67, a strong defensive position. The marines cleared fields of fire, rigged booby traps, and laid personnel and antitank mines in front. Several

37-mm. antitank guns, with 75-mm. tank destroyers concealed near by in support, covered the sand bar, which was illuminated at night by headlights salvaged from damaged amphibian tractors. There were not enough troops to hold the beach and jungle between the forward Matanikau position and the perimeter defense; patrols covered the gaps each day.

The arrival of the 164th Infantry on 13 October permitted General Vandegrift to make further changes in the Lunga perimeter defense. The 22,000-yard-long perimeter line was divided into five regimental sectors.[28] As it was believed that the enemy would be most likely to attack from the west, the heaviest strength was concentrated in the western sectors. In Sector One, 7,100 yards of beach on Lunga Point, the 3d Defense Battalion, with the 1st Special Weapons Battalion attached, had tactical command, and co-ordinated the related functions of beach defense and antiaircraft fire. The amphibian tractor, engineer, and pioneer troops continued to hold the beach lines at night.

The 164th Infantry, Col. Bryant E. Moore commanding, and elements of the 1st Special Weapons Battalion were assigned to Sector Two, the longest infantry sector. This 6,600-yard line extended along the beach from the 3d Defense Battalion's right flank to the Ilu River, inland along the Ilu about 4,000 yards, and west through the jungle to the left flank of the 7th Marines. The 7th Marines (less one battalion) occupied Sector Three, about 2,500 yards of jungle between the 164th Infantry's right and the Lunga River, including the south slopes of Bloody Ridge. The 1st Marines (less one battalion) held Sector Four, about 3,500 yards of jungle between the Lunga and the left flank of the 5th Marines, who held Sector Five, the western corner of the perimeter.

The 3d Battalions of both the 1st and 7th Marines held the Matanikau line, and were supported by parts of the 1st Special Weapons Battalion and one battalion of the 11th Marines. The 1st Air Wing was to continue to provide air cover, close ground support, and longer-range bombardment and reconnaissance. The 1st Tank Battalion, then held in division reserve, was to continue to reconnoiter areas suitable for tank action. Each sector was placed under the command of the respective regimental commander. Division headquarters again directed each sector commander to maintain one battalion in reserve to be available to the division if needed.[29] These were the defenses with which the Lunga garrison was to meet the Japanese counteroffensive in October.

[28] 1st Mar Div Opn Ord No. 12–42, 13 Oct 42, in 1st Mar Div Rpt, V, Annex G.
[29] 1st Mar Div Rpt, V, 15.

JAPANESE ATTACKS ON THE AIRFIELD *by daylight bombers and "Tokyo Express" warships created scenes such as this explosion of a large enemy bomb near a hanger. The raids were a constant danger on Guadalcanal during October, 1942.*

AMERICAN DEFENSE POSITIONS *along the east bank of the Matanikau were established by the Marines shortly after the 7–9 October offensive. Heavily sandbagged and roofed over with logs, this 37-mm. position dominated the important sand bar at the mouth of the river.*

Air and Naval Preparations

While the *17th Army* troops had been landing on Guadalcanal's north coast, Japanese fleet units had been preparing to execute their part of the plan. The strongest Japanese naval force assembled since the Battle of Midway left Truk to assemble at Rabaul for the offensive. Bombers from the Southwest Pacific had been attacking Rabaul regularly, but they had inflicted little damage and presented no great threat to the assembling fleet.[30] Japanese submarines had deployed southward in August and September to try to cut the American supply lines leading to Guadalcanal,[31] and warships escorted *17th Army* convoys to Guadalcanal and shelled the airfield almost every night. As long as American aircraft could operate from Henderson Field the Japanese could not safely bring troops and heavy equipment to Guadalcanal in transports and cargo ships. The nocturnal Tokyo Express could deliver troops in relative safety but could not carry heavy equipment or large amounts of supplies. The Tokyo Express warships and the daylight bombers therefore made a concerted effort in October to neutralize the Lunga airfield.

Admiral Ghormley's naval forces were still smaller than those that the Japanese could muster, but, determined to stop the nightly naval bombardments and the flow of enemy reinforcements to Guadalcanal, he ordered the four cruisers and five destroyers under Admiral Scott to sail from Espiritu Santo to Savo by way of Rennell to intercept any Japanese naval units moving on Guadalcanal. Scott's force was also to cover the left flank of the convoy carrying the 164th Infantry to Guadalcanal.

At 1345, 11 October, patrol planes from Guadalcanal discovered a Japanese force of four cruisers and one destroyer[32] sailing south through the Slot toward Guadalcanal. The Japanese had dispatched them to neutralize Henderson Field and thus provide greater safety for the landing of additional troops and supplies.[33] The force was sighted again at 1810 about 110 miles from Guadalcanal.

Informed of the approaching Japanese, Admiral Scott sailed from the vicinity of Rennell toward Cape Esperance to be in position to stop them about midnight. As Scott's force neared the channel between Cape Esperance and Savo about 2232,

---

[30] COMSOWESPAC to COMSOPAC, 0125 of 10 Oct 42. SOPAC War Diary; Miyazaki, Personal Account, p. 1.

[31] USSBS, *Interrogations,* II, 468.

[32] USSBS, *Campaigns of Pacific War,* App. 42, p. 117.

[33] USSBS, *Interrogations,* II, 456.

the screens of the radars on the cruisers *Boise* and *Helena* showed five Japanese ships 18,000 yards to the northwest. Search planes from the cruiser *San Francisco* also reported about 2300 that one Japanese transport and two destroyers were in Sealark Channel, but Scott decided to attack the larger force of cruisers and destroyers. The transport and the two destroyers escaped. The *Boise* and *Helena* reported the presence of the Japanese cruisers and destroyers by voice radio to Admiral Scott aboard the *San Francisco,* but he did not attack at once. The flagship's radar was older and less efficient than that aboard the other cruisers, and Scott was not sure of the location of the destroyers of his force. He feared that the destroyers reported by the *Boise* and *Helena* might be his own. The American destroyers, having recently changed their course, were then to starboard (north) of Scott's cruisers, which were sailing on a southwesterly course. The American destroyers thus lay between the opposing cruiser forces.

The *Helena* opened fire on the Japanese at 2346, 11 October; her fire was followed by that of the cruiser *Salt Lake City,* the *Boise,* and the destroyer *Farenholt.* The Japanese were caught completely by surprise. The American column executed the classic naval maneuver of crossing the enemy's T, by sailing in column at a right angle to, and ahead of, the approaching Japanese column. The entire American force was thus able to concentrate salvoes on each ship as it came forward. Each Japanese ship, on the other hand, masked the guns of the ships in its rear. Two Japanese vessels sank at once; the flagship *Aoba* was badly damaged, and the cruiser *Kinugasa* suffered light damage. The surviving Japanese ships retired northward after thirty-four minutes of battle. The destroyer *Marukamo* was joined by the destroyer *Natsugumo,* and they returned to Savo to rescue survivors in the water, but both were sunk the next morning by dive bombers and fighters from Henderson Field.

Scott's losses were light by comparison. The *Boise, Salt Lake City,* and *Farenholt* suffered damage. The destroyer *Duncan,* which had pulled close to fire torpedoes at the enemy, was caught between the American and Japanese forces, hit by fire from both, and sank on 12 October.[34]

The victory at Cape Esperance, whose flames lit the night skies west of the Lunga, cheered the men in the Lunga perimeter, but its effects were short-lived. Two days after Admiral Scott's force stopped the Tokyo Express, the Japanese hit the airfield with damaging blows. Guadalcanal's air situation had steadily improved during September, for more planes had been arriving. On 22 September

---

[34] USSBS, *Campaigns of Pacific War,* pp. 115–16.

Vandegrift reported to Ghormley that thirty F4F's, twenty-two SBD's, seven TBF's, and five P–400's were operational. The Naval Advanced Base at Kukum included an aviation unit and the 6th Construction Battalion. Air squadron personnel totaled 1,014—917 men of Marine Air Group 23, 33 of the 67th Fighter Squadron, and 64 from the naval carrier squadrons.[35] The P–400's had proved so valuable that Vandegrift requested more to support ground operations.[36]

By 10 October twelve P–39's of the 67th Fighter Squadron had reached Henderson Field but had not yet gone into action. B–17's were now occasionally being staged through Henderson Field.[37] But these operations were soon to end.

On 13 October there were ninety operational aircraft under General Geiger's command at Henderson Field—thirty-nine SBD's, forty-one F4F's, four P–400's, and six P–39's.[38] At 1200 twenty-two Japanese bombers, escorted by fighters, flew over to bomb Henderson Field from 30,000 feet. They were almost unchallenged. The P–400's could reach only 12,000 feet; the P–39's could climb to 27,000. The F4F, a relatively slow climber, could not reach the enemy in time to intercept him. Between 1330 and 1400 all the American planes were forced to land for more gasoline. While they were being refuelled, a second wave of about fifteen bombers attacked the field. The men of the 6th Construction Battalion worked throughout the afternoon in an effort to keep the field in operation. They had loaded their dump trucks with earth well in advance to speed the task of filling the bomb craters. But their efforts did not avail. The Japanese did not completely neutralize the runway on 13 October, but they inflicted such severe damage that General Geiger was forced to broadcast the information that Henderson Field could not be used by heavy bombers except in emergencies.[39]

After the last bomber had retired, the long-range 150-mm. howitzers which the Japanese had been landing opened fire on the airfield and Kukum Beach from positions near Kokumbona. They first made Kukum Beach untenable.[40] The 1st Marine Division had no sound-and-flash units to locate the enemy howitzers, or suitable counterbattery artillery with which to reply to "Pistol Pete," as the troops called the enemy artillery. The field artillery units were armed with 75-mm. pack and 105-mm. howitzers, and the 3d Defense Battalion had emplaced its 5-inch gun batteries on the beach. On 13 October and the days that followed,

---

[35] 1st Mar Div Rpt, V, Personnel Annex W, 2.
[36] CG 1st Mar Div to COMAIRSOPAC, 0323 of 2 Oct 42. SOPAC War Diary.
[37] Ltr, COMGENSOPAC to WDCSA, 10 Oct 42. OPD 381 PTO Sec. III (10-7-42).
[38] 1st Mar Div Rpt, V, Avn Annex Q, 3.
[39] COMAIRWING I to all CGs Island Bases, 0217 of 13 Oct 42. SOPAC War Diary.
[40] 1st Mar Div Rpt, V, Logistics Annex Z, 2.

the 5-inch guns and the 105-mm. howitzers attempted to silence Pistol Pete. But the trajectory of the 5-inch guns was too flat for effective counterbattery fire. Some of the 105's were moved up to the Matanikau River, but they were too light for effective counterbattery fire.[41] Aircraft also attempted to silence the Japanese artillery, but were no more successful than the artillery.

Shortly before midnight of 13 October, a Japanese naval force which included the battleships *Haruna* and *Kongo* sailed unchallenged into Sealark Channel. While a cruiser plane illuminated the target area by dropping flares, the task force bombarded the airfield for eighty minutes, the heaviest shelling of the campaign. The battleships fired 918 rounds of 360-mm. ammunition, of which 625 were armor-piercing and 293 high explosive. They covered the field systematically. Explosions and burning gasoline lit the night brightly. In the words of a Japanese report, "explosions were seen everywhere, and the entire airfield was a sea of flame."[42] Forty-one men were killed, and many aircraft damaged. When the shelling had ceased, enemy bombers raided the airfield intermittently until daylight. On 14 October only forty-two planes would fly—seven SBD's, twenty-nine F4F's, four P–400's and two P–39's.[43] An American report states:

When the men could finally come from their foxholes and survey the damage they knew what had hit them. They found jagged noses of shells measuring 14 inches in diameter—the shells from battleships' guns—and smaller pieces of shrapnel [sic]. Bits of clothing and equipment were hanging from telephone wires.

The field itself was in shambles. . . . The 67th [Fighter Squadron] was fortunate—only two P–39's were damaged, and, miraculously, not one of the old P–400's was hit.[44]

The next morning a few B–17's which had been operating temporarily from Henderson Field took off safely from the 2,000 feet of usable runway to return to Espiritu Santo.[45] The bombardments had rendered the airfield unusable as a base for heavy bombers. Moreover the presence of Japanese aircraft and warships over and in Sealark Channel prevented cargo ships from bringing in fuel, so that the perpetual shortage of aviation gasoline on Guadalcanal had now become more acute. As a result B–17's could no longer be staged through Henderson Field.

By the afternoon of 14 October Japanese bombing and shelling had knocked Henderson Field out of action. Pistol Pete prevented aircraft from using the run-

---

[41] 3d Def Bn, Action Rpt, pp. 2, 16; 1st Mar Div Rpt, V, Arty Annex R, 1; del Valle, "Marine Field Artillery on Guadalcanal," p. 730.

[42] ATIS, SCAP, Hist Rpts, Naval Opns: Rpt Bombardment Allied Beachhead on Guadalcanal (Doc No. 16567–B, 5 Apr 46).

[43] 1st Mar Div Rpt, V, Avn Annex Q, 3.

[44] 67th Fighter Sq Hist, Mar–Oct 42, p. 24.

[45] Guadalcanal and the Thirteenth Air Force, p. 35.

AFTERMATH OF THE 13–14 OCTOBER ATTACK ON THE LUNGA PERIMETER

when Japanese bombing and shell fire tore great holes in the Marsden-matted runway (above) and wrecked many buildings. The shambles below was a U.S. radio station.

way. Fortunately the construction battalion had laid out a rough grassy runway southeast of Henderson Field. When dry this runway, Fighter Strip No. 1, could be used by light planes and it served for a week as the main airfield.

Aviation gasoline supplies had fallen to a critically low level. On the afternoon of 14 October a Marine staff officer informed the 67th Fighter Squadron that there remained just enough gasoline to mount strikes against a Japanese force, including transports, which patrolling SBD's had found sailing toward Guadalcanal. The 67th was ordered to load its planes with 100-pound bombs and to join the SBD's in striking at the oncoming ships. The aircraft took off and located the enemy before nightfall. They sank one ship and set another on fire, but failed to halt the convoy, which continued on toward Guadalcanal under cover of darkness.[46]

When day broke on 15 October, five Japanese transports and their eleven escorting warships were plainly visible from Lunga Point as they lay ten miles away at Tassafaronga unloading troops, weapons, supplies, and ammunition.[47] The runway was pitted with shell and bomb craters. Only by searching wrecked planes and hunting in the jungles beside the runway for stray gasoline drums was enough fuel obtained for the planes to take off from the pitted runway to strike at the ships. The searches had yielded 400 drums, or about enough for two days' operations.[48] On the same day Army and Marine Corps transport planes (C-47's) began flying gasoline from Espiritu Santo to Guadalcanal, despite the fire from Pistol Pete. Each C-47 carried twelve drums. The seaplane tender *MacFarland* also ran in a load of gasoline from Espiritu Santo. Caught by Japanese planes in Sealark Channel on 16 October, she was seriously damaged but was salvaged by her crew in an inlet on Florida Island.[49]

American fighters and dive bombers attacked the Japanese ships on 15 October, and, despite antiaircraft fire and the opposition of Japanese planes, sank one transport and set two more afire by 1100. The remaining ships and their escorts, under attack from both Guadalcanal aircraft and B-17's and SBD's from Espiritu, then put out to sea. One ship fell victim to the B-17's near Savo.[50]

Although the air attacks seriously damaged the Japanese transports, they

---

[46] 67th Fighter Sq Hist, Mar–Oct 42, pp. 26–27; 1st Mar Div Rpt, V, 16.

[47] *Ibid.*; CG 1st Mar Div to COMSOPAC, 0005 of 16 Oct 42. SOPAC War Diary; USSBS, *Allied Campaign Against Rabaul*, p. 44. The latter source states there were six ships unloading.

[48] 1st Mar Div Rpt, V, Logistics Annex Z, 9, 10.

[49] See ONI, USN, Combat Narratives: Miscellaneous Actions in the South Pacific, 8 August 1942–22 January 1943 (Washington, 1943).

[50] 1st Mar Div Rpt, V, 17.

succeeded in landing all the troops—between 3,000 and 4,000 men[51]—and 80 percent of their cargo. The soldiers included part of the *230th Infantry* of the *38th Division* as well as seven companies of the *16th Infantry* of the *2d Division,* the last Japanese infantry units to land prior to the opening of the ground offensive against Lunga perimeter.

That the Japanese were preparing to attack in force was all too obvious. General Vandegrift radioed to South Pacific Headquarters to stress his need for the greatest possible amount of air and surface support.[52] Admiral Ghormley, fully aware of the situation, requested General MacArthur to have Southwest Pacific aircraft search the western approaches to the southern Solomons for enemy aircraft carriers.[53] When the B–17's were forced off Henderson Field, Rear Adm. Aubrey W. Fitch, commanding South Pacific land-based aircraft, suggested that Southwest Pacific aircraft relieve the pressure on Guadalcanal by intensifying their attacks on Rabaul, Kahili, and Buka.[54]

On 16 October, Admiral Ghormley warned Admiral Nimitz that the Japanese effort appeared to be "all out." South Pacific forces, he stated, were "totally inadequate," and needed air reinforcements.[55] Naval strength had been seriously weakened by combat losses. The *Enterprise, Saratoga,* and *North Carolina* were in Pearl Harbor undergoing repairs. Admiral Nimitz ordered that work on the *Enterprise* be rushed, and on 16 October the veteran carrier was able to leave Pearl Harbor for the South Pacific with the *South Dakota* and nine destroyers.[56] Meanwhile Fitch's force at Espiritu Santo was increased to eighty–five patrol planes and heavy bombers. Southwest Pacific aircraft continued to support Guadalcanal by patrolling, and by bombing Rabaul and the fields in the northern Solomons.

The Ground Offensive

Japanese Tactical Plans

General Hyakutake's units had meanwhile been confidently preparing to execute their part of the plan—an assault directed at the seizure of the airfield. The *17th Army* issued tactical orders to the *2d Division* on 15 October. The

---

[51] USSBS, *Allied Campaign Against Rabaul,* p. 44.

[52] CG 1st Mar Div to COMSOPAC, 1942 of 14 Oct 42. SOPAC War Diary.

[53] COMSOPAC to COMSOWESPAC, 0730 of 14 Oct 42. SOPAC War Diary.

[54] COMAIRSOPAC to COMSOPAC, 2225 of 14 Oct 42. SOPAC War Diary.

[55] COMSOPAC to CINCPAC, 0440 of 16 Oct 42. SOPAC War Diary.

[56] See ONI, USN, Combat Narratives: Solomon Islands Campaign, V, Battle of Santa Cruz Islands, 26 October 1942 (Washington, 1943) for a more complete account of naval activities.

main body of the *2d Division,* then in the vicinity of Kokumbona, was to deliver a surprise attack against the south flank of the American position on X Day, then tentatively set for 18 October. While the main body of the *2d Division,* commanded by Lt. Gen. Masao Maruyama, was pushing inland to reach its line of departure south of the airfield, a force west of the Matanikau under command of Maj. Gen. Tadashi Sumiyoshi, commander of *17th Army* artillery, was to cover its rear, divert the Americans, and shell the Lunga airfields and artillery positions. An amphibious attack by the *1st Battalion, 228th Infantry,* was still a part of the plan, but it was later discarded. American morale and strength, the Japanese believed, were declining.[57]

The coast force under Sumiyoshi's command consisted of five infantry battalions of about 2,900 men, one tank company, fifteen 150-mm. howitzers, three 100-mm. guns, and seven field artillery pieces.[58] The units in Sumiyoshi's force included the *4th Infantry* as well as elements of the *4th, 7th,* and *21st Heavy Field Artillery Regiments* and several mountain artillery and antiaircraft artillery units, and perhaps tanks and part of the *124th Infantry.*[59]

The enveloping force under Maruyama which was to attack Henderson Field from the south consisted of eight or nine infantry battalions totaling 5,600 men, plus artillery, engineer, and medical troops. This force was divided into two wings. The right wing, under Kawaguchi, consisted of one battalion of the *124th Infantry,* two battalions of the *230th Infantry,* parts of the *3d Light Trench Mortar Battalion* and the *6th* and *9th Independent Rapid Fire Gun Battalions,* the *20th Independent Mountain Artillery,* and engineers and medical troops. The left wing, under Maj. Gen. Yumio Nasu, was composed of the *29th Infantry,* the *3d Light Trench Mortar Battalion* (less detachments), a *Rapid Fire Gun Battalion,* a *Mountain Artillery Battalion,* and engineers. In reserve were the *16th Infantry* and additional engineer units.[60]

[57] Interrog of Maruyama, Miyazaki, Konuma, and Tajima, App. Gist of *17th Army* Ord of 15 Oct 42; XIV Corps Trans, 21 Feb 43, of *2d Div* plan of attack; *17th Army* Opns, I. Both the *17th Army* and the *2d Division* issued many orders during this period, most of which revised the original plan slightly. Subsequent accounts of this operation given by Japanese officers are often contradictory. The account given here is based on the best sources available, but may err in detail.

[58] ATIS, SCAP, reproduction of *1st Demob Bureau* map of *17th Army* Oct 42 opns.

[59] *17th Army* Opns, I, does not show the tanks or any part of the *124th Infantry* under Sumiyoshi's command, although they must have been, as the results of the interrogations of former *17th Army* officers clearly show. *17th Army* Opns, I, terms the 150-mm. artillery units as medium, but contemporary documents called them heavy field artillery units.

[60] Interrog of Hyakutake, Maruyama, Miyazaki, and Tamaki, *1st Demob Bureau* data; *Bureau's* map; *17th Army* Opns, I.

Kawaguchi's wing, after working inland from Kokumbona, was to attack northward under cover of darkness from east of the Lunga to capture the airfield and destroy the American forces east of the Lunga. Nasu's left wing was to attack northward from a point between Kawaguchi and the Lunga River.

Supremely confident that these soldiers could retake Lunga Point, General Hyakutake left the main body of the *38th Division* at Rabaul and in the northern Solomons in readiness for operations in New Guinea. Capture of the field would be heralded by the code signal BANZAI.[61] He directed his troops to continue "annihilating" the enemy until General Vandegrift, with staff officers, interpreters, one American flag and one white flag, had advanced along the coast toward the Matanikau to surrender.[62]

To get troops, guns, ammunition, and supplies into position for the attack, the engineers built and improved roads leading from the landing beaches eastward to Kokumbona. Engineers and combat troops had also begun work in September on an inland trail by which the *2d Division* could get into position south of Henderson Field. This trail, commonly known as the Maruyama Trail, ran southward from the *17th Army* assembly area at Kokumbona, then turned east to cross the Matanikau and Lunga Rivers south of Mount Austen, and followed the Lunga River downstream (north) to a point near the American perimeter.[63] It covered a distance of about fifteen miles. The Maruyama Trail led through the thickest of tropical jungles, where giant hardwood trees, vines, and undergrowth are so thick that a man cannot easily walk upright or see more than a few yards. The route south of Mount Austen led over an almost unbelievably tangled series of ridges and ravines. As sunlight never penetrates the treetops, the earth underfoot is wet and swampy. The Japanese had no heavy road-building equipment but hacked their way by hand, using axes, saws, and machetes. At best they could have cleared only a path through the undergrowth, making no attempt to cut down the trees. Mount Austen's bulk, plus the jungle, would hide the advancing column from Lunga Point, and the overhead growth provided security from aerial reconnaissance.

Since the Japanese had brought no horses and almost no motor transport on the Tokyo Express, supplies had to be brought forward by hand from as

---

[61] *17th Army* Opns, I.

[62] XIV Corps, Enemy Opns, *17th Army* Hist, pp. 5–6.

[63] Interrog of Hyakutake, Miyazaki, Maruyama, and Obara. The exact trace of the trail is not now known. The Japanese had no military maps of the area at the time, and the interrogated officers could not plot the trail on the map furnished by the author.

far away as Cape Esperance. About 800 tons of supplies had to be hand-carried forward.[64] The artillery pieces assigned to Maruyama were hauled forward by manpower. General Maruyama also ordered each soldier to carry, in addition to his regular equipment, one shell,[65] apparently from the supply dump near Kokumbona.

On 16 October, after assembling at Kokumbona, Maruyama's troops set out on their grueling march toward the line of departure east of the Lunga River, "crossing mountains and rivers with much difficulty due to the bad roads and heavy terrain."[66] Progress was slow. Since the trail was narrow, the men marched, single file, in a long straggling column. The van would begin the march early each morning, but the rear elements usually could not move until afternoon, with the result that the *2d Division* inched along like a worm. Torrential rains fell during most of the march. The troops, subsisting on half rations of raw rice,[67] burdened with shells and full combat equipment, had to use ropes to scale some of the cliffs. They also used ropes to pull the artillery pieces, machine guns, and mortars along the trail. As carrying and hauling the artillery pieces by manpower proved impossible, these guns were abandoned along the line of march.[68]

Hyakutake's confidence was somewhat justified, for he enjoyed significant advantages. The 150-mm. howitzers in Kokumbona outweighed the heaviest American howitzers on Guadalcanal. Almost nightly Japanese warships were sailing into Sealark Channel with impunity. The majority of the 20,000 Japanese troops were fresh, while many of General Vandegrift's 23,000 men were suffering from malaria and malnutrition. The Japanese could reasonably expect to surprise the Americans, since the wide envelopment by Maruyama's division through jungled, mountainous terrain was hidden from ground or aerial observation.

On the other hand, the Americans were entrenched in prepared positions, were expecting an attack, and could place artillery fire in front of any threatened sector of the perimeter. The Japanese had no near-by airfields, and American planes, though few in number, possessed local control of the air when they had enough gasoline, and thus limited the amount of heavy materiel which the

---

[64] XIV Corps, Enemy Opns, Hist and Inf of Misc Units, p. 8.

[65] XIV Corps Trans, 21 Feb 43.

[66] *Ibid.*, 14 Jul 43.

[67] 1st Mar Div Rpt, V, Int Annex N, 11.

[68] Interrog of Hayukutake, Miyazaki, and Maruyama.

enemy could safely land. The Japanese lacked sufficient transport. Hyakutake had committed his main force to a wide enveloping march through wild, track-less jungle, with all the difficulties of communication, co-ordination, and control attendant upon such a maneuver. Finally, it is doubtful that Hyakutake had enough reserves immediately available to exploit a break-through, even if the assault forces were able to penetrate the perimeter defense in strength.

Action on the Matanikau

The landing of the Japanese from transports on 15 October had alerted the 1st Marine Division to a major attack by infantry. A captured map indicated the possibility of a triple-pronged assault by three enemy divisions from the east, west, and south.[69] But there were no indications that fresh Japanese forces had landed east of the perimeter. Air and ground patrols had not found any organized bodies of Japanese troops along the upper Lunga but only dispirited groups of hungry stragglers, most of whom were promptly killed. On the other hand, the increasing artillery fire and growing Japanese troop strength west of the Matanikau convinced the Lunga defenders that the brunt of the attack would fall in the west.

Maruyama's forces, unknown to the Americans, were meanwhile slowly approaching the perimeter. Without good military maps, the Japanese commanders were meeting difficulty in finding their way. When advance elements of the enveloping force failed to cross the upper Lunga before 19 October, Maruyama postponed the assault date until 22 October.[70]

The first ground action occurred in the Matanikau area on 20 October when a Japanese combat patrol from Sumiyoshi's force approached the west bank of the river. The patrol, which included two tanks, withdrew after a 37-mm. gun in the sector of the 3d Battalion, 1st Marines, hit one tank. At sunset the next evening, after heavy Japanese artillery fire, nine Japanese tanks supported by infantry came out of the jungle on the west bank to attempt to drive east over the sand bar. But 37-mm. fire knocked out one tank and the force pulled back to the west.

No Japanese infantry appeared on 22 October, but Sumiyoshi's artillery kept firing. On 22 October Maruyama, still short of his line of departure, put off the attack date to 23 October; on that date he postponed it until 24 October.

The twenty-third of October was a quiet day until 1800, when Sumiyoshi's artillery began to fire its heaviest concentrations up to that time—an orthodox

[69] 1st Mar Div Rpt, V, 21.
[70] XIV Corps Trans, 14 Jul 43.

preparation on the Matanikau River line, the rear areas, and the coast road. When the fire ceased a column of nine 18-ton medium tanks[71] appeared out of the jungles to try to smash a passage across the sand bar to penetrate the defenses of the 3d Battalion, 1st Marines, while the *4th Infantry* assembled in the jungle west of the river. (*Map VII*) To halt the infantry, the 11th Marines immediately began firing a series of barrages to cover a 600- to 800-yard-wide area between the Matanikau River and Point Cruz,[72] while the 37-mm. guns on the Matanikau engaged the tanks. Not one enemy infantryman succeeded in crossing to the east bank of the river. The antitank guns meanwhile wrecked eight tanks as they rumbled across the sand bar. One tank eluded the 37-mm. fire and crossed the bar to break through the wire entanglements. A marine rose out of his foxhole and threw a grenade into the tank's tracks. A 75-mm. self-propelled tank destroyer then approached to fire at close range. The tank ran down the beach into the water, where it stalled, and was finished off by the tank destroyer. The assault having been stopped so abruptly, the surviving Japanese infantrymen withdrew to the west. About midnight a second Japanese attempt to cross the river farther upstream was easily halted.

The jungles west of the river were filled with Japanese corpses, and many enemy dead lay on the sand bar. The 1st Marines, with 25 killed and 14 wounded, estimated Japanese losses at 600.[73] Marine patrols later found three more wrecked tanks west of the river. They had apparently been destroyed by the 11th Marines' fire before they could reach the Matanikau.

Sumiyoshi had sent one tank company and one infantry regiment forward to attack a prepared position over an obvious approach route while the Americans were otherwise unengaged. The Maruyama force, still moving inland, had not reached its line of departure. In 1946, the responsible commanders gave different reasons for the lack of co-ordination and blamed each other. According to Hyakutake, this piecemeal attack had been a mistake. The coastal attack was to have been delivered at the same time as Maruyama's forces struck against the southern perimeter line. Maruyama, according to Hyakutake, was to have notified the *4th Infantry* when he had reached his line of departure on 23 October, and he so notified the *4th Infantry*. That regiment then proceeded with its attack.[74]

[71] Japanese medium tanks are comparable with U. S. light tanks. These were later identified as Model 2598 Ishikawajima Tankettes and Model 98 medium cruisers. 1st Mar Div Rpt, V, Int Annex N, 9.

[72] del Valle, "Marine Field Artillery on Guadalcanal," p. 730.

[73] 1st Mar Div Rpt, V, Annex O (1st Mar Regt Hist), 2.

[74] Interrog of Hyakutake, Miyazaki, and Maruyama.

WRECKAGE ON THE MATANIKAU SAND BAR, *torn jungle and a few enemy corpses were all that remained of the Japanese attempt to breach Marine defenses east of the river 23 October. Above are five of the nine tanks which reached the open. The next morning the Marines (below), still in possession of the river mouth, nicknamed the area "Hell's Corner."*

Maruyama disclaimed responsibility for the blunder, and blamed *17th Army Headquarters*. His forces, delayed in their difficult march, had not reached their line of departure on 23 October. The *17th Army*, he asserted, overestimated the rate of progress on the south flank and ordered the coast forces to attack on 23 October to guarantee success on the south flank.[75]

Sumiyoshi was vague. He claimed that throughout the counteroffensive he had been so weakened by malaria that he had found it difficult to make decisions. Despite an earlier statement that he did not know why the attack of 23 October had been ordered, he declared that he had attacked ahead of Maruyama to divert the Americans. Communication between the two forces, he claimed, had been very poor. Radio sets gave off too much light, and thus had been used only in the daylight hours. Telephone communication had been frequently disrupted. As a result the coast force had been one day behind in its knowledge of Maruyama's movements.[76]

The Main Attacks

On 24 October, the day after Sumiyoshi's abortive attack, the Lunga perimeter was fairly quiet during the morning hours. Japanese artillery fire continued intermittently during the entire day, and killed six and wounded twenty-five marines. In the afternoon two events indicated that the situation was becoming serious for the Americans. Men of the 3d Battalion, 7th Marines, holding the southeast line of the forward Matanikau position along Hill 67, observed a Japanese column passing eastward over Mount Austen's open foothills about 1,000 yards south of their lines. This column, whose exact composition is doubtful, is reported to have been commanded by Colonel Oka. It had apparently crossed the upper Matanikau in an effort to outflank the forward Matanikau position.[77] Battalions of the 11th Marines immediately put fire on the area, and aircraft rose to strafe and bomb it. But the column had disappeared among jungled ravines, and the effects of the bombing and shelling were probably slight.

As earlier patrols had reported that the upper reaches of the Lunga River were clear of the enemy, the 2d Battalion of the 7th Marines had been withdrawn from Sector Three east of the Lunga prior to Sumiyoshi's attack on 23

---

[75] *Ibid.*

[76] Interrog of Sumiyoshi; *17th Army* Opns, I, slurs over the blunder, but asserts that Hyakutake approved postponing the *2d Division's* attack from 23 to 24 October.

[77] According to *1st Demob Bureau's* map, this column, commanded by Colonel Oka, consisted of 1,200 troops of the *124th Infantry* (less *3d Battalion*) and the *3d Battalion, 4th Infantry*. This movement had apparently not been ordered in the original plan of campaign.

October The entire 2,800-yard front, from the Lunga River over Bloody Ridge to the right flank of the 164th Infantry, was turned over to the 1st Battalion of the 7th Marines, commanded by Colonel Puller. The 2d Battalion of the 7th was ordered to the Matanikau to relieve the 3d Battalion of the 1st Marines. But following the Sumiyoshi attack on 23 October and the observation of the enemy column the next afternoon, the 2d Battalion of the 7th Marines, on 24 October, moved hastily into position to cover the gap between the Matanikau line and the Lunga perimeter. It held over 4,000 yards of front along the line between the left flank of the 3d Battalion, 7th, and the 5th Marines in the Lunga perimeter.

The discovery of Oka's column east of the Matanikau was followed by evidence that another sector was in danger. A straggler from a 7th Marines patrol returned to the perimeter in the late afternoon to report that he had seen a Japanese officer studying Bloody Ridge through field glasses. At the same time a marine from the Scout-Sniper Detachment reported that he had seen the smoke of "many rice fires" rising from the jungle near the horseshoe bend of the Lunga River, about 1¾ miles south of the southern slopes of Bloody Ridge.[78] It was too late in the day for further defensive measures, and the 1st Battalion of the 7th Marines, spread thinly over its long front, awaited the attack. There were then available few troops which were not already in the front lines. The motorized division reserve, bivouacked north of Henderson Field, consisted of the 3d Battalion, 2d Marines. The only other uncommitted infantry troops in the perimeter were the reserve battalions in each regimental sector.

By 24 October Maruyama's infantry forces had finally crossed the Lunga River and moved into position in the dark jungles east of the Lunga and south of Bloody Ridge. On the left (west) the *29th Infantry,* with the *16th* in reserve, prepared to attack on a narrow front, while the *Kawaguchi Force,* now commanded by Col. Toshinari Shoji, prepared to attack farther east.[79] The heaviest weapons for supporting the infantry were machine guns. All the artillery pieces and mortars had been abandoned along the line of march. Maruyama hoped that bright moonlight would provide enough light for his assaulting troops to maintain their direction, but clouds and heavy rainfall made the night black.[80]

---

[78] 1st Mar Div Rpt, V, 23.

[79] *17th Army* Opns, I. According to Sumiyoshi and Tamaki (*2d Div* CofS), Kawaguchi, who had advocated attacking from the southeast, had fallen out with his superiors over the plan and had been relieved before the battle. Neither Hyakutake, Miyazaki, nor Maruyama mentioned this.

[80] XIV Corps Trans, 14 Jul 43.

The early evening hours of 24 October were quiet. A Marine listening post east of Bloody Ridge briefly opened fire about 2130. The front then lay quiet until half an hour after midnight, when Japanese infantrymen, firing rifles, throwing grenades, and shouting their battle cries, suddenly sprang out of the jungle to try to cross the fields of fire on the left center of the 1st Battalion of the 7th Marines east of Bloody Ridge. This was the *29th Infantry's* assault, the only attack delivered by the Japanese that night. Shoji's wing, attempting to reach the perimeter in the black, rainy night, had lost direction and got in behind the *29th Infantry*. The confused battalions were immediately ordered to the front but arrived too late to participate in the night's action.[81]

At the first attacks by the *29th Infantry,* troops on the right flank of the 2d Battalion of the 164th Infantry opened fire to assist the 1st Battalion, 7th Marines. Division headquarters correctly assessed the significance of the Japanese attack. It immediately ordered the 3d Battalion of the 164th Infantry, then in regimental reserve in the 164th's sector, to proceed to the front and reinforce the Marine battalion by detachments,[82] for the 1st Battalion, 7th, was holding a long front against heavy odds. The division reserve was not committed. The Army battalion, commanded by Lt. Col. Robert K. Hall, was then in bivouac south of Henderson Field about one mile from the front lines. The rain was still falling heavily, and visibility was poor. By 0200 the assembled battalion, about to engage the Japanese infantry for the first time, had marched out of its bivouac area. While the Marine battalion continued to hold back the Japanese, the soldiers entered the lines by detachments between 0230 and 0330, 25 October.[83] The night was so dark that the marines guided the soldiers into position practically by hand. The two battalions, as disposed that night, did not defend separate sectors, but were intermingled along the front.

In the first wild minutes of battle the *29th Infantry* overran some of the American positions. One platoon captured two mortar positions but was immediately destroyed by Puller's forces.[84] The 11th Marines began firing barrages in depth in front of the threatened sector and maintained the fire throughout the engagment.

The Japanese attacked with characteristic resolution all through the night, but every charge was beaten back by the concentrated fire of American small

---

[81] Interrog of Hyakutake, Miyazaki, and Maruyama.
[82] 1st Mar Div Rpt, V, 24; 164th Inf Unit Rpt, 25 Oct 42.
[83] 164th Inf, Rpt Action Against the Enemy, p. 1.
[84] XIV Corps Trans, 14 Jul 43.

arms, heavy weapons, and artillery. The rifle companies were supported by the Marine heavy weapons and artillery, by the weapons of M Company, by one heavy machine-gun section of H Company, and by 37-mm. antitank guns of the 164th Infantry. That night M Company fired 1,200 81-mm. mortar rounds.[85] The line threw back a series of separate infantry assaults. It neither broke nor retreated, although some Japanese, including Col. Masajiro Furumiya of the *29th Infantry,* penetrated to the jungle behind the American lines.[86] By 0700, 25 October, the Japanese attacks had temporarily ceased. Maruyama was withdrawing his battalions to regroup and prepare for another assault.

The front lines remained quiet throughout the daylight hours of Sunday, 25 October. Japanese artillery and aircraft were so active, however, that veterans of Guadalcanal have named the day "Dugout Sunday." Pistol Pete opened up at 0800, to fire for three hours at 10-minute intervals. Strong enemy naval forces, which were engaged the next day in the Battle of Santa Cruz, were known to be approaching, and the early hours of Dugout Sunday had found all Guadalcanal aircraft grounded. Fighter Strip No. 1, without matting or natural drainage, had been turned into a sticky bog by the heavy rains. Japanese planes bombed and strafed Lunga Point in seven separate attacks.[87]

Some Japanese pilots, resolutely dive bombing a group of planes parked in regular formation along the edge of Henderson Field, destroyed a considerable number. These conspicuous targets, however, were non-flying hulks from the "boneyard" left in the open to deceive the enemy. The operational aircraft had been dispersed and camouflaged.[88]

During the morning three Japanese destroyers, having entered Sealark Channel from the north, caught two World War I, flush-decked, American destroyer-transports off Kukum. Outgunned, the American vessels escaped to the east. The Japanese then opened fire on two of the harbor patrol boats from Tulagi, set them ablaze, and ventured within range of the 3d Defense Battalion's 5-inch batteries on the beach. The batteries hit the leading destroyer three times, and the enemy ships then pulled out of range. The sun had dried the airfield slightly, and three fighters succeeded in taking off to strafe the destroyers, which escaped to the north.

[85] Lt Col Samuel Baglien (former ExO, 164th Inf), "The Second Battle for Henderson Field," *Infantry Journal,* May 1944 (LIV, 5), 5.

[86] See extracts from Furumiya's diary in 1st Mar Div Rpt, V, Annex I.

[87] 3d Def Bn Air Action Rpt, 25 Oct 42.

[88] 1st Mar Div Rpt, V, 24–25.

STRENGTHENING THE LUNGA PERIMETER, *Marines prepared mortar positions and set up their tents in the open (above) while patrols covered the southern flanks. Below: a detachment rests in the shade before pushing into the jungle.*

As the runways became drier more American planes were able to take to the air to challenge the Japanese overhead, until by evening they had shot down twenty-two planes in addition to five destroyed by antiaircraft fire.

Along the perimeter the Americans reorganized their lines. The 1st Battalion of the 7th Marines and the 3d Battalion of the 164th Infantry, which had been intermingled during the night, divided the front between them. The Marine battalion, occupying the sector from the Lunga River to a point about 1,400 yards to the east, covered the south slopes of Bloody Ridge. Hall's battalion took over the sector in low-lying, rough jungle between the marines' left (east) flank and the right flank of the 2d Battalion of the 164th Infantry. The 3d Battalion, 164th, prepared to defend its sector with three companies in line —L on the left, K in the center, and I on the right. The 60-mm. mortars were emplaced behind the lines to put fire directly in front of the barbed wire; 81-mm. mortars, behind the light mortars, were to hit the edge of the jungle beyond the cleared fields of fire, which ranged in depth from 60 to 100 yards. Four 37-mm. guns covered the junction of the 2d and 3d Battalions of the 164th Infantry, where a narrow trail led north to the Lunga road net. The 164th Infantry regimental reserve, consisting of 175 men of the Service and Antitank Companies, bivouacked in the 3d Battalion's old positions.[89] To the west, in Sector Five, the 5th Marines swung their line southwestward to close with the left flank of the 2d Battalion, 7th Marines. During the day the soldiers and marines, besides strengthening their positions, improving fields of fire, and cleaning and siting their weapons, hunted down a number of Japanese who had penetrated the perimeter during the night.

Hidden in the jungles south of the perimeter, Maruyama was preparing to attack again. Acting on a false report that an American force was approaching his right (east) flank, he deployed Shoji's wing on the right to cover his supposedly threatened flank. The attack against the perimeter was to be delivered by two infantry regiments in line—the *16th* on the right and the *29th* on the left.[90]

After nightfall on Dugout Sunday, Maruyama's forces struck again in the same pattern as on the previous night. The *16th* and *29th Infantry Regiments* attacked along the entire front of the two American battalions which had defeated the *29th Infantry* the night before. Supported by machine-gun fire, groups of from 30 to 200 assaulted the perimeter in the darkness. They executed

---

[89] Baglien, "The Second Battle for Henderson Field," p. 25.
[90] Interrog of Hyakutake, Miyazaki, and Maruyama.

one strong attack against the point of contact of the 2d and 3d Battalions of the 164th Infantry where the trail led northward. Two enemy heavy weapons companies covered by riflemen repeatedly drove in toward the trail, but they were driven off or killed by canister from the 37-mm. guns and by fire from the weapons of the 3d and 2d Battalions of the 164th Infantry. About 250 Japanese were killed in their attempt to seize the trail.[91] One company of the division reserve went forward to support L Company of the 164th, and one platoon of G Company, 164th, moved south to support L Company and E Company, on L's left. The 164th regimental reserve was alerted in the event of a breakthrough, but again the lines held. The *16th* and *29th Regiments* pressed their attacks until daylight, but every one was beaten off. As day broke on 26 October, the shattered Japanese forces again withdrew into the cover of the jungle. Hyakutake's main effort had failed.

Elsewhere during the night of 25–26 October the enemy attacked with slightly greater immediate success. Oka's force, which had been observed crossing Mount Austen's foothills the day before, struck north at the attenuated line of the 2d Battalion of the 7th Marines east of Hill 67. The Japanese broke through at one point, but before they could consolidate their positions, Maj. Odell M. Conoley, a Marine staff officer, leading headquarters personnel, special weapons troops, bandsmen, and one platoon of the 1st Marines, hastily contrived a counterattack and drove the Japanese off the ridge.[92]

The unsuccessful night attacks of 25–26 October marked the end of the ground phase of the October counteroffensive. The Japanese forces began a general withdrawal about 29 October.[93] There were no more infantry assaults.[94] American patrols were able to advance 2,500 yards south of the perimeter without encountering any organized Japanese forces. They found only sniping riflemen, small patrols, and bands of stragglers. The defeated enemy forces were retreating eastward and westward to Koli Point and to Kokumbona.

The Americans had won the battle handily. Their employment of their weapons had been skillful and effective. The infantrymen, though outnumbered, had stayed at their posts in the face of determined enemy attacks. The soldiers of the 164th Infantry had done well in their first action. Colonel Hall's

[91] 164th Inf, Rpt Action Against Enemy, pp. 1–2.

[92] USMC, Guadalcanal Campaign, p. 80; 1st Mar Div Rpt, V, Annex O (1st Mar Regt Hist), 2.

[93] Interrog of Hyakutake, Miyazaki, and Maruyama.

[94] L Company, 164th Infantry, fired for 30 minutes at a suspected enemy force in the jungle in front of the lines on the night of 27–28 October. See Baglien, "The Second Battle for Henderson Field," p. 28.

battalion had, in the words of General Vandegrift, "arrived in time to prevent a serious penetration of the position and by reinforcing the 1st Battalion, 7th Marines throughout its sector, made possible the repulse of continued enemy attacks. The 1st Division is proud to have serving with it another unit which has stood the test of battle and demonstrated an overwhelming superiority over the enemy."[95]

The Japanese counteroffensive, which had been begun with such high hopes, was a costly failure. The 1st Marine Division conservatively reported that some 2,200 Japanese soldiers had been killed. A later Army report estimated that the combat strength of the *16th* and *29th Regiments* had been reduced by 3,568. By November, effective strength of the *4th Infantry* numbered only 403.[96] Over 1,500 decaying Japanese bodies lay in front of the 1st Battalion, 7th Marines, and the 3d Battalion, 164th Infantry.[97] The latter regiment buried 975 enemy bodies in front of K and L Companies alone.[98] Among the dead Japanese were General Nasu and Colonels Furumiya and Toshiro Hiroyasu (commanding the *29th* and *16th Regiments,* respectively.) By comparison American losses had been light. The 164th Infantry reported twenty-six killed, four missing, and fifty-two wounded throughout October.

The bombardment of the Lunga airfields had been by far the most successful phase of the Japanese counteroffensive. However, the Japanese might have achieved greater success had the air and naval bombardments been delivered simultaneously with the infantry attacks. The infantry assaults, usually delivered against battalions by forces in regimental strength, had failed completely. Japanese co-ordination, as exemplified by the operations of Sumiyoshi and Maruyama, had been poor, and the assaults had been delivered in piecemeal fashion. If Oka's attack had been intended to divert the Americans, it came forty-eight hours too late to be effective. The fact that Maruyama was able to move his troops inland around Mount Austen in secret was a signal demonstration of the skill and doggedness of the Japanese soldier, but the terrain over which the intended envelopment had been executed had prevented the movement of artillery. The heavy artillery in Kokumbona does not appear to have been used in direct support of Maruyama's attacks. Maruyama's night attacks

---

[95] 1st Mar Div Bull No. 64a–42, 29 Oct 42, attached to 164th Inf Opn Rpt, 24–31 Oct 42, in USAFISPA G–3 Periodic Rpts, in Org Rec Br, AGO, St. Louis, Mo.

[96] XIV Corps, Enemy Opns, *17th Army* Hist, pp. 2, 7.

[97] 1st Mar Div Rpt, V, Int Annex N, 10.

[98] 164th Inf Rpt Action Against Enemy, p. 2.

were thus made by infantrymen against prepared positions supported by artillery and heavy weapons. As the circular perimeter line possessed no open flanks, the Japanese delivered frontal assaults. The Lunga airfields, though seriously threatened, were saved by a combination of Japanese recklessness and American skill and bravery.

The Battle of the Santa Cruz Islands

The naval phase of the October counteroffensive was concluded almost anticlimactically by the Battle of the Santa Cruz Islands on 26 October. South Pacific naval forces had been preparing to meet the attack since early October. On 20 October the Joint Chiefs of Staff transferred the submarines of the Southwest Pacific naval forces to the South Pacific until the completion of the Guadalcanal campaign,[99] and Admiral Nimitz promised to send more submarines from the Pacific Fleet.[100] The Southwest Pacific submarines were ordered to attack warships, tankers, transports, and supply ships in the vicinity of Faisi, Rabaul, Buka, northern New Georgia, Kavieng, Bougainville Strait, Indispensable Strait, and Cape Cretin on the Huon Peninsula in New Guinea.[101] On 24 October the *Enterprise* and her escorts rendezvoused with the *Hornet* task group northeast of the New Hebrides. The task force thus assembled, commanded by Rear Adm. Thomas C. Kinkaid, included the two carrier groups—the *Enterprise, South Dakota,* one heavy cruiser, one light antiaircraft cruiser, and eight destroyers—and the *Hornet* with two heavy and two light antiaircraft cruisers and six destroyers.

A strong Japanese fleet, consisting of four carriers, four battleships, nine cruisers, twenty-eight destroyers, four oilers, and three cargo ships,[102] had meanwhile been maneuvering off the Santa Cruz Islands in support of the *17th Army.* At 0110 of 26 October, while the *17th Army* forces were attacking Lunga Point, a patrolling plane reported to Admiral Kinkaid's force that it had discovered part of the enemy fleet near the Santa Cruz Islands. Kinkaid moved in to attack. The ensuing engagement, a series of aircraft attacks against both planes and surface ships, was less decisive than the ground operations on Gua-

---

[99] COMINCH TO CINCPAC, COMSOPAC, COMSOWESPAC, 0736 of 20 Oct 42. SOPAC War Diary.

[100] CINCPAC to COMSOPAC, 2215 of 20 Oct 42. SOPAC War Diary.

[101] COMSOPAC to CTF 42, 0232 of 24 Oct 42. SOPAC War Diary. Cape Cretin, through an apparent garble, is given as Cuttin in the message.

[102] USSBS, *Campaigns of Pacific War,* App. 44, p. 123.

THE BATTLE OF THE SANTA CRUZ ISLANDS. *A Japanese aircraft (above) having just made an unsuccessful run on the aircraft carrier* Enterprise *can be seen diving into heavy fire from the U.S.S.* South Dakota. *Below, a near miss bomb hits the water off the starboard bow of the U.S.S.* Hornet, *one of several hits which sent the carrier to the bottom during the Santa Cruz action 26 October 1942.*

dalcanal. The outnumbered American force lost twenty planes to the enemy, and fifty-four more from other causes. The *Hornet* and the destroyer *Porter* were sunk, and the *Enterprise,* the *South Dakota,* and the light antiaircraft cruiser *San Juan* and the destroyer *Smith* suffered damage. All the enemy ships remained afloat, but three carriers and two destroyers were damaged. The Japanese lost 100 planes, a loss which may have limited the amount of air cover they were able to provide to their convoys in November.[103] At the conclusion of the day's action the Japanese fleet withdrew and returned to Truk,[104] not because it had been defeated but because the *17th Army* had failed.[105] The Santa Cruz engagement proved to be the last action of the Guadalcanal campaign in which the Japanese employed aircraft carriers in close support.

Thus far in the campaign, Allied air and naval forces had fought valiantly, but had not yet achieved the result which is a requisite to a successful landing on a hostile island—the destruction or effective interdiction of the enemy's sea and air potential to prevent him from reinforcing his troops on the island, and to prevent him from cutting the attacker's line of communication. This decisive result was soon to be gained.

[103] *Ibid.*; USSBS, *Interrogations,* II, 462.
[104] *Ibid.*, I, 79.
[105] Battle of Santa Cruz, p. 58.

CHAPTER VII

Decision at Sea

On 18 October Admiral Ghormley was relieved and the South Pacific Area received a new commander—Admiral William F. Halsey, Jr.[1] Admiral Halsey, then fifty-nine years of age, was one of the most experienced officers of the U. S. Navy. Graduated from the U. S. Naval Academy in 1904 as a passed midshipman, Halsey was commissioned as an ensign in 1906. During World War I he commanded destroyers in British waters. He attended the Navy and Army War Colleges in 1933 and 1934, and then successfully completed the naval aviator's course at Pensacola.

His career thereafter had been chiefly concerned with aircraft and aircraft carriers. Fom 1935 to 1937 he commanded the carrier *Saratoga*. After serving for a year as commanding officer at Pensacola, he took command, as a rear admiral, of Carrier Division 2 (*Yorktown* and *Enterprise*) in 1938. The next year he led Carrier Division 1 (*Saratoga* and *Lexington*), and in 1940, a vice admiral, he led the Aircraft Battle Force of the Pacific Fleet. Halsey had been on the high seas with a carrier task force at the time the Japanese struck Pearl Harbor on 7 December 1941, and his undamaged task force was fortunately available for a series of raids against the Gilbert, Marshall, Wake, and Marcus Islands in the spring of 1942. He also commanded the task force which took Lt. Col. James H. Doolittle's medium bombers to within striking distance of Tokyo in April 1942. Illness had kept him out of the Battle of Midway. But the aggressive admiral had now returned to active service, and his audacious spirit was to have a dynamic effect upon the South Pacific.

Although he was unable to visit Guadalcanal until 8 November, Admiral Halsey was well aware of the difficulties which faced him. He had at once to decide whether Guadalcanal should be evacuated or held. On 20 October, following the heavy bombardments and the landings of Hyakutake's troops, Gen-

---

[1] COMSOPAC to all CGs Island Bases SOPAC, CTFs 16 and 17, all CTFs SOPAC, COMSOPAC Admin, COMGENSOPAC, 1350 of 18 Oct 42. SOPAC War Diary. Halsey was a vice admiral on 18 October, but was promoted to admiral shortly afterward.

ADMIRAL WILLIAM F. HALSEY *photographed during a shipboard conference.*

eral Vandegrift had reported in person to Admiral Halsey aboard the flagship *Argonne* in Noumea Harbor. Present at the meeting were Lt. Gen. Thomas H. Holcomb, the Commandant of the Marine Corps, who was on a tour of inspection, General Harmon, Admiral Turner, and Maj. Gen. Alexander M. Patch, who commanded the American Division. Vandegrift informed Halsey that he could hold Guadalcanal if he was given stronger support. The Admiral knew that Guadalcanal must be held, and promised the support of all his available forces. One of his first orders sent Kinkaid's force to the Santa Cruz Islands where it engaged the Japanese on 26 October.[2]

The South Pacific Area was soon to receive additional means by which the aggressive spirit could be transformed into action. President Roosevelt and the Joint Chiefs of Staff recognized that the situation on Guadalcanal was extremely serious. On 21 October Admiral King, after an urgent request from the South Pacific for more forces, notified Admiral Nimitz that the Joint Chiefs of Staff had approved a much stronger air establishment for the South Pacific, to be based there by 1 January 1943.[3] On 24 October President Roosevelt, in a memorandum for the Joint Chiefs of Staff, expressed a desire that the Joint Chiefs send every possible weapon to Guadalcanal and North Africa even if additional shipments meant reducing commitments elsewhere.[4] In reply, Admiral King stated that a considerable force would be diverted, including one battleship, six cruisers, two destroyers, and twenty-four submarines, plus torpedo boats, seventy-five fighter aircraft, forty-one dive and fifteen torpedo bombers. Thirty transports had been allocated to the South Pacific for November, and twenty additional 7,000-ton ships would be diverted later.[5]

In his reply to the President, General Marshall stated that the situation in the South Pacific depended upon the outcome of the battle then in progress for Guadalcanal. The ground forces in the South Pacific were sufficient for security against the Japanese, he felt, and he pointed out that the effectiveness of ground troops depended upon the ability to transport them to and maintain them in the combat areas. Total Army air strength in the South Pacific then consisted of 46 heavy bombers, 27 medium bombers, and 133 fighters; 23 heavy bombers were being flown and 53 fighters shipped from Hawaii to meet the emergency.

[2] William F. Halsey and Julian Bryan, III, *Admiral Halsey's Story* (New York, 1947), p. 117.

[3] COMSOPAC to CINCPAC, 1230 of 17 Oct. 42; COMINCH to CINCPAC, 1523 of 21 Oct. 42. SOPAC War Diary.

[4] Disp, Pres Franklin D Roosevelt to JCS, 24 Oct 42. OPD 381 PTO Sec. III (10–24–42).

[5] Memo, COMINCH for Pres Franklin D Roosevelt, 26 Oct 42. OPD 381 PTO Sec. III (10–7–42). The 24 submarines included 12 submarines from the Southwest Pacific Area.

MacArthur had been directed to furnish bomber reinforcements and P–38 replacement parts to the South Pacific. General Marshall had taken the only additional measures which, besides the possible diversion of the 25th Division from MacArthur's area to the South Pacific, were possible—the temporary diversion of three heavy bombardment squadrons from Australia to New Caledonia, and the release of P–40's and P–39's from Hawaii and Christmas Island.[6]

Reinforcements

Air Power

In October the Japanese had come perilously close to destroying American air strength on Guadalcanal. Despite their utmost efforts the airfield remained in American hands and recovered from the heavy blows, although Guadalcanal's air strength, impaired by operational losses and Japanese bombardment, remained low during the rest of October. Only thirty-four aircraft were fit to fly on 16 October, but were reinforced on that date by the arrival of twenty F4F's and twelve SBD's.[7] By 26 October, after a series of bombing raids and shellings, there were but twenty-nine operational aircraft at Henderson Field—twelve F4F's, eleven SBD's, three P–400's, and three P–39's.[8]

By the end of November, with the lessening of Japanese attacks against the Lunga area and the increase of Allied strength in the South Pacific, the Guadalcanal air force had increased in size although as late as 10 November the shortage of fuel prevented heavy bombers from using Henderson Field. General MacArthur on 14 November promised to send eight P–38's to the South Pacific.

By the middle of November a total of 1,748 men in the aviation units were operating at the Lunga airfields—1,261 of Marine Air Group 14; 294 of Marine Air Group 142; 33 naval pilots; 144 of the 347th (Army) Fighter Group, and 16 of the 37th (Army) Fighter Squadron.[9] By 21 November the entire 5th (Army) Heavy Bombardment Group, which like the 11th had participated in the Battle of Midway, had reached the South Pacific to operate from Espiritu Santo.[10] P–38's had reached Guadalcanal to be based there permanently, and

---

[6] Memo, WDCSA for Pres Franklin D Roosevelt, 26 Oct 42. OPD 381 PTO Sec. III (10–7–42).

[7] 1st Mar Div Rpt, V, Avn Annex Q, 3.

[8] CG 1st Mar Div to COMSOPAC, 2311 of 25 Oct 42. SOPAC War Diary.

[9] 1st Mar Div Rpt, V, Personnel Annex W, 2.

[10] 5th Bomb Gp (H) Hist, p. 7. AF Hist Sec Archives.

B–17's were using the field regularly although the fuel shortage still limited operations.[11] On 24 November 94 aircraft on Guadalcanal were operational, including 15 P–39's, 1 P–40, 8 B–17's, 11 P–38's, 9 TBF's, 6 New Zealand Hudsons, 29 F4F's, and 15 SBD's, and by 30 November additional reinforcements had increased the total to 188 planes of all types.[12]

Aola Bay

By November plans for building an additional airfield on Guadalcanal were ready to be put into effect. Prior to Admiral Halsey's assumption of command, the 1st Battalion of the 147th Infantry, a separate regiment, had sailed from Tongatabu with the mission of occupying Ndeni. General Harmon had not changed his conviction that the occupation of Ndeni would be a needless waste of effort. He presented his opinions to Halsey, who, after conferring with his subordinates, accepted Harmon's views. On 20 October he directed the 147th Infantry to Guadalcanal.[13] The Ndeni operation was never carried out.

Halsey decided to send the 147th Infantry to Guadalcanal to cover the construction of an air strip at a point far enough east of the Lunga to give fighter planes at Lunga Point enough time to rise to the attack if the Japanese attacked the eastern field. Aola Bay, lying about thirty-three miles east-southeast of Lunga Point, was selected by Admiral Turner as the landing and airfield site. The Aola Bay landing force, as finally constituted, was under command of Col. W. B. Tuttle and included 1,700 men of the 1st Battalion, 147th Infantry; two companies of the 2d (Marine) Raider Battalion; a detachment of the 5th Defense Battalion; Provisional Battery K of the 246th Field Artillery Battalion of the American Division, which was equipped with British 25-pounders; and 500 naval construction troops.[14]

While the practicality of taking Ndeni was being considered, Halsey's headquarters had completed plans for moving strong reinforcements to Lunga Point. On 29 October Admiral Turner informed General Vandegrift that his requests for more ammunition, materiel, and support were being seriously considered. The admiral planned to have two ships land stores, ammunition, and two batteries of 155-mm. guns on 2 November. Provision for the movement of the 8th Marines of the 2d Marine Division to Guadalcanal was being given the

---

[11] COMAIRSOPAC to COMSOPAC, 0207 of 21 Nov. 42. SOPAC War Diary.

[12] CG 1st Mar Div to COMSOPAC, 2156 of 23 Nov 42; 2328 of 29 Nov 42. SOPAC War Diary.

[13] Army in the South Pacific, p. 3. See also *Admiral Halsey's Story*, p. 119, which contains some minor errors.

[14] COMAMPHIBFORSOPAC War Diary, 30 Oct 42. A shortage of artillery pieces had led to the equipping of K Battery with British field howitzers temporarily.

highest priority, and that regiment was to land on 3 November. Turner expressed the desire, somewhat gratuitously, that Vandegrift take the offensive after the arrival of the 8th Marines. Another Army regiment and the 1st (Marine) Aviation Engineer Battalion, Turner announced, were to arrive about 10 November, and the 2d Raider Battalion might possibly land at Beaufort Bay on the south coast about the same time.[15] A task force commanded by Rear Adm. Daniel J. Callaghan was constituted to transport the 8th Marines and the Aola Force to Guadalcanal.

The Aola Force, carried on three transports and two destroyer-transports, landed unopposed at Aola Bay on 4 November. It established a 600-yard-long beachhead a short distance east of the Aola River. When the beachhead had been established, command of Colonel Tuttle's landing force passed from Admiral Callaghan to General Vandegrift. The transports unloaded continuously until 0200, 6 November, and then withdrew. Admiral Halsey directed the raider companies to remain at Aola Bay, instead of leaving with the transports as originally planned.[16]

The troops established a perimeter defense, and on 29 November four transports landed the 3d Battalion of the 147th Infantry, additional elements of the 246th Field Artillery Battalion, part of the 9th (Marine) Defense Battalion, and more Seabees.

The Seabees had begun work on an airfield immediately after the landing on 4 November, but the entire area proved to be unsatisfactory. The earth was swampy, and tree stumps with deep, tangled roots slowed the process of clearing the ground. On 22 November Vandegrift, who from the first had opposed the selection of Aola Bay, recommended to Turner that the area be abandoned.[17] Admiral Fitch, the commander of South Pacific land-based aircraft, also disapproved of the Aola Bay site; Halsey assented to its abandonment, and the Aola Force, less the 2d Raider Battalion, was later removed to Volinavua at Koli Point to build an airfield on a grassy plain.[18] The movement to Koli Point was completed by 3 December,[19] and there the force was joined by the 18th Naval Construction Battalion and the rest of the 9th Defense Battalion.

---

[15] COMAMPHIBFORSOPAC to rad Guadalcanal, 1025 of 29 Oct 42. SOPAC War Diary.

[16] CTF 62 to *McKean, Manley*, 0435 of 29 Oct 42; CTF 62 to CTG 65.5, 0235 of 4 Nov. 42. SOPAC War Diary.

[17] CG 1st Mar Div to CTF 62, 0555 of 22 Nov. 42. SOPAC War Diary.

[18] 1st Mar Div Rpt, V, Int Annex N, 16.

[19] Rpt, G–3 USAFISPA to COMGENSOPAC, period 28 Nov–15 Dec 42, 16 Dec 42, in USAFISPA G–3 Worksheet File, 28 Nov–15 Dec 42, in Org Rec Br AGO.
G–3 Worksheet File, 28 Nov–15 Dec 42, in Org Rec Br AGO.

THE SITE FOR ANOTHER AIRFIELD *was first planned to be at Aola Bay (above), but terrain conditions forced a move westward to the flat plain at Koli Point, where the lower picture was taken some time after the battle. The completed air base there can be seen at left, with numerous U.S. Navy craft lying offshore.*

Reinforcement of the Lunga Garrison, 2–4 November

While the initial landings at Aola Bay were being effected on 4 November, more American troops and weapons were strengthening Lunga Point. The *Alchiba* and the *Fuller* landed stores and ammunition, together with one Army and one Marine Corps 155-mm. gun battery at Lunga Point on 2 November. These batteries—F Battery of the 244th Coast Artillery Battalion, and another battery of the 5th Defense Battalion—brought in the heaviest American artillery which had been sent to Guadalcanal up to that time, the first suitable for effective counterbattery fire.[20]

After the landing of a Japanese force east of Koli Point on the night of 2–3 November, Vandegrift asked Halsey to hurry the arrival of the 8th Marines. Callaghan's task force, which had been delayed by the proximity of enemy forces, sailed into Sealark Channel on 4 November to debark the reinforced 8th Marines, including the 75-mm. pack howitzers of the 1st Battalion, 10th Marines, and the Aola Force as shown above. The regular noon Japanese air attack forced the transports to disperse, and the Lunga Point section of Callaghan's task force withdrew to the southeast for the night. It returned the next morning to complete the unloading before sailing for Noumea.[21]

The Naval Battle of Guadalcanal

Japanese Plans

Following their defeat in the night battles of 23–26 October, the Japanese began preparing for a second major counteroffensive. Staff representatives from the *Combined Fleet* hurried to Guadalcanal by destroyer to help complete the plans. On 26 October General Hyakutake decided to send the *38th Division,* commanded by Lt. Gen. Tadayoshi Sano, and its heavy equipment from Rabaul to Guadalcanal on transports instead of aboard the Tokyo Express. Admiral Isoroku Yamamoto, commanding the *Combined Fleet,* approved of these plans.[22]

The Japanese organized four naval task forces for the November operation. Two bombardment forces were to neutralize Henderson Field; a third was to

---

[20] The elements of the 5th Defense Battalion which had been landed from time to time were designated as the 14th Defense Batallion on 15 January 1943. Turner's reports refer to the battery which landed on 2 November 1942 as A Battery, 14th Defense Battalion.

[21] CTF 65 to COMSOPAC, 0330 of 4 Nov 42; CTF 65 to CTF's 63, 64, 62, 16, COMSOPAC, 1747 of 5 Nov. 42. SOPAC War Diary.

[22] USSBS, *Interrogations,* II, 468–469.

STRATEGIC AIR ACTIONS *during October were carried out against Japanese positions on Gizo Island (above), where one of a flight of B–17's is seen leaving the target after the bombing, and against enemy shipping (below) lying off Buin, Bougainville Island. A salvo of bombs has bracketed a small Japanese freighter as another ship (right) maneuvers to escape the attack. Light areas near top right evidence an earlier, less successful strike. White spots are enemy machine gun tracers.*

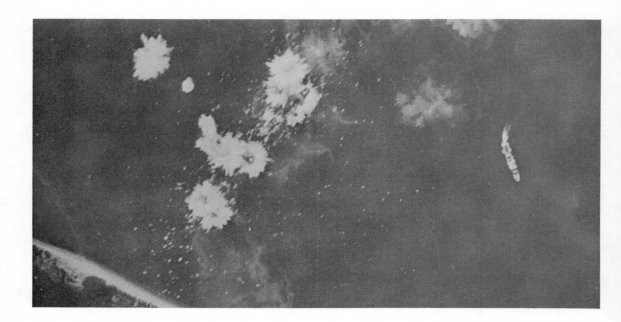

transport the *38th Division* and heavy equipment from Rabaul to Guadalcanal, while a fourth force from the *Combined Fleet* gave general support.

The *17th Army* had first decided to land the *38th Division* at Koli Point, whereupon the entire *17th Army* was to attack the Lunga area from the east and west. But *Imperial General Headquarters,* disapproving of the dispersion of forces, directed that the *38th Division* deliver its attack from the Matanikau area, where it could receive the maximum support from *17th Army* artillery. The *17th Army,* however, did land a small force at Koli Point in early November to deliver supplies to some of Shoji's troops who had retreated there after the October disaster. Orders directing these forces to build an airfield on the flat plain south of Koli Point were also issued.[23] A part of the *230th Infantry* of the *38th Division* had already landed on Guadalcanal in October and on 2–3 November, and the Tokyo Express landed elements of the *228th Infantry* along the beaches from Kokumbona to Cape Esperance between 28 October and 8 November.[24]

Japanese naval units assembled in the harbors between Buin and Rabaul during the first days of November. By 12 November Allied reconnaissance planes reported that two aircraft carriers, four battleships, five heavy cruisers, and thirty destroyers, besides transports and cargo ships, had been assembled. There were sixty vessels in the Buin–Faisi–Tonolei anchorages alone.[25] But there was to be one vital difference between the October and November counteroffensives. The Japanese, who had previously been using their aircraft carriers with some success, did not commit them to action in November.

American Plans

American naval forces, though still inferior in number to those of the Japanese, were again to prove their effectiveness. Twenty-four submarines had been patrolling the Tokyo Express routes, and had destroyed or damaged a number of Japanese ships. Besides the submarines, the naval forces under Halsey's command included the aircraft carrier *Enterprise,* two battleships, three heavy cruisers, one light cruiser, one light antiaircraft cruiser, twenty-two destroyers, and seven transports and cargo ships, organized into two task forces. Because the lack of gasoline at Henderson Field was limiting the operations of

---

[23] *17th Army* Opns, I. USSBS, *Interrogations,* II, 470, states that the plan to land the *38th Division* at Koli Point was cancelled when the Americans gained control of the point in the first days of November.

[24] Amer Div Int Rpt, Tab A.

[25] For a more complete account of naval action see ONI, USN, Combat Narratives: Solomon Islands Campaign, VI, The Battle of Guadalcanal, 11–15 November 1942 (Washington, 1944).

B–17's, Admiral Halsey requested the Southwest Pacific Air Forces to bomb shipping around Buin, Tonolei, and Faisi between 11 and 14 November, as well as to reconnoiter the approaches to Guadalcanal.[26] Beginning on 10 November, South Pacific land-based aircraft, including those at Henderson Field, were to cover the northern and western approaches and to protect the Lunga area. The plans for the land-based aircraft of the South Pacific did not assign to them new missions, but restated their continuing missions in specific terms.

On Guadalcanal the situation was more hopeful than it had been in October. Pistol Pete could no longer shell the airfields with impunity. The arrival on 2 November of the 155-mm. guns of F Battery, 244th Coast Artillery Battalion, and the battery of the 5th Defense Battalion had provided effective counter-battery artillery.[27] Less than four hours after it had begun debarkation at Lunga Point, F Battery of the 244th was in action against Pistol Pete.[28] Troop strength had increased with the addition of the 8th Marines on 4 November, and still more reinforcements were expected soon.

The addition of more New Zealand troops and of the first elements of the 43d (U. S.) Division to the South Pacific force had made it possible to relieve the Americal Division of its mission of defending New Caledonia. The complete division was to be committed to Guadalcanal, where one of its regiments, the 164th Infantry, was already engaged.

Reinforcement by the 182d Infantry

The next Americal Division unit to be shipped to Guadalcanal was the 182d Regimental Combat Team, less the 3d Battalion which was still in the New Hebrides. The movement of this unit to Guadalcanal by Turner's task force was to be a larger operation than the dispatch of the Aola Bay Force and the 8th Marines.

One of the two South Pacific naval task forces, under command of Admiral Turner, was charged with the dual responsibility of defending Guadalcanal and of transporting troops and supplies to the island. Admiral Kinkaid's carrier task force at Noumea was available to support Turner's force. These forces, though limited in numbers, had to stop the Japanese unless the U. S. Navy was to be driven out of the Solomons.[29]

---

[26] *Ibid.*, p. 4.

[27] 1st Mar Div Rpt, V, Arty Annex R; 1st Mar Div Rpt, V, 21, implies that 155-mm. guns had arrived by 23 October, which is not correct.

[28] 1st Mar Div Rpt, V, Arty Annex R.

[29] Battle of Guadalcanal, p. 4.

Turner's task force was organized into three groups. Three transports, one cruiser, and four destroyers under Admiral Scott constituted one group. Scott's ships were to carry marines, ammunition, and rations from Espiritu Santo to Guadalcanal. Admiral Callaghan commanded the second group of five cruisers and ten destroyers which were to operate out of Espiritu Santo and cover the movement of the third group from Noumea to Guadalcanal. Admiral Turner assumed direct command of the third group, consisting of four transports which were to transfer the 182d Regimental Combat Team (less the 3d Battalion), Marine replacements, naval personnel, and ammunition from Noumea to Guadalcanal.

Admiral Kinkaid's force at Noumea, consisting of the carrier *Enterprise,* two battleships, two cruisers, and eight destroyers, was to support Turner's force. In addition all aircraft in the South Pacific were to cover the movement of Turner's ships and to strike at any approaching Japanese vessels. Turner expected that a Japanese invasion fleet would soon be approaching Guadalcanal. He planned to land the 182d Infantry at Lunga Point and move the transports out of danger before the enemy could arrive. The ships under his direct command sailed from Noumea at 1500, 8 November. The next day Scott's group left Espiritu Santo; Callaghan's warships followed on 10 November. Callaghan's and Turner's groups rendezvoused off San Cristobal the next morning.

Scott's group arrived off Guadalcanal at 0530 on 11 November. The *Zeilin, Libra,* and *Betelgeuse* began unloading but were interrupted twice during the day by enemy bombers which damaged all three ships. At 1800 the group withdrew to Indispensable Strait. Damage to the *Zeilin* was found to be serious, and with one destroyer as escort she returned to Espiritu Santo. Scott's warships, at 2200, joined Callaghan's group, which had been preceding the advance of Turner's transports. The *Libra* and *Betelgeuse* later joined Turner's group. The warships, under Callaghan's command, then swept the waters around Savo Island, and remained in Sealark Channel for the rest of the night of 11–12 November.

The transports anchored off Lunga Point at 0530, 12 November. Covered by the warships, they began discharging troops and cargo. A Japanese shore battery in the vicinity of Kokumbona opened fire on the *Betelgeuse* and *Libra* at 0718 but missed; it ceased firing when one cruiser, two destroyers, and counter-battery artillery on shore replied. About twenty-five enemy torpedo bombers attacked in the afternoon, and forced the ships to cease unloading and get under way. The cruiser *San Francisco,* which was Callaghan's flagship, and the

LANDING OF THE 182D REGIMENTAL COMBAT TEAM 12 NOVEMBER *was carried out smoothly during the morning as troops hauled their equipment ashore (above). During the afternoon enemy air attacks temporarily interrupted operations. The cruiser* San Francisco *was hit (under smoke in distance, lower photo), but the transport shown and others were undamaged.*

destroyer *Buchanan* were damaged but the transports were not hit, and all but one bomber were shot down. The transports re-anchored at 1525, having been forced to halt unloading for two hours.

At 1035 on the same morning American planes patrolling north of Malaita sighted a Japanese force, including two battleships, sailing south toward Guadalcanal. A convoy of transports carrying the *38th Division* troops, replacements, and naval troops followed farther to the north. By late afternoon Admiral Turner had concluded that 90 percent of the supplies carried by the ships under his direct command could be unloaded that day, but that several more days would be required to unload the *Betelgeuse* and *Libra*. To avoid destruction by the enemy battleships, he decided to withdraw all the cargo ships and transports. The warships were to remain to engage the approaching enemy.

The cargo ships and transports, escorted by destroyers, withdrew at 1815, 12 November.[30] Callaghan's and Scott's warships preceded them to Indispensable Strait, then reversed their course and returned to protect Guadalcanal. The *McCawley* and the *President Jackson* had been completely unloaded; 80 percent of the *President Adams'* cargo had been landed, 50 percent of the *Crescent City's*, 40 percent of the *Betelgeuse's*, and 20 percent of the *Libra's*. All the troops, numbering about 6,000 men, had debarked.[31] The forces which had been landed by Scott's group consisted of the 1st (Marine) Aviation Engineer Battalion, ground crews of the 1st Marine Air Wing, and marine replacements. Turner's ships had landed 1,300 marine replacements, 372 naval personnel, L Battery, 11th Marines (155-mm. howitzers), some 164th Infantry casuals, and the 182nd Infantry Regimental Combat Team. The combat team was made up of the 1st and 2d Battalions, 182d Infantry; the 245th Field Artillery Battalion (105-mm. howitzers), plus engineer, medical, quartermaster, and ordnance personnel—3,358 men.[32]

Cruisers Versus Battleships, 12–13 November

The Japanese force which had been sighted consisted of the battleships *Hiei* and *Kirishima,* one light cruiser, and fifteen destroyers.[33] This force had orders to enter Sealark Channel and neutralize the airfields on Guadalcanal by

[30] COMAMPHIBFORSOPAC, Rpt Opns TF 67 and TF 62.4, Reinf Guadalcanal 8–15 Nov 42 and Summary Third Battle Savo, Ser 00469, 3 Dec 42. This report is filed in the Office of Naval Records and Library.

[31] CTF 67 to COMSOPAC, 0140 of 13 Nov 42. SOPAC War Diary.

[32] TF 6814 and Amer Div, Hist Data, Inc 8, pp. 1–2. The bulk of Americal Division records when consulted were in HRS DRB AGO.

[33] USSBS, *Campaigns of Pacific War, App.* 46, p. 127; *Interrogations,* II, 469, lists 2 battleships and 13 destroyers.

bombardment. Once enough aircraft and supplies had been destroyed, and the airfield pitted, Japanese troops could be transported to Guadalcanal in safety.[34] The fact that the battleships carried high explosive ammunition for bombarding the airfield instead of armor-piercing shells reduced the margin of superiority of their 14-inch guns in the ensuing battle, for the battleships' shells did not always penetrate the cruisers' armor plate. This was fortunate, for to withstand the enemy force Admiral Callaghan had only two 8-inch gun cruisers, one 6-inch gun cruiser, two light antiaircraft cruisers, and eight destroyers.

Callaghan led his light forces toward Savo after dark to engage the battleships. At 0124 on 13 November *Helena's* radar located Japanese ships 27,000 yards away, between Savo and Cape Esperance. A warning was immediately transmitted to the flagship *San Francisco,* but the cruiser's search radar was inadequate. As a result Admiral Callaghan, like Admiral Scott at Cape Esperance one month earlier, did not know the exact location of either his own or the enemy ships.

The American destroyers closed to short range to fire torpedoes. The vans of the opposing forces intermingled, and the American column penetrated the Japanese formation. The Japanese illuminated the American cruisers, then opened fire at 0148. The outnumbered Americans replied, firing to port and starboard. The American column became disorganized as destroyers maneuvered to fire torpedoes, and both cruisers and destroyers swerved off their courses to avoid collisions. The engagement became a melee in which the desperate American ships engaged the enemy individually. In the confusion both sides occasionally fired on their own vessels. As far as they could, the American ships concentrated their fire on the battleship *Hiei.*

Admiral Scott, aboard the *Atlanta,* was killed by fire from a cruiser. Later a salvo from the *Hiei* struck the *San Francisco* and killed, among others, Admiral Callaghan, and mortally wounded her commanding officer, Capt. Cassin Young. The *San Francisco* continued to engage the *Hiei* as long as her main battery would bear. The *Hiei* fired several salvos, then ceased. The *San Francisco,* having received fifteen major hits from heavy guns, withdrew. The *Atlanta* caught fire, and several American destroyers blew up, but about 0300 the Japanese abandoned their attempt to break through the tenacious American force, and retired northward. Two Japanese destroyers had been sunk, and four were damaged.

[34] *Ibid.,* 470.

The gallantry of the light American forces in this desperate action had saved Henderson Field from a battleship bombardment, but the cost was heavy. Of the thirteen American ships, twelve had been either sunk or damaged. The antiaircraft cruisers *Atlanta* and *Juneau,* and the destroyers *Barton, Cushing, Laffey,* and *Monssen* sank in the channel. The heavy cruisers *San Francisco* and *Portland* and the destroyers *Aaron Ward, O'Bannon,* and *Sterrett,* which all had suffered serious damage,[35] retired with the two other surviving ships toward Espiritu Santo during the morning of 13 November.

The battleship *Kirishima* had escaped, but at daylight on 13 November American air forces located the battleship *Hiei* near Savo. Crippled and on fire, she was cruising slowly in circles. The *Hiei,* the principal American target, had been struck eighty-five times in the battle, and was out of control. Planes from Henderson Field attacked her steadily all day, and on the night of 14 November she was scuttled by her crew.

Bombing the Japanese Transports, 14 November

Meanwhile Admiral Kinkaid had led his carrier task force from Noumea toward Guadalcanal. At daylight on 14 November search planes from the *Enterprise* sighted a group of Japanese cruisers near New Georgia. These ships belonged to a second Japanese force which, consisting of three heavy and two light cruisers and four destroyers from the *Outer South Seas Supporting Unit* of the *8th Fleet,* had entered Sealark Channel early on the morning of 14 November. When American motor torpedo boats sortied from Tulagi, the Japanese retired without having inflicted much damage to Henderson Field. Later, when the search planes found this force, aircraft from Guadalcanal and from the carrier attacked it and sank one heavy cruiser and damaged one heavy and one light cruiser and a destroyer.

After these attacks the planes from the *Enterprise* flew to Guadalcanal to operate temporarily from Henderson Field. This permitted the *Enterprise,* the only remaining carrier in the South Pacific, to withdraw to the south out of range of hostile aircraft.[36]

Disregarding the fact that the American airfields on Guadalcanal were still in operation, the Japanese determined to bring the troop convoy to Guadalcanal. On 14 November it left the waters near northern New Georgia, where it had been standing by since 13 November, to sail southward down the Slot. Con-

[35] USSBS, *Campaigns of Pacific War,* App. 46, p. 127. *Campaigns of Pacific War* erroneously states that the *Helena* sank on her withdrawal to the south.

[36] *Ibid.,* p. 126.

sisting of eleven transports and cargo ships and twelve escorting destroyers,[37] this convoy was the largest the Japanese had yet employed in the Solomons. The ships carried about 10,000 troops of the *229th* and *230th Regiments* of the *38th Division,* artillerymen, engineers, replacement units, a naval force of between 1,000 and 3,500 men, weapons, and 10,000 tons of supplies.[38] The Japanese had not committed aircraft carriers to close support of operations, and the convoy's air cover was weak.

A Southwest Pacific patrol plane, lending support to the South Pacific, discovered the convoy at 0830, 14 November, about 150 miles from Guadalcanal. Guadalcanal aircraft and the *Enterprise* air group made ready to attack with torpedoes, bombs, and machine guns. Ground crews servicing the planes rolled bombs across the muddy runways, lifted them into the bays, and fuelled the planes entirely by hand. The planes took off and struck the transports continuously throughout the day with outstanding success. They hit nine transports. Seven sank at sea, and the four remaining afloat sailed on toward Guadalcanal under cover of darkness.

Night Battleship Action, 14–15 November

Strengthened and reorganized, the heavy bombardment force which had fought the American cruisers on the night of 12–13 November turned back toward Guadalcanal to cover the approach of the transports. It consisted of the battleship *Kirishima,* two heavy and two light cruisers, and nine destroyers. To combat this force and to attack any surviving transports, Admiral Halsey sent the battleships *Washington* and *South Dakota* and four destroyers from Kinkaid's force to the north. Under the command of Rear Adm. Willis A. Lee, Jr., the two battleships and four destroyers passed the southeastern tip of Guadalcanal about noon on 14 November. Shortly before midnight, they entered the channel. As the *Washington* neared Savo in the darkness at 0001, 15 November, her radar located an enemy ship. The *Washington* opened fire at 0016, at a range of 18,500 yards, and the *South Dakota* and the destroyers entered the action immediately thereafter. The Japanese fought back vigorously, but by 0142 the long-range gun fight in the narrow waters had ended. It was one of the few engagements between battleships of the entire war. The Japanese retired northward, having again failed to hit the airfields. The badly damaged *Kirishima* was

---

[37] USSBS, *Interrogations,* II, 469.

[38] *Ibid.; Campaigns of Pacific War,* p. 125, and App. 46, p. 128; *Allied Campaign Against Rabaul,* p. 108; *17th Army Opns I; 3d Battalion, 229th Infantry,* landed in New Guinea at this time. ATIS, SWPA, Enemy Pub No. 29: Orders of Giruwa Def Area, p. 10.

JAPANESE TRANSPORTS BEACHED AND BURNING 14 NOVEMBER. *Three of the four enemy transports which succeeded in reaching Guadalcanal. The* Kinugawa Maru, *seen still burning just east of the Bonegi River mouth at Tassafaronga Point. In the distance near Bunina Point is a third hulk, shown in the lower photo with wrecked Japanese landing barge in the foreground.*

scuttled by her crew; one Japanese destroyer sank. Three of the American destroyers sank, and the *South Dakota* and the other destroyer suffered damage.[39]

When day broke on 15 November the Americans saw, lying at Tassafaronga in plain view, the four surviving transports of the force which had been hit the day before. The transports had no air cover. Three were beached and unloading, while the fourth was slowly pulling northward toward Doma Reef. F Battery of the 244th Coast Artillery Battalion had moved two of its guns from their field artillery positions on the west bank of the Lunga to the beach. These guns opened fire at 0500 and hit one beached transport 19,500 yards away; the ship began to burn.[40] The 3d Defense Battalion's 5-inch batteries opened fire forty-five minutes later on a second ship 15,800 yards away and hit her repeatedly. The beached target burned and listed to port.[41] The destroyer *Meade* sailed over from Tulagi to shell both the ships and the landing areas,[42] while aircraft from Henderson Field and bombers from Espiritu Santo attacked the remaining ships. By noon all four had been turned into burning, useless hulks which were abandoned to rust in the shallow water. The planes then turned their attention to the Japanese supplies which had been landed, and started tremendous fires among the piles of materiel. One blaze was 1,000 yards long.[43]

Cost and Results

Of the ill-fated convoy's 10,000 or more troops, about 4,000 had landed safely on Guadalcanal,[44] but without sufficient supplies and rations. Only five tons of the 10,000 tons of supplies aboard the ships were landed safely.[45] Of the rest of the troops, some had drowned at sea, but a large number were rescued by the Japanese.[46]

The destruction of the convoy brought the November counteroffensive to a quick end. For the Japanese the failure had been expensive. Besides the troops and supplies lost at sea, they had lost two battleships, one heavy cruiser, and three destroyers sunk. Equally serious had been the destruction of the eleven ships in the convoy, a total loss of 77,609 shipping tons.[47] Two heavy cruisers,

---

[39] *Campaigns of Pacific War*, App. 46, p. 129.

[40] 259th (formerly 244th) Sep CA Bn (HD) Hist, 1 Jan 42–30 Jun 42 (np), in HRS DRB AGO.

[41] 3d Def Bn, 5-inch Rpt, p. 4.

[42] COMAMPHIBFORSOPAC War Diary, 15 Nov 42.

[43] 1st Mar Div Rpt, V, 33.

[44] *Allied Campaign Against Rabaul*, p. 93.

[45] *Ibid.*, p. 108.

[46] USAFISPA, Japanese Campaign in the Guadalcanal Area, pp. 29–30, estimates that 7,700 troops had been aboard, of whom 3,000 drowned, 3,000 landed on Guadalcanal, and 1,700 were rescued.

[47] USSBS, *Interrogations*, II, 470.

one light cruiser, and six destroyers had been damaged. The U. S. Navy had lost one light cruiser, two light antiaircraft cruisers, and seven destroyers sunk, and one battleship, two heavy cruisers, and four destroyers damaged.

This was the last major effort by the Japanese Army and Navy to recapture the Lunga area by a co-ordinated attack. The November battle had made the task of reinforcing Guadalcanal much less dangerous. The movement of the 182d Infantry was the last shipment of troops to Guadalcanal in the face of enemy forces. Thereafter American troops were to be landed on Guadalcanal fairly regularly, and although enemy air attacks continued, and the *Alchiba* was torpedoed by a submarine on 28 November, the danger of attack by enemy warships lessened. The Lunga area was now securely held, for by the end of November Vandegrift's force totaled 39,416 men.[48]

The November battle had been the most decisive engagement of the Guadalcanal campaign. It had almost "sealed off" the Japanese on the Guadalcanal battlefields from their rear bases. After November, the most important factor of the campaign was to be the long hard ground fighting on the island itself.

[48] 1st Mar Div Rpt, V, Personnel Annex W, 3.

CHAPTER VIII

Advances Toward Kokumbona

In November, General Vandegrift had been able to resume the attempt to extend the western line beyond Kokumbona. The *17th Army* had been decisively defeated in October, and was unable to mount another counteroffensive until it could receive strong reinforcements. More American troops and planes were soon to be sent to Guadalcanal, and the offensive could be resumed with good prospects of ultimate success.

Operations 1–11 November

Kokumbona Offensive, 1–4 November

The first offensive move was begun before the mid-November naval battle. The objectives were about the same as those of the Marine offensive which opened on 7 October—first, the trail junction and landing beaches at Kokumbona, over 8,000 yards west of the Matanikau, and second, the Poha River, about 2,600 yards beyond Kokumbona. Once the Poha River line had been gained, the Lunga airfields would be safe from enemy artillery fire.

The infantry forces selected for the attack were the 5th Marines, the 2d Marines (less the 3d Battalion), and the Whaling Group, which now consisted of the Scout-Sniper Detachment and the 3d Battalion, 7th Marines. Supporting the offensive were to be the 11th Marines and attached Army artillery battalions, aircraft, engineers, and a boat detachment from the Kukum naval base.

The infantry forces were to attack west in column of regiments on a 1,500-yard front from the Matanikau River, the line of departure. The 5th Marines, closely followed by the 2d Marines in reserve, would make the assault. The Whaling Group would move out along the high grassy ridges on the left (south) of the assault forces to protect the left flank. Colonel Edson was to command the attacking force. The time for the attack was set for 0630, 1 November.

Full use was to be made of supporting artillery and mortar fire. The 11th Marines and attached battalions were to mass fire first in front of the 5th

OPENING THE KOKUMBONA OFFENSIVE. *Col. Merritt A. Edson (seated at desk, above) discusses plans for the 1 November attacks beyond the Matanikau River. Part of the plan was the construction of fuel-drum ponton footbridges across the stream (below), where Marines are seen crossing en route to the front lines.*

Marines. Artillery and mortar fire were to be placed on each objective and on each ravine and stream approached by the infantry. At least two battalions of artillery were to fire at targets as far west as the Poha, displacing their howitzers forward as the need arose. Aircraft were to strike enemy troop concentrations and artillery positions. Spotting planes for the division artillery would be furnished by the 1st Marine Air Wing.

On the night before the assault, the 1st Engineer Battalion was to construct footbridges across the Matanikau, and an additional bridge suitable for vehicles on the day of the attack. The naval boat detachment was to provide boats for amphibious supply and evacuation as the troops advanced up the coast.[1]

In preparation for the attack, the 1st and 2d Battalions of the 2d Marines were brought to Guadalcanal from Tulagi. The 3d Battalion, which had served as division mobile reserve for six weeks, was sent to Tulagi to rest. The 5th Marines moved to the forward Matanikau position to relieve the 2d Battalion, 7th Marines, and the 3d Battalion, 1st Marines; responsibility for the 5th Marines' old sector in the perimeter defense was assigned to the 2d Battalion of the 7th Marines. Detachments from the heavy weapons companies of the 3d Battalion, 1st Marines, and from the 2d Battalion, 7th Marines, remained in position along the Matanikau to cover the attacking forces as they made the crossing on 1 November. The 2d Marines (less the 3d Battalion) meanwhile moved into bivouac east of the Matanikau River.

The engineers salvaged and prepared material for the bridges between 25 and 31 October. On the afternoon of 31 October they hauled the material to the east bank of the river. Early on the morning of 1 November E Company of the 5th Marines crossed the river to outpost the west bank in order to cover the troops constructing the bridges. Between 0100 and 0600, 1 November, A, C, and D Companies of the 1st Engineer Battalion laid three footbridges over the river. Each bridge had a 40-inch-wide treadway which was supported by 2-by-4-inch stringers lashed to a light framework which in turn was lashed to floating fuel drums.

At daybreak on 1 November the 11th Marines, assisted by the 3d Defense Battalion's 5-inch guns, fired the preliminary bombardment. The cruisers *San Francisco* and *Helena* and the destroyer *Sterrett* had been sent up by Admiral Halsey, and they shelled the areas west of Point Cruz.[2] P-39's and SBD's from

---

[1] 1st Mar Div Opn Ord No. 13–42, 30 Oct 42, in 1st Mar Div Rpt, V, Annex K.
[2] CTF 65 to COMSOPAC, 0330 of 4 Nov 42; CG 1st Mar Div to COMSOPAC, 2131 of 1 Nov 42. SOPAC War Diary.

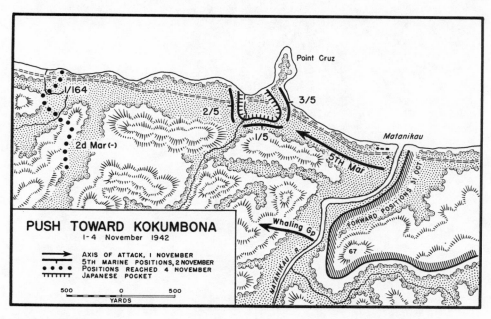

MAP NO. 9

Henderson Field struck Japanese artillery positions, while nineteen B–17's from Espiritu Santo dropped 335 100-pound bombs on Kokumbona.[8]

When the artillery fire lifted, the three battalions of the 5th Marines started across the Matanikau bridges. (*Map 9*) By 0700 the move had been completed successfully, and the 1st and 2d Battalions, on the right and left respectively, deployed to the attack. Their left was covered by the Whaling Group, which had crossed the river farther upstream. The 1st Battalion of the 5th, advancing over the flat ground along the beach, met the heaviest opposition as the Japanese, yielding ground slowly and reluctantly, fought a delaying action. The 2d Battalion, moving over higher ground, pushed ahead rapidly and lost contact with the 1st shortly after 1230. The advancing forces halted for the night short of Point Cruz, having gained slightly more than 1,000 yards in the day's action.

During the day the engineers, using a 10-ton temporary pier, had put a vehicular bridge across the Matanikau about 500 yards from the mouth. Although completed that day the bridge could not be used until the following afternoon, when a new road from the coast road to the bridge was completed.

[8] COMAIRSOPAC to COMSOPAC, 0705 of 1 Nov 42. SOPAC War Diary.

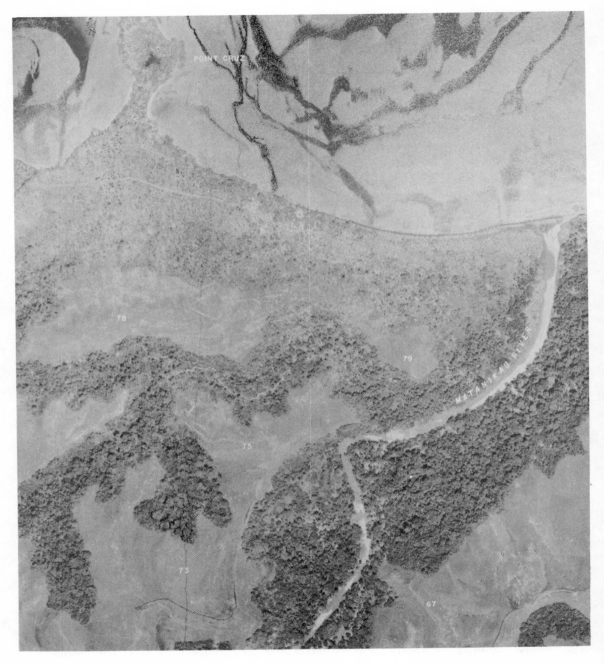

THE POINT CRUZ TRAP *into which the Japanese were pushed by the advance of 1–4 November, is shown at the top of this vertical aerial photograph. Bridging the Matanikau in the vicinity of the sharp river bend, the 5th Marines moved along the flat coastland north of Hills 78 and 79 while the Whaling Group crossed near Hill 67 and fought westward over the terrain of Hills 73–75.*

The next morning Colonel Edson committed the reserve 3d Battalion to assist the 1st Battalion on the right, while the 2d Battalion, having advanced beyond Point Cruz, turned to the right to envelop the enemy by attacking northward. By 1042 the 2d Battalion had reached the beach west of the Point and trapped the Japanese who were still opposing the 1st and 3d Battalions.[4]

During the afternoon of 2 November the two battalions of the 2d Marines passed by on the left of the 5th Marines to continue the westward push the next day. On 3 November the 1st Battalion, 2d Marines, and the Whaling Group, which had continued its advance inland, led the assault. The 2d Battalion, 2d Marines, and the 1st Battalion, 164th Infantry (Lt. Col. Frank C. Richards commanding), which had been ordered forward from its positions on the Ilu River, were in reserve. Meanwhile the 5th Marines successfully reduced the pocket at Point Cruz; the regiment killed about 350 Japanese and captured twelve 37-mm. guns, one field piece, and thirty-four machine guns. In the final phases of the mop-up the 5th Marines delivered three successful bayonet assaults,[5] and drove the surviving Japanese into the sea.[6] After the reduction of the pocket the 5th Marines and the Whaling Group were ordered back to the Lunga area, and Colonel Arthur, commanding the 2d Marines, took over tactical direction of the offensive from Colonel Edson.

The next day the 1st Battalion of the 164th Infantry and the 2d Marines (less the 3d Battalion) resumed the advance. By afternoon they had moved forward against the retreating Japanese to a point about 2,000 yards west of Point Cruz, or about 4,000 yards short of Kokumbona. At that point division headquarters halted the advance. Enemy troops had landed east of the perimeter defense, and there could be no further westward movement until the threat had been removed. At 1500 the three battalions dug in at Point Cruz to hold part of the ground they had gained.

Koli Point

Division headquarters had been expecting a Japanese landing in early November at Koli Point east of the Lunga perimeter.[7] To forestall the attempt, the 2d Battalion of the 7th Marines, Lt. Col. H. H. Hanneken commanding, had been ordered out of the Lunga perimeter to make a forced march to the Metapona River, about thirteen miles east of the Lunga. By nightfall of 2 November,

---

[4] 1st Mar Div Rpt, V, Annex P (5th Mar Record), 9–10.

[5] 1st Mar Div Rpt, V, 28.

[6] Rpt, OPD Obs to OPD, 13 Mar 43, App. III. OPD 381 SOPAC Sec. III PTO (3–13–43).

[7] CG 1st Mar Div to COMSOPAC, 0005 of 1 Nov 42. SOPAC War Diary.

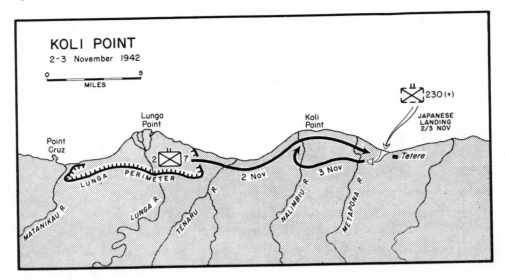

MAP NO. 10

when the 5th Marines had reduced the Point Cruz pocket, the battalion had established defensive positions east of the Metapona's mouth near the village of Tetere. (*Map 10*) About 2200 on 2 November the silhouettes of one Japanese cruiser, one transport, and three destroyers appeared offshore in the rainy darkness to land supplies and about 1,500 soldiers[8] from the *230th Infantry* at Gavaga Creek, about one mile east of Colonel Hanneken's position. Hyakutake had ordered these troops, with ammunition and provisions for 2,000 men, to land, join Shoji's force in the vicinity of Koli Point, and build an airfield.[9]

By the time the Japanese were landing, Colonel Hanneken's radio communication had failed, and he was unable to inform division headquarters of his situation. The next morning the Japanese force moved west. The Marine battalion engaged the enemy, and was hit by artillery and mortar fire. When one Japanese unit pushed southwest to outflank the marines, the battalion, fighting

---

[8] CG 1st Mar Div to COMSOPAC, 2205 of 17 Nov 42. SOPAC War Diary.

[9] *17th Army* Opns, I; Amer Div Int Rpt, Tab A; XIV Corps, Enemy Opns, which states that landing craft brought the Japanese from the western beaches of Guadalcanal, asserts that two battalions landed. Brig. Gen. E. B. Sebree, when Military Attache to Australia, interrogated the prisoner of war Maj. Gen. Takeo Ito (former CG, *38th Div* Inf Gp) at Rabaul in 1947. Ito stated that the only troops at Koli Point then were the *230th Infantry* survivors who had come there in October; the ships landed only supplies on the night of 2–3 November 1942. Interv with Gen Sebree, 19–20 Jun 43, who lent his notes of the interrogation of Ito to the author.

as it went, withdrew slowly westward along the coast, crossed the Nalimbiu, and took a stronger position on the west bank. Colonel Hanneken, whose troops were running short of food, attempted to radio information about his situation to division headquarters but was not able to get his message through until 1445.[10]

When headquarters received Hanneken's message, arrangements for support and reinforcement were quickly completed. Aircraft from the Lunga airfields bombed and strafed enemy positions, but as no targets were visible from the air results were probably insignificant.[11] The cruisers *San Francisco* and *Helena* and the destroyers *Sterrett* and *Lansdowne,* which had been supporting the Kokumbona attack, sailed eastward to shell Koli Point.[12] The 1st Battalion, 7th Marines, with the regimental commander Col. Amor L. Sims, immediately embarked on landing craft to reinforce the 2d Battalion at Koli Point. (*Map VIII.*) The 164th Infantry (less the 1st Battalion) was ordered out of its positions along the Ilu to march east to a point about 4,000 yards south of the 7th Marines at Koli Point to be in position to envelop the Japanese left (south) flank.[13]

General Rupertus, assistant commander of the 1st Marine Division, took command of the Koli Point operation, his first tactical experience on Guadalcanal. On 4 November, the day on which the Kokumbona attack was halted, the Lunga perimeter command was reorganized. General Rupertus was transferred from the relative quiet of Tulagi to Guadalcanal. The Lunga area was divided into two separate sectors, one east of the Lunga and one west of the river. General Rupertus took the east sector. Brig. Gen. Edmund B. Sebree, assistant commander of the American Division, who had just landed on the island to prepare for the arrival of the remainder of his division, took the west sector. Both generals reported directly to division headquarters, which thus operated as a small corps headquarters.

On 4 November General Rupertus, and regimental headquarters and the 1st Battalion of the 7th Marines reached Koli Point. The 164th Infantry (less the 1st Battalion) and B Company of the 8th Marines left the Ilu River line at 0600 to march to their objective about seven miles to the east. General Sebree accompanied the 164th to gain close experience with jungle warfare. At the same time, 1st Marine Division headquarters issued orders to the 2d Raider Battalion,

---

[10] 1st Mar Div Rpt, V, Annex U, (D-3 Journal), 25; 1st Mar Div Rpt, V, 29.
[11] 1st Mar Div Rpt, V, Int Annex N, 15.
[12] CTF 65 to COMSOPAC, 0330 of 4 Nov 42. SOPAC War Diary; 1st Mar Div Rpt, V, Int Annex N, 15.
[13] 164th Inf Opn Rpt, 31 Oct–7 Nov 42, in USAFISPA G–3 Periodic Rpts, 29 Oct–16 Nov 42.

which had just landed at Aola Bay with the 147th Infantry, to advance overland toward Koli Point to intercept any Japanese detachments moving eastward.

The 164th Infantry progressed slowly on its inland march through swampy jungles and hot stretches of high kunai grass. As there were no inland roads, trucks carried some supplies along the coast to Koli Point, but inland the soldiers of the 164th Infantry, wearing full combat equipment, had to hand-carry all their weapons and ammunition. It was noon before the regiment reached the first assembly area on the west bank of the Nalimbiu River. While regimental headquarters and the 3d Battalion bivouacked for the night, the 2d Battalion advanced northward in column of companies along the west bank of the Nalimbiu. After advancing about 2,000 yards, the 2d Battalion bivouacked. It had not established contact with the 7th Marines. Patrols had met only a few small Japanese units.

On the following morning, 5 November, General Rupertus ordered the 164th Infantry (less the 1st Battalion) to cross to the east bank of the Nalimbiu, and then to advance north to Koli Point to destroy the Japanese facing the 7th Marines at Koli Point. The 3d Battalion crossed the flooded Nalimbiu about 3,500 yards south of Koli Point, then swung north to advance along the east bank. Again no large organized enemy force appeared. The battalion advanced against occasional rifle and machine-gun fire. Machine-gun fire halted two platoons of G Company for a time until American artillery and mortar fire silenced the enemy guns. The 2d Battalion of the 164th Infantry, which had withdrawn to the south from its bivouac positions, followed on the right and rear of the 3d Battalion.

Action on 6 November was indecisive. The 7th Marines crossed the flooded Nalimbiu with difficulty, while the 164th Infantry's battalions moved slowly through the jungle. The 3d Battalion found an abandoned Japanese bivouac about 1,000 yards south of Koli Point, but the enemy had escaped to the east. The 3d Battalion reached Koli Point at night on 6 November and was followed by the 2d Battalion the next morning. During the night of 5–6 November the 2d and 3d Battalions, mistaking each other for the enemy, exchanged shots.[14] Regimental headquarters and the Antitank and E Companies of the 164th Infantry, together with B Company of the 8th Marines, followed a more circuitous route, and reached Koli Point later in the morning.

The combined force then advanced eastward to a point about one mile west

[14] Interv with Gen Sebree.

of the wide mouth of the Metapona River. Again there was no enemy resistance, possibly because the Japanese were preparing defenses east of the Metapona to permit the main body to escape.[15] The Americans dug in to defend the beach west of the Metapona against an expected landing on the night of 7–8 November, but it failed to materialize. On 8 November the 2d Battalion of the 164th Infantry was attached to the 7th Marines and placed in reserve. To surround the Japanese, who had dug in along Gavaga Creek at Tetere about one mile east of the Metapona, the three battalions left their positions west of the wide, swampy mouth of the Metapona and advanced to the east and west of Gavaga Creek. The 1st Battalion, 7th Marines, occupied the west bank and took positions running inland from the beach. The 2d Battalion, 7th Marines, was posted on the east to hold a shorter line between the east bank of Gavaga Creek and the beach. When dengue fever put General Rupertus out of action on 8 November, General Sebree took command on orders from Vandegrift.

With the Japanese force located and surrounded, the size of the American force at Koli Point could be safely reduced. Since General Vandegrift desired to commit a large part of the 164th Infantry to the attack against Kokumbona, regimental headquarters, the Antitank Company, and the 3d Battalion of the 164th Infantry and B Company of the 8th Marines were brought back to the Lunga perimeter by boat and truck on 9 November.

On that day, at Koli Point, the 2d Battalion (less E Company) of the 164th Infantry took positions on the right of the 1st Battalion, 7th Marines. During the night E Company was committed to the left flank of the 2d Battalion of the 7th Marines. The Americans now held a curved line from the beach around a horseshoe bend in Gavaga Creek. The Japanese, blocked on the east and west, repeatedly attempted to break out of the trap. They used machine guns, mortars, and hand grenades in their attempts to drive the Americans back. One gap in the American lines remained open in the south, for F and E Companies of the 164th, which were separated by the swampy creek, had failed to make contact. Although wounded seven times by mortar shell fragments, Colonel Puller remained in command of the 1st Battalion of the 7th Marines.

The marines and soldiers, supported by 155-mm. gun batteries, two 75-mm. pack howitzer batteries, and aircraft, began to reduce the pocket. The Japanese resisted vigorously with grenades, mortars, automatic weapons, and small arms. On 10 November F Company of the 164th Infantry attempted to close the gap

---

[15] 164th Inf Opn Rpt.

and join flanks with E Company. The attempt failed, and the commander of the 2d Battalion of the 164th was relieved.[16] On the next day G Company drove east to close the gap. As the Marine battalions closed in from the east and west, the 2d Battalion of the 164th Infantry pushed north to reach the beaches in the late afternoon of 11 November. By 12 November the pocket had been entirely cleared. About forty Americans had been killed, 120 wounded; 450 Japanese had been killed.[17] The captured materiel included, besides stores of rations and fifty collapsible landing boats, General Kawaguchi's personal effects.

Hyakutake apparently abandoned the idea of building an airfield near Koli Point, for he ordered Shoji's troops to return via the inland route to Kokumbona.[18] Some of the Japanese had escaped through the gap between the two companies, and some others had apparently withdrawn inland about 7 November. These forces, retreating south and west toward Mount Austen, were harried by Lt. Col. Evans F. Carlson's 2d Raider Battalion which had marched west from Aola Bay. The raiders, in a remarkable 30-day march outside the American lines, covered 150 miles, fought 12 separate actions, and killed over 400 enemy soldiers at a cost of only 17 raiders killed before they finally entered the Lunga perimeter on 4 December.[19] Of the estimated 1,500 Japanese soldiers who may have landed at Koli Point, probably less than half survived to rejoin the main forces at Mount Austen and the hills to the west.

Resumption of the Kokumbona Offensive

On 10 November, with the trapping of the Japanese at Koli Point, it became possible to renew the westward offensive toward Kokumbona. Under Colonel Arthur's command, the 1st Battalion of the 164th Infantry, the newly arrived 8th Marines, and the 2d Marines (less the 3d Battalion) moved west from Point Cruz on 10 November. Supported by fire from the 1st, 3d, and 5th Battalions of the 11th Marines, the composite force executed a frontal attack on a three-battalion front. The 1st Battalion, 164th Infantry, advanced on the right along the beach; the 2d Battalion, 2d Marines, advanced in the center, and the 1st Battalion, 2d Marines, was echeloned to the left and rear in the attack. On 11 November the advance was resumed against rifle, machine-gun, and mortar fire. By noon the troops had fought their way to a point slightly beyond that which they had reached on 4 November.

---

[16] Interv with Gen Sebree.
[17] 1st Mar Div Rpt, V, 30.
[18] *17th Army* Opns, I, which does not mention the engagement at Koli Point.
[19] 1st Mar Div Rpt, V, 30–31.

CARLSON'S RAIDERS, LANDING AT AOLA BAY *the morning of 4 November, moved toward Koli Point to intercept Japanese forces which had come ashore east of the Lunga perimeter. Enemy positions were beyond Taivu Point, seen on the far horizon.*

JAPANESE COLLAPSIBLE LANDING BOATS *of the type shown in this picture taken later in the Guadalcanal campaign, were part of the materiel captured at Koli Point. With the stern section removed, the boat's sides can be compressed as the rubber bottom folds.*

The Japanese were grimly determined to prevent the Americans from taking Kokumbona. This village was the site of the *17th Army* command post, and also the terminus of the main supply trail to the positions which the Japanese were secretly preparing on Mount Austen. Accordingly Hyakutake assigned the mission of halting the American attack to a new general, Maj. Gen. Takeo Ito, Infantry Group commander of the *38th Division* and a veteran of the fighting in China. Ito had landed at Tassafaronga from a destroyer on 5 November to take command of a reserve force of 5,000 men. Believing that the American front west of Point Cruz was so narrow that he could easily outflank it, he moved his force to a concealed position in the jungled hills on the left flank of the Americans, about 5,000 yards south of the beach. From this point he planned to strike the American left flank and rear.[20]

Before Ito could attack, and before the Americans were even aware that their left was in danger, Vandegrift was once more forced to halt the offensive when he received word that the Japanese were preparing to bring large troop convoys to Guadalcanal in mid-November. To meet the threat of another counteroffensive, all troops were needed within the Lunga perimeter.

The battalions disengaged; the 2d and 8th Marines retired toward the Matanikau, covered by the 1st Battalion of the 164th Infantry. The marines recrossed the Matanikau on 11 November, followed next day by the Army battalion. The entire 164th Infantry, having returned from its operations across the Matanikau and Metapona Rivers, went into division reserve. Once safely across the Matanikau, the Americans destroyed the bridges and held their lines while the air and naval forces fought desperately to keep the Japanese away.

Push Toward the Poha

As a result of the naval victory in mid-November and the arrival of the 182d Infantry, commanded by Col. Daniel W. Hogan, the offensive toward Kokumbona and the Poha Rivers was resumed. The 1st Marine Division headquarters, which ordered the attack, placed General Sebree, commander of the western sector, in tactical command. Available troops in the west sector included the 164th Infantry, the 8th Marines, and the two battalions of the 182d Infantry. To support operations in any direction, all artillery battalions remained grouped within the perimeter under del Valle's command.

[20] Interv with Gen Sebree.

General Sebree planned first to gain a line of departure far enough west of the Matanikau and far enough south of the beach to provide sufficient room for the regiments to maneuver. Once the line of departure had been gained, a full-scale offensive could be opened. The line which General Sebree planned to capture first ran about 2,500 yards inland from Point Cruz to the southernmost point (Hill 66) of a 1,700-yard-long ridge (Hills 66–81–80).

It was thought that the west bank of the Matanikau was not occupied by the Japanese during the second week of November. This belief was confirmed by infantry and aerial reconnaissance patrols, and General Sebree and Colonel Whaling of the Marines personally patrolled the ground as far west as Point Cruz without meeting any Japanese.

Once the line of departure had been gained, the assault units were to move west, followed by the 1st Marines on the inland flank. The latter regiment was to turn northward to envelop any Japanese pockets as the 5th Marines had done so successfully earlier in the month, while the assault units continued to advance westward. This part of the plan was canceled when the 1st Marine Division was alerted for departure from Guadalcanal.[21]

The 2d Battalion of the 182d Infantry was to cross the Matanikau on 18 November to seize Hill 66, the highest ground north of the northwest Matanikau fork, and the 1st Battalion of the 182d Infantry would advance across the river and west to Point Cruz the next day. As the American forces which had withdrawn on 11–12 November had destroyed all the Matanikau bridges, engineers were to bridge the river, improve the coast road, and build a trail over the ridges to Hill 66.

The terrain west of the Matanikau differs from the deep jungles of the inland areas. The coast is flat and sandy. South of the beach rocky ridges, covered with brush and coarse grass, thrust upward to heights of several hundred feet. These ridges, running from north to south, rise near the beach and increase in height toward the south. Between these steep ridges are deep, jungled ravines which the Japanese could exploit to good advantage. The ridge line formed by Hills 80, 81, and 66 faces northwest and turns sharply eastward at Hill 66 toward the Matanikau River's main stream. It is separated from the high hills on the south by the valley cut by the northwest Matanikau fork.

Unknown to the Americans, the *17th Army* had also been planning for local offensive action. While the shattered *2d Division* assembled near Kokum-

[21] *Ibid.;* interv with Col Paul A. Gavan (former G–3, Amer Div), 14 Nov 46. No formal field order was published.

bona, the *38th Division* had been ordered to advance east from Kokumbona, cross the Matanikau, and seize the high ground on the east bank for artillery positions and as a line of departure for another assault against the Lunga airfields. At the same time troops under Ito's command had been ordered to occupy Mount Austen.[22]

On 18 November the 2d Battalion of the 182d Infantry (Lt. Col. Bernard B. Twombley commanding), covered by the 8th Marines on the east bank of the Matanikau, crossed a footbridge about 700 yards from the Matanikau's mouth to seize Hill 66. (*Map IX*) The battalion climbed to the top of the first ridge on the west bank (Hill 75) and advanced southwest behind the ridge crest toward Hill 66, about 2,000 yards from Hill 75. There were no Japanese on the ridges, but the inexperienced battalion made slow progress. The men, having landed only six days before, were not yet accustomed to the moist heat. Since landing, most of them had been unloading ships and moving their supplies. They carried full loads of ammunition, water, and food. Many who had not swallowed salt tablets collapsed, exhausted from the hard climb. The 2d Battalion did not reach Hill 66 until noon.[23] Having taken the objective, the men dug foxholes and gun emplacements on the west and south military crests of Hill 66. On the left was G Company, and F on the right. Battalion reserve consisted of E Company, and H Company put its mortars in a gully behind the battalion command post.[24]

In the afternoon a detail of two officers and thirty enlisted men from G Company went into the valley on the south to fill canteens at a water hole. They reached the spring safely, but failed to post sentries as they filled the clanking canteens. As one man in the group glanced up, he saw a Japanese officer and about twenty soldiers deploying in the jungle near by. The Japanese promptly opened fire. The water detail scattered, each man taking cover as best he could. When a rescue party from the 2d Battalion later made its way to the spring, the enemy patrol withdrew and the water party straggled back to the crest of Hill 66. One officer and one enlisted man had been killed.[25] There were no more encounters with the Japanese that day.

The 1st Battalion of the 182d Infantry, commanded by Lt. Col. Francis F.

---

[22] *17th Army* Opns, I; Interrog of Hyakutake, Miyazaki, and Maruyama.

[23] Interv USAFISPA Hist Off with Col William D. Long (former G-2, Amer Div), 31 May 44; interv, author, with Col Long, 26 Mar 46.

[24] 2d Bn, 182d Inf, S-2 Journal, 18 Nov 42.

[25] Interv with Col Long.

MacGowan, crossed the Matanikau the next morning (19 November). The battalion advanced along the flat ground between the northernmost hills and the beach, while B Company of the 8th Marines, acting on Sebree's orders, advanced over the most northerly hill (Hill 78) to cover the battalion's left flank. About 400 yards west of the river the battalion met fire from small enemy groups, but there was no heavy fighting. The battalion moved slowly and cautiously, fighting a series of skirmishes as it moved toward Point Cruz.[26]

B Company of the 8th Marines also met enemy fire west of Point Cruz and withdrew to the vicinity of Hill 78 to take cover. The company again attempted to advance, but could not gain ground.[27] About noon Colonel MacGowan's battalion halted just east of Point Cruz; it dug in along a 700-yard line from the beach east of the point to the west tip of Hill 78, refusing the left flank eastward a short distance along the south slopes of the hill. The Marine company then withdrew across the Matanikau to rejoin its regiment. The 1st and 2d Battalions of the 182d Infantry were then separated by a gap of over 1,000 yards.

Japanese troops had been secretly moving east from Kokumbona.[28] These forces took positions west of the 1st Battalion during the night of 19–20 November, while artillery and mortars fired on the American lines. About dawn on 20 November part of this force struck suddenly at the 1st Battalion's left flank. The troops holding high ground on the battalion's left held their line, but as the attack developed along the 1st Battalion's line the troops on the low ground fell back about 400 yards. General Sebree, Lt. Col. Paul A. Gavan, the operations officer, and Lt. Col. Paul Daly, the assistant intelligence officer, of the Americal Division, came forward and found the battalion "somewhat shaken." They halted the withdrawal and reorganized the companies.[29]

Planes and artillery then struck at the Japanese, who had not exploited their advantage by advancing east of Point Cruz, and the 1st Battalion again moved west and by 0900 had regained its position.[30]

C and A Companies of the 182d attacked west after the recapture of the initial line and advanced to the beach just west of Point Cruz. There the attack stalled after the companies had been hit hard by Japanese artillery and mortar

---

[26] Interv with Col Gavan.

[27] Amer Div Narrative of Opns, p. 3.

[28] XIV Corps, Enemy Opns, pp. 4–5.

[29] Lt Col Paul A. Gavan, Personal Experience Account of ACofS, G–3, Amer Div, p. 1; interv with Col Gavan.

[30] Intervs with Gen Sebree and Col Gavan.

fire. There was "considerable confusion and some straggling" in the 182d Infantry, and it was only after order had been restored that the 1st Battalion organized a disciplined firing line.[31] The Japanese retained Point Cruz itself.

By afternoon on 20 November it had become obvious that more American
troops were needed west of the Matanikau. The Japanese were known to be
moving more troops forward into the engagement.[32] General Sebree therefore ordered the more experienced 164th Infantry out of reserve to fill the gap
between the two battalions of the 182d Infantry. The 164th Infantry was to
enter the line under cover of darkness and attack the next morning. The 1st
Battalion of the 164th Infantry entered the line on the left of the 1st Battalion
of the 182d Infantry, and the 3d Battalion of the 164th moved in between the
2d Battalion, 182d Infantry, and the 1st Battalion, 164th. Each battalion of the
164th took over about 500 yards of the line, and the 182d Infantry battalions,
on either side of the 164th Infantry, extended their flanks to join with those of
the 164th.

During the first three days of the operation supplies for the units west of
the Matanikau had been carried forward by hand from the river line. The engineers finally succeeded in building a footbridge over the flooded Matanikau,
but the bridge for heavy vehicles was not completed until 21 November.[33]

The 1st Battalion of the 182d attacked west from the Point Cruz area on
21 November. It met heavy artillery and mortar fire, as well as small-arms fire
from some Japanese entrenched on Point Cruz itself, the beach on the west,
and the near-by hills and ravines. The battalion reduced Point Cruz, but failed
to advance west.[34]

The battalions of the 164th Infantry also attacked to the west on 21 November from the Hill 80–81 ridge line. A ravine about 200 feet deep, varying in
width from 150 to 300 feet, lay directly in front of Hills 80 and 81. A series of
steep ridges (Hills 83 and 82) lay west of the ravine. To get through the ravine
and gain the ridges on the west, it would be necessary for the 164th Infantry to
cross about fifty yards of open ground on the ridge. Between 11 and 18 November the Japanese had built strong positions, containing a large number of
automatic weapons, in the hills and ravines and on the flat ground west of
Point Cruz. The hill positions, well dug in on the reverse slopes, were defiladed

[31] Amer Div Narrative of Opns, p. 3.
[32] Gavan, Personal Experience Account, p. 2.
[33] Intervs with Col Long.
[34] 182d Inf Opn Rpt, pp. 3–4.

THE RAVINE IN FRONT OF HILLS 80–81, *where the 164th Infantry attacks stalled on 23 November, was well defended by Japanese dug into defiladed positions in Hills 83 and 82. American troops were halted on the line of Hills 66, 81, 80.*

from American artillery and mortar fire. Machine guns sited at the head of each ravine could put flanking fire into advancing troops. The ravine in front of Hills 81–80 was especially well defended. On the flat ground in places where a thin layer of earth covered a coral shelf, the Japanese had dug shallow pits with overhead cover, as well as foxholes under logs and behind trees. These positions, organized in depth, were mutually supporting. Small arms supported the automatic weapons, and artillery and mortars could cover the entire American front.[35]

Japanese fire quickly halted the 164th Infantry after it had made an average gain of less than forty yards. The 182d and 164th Regiments attacked again on 22 November but failed to make progress. In the afternoon the 8th Marines was notified that it was to pass through the 164th Infantry the next day to attack toward Hill 83.

After the infantry had withdrawn 300 yards behind the front lines early on 23 November, the 245th Field Artillery Battalion and L Battery and the 1st and 2d Battalions of the 11th Marines fired a 30-minute concentration on the Japanese lines. The 8th Marines then passed through the 164th Infantry and delivered successive attacks against the Japanese throughout the day. The regiment was supported by the artillery which fired 2,628 rounds of all calibers.[36] During the bombardment, Hyakutake and the *17th Army* chief of staff were slightly injured at their command post near Kokumbona.[37] The American forces failed to gain. The Japanese, defending vigorously, put fire all along the entire American lines. The 3d Battalion of the 164th Infantry was hit by accurate fire. In the afternoon of 23 November mortar fire struck the command posts of L, I, and K Companies, and killed the battalion surgeon, four lieutenants, and one 1st sergeant.[38]

American headquarters concluded that "further advance would not be possible without accepting casualties in numbers to preclude the advisability of [continuing] this action."[39] The troops were ordered to dig in to hold the Hill 66–80–81–Point Cruz line. The attack had ended in a stalemate.

Operations up to 23 November had demonstrated that frontal assault would be costly. By 25 November less than 2,000 men of the 164th Infantry were fit

[35] Intervs with Col Long.
[36] 1st Mar Div Rpt, V, Arty Annex R, 3.
[37] *17th Army* Opns, I.
[38] 164th Inf Unit Rpt, 23 Nov 42. Colonel Hall, 3d Battalion commander, was wounded and evacuated from the island the next day.
[39] Amer Div Narratives of Opns, p. 3.

for combat. Between 19 and 25 November 117 of the 164th had been killed, and 208 had been wounded. Three hundred and twenty-five had been evacuated from the island because of wounds or illness, and 300 more men, rendered ineffective by wounds, malaria, dysentery, or neuroses, were kept in the rear areas.[40] The 1st Marine Division was soon to be relieved, and its impending departure would reduce American troop strength too greatly to permit the execution of any flanking movements over the hills south of Hill 66. Until reinforcements could be brought in, the westward offensive had to be suspended.

The attacks on 18–23 November had, however, achieved some success. Hyakutake's plan to recapture the Matanikau's east bank had been thwarted, although in November he secretly began to increase his strength on Mount Austen.[41] American troops had finally established permanent positions west of the Matanikau. The Americans and the Japanese now faced one another at close ranges, the Americans on high ground, the Japanese on reverse slopes and in ravines. Each side could cover the opponent's lines with rifle, automatic, mortar, and artillery fire, and put mortar and artillery fire on the trails and rear areas. Americans and Japanese were to hold these static but dangerous lines until the beginning of the XIV Corps' general offensive in January.

[40] 164th Inf S–1 Journal, 25 Nov 42.

[41] On 30 November 1942, 8 enemy destroyers attempted to land reinforcements and supplies. Intercepted by 5 U.S. cruisers and 6 destroyers off Tassafaronga, they failed, but sank 1 and damaged 3 American cruisers, suffering 1 destroyer sunk and 1 damaged. See USSBS, *Campaigns of Pacific War,* pp. 139–40, and ONI, USN, Combat Narratives: Solomon Islands Campaign, VII, Battle of Tassafaronga, 30 November 1942 (Washington, 1944).

CHAPTER IX

The Situation in December

General Patch Takes Command

By the end of November, the higher commanders in the Pacific clearly recognized that the 1st Marine Division needed to be relieved and evacuated to a healthier climate. The division had begun the first offensive undertaken by American ground troops in World War II. Despite the lack of the powerful air and surface support that American infantrymen in later campaigns were to take almost for granted, and in spite of air raids, naval bombardments, inadequate diet, inadequate armament, and resolute Japanese infantry attacks, it had captured and successfully defended an airfield of great importance. Its achievements were rewarded by the Presidential Unit Citation.

Marine battle casualties had not been excessive. Over 600 men of the division were killed in action or died of wounds and other causes between 7 August and 10 December 1942. During the same period the dead of other American units on Guadalcanal totaled 691. Over 2,100 sick and wounded men of the 1st Division had already been evacuated.

In the Solomons battle casualties did not accurately reflect a unit's losses. Hospital admissions resulting from sickness must also be taken into account. Up to 10 December 1942, of the 10,635 casualties in the division, only 1,472 resulted from gunshot wounds; 5,749 malaria cases had put men out of action. In November malaria alone sent 3,283 into the hospital. Gastro-enteritis, which had struck nearly 500 men during August and September, materially decreased during the following months and in December only 12 cases appeared. War neuroses afflicted 110 during October when enemy bombardments had been heaviest, but in November only 13 were affected.[1] These figures are not necessarily mutually exclusive. Many malaria victims were hospitalized more than once; many of the same men were also later killed or wounded. Thus the number of men in the division who were not hospitalized may have been larger

---

[1] 1st Mar Div Rpt, V, Annex X, 1.

RELIEF FOR THE MARINES AND A CHANGE OF COMMAND *were major decisions acted upon at Guadalcanal in December, 1942. The 1st Marine Division, while still fighting hard, had lost many men and the makeshift sick bays (above) were handling a capacity of cases. General Patch (wearing glasses, lower photo) succeeded Marine General Vandegrift (right), with whom he is shown in conference. At left is Col. R. Hall Jeschke, USMC.*

than the statistics indicate. Yet many other malaria victims did not report for treatment, and many milder cases were not hospitalized.

The men who had remained on duty were ready for relief. They had endured months of intermittent combat, air raids, and naval attacks. Inadequate diet had caused nearly every man to lose weight. Secondary anemia was common. Weakness resulting from malnutrition, heat, and disease was causing an excessive number of march casualties in all units. Merely living in the Lunga perimeter was an ordeal in itself. Water was insufficient for bathing and laundry, and fungi frequently infected those who bathed in the rivers. The old October perimeter had included less than thirty square miles, so there were no real rest areas, nor any recreational facilities. Flies, attracted by unburied enemy corpses lying beyond the perimeter, harassed the troops constantly. They clustered so thickly that men messing in the open had to brush flies off their food with one hand while eating with the other.

As early as 3 November Halsey had wished to relieve the worn-out division, but he was unable to do so until he could send more fresh troops to Guadalcanal. The 43d Division was already on its way to the South Pacific; the first elements of the division had arrived in the area in early October. On 3 November Harmon repeated an earlier request that General Marshall send the 25th Division, then assisting in the defense of the Hawaiian Islands, to the South Pacific.[2] While General Marshall had alerted the 25th Division for movement as early as 19 October, it was not then definitely decided whether the division was to go to the South or to the Southwest Pacific Area. One combat team of the 25th Division was to have left Pearl Harbor in November,[3] but it was delayed when the ship aboard which it was to sail, the *President Coolidge,* sank on 26 October when it struck two U. S. mines off Espiritu Santo.[4] The *Coolidge* was carrying the 172d Regimental Combat Team of the 43d Division.

On 30 November the Joint Chiefs of Staff decided to send to the South Pacific the 25th Division, commanded by Maj. Gen. J. Lawton Collins. The 1st Marine Division was to be relieved, with the first echelon leaving in early December. It was to go to the Southwest Pacific Area to be rehabilitated and to provide General MacArthur with a division having amphibious training.[5]

[2] COMGENSOPAC to WDCSA, 1028 of 3 Nov 42. SOPAC War Diary.

[3] OPD memo for record, 19 Oct 42. OPD 370.5 PTO Sec. I Case 34.

[4] Memo, ACofS OPD for WDCSA, 29 Oct 42, sub: Delay in Movement 25th Div, and OPD memo for record, 30 Oct 42. OPD 370.5 PTO (10–30–42) Case 45.

[5] OPD memo for record, 30 Nov 42, sub: Change Destination 25th Div and 1st Mar Div. OPD 370.5 PTO (11–30–42) Case 45.

On Guadalcanal staff officers of the Americal Division, who had arrived in November and been working closely with the Marine division staff, were preparing to take over. At the beginning of December they moved into the Marine staff sections to acquaint themselves with the problems peculiar to Guadalcanal. The Americal Division's supply sections completed an inventory of the stocks on the island, and on 1 December they assumed responsibility for supply. By 8 December all Army staff officers had assumed complete responsibility.

The selection of a commander to succeed General Vandegrift was left to General Harmon. He chose Maj. Gen. Alexander M. Patch, commanding general of the Americal Division, to direct tactical operations on Guadalcanal.[6] On 9 December General Patch relieved General Vandegrift, who was to leave with his division.[7] The evacuation of the 1st Division began on the same day, when three ships carrying the 5th Marines sailed out of Sealark Channel for Australia.[8] By the end of the month the rest of the division had followed.

General Patch, the new commander, born in 1889, was graduated from the U. S. Military Academy in 1913. He saw active service in France during World War I, taught military science and tactics at Staunton Military Academy in Virginia during three separate tours of duty, and was graduated from the Command and General Staff School and from the Army War College. From 1936 to 1941, he served on the Infantry Board at Fort Benning, with the 47th Infantry, and commanded the Infantry Replacement Training Center at Camp Croft in South Carolina. Early in 1942 he had been ordered, as a brigadier general, to command the American force which had been organized to defend New Caledonia.

On 10 December 1942 the Guadalcanal–Tulagi area assumed somewhat the same status as the other island commands in the South Pacific. General Harmon became responsible for providing supplies for the troops. Admiral Turner was relieved of responsibility for defending Guadalcanal but was to retain responsibility for transporting troops and supplies to the area.[9] General Patch was responsible to Admiral Halsey. His command included the Guadalcanal airfields, the seaplane base at Tulagi, and the naval bases as well as the troops of

[6] COMSOPAC to CG Guadalcanal, 1228 of 8 Dec 42. SOPAC War Diary; Harmon, Army in the South Pacific, p. 5; Halsey, Narrative Account of the South Pacific Campaign, p. 5.

[7] CG 1st Mar Div to COMSOPAC, 0417 of 9 Dec 42. SOPAC War Diary.

[8] COMAMPHIBFORSOPAC War Diary, 9 Dec 42.

[9] COMSOPAC to COMAMPHIBFORSOPAC, CG Guadalcanal, CG I MAC, COMNAVBAS SOPAC, COMINCH, CINCPAC, COMGENSOPAC, COMAIRSOPAC, COMSERONSOPAC, 0446 of 7 Dec 42. SOPAC War Diary.

all services.[10] The troops were then occupying Tulagi, the adjacent islands, and Koli Point, Lunga Point, and the Matanikau River–Point Cruz area on Guadalcanal. The mission given him was clear and direct: "eliminate all Japanese forces" on Guadalcanal.[11]

Troop Strength

For the Americans on Guadalcanal October and November had been primarily periods of stubborn defense interspersed with hard-fought local offensives. The first half of December was a period of transition, a time of organization for offensive action while reinforcements were on their way.

Prior to the relief of the 1st Marine Division American forces had included almost 40,000 men.[12] Although in December there were about 25,000 Japanese troops on Guadalcanal, the Americans were not sure of the *17th Army's* precise strength or dispositions,[13] and there always remained the dangerous possibility that it might be reinforced by the nocturnal Tokyo Express.

Prior to his assumption of command General Patch had estimated that he would require at least two reinforced divisions to hold the airfields, and three to prevent the Japanese from making any more landings.[14] But there were then no other divisions in the South Pacific which could be spared. The 37th Division, the only other complete U. S. Army division in the South Pacific except the American, was then holding the strategically important Fiji Islands and could not be moved.[15] The departure of the 1st Marine Division reduced troop strength so much that no major offensives could be undertaken until the 25th Division arrived. The American Division, the 147th Infantry, the reinforced 2d and 8th Marines of the 2d Marine Division, and the Marine defense battalions were the only ground forces available to General Patch during most of December, and most of these were needed to hold the ground already gained.

Most of the remaining units of the American Division reached Guadalcanal in December. The 132d Regimental Combat Team (less the 1st Battalion and A Battery of the 247th Field Artillery Battalion) landed on 8 December.[16]

---

[10] *Ibid.*

[11] Army in the South Pacific, p. 5.

[12] Amer Div Strength Rpt, 11 Dec 42.

[13] G–2, Amer Div, draft rpt to G–2, USAFISPA, in misc ltrs and memos, G–2, Amer Div.

[14] Ltr, CG Amer Div to COMGENSOPAC, cited in USAFISPA Guadalcanal ms No. 2, Ch. VIII, p. a2.

[15] Army in the South Pacific, p. 5.

[16] COMAMPHIBFORSOPAC War Diary, 8 Dec 42.

The 2d Marine Division Signal Company and the 18th Naval Construction Battalion landed on 12 December, followed on 13 December by the 3d Battalion, 182d Infantry, and C Company, 2d (Marine) Engineer Battalion. The next day more Americal Division units landed—the Mobile Combat Reconnaissance Squadron, the 1st Battalion, 132d Infantry, A Battery of the 247th Field Artillery Battalion, and a detachment of the 39th Military Police Company. The 221st Field Artillery Battalion did not arrive until January 1943. These units were inexperienced, but the 164th and 182d Regiments had seen heavy fighting.

The Americal Division was a unique Army unit, for it bore a name instead of a number and had been activated in New Caledonia instead of on United States territory. The name "Americal" is a contraction of the words *America* and *New Caledonia*. The division, activated in May 1942, was composed of elements of the force sent to defend New Caledonia in the early months of the war.

Composed of infantry, artillery, and supporting units and led by General Patch, this task force had left the United States on 23 January 1942. After a short stay at Melbourne, Australia, it had reached Noumea, New Caledonia, on 12 March, to occupy and defend that island.[17] New Caledonia, valuable as a military base and source of nickel, was a French colony held by the Vichy government during the first years of World War II until a popular uprising overthrew the Vichy governor and installed a member of Gen. Charles de Gaulle's Fighting French Forces. In co-operation with the Fighting French authorities, General Patch's force had organized the defense of New Caledonia.[18]

The main units of the Americal Division were the 132d, 164th, and 182d Infantry Regiments; the 221st, 245th, 246th, and 247th Field Artillery Battalions; the 57th Engineer Combat Battalion; the 101st Quartermaster Regiment; the 101st Medical Regiment; the 26th Signal Company, and the Mobile Combat Reconnaissance Squadron. The division, which had been widely dispersed in New Caledonia, was to operate on Guadalcanal as a complete division for the first time.

The first element of the division to land on Guadalcanal was the 164th Infantry, a part of the North Dakota National Guard. It was followed by a Massachusetts National Guard regiment, the 182d Infantry. The units of the Americal

---

[17] TF 6814 and Amer Div, Hist Data, p. 1.

[18] Although the troops had received some jungle training in New Caledonia, divisional maneuvers had not been possible.

AMERICAL DIVISION REINFORCEMENTS LANDED 8 DECEMBER *to bring Army forces in Guadalcanal to almost full division strength. These two pictures show troops of the 132d Regimental Combat Team bringing ashore their weapons and equipment, including a mobile pigeon loft, along the Kukum beaches.*

which served with the 1st Marine Division also received the Presidential Unit Citation. The 132d Infantry, of the Illinois National Guard, arrived last. The division's artillery battalions came from the old 72d and 180th Field Artillery Regiments. The Mobile Combat Reconnaissance Squadron, equipped with jeeps, rifles, machine guns, automatic rifles, mortars, and 37-mm. antitank guns, was a special unit which had been organized in New Caledonia by Lt. Col. Alexander M. George to provide a mobile striking force to strengthen the defense of the island.[19] Guadalcanal's terrain was too rough and densely jungled for motorized combat units, however, and the squadron fought on foot.

Brig. Gen. Edmund B. Sebree, then assistant division commander and soon to command the division, was by December a veteran of Guadalcanal. He had reached the island in early November, had conducted the closing phase of the Koli Point action, and had commanded part of the perimeter defense. On General Vandegrift's order he had directed the offensive of 18 November which, though it bogged down short of the Poha River, succeeded in establishing the American lines west of the Matanikau River.

There were no experienced fresh troops on Guadalcanal in early December. The 132d Infantry was fresh but untried, and the veteran Marine and Army units were in little better condition than the 1st Marine Division. All were suffering from general debility, battle weariness, and malaria, and most of the Americal Division units were understrength. On 11 December the Americal Division numbered 13,169 men—23 officers and 3,102 enlisted men below full strength. The 132d, 164th, and 182d Infantry Regiments, with an authorized strength of 3,325 men each, lacked 329, 864, and 869 men, respectively.[20]

General Harmon resorted to emergency measures to increase the strength of the forces on Guadalcanal. With Admiral Halsey's approval, he ordered the ships bearing the 25th Division from Hawaii to sail to Guadalcanal without reloading at New Caledonia. In doing so General Harmon knowingly took a risk, for, as General Marshall warned him on 7 December, shipping space had been too limited for combat-loading, or even unit-loading the ships before they left Pearl Harbor. Discharging these ships in the forward area would be dangerous.[21] But in view of General Patch's urgent need for more troops, combat-loading the 25th Division's ships at Noumea, where dockside congestion had caused a crisis, would delay the landing of the division on Guadalcanal by six

---

[19] Mob Combat Recon Sq, Amer Div, Hist, p. 12.
[20] Amer Div Strength Rpt, 11 Dec 42.
[21] Rad, WDCSA to COMGENSOPAC, 7 Dec. 42. OPD 370.5 PTO Sec. I.

weeks—until early February 1943.[22] General Harmon therefore carried out his plan despite the dangers involved, and the 25th Division, protected by air and surface forces, went to Guadalcanal without taking time to reload at Noumea. The 35th Regimental Combat Team landed at Beach Red on 17 December; it was followed by the 27th Regimental Combat Team on 1 January 1943, and by the 161st Regimental Combat Team on 4 January. All units landed without loss. On 4 January 2d Marine Division headquarters and the 6th Marines, Reinforced, having moved up from New Zealand, also landed, thereby bringing the 2d Marine Division to nearly full strength. General Patch had now, in addition to miscellaneous units, three divisions.

The additional duties assumed by General Patch's staff during December imposed heavy burdens upon it. American Division headquarters, the highest headquarters on Guadalcanal in December, had been acting as a full corps headquarters—acting simultaneously as island headquarters, American Division headquarters, and headquarters for part of the 2d Marine Division. To remedy this situation, General Harmon recommended to General Marshall that a corps headquarters be designated for the Guadalcanal–Tulagi area. General Marshall, who on 5 December had informed General Harmon that all Army Air Force units in the South Pacific Area were to be designated the Thirteenth Air Force, acceded to this request, and on 2 January 1943 General Harmon activated the XIV Corps.[23] The Corps consisted of the American and 25th Divisions, with the 2d Marine Division and other Marine ground forces attached.

General Patch was given the command of the XIV Corps, and General Sebree succeeded to command of the American Division. Headquarters and Headquarters Company, VIII Corps, then in the United States, was redesignated and assigned to the XIV Corps, and in late December Brig. Gen. Robert L. Spragins arrived to assume his duties as XIV Corps chief of staff. The XIV Corps' staff section chiefs assumed their duties on 5 January 1943, but most of the posts at XIV Corps headquarters were manned by American Division staff officers. The American Division staff section chiefs acted simultaneously for their division and as assistant staff section chiefs for the Corps.[24] As late as 1 February 1943 XIV Corps headquarters proper consisted of only eleven officers

---

[22] Hist USAFISPA, Pt. III, II, 646; see also ltr, COMGENSOPAC to WDCSA, 15 Dec 42. OPD 381 PTO Sec. III (12–15–42).

[23] Hist USAFISPA, Pt. I, I, 142. Prior to the activation of the XIV Corps, General Patch's command on Guadalcanal has been informally termed the CACTUS Corps.

[24] Interv with Col Gavan, 14 Nov 46.

Strength of American Forces at Guadalcanal, 7 January 1943 [a]

Unit	Total	Officers	Enlisted men
All units	50,078	2,402	47,676
Americal Division	16,196	837	15,359
132d Infantry Regiment	2,828	122	2,706
164th Infantry Regiment	2,483	116	2,367
182d Infantry Regiment	2,638	125	2,513
147th Infantry Regiment (attached)	2,233	81	2,152
Mobile Combat Reconnaissance Squadron	542	34	508
221st Field Artillery Battalion	[b]532	[b]34	[b]498
245th Field Artillery Battalion	521	29	492
246th Field Artillery Battalion	516	34	482
247th Field Artillery Battalion	482	28	454
Other units[c]	3,421	234	3,187
25th Division	12,629	605	12,024
27th Infantry Regiment	3,315	139	3,176
35th Infantry Regiment	3,306	133	3,173
161st Infantry Regiment	2,065	99	1,966
8th Field Artillery Battalion	572	30	542
64th Field Artillery Battalion	578	30	548
89th Field Artillery Battalion	566	28	538
90th Field Artillery Battalion	128	10	118
Other units[c]	2,099	136	1,963
2d Marine Division	[d]14,733	[d]657	14,076
2d Marines	3,626	154	3,472
6th Marines	4,430	196	4,234
8th Marines	3,605	169	3,436
Other units[c]	3,072	138	2,934
Air units	[d]1,607	[d]157	1,450
Naval units	[d]4,913	146	[d]4,767

[a] Represents effective strength of organic and attached units. Does not include strength of XIV Corps Headquarters troops, data for which are not available.

[b] Represents strength as of 1 February 1943. The 221st FA Battalion landed on 4 January 1943, but was not included in strength report for 7 January.

[c] Consists chiefly of service units, headquarters troops, and miscellaneous attached units.

[d] Adjusted to correct obvious errors in source data.

Source: XIV Corps Strength Reports for 7 January and 1 February 1943. Strength Reports — Americal Division, 11 December 1942–February 1943.

and two enlisted men. The Corps was not only insufficiently staffed, but also lacked service troops and organic corps artillery. It used the 155-mm. guns of the defense battalions and the Army coast artillery battery as corps artillery.

The arrival of reinforcements in late December and early January increased American strength on Guadalcanal sufficiently to make possible the opening of large-scale offensive operations. By 7 January 1943 Allied air, ground, and naval forces in the Guadalcanal area totaled about 50,000 men. The Americal Division numbered about 16,000; the 25th Division, 12,629; the 2d Marine Division, 14,733.[25]

Air Power

By December the difficulties and shortages which had limited the campaigns in the South and Southwest Pacific were partially overcome. In the Solomons, Allied air strength was on the increase. Control of the air and the sea in the southern Solomons enabled Halsey and Turner to send troops and supplies to Guadalcanal regularly. The number of heavy Army bombers in the South Pacific had increased. The veteran 11th Heavy Bombardment Group had been operating in the theater since July, and in November it was reinforced by the 5th Heavy Bombardment Group and the 12th and 44th Fighter Squadrons, which arrived at Espiritu Santo from Hawaii. By November forty B-17's of the two groups were operating in the Solomons, and General Harmon released heavy bombers of the 90th Bombardment Group which he had been authorized to divert en route to the Southwest Pacific. On 20 October twin-engined Army fighter planes (P-38's) had arrived in the South Pacific, but not until November, when Henderson Field was safe from shell fire, could they be based at Guadalcanal. When heavy bombers from Henderson Field raided Buin on 18 November, P-38's escorted the B-17's all the way for the first time.

Unfortunately the B-17's frequently had to be diverted from bombardment to patrol missions. The Navy's twin-engined flying boats (PBY's) were too vulnerable to enemy attack.[26] The B-17's, on the other hand, could patrol over long stretches of water, locate enemy convoys, and beat off attacking Japanese fighter planes. The effectiveness of heavy bombers was also diminished by the fact that most fixed enemy objectives lay beyond the range of bombers based at Espiritu Santo. The heavy bombers when not flying patrol missions were usually limited to the bombardment of shipping and thus did not meet with conspicu-

---

[25] XIV Corps Strength Rpt, 7 Jan 43, in Amer Div Strength Rpt. Figures in the Corps report, incorrectly totaled, have been corrected. The Corps' report does not show the 221st Field Artillery Battalion, which landed on 4 January 1943. As strength figures for this battalion for 7 January 1943 have not yet been found, those for 1 February 1943 have been used to reach the approximately correct figure.

[26] Guadalcanal and the Thirteenth Air Force, p. 78. The Navy's more powerful PB4Y's were not to reach the South Pacific until 1943.

ous success as compared with the dive bombers and torpedo bombers which the Navy had designed for just such work. A sustained air offensive against the enemy in the northern Solomons could not be mounted until a strong bomber force was permanently based at Henderson Field.

Allied air power on Guadalcanal had greatly increased since the grim days in October. On 23 November General Vandegrift reported that eighty-four U. S. Army, Navy, Marine Corps, and Royal New Zealand Air Force planes were operating from Guadalcanal. By 29 November there were 188 aircraft of all types.[27] By December the 1st Marine Air Wing included Marine Air Group 14, with elements of the 12th, 68th, and 339th Fighter Squadrons and of the 70th Medium Bombardment Squadron (equipped with B–26's) of the Army Air Forces attached. The advance elements of Brig. Gen. Francis P. Mulcahy's 2d Marine Air Wing, which was to relieve the 1st Wing, arrived on 26 December.

By December, in spite of all difficulties, air and naval power had almost, but not completely, isolated the Japanese on Guadalcanal. The Tokyo Express could slip through on occasion, but the island's air forces limited its trips. Allied air power was also able to prevent Japanese aircraft from successfully attacking ground installations in force during daylight and from using aircraft for daylight reconnaissance.[28]

Henderson Field was in fair condition by December. Although its operational facilities were still crude, it could support the efficient operation of eighty planes. On returning to the United States after his tour of duty as commander of land-based aircraft in the South Pacific, Admiral McCain had recommended building gasoline storage tanks with a minimum capacity of half a million gallons. He had recommended storage tanks with a million-gallon capacity if Guadalcanal was to be used as a base for further advances,[29] and by December construction of storage tanks with that capacity had begun.[30] Henderson Field could be used in all weathers. By 10 January steel mats had been laid over 320,750 square feet of runway but 600,000 square feet remained without mats. Fighter Strip No. 1, east of Henderson, was being regraded in December but 1,800,000 square feet of matting were required.[31] It was later to serve Navy and

[27] CG 1st Mar Div to COMSOPAC, 2156 of 23 Nov 42; 2328 of 29 Nov 42. SOPAC War Diary.

[28] Amer Div Int Rpt, p. 3.

[29] JPS Minutes, 9 Oct 42.

[30] CINCPAC, Solomons Campaign, 30 Nov 42 to 4–5 Jan 43.

[31] Rad, Guadalcanal to COMAIRSOPAC, 10 Jan 43, XIV Corps G–3 Journal; Guadalcanal and the Thirteenth Air Force, p. 164.

Marine Corps aircraft. The coral-surfaced Fighter Strip No. 2 southwest of Kukum was nearly complete by the end of December. It was to furnish U. S. Army and Royal New Zealand Air Force pilots with an excellent runway. At Koli Point naval construction forces, unhindered by enemy ground forces, had nearly completed the bomber strip, Carney Field.[32]

The daylight air attacks, naval shellings, and artillery fire that had pounded Henderson Field so heavily in October were over, although harassing air raids continued to take place at night. Antiaircraft guns of the Marine Corps defense battalions and, until its relief, of the 1st Special Weapons Battalion defended the airstrips. Automatic weapons ranging in size from .30-caliber water-cooled antiaircraft machine guns to 20-mm. and 37-mm. antiaircraft guns beat off strafers and dive bombers, and 90-mm. guns and searchlights defended the field against high-level bombers.

One of the features of the campaign was the nightly nuisance attacks by the Japanese planes, which the troops called "Louie the Louse," or from the engines' sound, "Washingmachine Charley" and "Maytag Charley." Charley bombed at random and caused little damage, but the bombs forced the troops to take cover in dugouts and foxholes, losing sleep and exposing themselves to malarial mosquitoes. Charley was a difficult target for the antiaircraft guns since he usually flew high and maneuvered violently when searchlights and guns went into action. Night fighting, radar-equipped planes, which would have been effective against him, were not to reach the South Pacific until late in February 1943. On several occasions air forces and antiaircraft batteries successfully co-ordinated fighter attacks with searchlight illumination.

The long-range radar used on Guadalcanal, the SCR 270, functioned fairly well, although the antiaircraft batteries' fire control radar, the SCR 268, was too primitive for accurate fire control. The coastwatching stations supplemented radar to warn the Lunga area of approaching enemy planes, for the enemy occasionally attacked Lunga Point from the south and southwest over the mountains which screened the planes from radar beams.

The American Situation on Guadalcanal

The area of Guadalcanal which was held by American troops in December was not much greater than that captured in the assault landing. The Lunga

---

[32] Rad, CG Guadalcanal to COMAIRSOPAC, 13 Dec 42. Amer Div G–3 Journal.

perimeter had been enlarged in the November offensive to include the Matanikau River and the area west to Point Cruz. By December the American lines extended from Point Cruz south to Hill 66, from there were refused east across the Matanikau River, and joined the old Lunga perimeter line east of the river. At Koli Point Colonel Tuttle's 147th Infantry, the 9th (Marine) Defense Battalion, and the naval construction battalion had established a perimeter defense.

Tulagi, Gavutu, and Tanambogo, successfully stormed on 7–8 August, were in American hands. The Japanese had shelled and bombed these islands but had directed all their ground assaults against Henderson Field. Tulagi Harbor provided a good anchorage for warships and transports. American patrols from Tulagi regularly visited Florida Island across the channel from Guadalcanal, to check on possible enemy forces.

The fundamental importance of health and supply in the American situation on Guadalcanal had not diminished. But by December supply had greatly improved over that of the early days, and a major crisis at Noumea had been surmounted. In November, a break-down in the handling of incoming ships at Noumea threatened to cut off supplies for the Army troops on Guadalcanal. The South Pacific Amphibious Force was already short of ships, and with the torpedoing of the *Alchiba* off Guadalcanal in November Admiral Halsey reported that only four undamaged cargo ships were left in the South Pacific Force.[33] At Noumea the increased flow of supplies and troops from the United States had resulted in a serious congestion of the harbor, where 91 vessels carrying 180,000 tons of cargo were waiting to be unloaded. Eighty-three of the vessels carried supplies and equipment which were to be trans-shipped to the New Hebrides and to Guadalcanal. Noumea, like the few other partially developed ports in the South Pacific, lacked enough men, equipment, and storage and berthing space to unload the ships. Army, Navy, and Marine Corp units had formerly each handled their own supplies, but in late November Admiral Halsey suggested that the Army assume responsibility for loading and unloading ships at Noumea. The Army took over the task immediately. In November 34,327 long tons of cargo had been discharged at Noumea, and in December the amount rose to 126,216 long tons. Cargo shipments to Guadalcanal, which had totaled 5,259 long tons in November, increased to 7,271 long tons in December.[34]

Once supplies reached Guadalcanal, however, further difficulties arose. In the absence of docks, all supplies had to be unloaded from ships standing off-

[33] COMSOPAC to CINCPAC, 0841 of 30 Nov 42. SOPAC War Diary.
[34] Hist USAFISPA, Pt. III, II, 645–48.

SUPPLY TROUBLES *were accentuated by lack of men and equipment to handle incoming shipments of materiel. At Guadalcanal (above) all spare troops were kept busy manhandling supplies from barges to the beach. The rear area supply center at Noumea, New Caledonia, became overburdened and crates were stacked wherever space could be found.*

shore, lightered to the beaches, unloaded, reloaded on trucks and hauled inland to the dispersed dumps. Since the shortage of shipping space stripped units traveling to Guadalcanal of much of their motor transport, there were never enough trucks. As the number of service troops was also inadequate, combat troops as well as native laborers were forced to handle cargo, a duty for which the combat soldiers showed a marked lack of enthusiasm. As General Patch wrote, combat troops were "apathetic toward labor."[35]

Moreover, poor roads hindered the movement of supplies inland. Engineers and pioneers of the 1st Marine Division had built roads and some bridges, and the 57th Engineer Battalion was continuing the work. Known before the war as Government Track, the coast road served as the main route between the Ilu River and Point Cruz. An additional road net served Henderson Field and the infantry positions to the south. The marines had begun a jeep trail southwest from the perimeter toward Mount Austen; the 57th Engineers were to complete this trail, over which supplies for the forthcoming attack on Mount Austen were to be carried. A permanent motor bridge enabled heavy vehicles using the coast road to cross the Matanikau. The coast road supplied the troops near Point Cruz, while jeeps carried supplies to Hill 66 on a trail leading over Hills 73 and 72.

These roads, which rain turned into mudholes, were never completely adequate even in dry weather for the supply of front-line units. Before the American invasion no real motor roads had existed. The Japanese had hacked trails through the jungle but many had been obliterated by the trees and undergrowth. When American troops advanced, the engineers would build supply roads behind them, but since they were muddy and narrow, small supply dumps, widely dispersed as a protection against bombing and shell fire, were situated well forward. Jeeps and hand-carriers usually brought supplies to the units in the front lines. Despite these efforts, American troops in January were frequently to outrun their supplies and in some instances were even to fight for considerable periods without water.

Malaria, too, affected operations. By December 1942 the problem of malaria control had not been solved, nor was it to be solved until after the campaign. Malaria, the greatest single factor reducing the effectiveness of South Pacific troops, caused five times as many casualties as enemy action in the South Pacific. No malaria control personnel had been permitted on Guadalcanal until

[35] Ltr, CG XIV Corps to COMSOPAC, 20 Jan 43, quoted in *ibid.*, 650.

BRIDGES AND ROADS *in Guadalcanal were virtually non-existent when American forces landed. Engineers used native materials, supplemented by imported materials (above) to put a permanent bridge over the Matanikau River, but were unable to do much about jungle roads (below) when it rained.*

mid-November. The island had been occupied almost a year before sufficient aerosol dispensers and insect repellent were available. Quinine was scarce; suppressive atabrine treatment had been inaugurated but had not halted the spread of the disease. Many men swallowed atabrine tablets reluctantly if at all. Many falsely believed that it was poisonous, that it caused sexual impotence, or that it stained the skin permanently. Little had been done to check the breeding of mosquitoes. The natives were all heavily infected, as were the Japanese. Each rain filled the numerous swamps, streams, lagoons, craters, and foxholes, and provided ideal breeding areas for mosquitoes. Malaria discipline had been lax in all units.[36]

Of the ineffective troops in the Army units on Guadalcanal, nearly 65 percent were put out of action by disease as compared with about 25 percent wounded in action.[37] The rate of malaria per 1,000 men per year for units of all services on Guadalcanal was high. It rose from 14 cases per 1,000 in August to 1,664 per 1,000 in October, 1,781 in November, 972 in December, and 1,169 in January 1943.[38] The hospital admission rate from malaria in Army units alone on Guadalcanal from 1 November 1942 to 13 February 1943 averaged 420 admissions per 1,000 men per year.[39]

The Japanese Situation

As the American situation on Guadalcanal improved, the enemy's situation correspondingly deteriorated. By piecemeal commitment the Japanese had dissipated their air, surface, and troop strength. Hard fighting with Americans of all services had cost the enemy dearly, as had his own lack of perception, demonstrated by repeated attacks, without sufficient artillery support, against superior forces. Malnutrition and disease exacted a heavy toll from the enemy on Guadalcanal.

The Japanese Army command in the South Pacific was altered in December when a higher headquarters than that of the *17th Army* moved into Rabaul. On the orders of *Imperial General Headquarters,* Gen. Hitoshi Imamura, commanding the *8th Area Army,* left Java for Rabaul to assume command of

---

[36] *Ibid.,* pp. 618–28. See also Col Dale G. Friend, Rpts, in 101st Med Regt Hist and Rpts, in SGO Files.

[37] SGO, ASF Monthly Prog Rpt, Sec. 7: Health, Jan 45, p. 16.

[38] Hist USAFISPA, Pt. III, II, 632. See also WD Tech Bull Med 6, 15 Jan 44, "Data from Field on Malaria Control."

[39] Health, Jan 45, p. 18.

army operations. General Imamura reached Rabaul on 2 December 1942 and was followed later by his army.[40] On Guadalcanal the forward echelon of *17th Army Headquarters* continued to direct operations. General Hyakutake, the army commander, and his staff remained on the island until February 1943.[41]

In December, the *17th Army* kept the bulk of its combat forces between Point Cruz and Cape Esperance, while patrols covered the south coast. The Japanese front lines extended from the Point Cruz area to the high ground about 4,500 yards inland, curving east about 3,000 yards to include Mount Austen. The only Japanese troops east of the Lunga in December were stragglers. On the island were the remnants of General Maruyama's *2d Division,* General Sano's *38th Division,* and the *Kawaguchi* and *Ichiki Forces.* Maj. Gen. Takeo Ito, Infantry Group commander of the *38th Division,* commanded about 1,000 troops of the *124th* and *228th Infantry Regiments* and supporting units on an inland line extending from Mount Austen to a point about 3,000 yards west. Of this force, Maj. Takeyosho Inagaki with the *2d Battalion, 228th Infantry,* occupied the northeast slopes of Mount Austen. Colonel Oka, with part of the *124th Infantry* and other units, held the center of the line between Mount Austen and the Matanikau, while Col. Masaichi Suemura commanded the *1st* and *3d Battalions* of the *228th Infantry* on the high ground west of the Matanikau. In the coastal area, part of the *2d Division,* operating occasionally under *38th Division* command, and units of the latter division faced the Americans along the Point Cruz–Hill 66 line, while the rest of the *2d Division* was concentrated farther west.[42] In early December the Americans were not completely aware of Japanese strength and dispositions on Guadalcanal, especially on Mount Austen and the hills to the west.

Japanese troop strength had declined from the peak of 30,000 men, reached briefly in November, to average about 25,000 in December. Almost no reinforcements had arrived since the *38th Division* survivors had come ashore from their blazing transports on 15 November. During the entire campaign about 33,600 troops of the *17th Army* and 3,100 of the *Special Naval Landing Forces*

---

[40] USSBS, *Allied Campaign Against Rabaul,* p. 9. This source occasionally calls Imamura's command the *8th Group Army. 17th Army* Opns, I, states that *Headquarters, 8th Area Army* reached Rabaul on 22 November.

[41] *17th Army* Opns, I, II. Many Allied sources affirm that Hyakutake left the island well before February. According to the XIV Corps and Americal Division's intelligence reports, Maruyama directed operations in Hyakutake's absence.

[42] *17th Army* Opns, I; USAFISPA, Japanese Campaign in the Guadalcanal Area, p. 31; XIV Corps, Enemy Opns, p. 5; Amer Div Int Rpt, Tab B.

saw action on the island at various times.[43] In December the Americans underestimated the total strength of the Japanese on Guadalcanal; their estimates varied from 9,100 to 16,000.[44] But all Japanese units were understrength, and many soldiers were unfit for duty.

In all sectors the enemy, incapable of offensive action, had dug in for defense. The front-line troops especially were in poor physical condition. The increasing shortage of supplies had reduced rations to a bare minimum, to less than one-third the regular daily allowance.[45] Stealing of food was common. As the few supplies which were brought in were usually landed near Cape Esperance and carried by hand to the front, rear-area troops fared best. Front-line troops were often reduced to eating coconuts, grass, roots, ferns, bamboo sprouts, and what wild potatoes they could find.[46] There are even a few apparent instances of cannibalism on Mount Austen.[47]

But hunger was not the only serious problem. If malaria decimated the American ranks, it caused havoc among the enemy. Among the Japanese probably every man was a victim. They had no systematic malaria control, few mosquito nets, and inadequate field hospitals. While American troops operated and bivouacked on high open ground whenever possible, the enemy's need for security from air attack made him travel, bivouac, and fight in the jungles, where the Anopheles mosquito breeds in the sluggish streams and swamps. According to enemy figures, of 21,500 casualties, 9,000 died of disease—malaria, malnutrition, beri-beri, and dysentery.[48] Illness and malnutrition weakened the troops so much that late in the campaign one Japanese officer is reported to have classified his men in three groups: those who could move and fight, those who

[43] *17th Army* figures are taken from *17th Army* Opns, II, and from the interrog of Maruyama, Miyazaki, Konuma, and Tajima; those of the *Special Naval Landing Forces* are derived from a table, attached to the latter interrogation, prepared by the *1st Demob Bureau.*

[44] See G–2, Amer Div, draft rpt to G–2, USAFISPA; ltr, Lt Col W. D. Long to Lt Col E. J. Buckley (D–2, 1st Mar Div), 21 Mar 43, G–2, Amer Div, misc ltrs and memos; 1st Mar Div Rpt, V, Annex Y.

[45] *17th Army* Opns, I; Miyazaki, Personal Account, p. 14.

[46] CINCPOA, Weekly Intelligence, 25 Dec 42: Japanese Medical Problems in the South and Southwest Pacific, in MIS Library, Dept of the Army.

[47] Interv with Col Stanley R. Larsen, 19 Aug 46. Colonel Larsen commanded the 2d Battalion, 35th Infantry, on Mount Austen and saw butchered corpses. See also statements by Col R. B. McClure (CO, 35th Inf), 20 Jan 43; Lt Col James L. Dalton, II, 31 Jan 43; Maj Lorne S. Ward, 29 Jan 43; and Lt Col Stuart F. Crawford, (G–2, 25th Div), in 25th Div FO's, in misc USAFISPA docs in files of Hist Div, SSUSA.

[48] *1st Demob Bureau* table, attached to interrog of Hyakutake, et al. *17th Army* Opns, II, gives figures which substantially agree, but shows the total dead as 21,600. Amer Div Int Rpt, Tab B, gives 27,000 enemy dead; Japanese Medical Problems, p. 11, estimates that 2/3 of enemy deaths were caused by illness; XIV Corps, Enemy Opns, gives larger figures—42,554 committed; 24,330 killed; 3,000 evacuated; 14,724 died of wounds or sickness.

could fight only from emplacements, and those who could not fight at all.[49] In several instances when hospitals moved west during the retreats in January and February the medical personnel apparently evacuated only ambulatory patients. That the others were left behind to die or be captured was indicated by the fact that American troops, during the January offensives, were to find numbers of unwounded enemy corpses in abandoned hospital sites.

The Japanese troops lacked food because air and naval power had almost completely isolated them from their bases. They could not use transports for supply and reinforcements.[50] The nocturnal Tokyo Express was able to bring in only a scattering of supplies and reinforcements. The Express made about eleven trips to Guadalcanal between 16 November 1942 and 9 February 1943, and lost ten destroyers sunk and nineteen damaged in the process.[51] To deliver food to Guadalcanal, the Japanese at Rabaul packed rice in empty gasoline drums, roped fifty together, and loaded four of these 50-drum bundles on the deck of each destroyer. The destroyers would then sail down the Slot, arrive at Cape Esperance at night, and throw the drums overboard to float in with the morning tide. Destroyers transported over 20,000 drums, but the troops ashore recovered less than 30 percent. Some were destroyed on the coral reefs, the ropes often broke, and Allied fliers on dawn patrol strafed them whenever possible. When the drum method failed the Japanese tried supply by submarine, but with little success.[52] According to former *17th Army* officers, the Japanese on Guadalcanal not only failed to receive the greater part of their heavy equipment, but also lost all but 10 percent of their ammunition.[53]

Thus it was impossible for the Japanese to undertake offensive operations. Not only were the soldiers too weak, but ammunition stocks were too low. Enemy artillery lacked shells to hit Henderson Field, and Allied aircraft and counterbattery artillery made the extensive use of artillery dangerous.

Farther north, however, enemy activity was increasing. After their failure to retake the Lunga airfields in November, the Japanese had begun to build an airfield at Munda Point on New Georgia, just 207 miles from Henderson Field. It was so well camouflaged that it was not discovered by the Americans until 3 December. Despite almost daily attacks by aircraft, the field was completed by

[49] Amer Div Int Rpt, Tab A, Enemy Opns.

[50] Miyazaki, Personal Account, p. 13.

[51] Amer Div Int Rpt, p. 3.

[52] Miyazaki, Personal Account, p. 13.

[53] *1st Demob Bureau,* Table II.

29 December. Thereafter Guadalcanal-based aircraft struck it regularly to prevent its fighters escorting the Tokyo Express or intercepting Allied bombing formations bound for the Shortlands and Bougainville, and to discourage its bombers from attacking the Lunga airfields.[54]

An Allied victory on Guadalcanal seemed to be assured by December, but only at the cost of more hard fighting. Though weak from hunger and disease, the Japanese were not disposed to surrender and were to continue to fight with bravery and skill.

[54] Guadalcanal and the Thirteenth Air Force, p. 164; Joint Hq, 5th and 11th Bomb Gps (H), Periodic Int Rpt, 1–31 Dec 42, in 11th Bomb Gp Hist.

CHAPTER X

The December Offensive

Although the lack of sufficient troops limited American capabilities, December was not without some bitter fighting. As a preliminary to a corps offensive, American troops began a small offensive designed to capture Mount Austen. The necessity for capturing the mountain had been recognized even before the Marine landing. General Vandegrift had originally planned to capture it together with Lunga Point. He had changed his plans on the discovery that Mount Austen was much farther from Lunga Point than the first maps had indicated. Lacking sufficient troops, he had never tried to hold it permanently. General Harmon had always maintained that Henderson Field would not be secure until the mountain was in American hands. In November he had asked General Vandegrift when he intended to take it; the Marine commander replied, according to Harmon, that he would take it at the earliest opportunity.

Mount Austen, 15–30 December

Plans for the XIV Corps Offensive

The capture of Mount Austen was a necessary prelude to a full-scale corps offensive against the Japanese west of the Matanikau. In early December Admiral Halsey, stating that it would not be possible to "predict the ability of our naval surface forces and air to satisfactorily interdict the operation of Jap submarines and the Tokyo Express into Guadalcanal . . . ," ordered General Harmon to take action necessary to eliminate all Japanese forces on the island.[1] This order gave General Harmon, temporarily, direct authority over tactical operations which he had not previously possessed, for as commander of U. S. Army Forces in the South Pacific he had only administrative authority. In effect, Admiral Halsey had informally deputed to him part of his own tactical authority within a limited area. General Patch's authority over his troops was

[1] Army in the South Pacific, p. 5.

not limited or affected in any way. He was to direct operations on Guadalcanal subject to the direction of Harmon, who was acting for Halsey.

General Harmon immediately flew to Guadalcanal to confer with General Patch. Patch planned to capture Mount Austen immediately. (*Map X*) Once that mountain had been taken and sufficient forces had been assembled, two divisions would attack westward while a third division defended the airfields. While one of the attacking divisions swung over Mount Austen and the hill masses south of Hill 66 to outflank the Japanese, the other would resume the coastal push from the Hill 66–Point Cruz line. The flanking movement would extend the American line west of the Matanikau an additional 3,000 yards inland. The two divisions would continue attacking westward to trap and destroy the Japanese. General Harmon gave his approval to this plan.

Planners also discussed the possibility of sending amphibious expeditions around Cape Esperance to land on the south coast in the enemy's rear, block the trail that ran from Kokumbona over the mountains to Beaufort Bay, and to advance west toward the cape. But these bold shore-to-shore movements could not be executed until more landing craft could be assembled.[2]

Terrain and Intelligence

Mount Austen, a spur of Guadalcanal's main mountain range, juts northward between the Matanikau and Lunga Rivers toward Lunga Point. The 1,514-foot summit lies about six miles southwest of Henderson Field and dominates the surrounding area. It provided the enemy with an excellent observation post from which to survey activity at Lunga Point—traffic at Henderson Field and the fighter strips, unloading of ships, and troop movements. Just as the coastwatchers radioed information on enemy movements to the Allied forces, so Japanese observers could warn their northern bases when bombers left Henderson Field. From the hill they could see the American areas west of the Matanikau, and over the hills west of the mountain into Kokumbona, 9,000 yards to the northwest.[3]

Mount Austen, where the Japanese were to make their strongest defensive effort of the campaign, is not a single peak, but the apex of a confusing series of steep, rocky, jungled ridges. The main ridge forming the summit rises

---

[2] Information on plans in December is derived from: Ltr, Lt Col W. D. Long to Col Buckley; Ltr, COMGENSOPAC to WDCSA, 15 Dec 42. OPD 381 PTO Sec. III (12–15–42); interv with Col Gavan. See also ltr, CTF 62 to COMSOPAC, 2 Nov 42, sub: Outline Plan TF 62 Opns Subsequent to 3 Nov 42, Ser 00353 FE 25 A4–3, in files of Hist Sec, Hq, USMC.

[3] Amer Div Int Rpt, Tab A, Enemy Opns; 35th Inf Journal, 8 Jan 43, in misc USAFISPA docs.

MOUNT AUSTEN'S DOMINANT POSITION *over the Lunga Perimeter and the hills to the west made its capture vital to the American plan. Towering over Henderson Field (above), it was also a good vantage point from which the enemy could watch troop movements westward from the Matanikau line (below).*

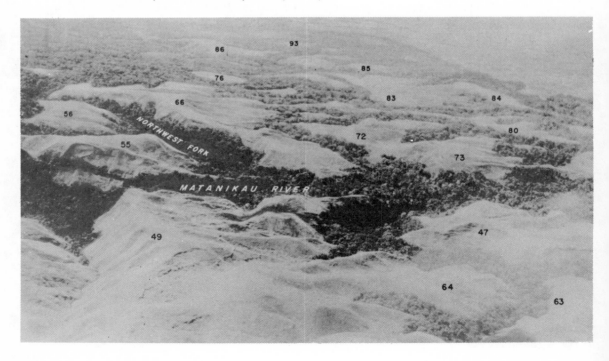

abruptly out of the foothills about two miles south of the shore, and east of the Matanikau River. Aerial photographs do not always give a clear picture of Mount Austen, for a dense forest covers the summit and much of the foothill area is covered by grass. The bare, grassy spaces are not separate hills, though for identification they were assigned numbers. No ridge is usually visible in a single vertical aerial photograph. The actual summit appears to be lower than the open, grassy areas. Hill 27, a separate rocky mound, 920 feet high, lies southwest of the summit. The crest rises just above the surrounding treetops, and is barely visible. Hill 31, a grassy area about 750 yards north of Hill 27, overlooks Lunga Point.

Fifteen hundred yards northwest of Mount Austen, across a deep gorge cut by the Matanikau, lies another hill mass (Hills 43 and 44). A third hill mass (Hills 55–54–50–51–52–53–57), about 900 feet high, lies just north of the first, and is clearly visible from Mount Austen. As General Patch intended to move one division over these hill masses in the southwesterly envelopment, it was first necessary to capture Mount Austen to deny it to the enemy, and to locate and partially roll up his east flank.

In late November and early December it was thought that the Japanese were not holding Mount Austen in strength. Patrols from the 132d Infantry, which was to attack Mount Austen, had confirmed the negative reports by earlier patrols from the 8th Marines and the 182d Infantry.[4] By 15 December, General Patch had reason to change this view. Intelligence reports indicated that the enemy might be building up strength in the south, and that he might attack in force from the south or raid the airfields.[5] On 12 December a night-raiding party had managed to steal through the lines to destroy one P–39 and a gas truck on Fighter Strip No. 2.[6] Two days later the 132d Infantry regimental intelligence officer, four other officers, thirty-five enlisted men, and ten native bearers reconnoitered Mount Austen's northwest slopes. Pushing east, they met fire from a force estimated to include one rifle platoon, four machine guns, and one or two mortars. Receiving orders by radio, the patrol withdrew. On his return to the Lunga perimeter the intelligence officer directed artillery fire on the enemy positions. From the patrol's experience it was concluded that the enemy had occupied Mount Austen. On 15 and 16 December the patrol went up Mount Austen's eastern slopes and reported finding only abandoned Japa-

---

[4] Amer Div Narrative of Opns, p. 5.
[5] Asst Div Comdr, Amer Div, memo, 15 Dec 42. Amer Div G–3 Journal.
[6] Guadalcanal and the Thirteenth Air Force, p. 161.

SUPPLY MOVEMENT TO MOUNT AUSTEN *was accomplished by groups of native bearers called the "Cannibal Battalion," (above) and over Wright Road. Photographed from Hill 29 in January 1943, the road is seen winding northward to the coast. Florida Island is on the right horizon.*

nese positions.[7] It had not found the enemy, who may have been lying quiet, unwilling to disclose his position.[8]

The commanders on Guadalcanal were not fully aware of the extent of the enemy's strength on Mount Austen. Colonel Oka's force, including understrength battalions from the *124th* and *228th Infantry Regiments,* and the *10th Mountain Artillery Regiment,* were then holding positions which extended to the northeast slopes of Mount Austen, and were concentrated in a 1,500-yard-long pillbox line west of the summit on a curved ridge lying between Hills 31 and 27. Supply and evacuation posed difficult problems for the Americans, but for the Japanese they were almost insoluble. They had to depend exclusively upon hand-carriers for rations and ammunition, and received a negligible quantity. There is no evidence to show that Oka's troops were ever reinforced after the 132d Infantry attacked. Most of the enemy wounded were apparently not hospitalized; they either fought on or died in their foxholes and pillboxes. The battalions of the *124th and 228th Regiments* had been on Guadalcanal for periods ranging from several weeks to three months; they had been affected by battle weariness, malnutrition, and disease.

Plans for Taking Mount Austen

By 16 December General Patch was ready to inaugurate preparations for the corps offensive in January by seizing Mount Austen. He ordered the 132d Infantry to occupy Mount Austen at once.[9] The operation was to be conducted under the control of the west sector commander, Col. John M. Arthur, USMC, who reported directly to General Patch.[10] The 132d Infantry, commanded by Col. LeRoy E. Nelson, had landed on Guadalcanal on 8 December, and was completely new to combat. The 3d Battalion, Lt. Col. William C. Wright commanding, was to lead the attack. Lt. Col. Earl F. Ripstra's 1st Battalion (less D Company) was to follow in reserve. The 2d Battalion, commanded by Lt. Col. George F. Ferry, was to remain in the Lunga perimeter defense.

Artillery support for the operation was to be provided initially by the 105-mm. howitzers of the 246th Field Artillery Battalion and the 75-mm. pack howitzers of the 2d Battalion, 10th Marines. Ample additional artillery support was available if needed. On 11 December 1942 there were twenty-eight 75-mm.

---

[7] 132d Inf Unit Repts, 15, 16, 17 Dec 42. Amer Div G–3 Journal.

[8] Interv with Col Gavan.

[9] Amer Div Opn Memo, 16 Dec 42. Amer Div G–3 Journal; 132d Inf Opn Memo No. 3, 16 Dec 42, in 132d Inf Msgs and Ords. No divisional field order has been found.

[10] Interv with Col Gavan.

pack howitzers, thirty-six 105-mm. howitzers, twelve 155-mm. howitzers, and six 155-mm. guns belonging to the Americal Division and attached units in the Lunga area.[11] The Marine Corps battalion moved its pack howitzers to the northwest slopes of Mount Austen, inside the perimeter defense, while Lt. Col. Alexander R. Sewall's 246th Field Artillery Battalion occupied the positions near Fighter Strip No. 2 that it had taken over from the 5th Battalion, 11th Marines. The 246th's positions were much farther from Mount Austen than those of the marines. The two battalions later fired some "Time on Target" (TOT) concentrations. To surprise the enemy troops and achieve the maximum possible destruction by having all initial rounds hit the target simultaneously, each battalion subtracted its shells' time of flight from the time its shells were to hit the target and fired its howitzers on the second indicated.[12] This was probably one of the earliest occasions during World War II when American artillerymen employed TOT in combat, although it should be emphasized that this was not a divisional artillery TOT.

To meet the difficulties of supply and evacuation, the 57th Engineer Battalion was building the rough, slippery, jeep track up the mountain from the coast road. By 20 December the engineers had reached Hill 35, about five miles southwest of Lunga Point. The 60-degree incline of Hill 35 slowed the engineers, for they then had no heavy equipment and only 40 percent of their authorized dump trucks. Jeeps were to carry supplies forward from the coast road to the terminus of the mountain road, from which available soldiers and the "Cannibal Battalion" of native bearers were to hand-carry supplies forward.

Preliminary Operations

The Mount Austen operation was opened on 17 December with a reconnaissance in force to the northeast slopes by L Company of the 132d Infantry, reinforced by about a hundred men from K Company. Patrols from these companies reported finding no Japanese.[13] Early on 18 December L Company marched up the road again ahead of the 3d Battalion's main body to the terminus at Hill 35. (*Map XI*) L Company advanced about 1,000 yards southwest from Hill 35, then swung left (southeast) to enter the jungle on the crest of the mountain. Patrols from L Company had pushed about 500 yards into the jungle by 0930, when fire from hidden enemy riflemen and machine gunners

---

[11] Amer Div Arty Strength Rpt, 11 Dec 42.

[12] Ltr, Lt Col Donald R. Tam (former S–3, 246th FA Bn) to author, 21 Apr 46. Colonel Tam could not remember the date of the TOT.

[13] 132d Inf Unit Rpt, 18 Dec 42.

forced them to take cover. Unable to see the enemy, the company awaited the arrival of the main body which joined it at 1130. At Colonel Wright's request the supporting artillery put fire on the suspected enemy position in front of the 3d Battalion, which did not close with the enemy. The battalion suffered only one casualty on 18 December, a shoulder wound. The troops were worn out, however, by the hard climb in the heat.[14] After the artillery fire the 3d Battalion killed three enemy soldiers, then established a perimeter defense just inside the jungle.[15]

The 132d Infantry continued to underestimate the strength of the enemy defenses. On 18 December, for example, it estimated that a determined westward advance by two battalions would drive the Japanese into the Matanikau River.[16] That this estimate was overly optimistic was soon to be demonstrated.

Three dive bombers (SBD's) bombed and strafed the enemy areas from 0725 to 0735 on 19 December; this was followed by a 5-minute artillery concentration 400 yards in front of the 3d Battalion. Colonel Wright and a three-man artillery liaison party from the 246th Field Artillery Battalion then reconnoitered west into the jungle in front of the 3d Battalion. About 0930 Colonel Wright, who was wearing his insignia of rank, was struck by enemy machine-gun fire. The three artillerymen stayed with him to administer first aid, but the enemy machine guns prevented medical aid men from reaching the colonel and halted all efforts to carry him to safety. He died from loss of blood shortly after noon, whereupon the artillerymen crawled back to the 3d Battalion's lines.

When Colonel Wright fell, the battalion executive officer, Lt. Col. Louis L. Franco, assumed command. At the time he took over the battalion he was 1,000 yards back with the rear echelon and unable to exercise control. The battalion, temporarily without a leader, was partly disorganized[17] and, in the words of one observer, its operations were "obscure."[18]

When Colonel Franco reached the front he organized the efforts of the battalion. Late in the afternoon he sent forward a combat patrol under the regimental intelligence officer. The patrol was guided by the artillery liaison party. Covered by the patrol's fire, the artillerymen crawled forward, rescued a

---

[14] 132d Inf Msg, 1249, 18 Dec 42.

[15] 25th Div Obs Notes, Attack Mt. Austen, in misc USAFISPA docs; 132d Inf Hist, 1 Jan 42–30 Jun 44, gives the same data, but errs in the dates; 132d Inf, Account, Battle Mt. Austen, gives the same data as 132d Inf Hist. 132d Infantry reports often use Hill 27 to mean Mt. Austen's western summit.

[16] 132d Inf Unit Rpt, 18 Dec 42.

[17] Amer Div Narrative of Opns, p. 4.

[18] Notes, Attack Mt. Austen, p. 2.

wounded man lying near by, and pulled Colonel Wright's body back.[19]

The 3d Battalion failed to gain ground on 19 December. Japanese riflemen harassed the troops with fire from concealed positions. A few infiltrated the American lines by slipping through the ravines to harass the supply parties and the engineers cutting the supply trail near Hill 35. At 1700 a concealed enemy automatic weapon opened fire and surprised the combined battalion command post, aid station, and ammunition dump. Simultaneously, at least two enemy riflemen also opened fire on the command post. The headquarters troops cleared the area hastily, and the command post was not reorganized until 1830.[20]

The regimental commander then ordered the reserve 1st Battalion (less D Company) to move southeast to join the left flank of the 3d Battalion south of Hill 19. Both battalions then dug in on a line which faced generally south from a point south of Hill 20, and extended east toward the eastern tip of Hill 21.

The night of 19–20 December was typical of the Mount Austen operation. It was noisy with artillery, small-arms, and automatic weapons fire. American artillery harassed the enemy throughout the night, while Japanese soldiers, attempting to infiltrate the 132d's line, employed noise-making ruses to tempt the Americans to fire and disclose their positions.

On 20 December the 1st Battalion sent out patrols in an unsuccessful effort to find the enemy's east flank, while Japanese riflemen and patrols harassed the 132d Infantry's flanks and rear.[21] On 21 December General Sebree ordered the 132d Infantry to cut the Maruyama Trail, which, he thought, lay across its left front.[22] Accordingly C Company advanced 1,000 yards to the south but found no enemy troops and no trail.

Meanwhile, getting supplies to the two front line battalions was proving difficult. Wright Road was a narrow, tortuous trail fit only for jeeps, and the heavy rains made its steep grades slick and dangerous. Jeeps could bring supplies to Hill 35, the point to which the engineers had pushed the road by 20 December, but beyond Hill 35 all ammunition, water, food, replacement parts, and medical supplies had to be hand-carried forward over rough, wooded slopes. Raiding enemy riflemen led the regimental commander, who was concerned about the security of the supply line, to request the Americal Division

[19] Amer Div G–3 Journal, 19 Dec 42.
[20] Notes, Attack Mt. Austen, p. 2.
[21] 132d Inf Unit Rpt, 20 Dec 42.
[22] Msg, Asst Div Comdr Amer Div to CO 132d Inf, 1440, 21 Dec 42. 132d Inf Journal.

headquarters to use the 2d Battalion, 132d Infantry, and the Mobile Combat Reconnaissance Squadron to protect the route.[23] Division headquarters, asserting that the supply line was not in serious danger, denied this request.[24]

The 101st Medical Regiment's Collecting Company, assisted by the 25th Division Collecting Company, was having trouble in evacuating wounded and sick. Litter bearers carried them to battalion aid stations 100 yards behind the firing line. Serious cases were carried in 100-yard relays to the forward collecting station on Hill 35, and from there jeep-ambulances carried them to the Lunga perimeter. Carrying the litters up and down ridges and through ravines was so exhausting that bearers had to be relieved and rested after one or two trips.[25] The medical aid men were fired on so frequently that they began to discard their arm brassards in favor of weapons. As carrying both wounded men and rifles at the same time proved awkward, two-man escorting parties armed with rifles and submachine guns escorted the litter bearers. Later in the operation, engineers and medical men fixed skids on litters to slide them down hills, and also rigged pulleys and steel cables to carry the litters across the deepest ravines.[26]

Resolute patrolling on 23 December produced more significant results than did the patrolling on 20 and 21 December. The 1st Battalion patrols covered 1,000 yards they had previously penetrated, then reconnoitered 500 yards farther toward the south and west. When they found neither Japanese nor trails, regimental headquarters concluded that the Maruyama Trail did not cross Mount Austen but circled along its southern slopes to reach the upper Lunga. In the north a 3d Battalion patrol advanced westward from the summit, skirting the southeast grassy area of Hill 30, and reached Hill 31, another grassy area more than 1,000 yards west of the 132d Infantry's line. The patrol, finding only abandoned enemy bivouacs around Hill 31, turned south and advanced a short distance before turning east to return to the American lines. On the return trip the patrol encountered small-arms fire. It returned the fire, killed one Japanese, and reached the lines without loss.[27]

As the patrol had found a safe route to Hill 31, Colonel Nelson changed the direction of his attack. At 2000, 23 December, he ordered the 3d Battalion

[23] Msg, CO 132d Inf to Hq Amer Div, 0950, 21 Dec 42. 132d Inf Journal.

[24] Msg, Asst Div Comdr Amer Div to CO 132d Inf, 1440, 21 Dec 42.

[25] Lt Col Raymond Bunshaw (25th Div), Recon Rpt, 31 Dec 42, in misc USAFISPA docs.

[26] Col Dale G. Friend, Rpt, in 101st Med Regt Hist and Rpts, in SGO files.

[27] 132d Inf Rpt, 23 Dec 42.

THE GIFU, *Japanese strong point in Mount Austen, lay on the jungled slopes between Hills 31 and 27, at the top of the picture. This scene was photographed from an airplane dropping supplies to troops on Hill 44 west of the Gifu, where a Japanese mortar burst shows. Hill 44 is separated from Mount Austen by the Matanikau River gorge.*

to move west over the patrol's route and prepare to attack toward Hill 27 from the north. The 1st Battalion was to follow the 3d Battalion west to cover the open areas (Hills 20, 28, 29, and 30) and to be in a position to assist the leading battalion, protect the supply route, and assist in carrying supplies forward.[28]

Attacks Against the Gifu Strong Point, 24–30 December

The 3d Battalion left its area at 0730, 24 December, in column of companies. L Company again led, followed by I and Headquarters Companies, the medical detachment, and M and K Companies. The battalion reached Hill 31 in the afternoon after routing some enemy riflemen who tried to oppose the advance. It then started a push south into the jungle. As the troops moved up the grassy, open slopes of Hill 31 they were halted by heavy machine-gun fire from well-concealed positions. The battalion had not suffered any casualties that day, but Colonel Franco, the battalion commander, decided that it was too late in the day to develop the enemy position and continue the attack. The 3d Battalion established a perimeter defense for the night in the ravine between Hills 31 and 32.[29]

Meanwhile the reserve 1st Battalion had completed its move. All companies were reported in position by 1230. B Company held the west spur of Hill 30, C Company, Hill 29, and A Company, Hill 20.[30]

The machine-gun fire which had halted the 3d Battalion's attack came from the strongest Japanese defensive position on Guadalcanal—the Gifu strong point. Its garrison, about five hundred men from Oka's forces, had given it the name of a prefecture in Honshu. The Gifu lay between Hills 31 and 27, west of the summit of Mount Austen. The strongest part of the area was a horseshoe-shaped line of about forty-five inter-connecting pillboxes between the two hills. Arranged in a staggered formation, they were mutually supporting. The pillboxes were made of logs, and were dug into the ground and revetted inside and out with earth. The roofs were three logs thick; the walls, two logs. Earth and foliage concealed and protected the pillbox tops, which rose less than three feet above the surface of the ground.

Each pillbox contained at least one and sometimes two machine guns, plus two or three riflemen. Supporting riflemen and light machine gunners outside

[28] 132d Inf Journal, 23 Dec 42.

[29] 132d Inf Unit Rpt, 24 Dec 42, states that the 3d Battalion had reached a point 450 yards from Hill 27. The battalion either mistook the summit for Hill 27, or overestimated its progress, for a point 450 yards north of Hill 27 was inside the Gifu.

[30] Overlay attached to 132d Inf Unit Rpt, 24 Dec 42.

the pillboxes had prepared positions under the bases of mahogany and banyan trees, and some were reported, probably erroneously, to have established themselves in the treetops. Foliage concealed the fire lanes, and in the thick, dark forest the well-camouflaged pillboxes were almost invisible. The machine guns in the positions covered all approaches with interlocking bands of fire, and the American infantrymen were to have great difficulty in finding their exact locations. When one machine gun was knocked out the Japanese would redistribute their automatic weapons.[31]

Mortar fire usually did little damage to the Gifu. The 105-mm. howitzer was to prove more effective, but only direct hits could damage the pillboxes. Anything lighter was ineffective, and less plunging fire burst in the trees.[32] Fuzed charges of high explosive could have destroyed the pillboxes had the soldiers been able to get close enough to place them. Flame throwers were not then in use. The attacking troops, of course, did not possess exact knowledge about the Gifu. Whenever they moved into the jungle, heavy fire would force them down before they could close in to locate the pillboxes.

The enemy position, though strong, was not invulnerable. It was a fixed position, but the Japanese were unable to supply or reinforce it. The attacking American forces had a preponderance of artillery support, while the Japanese, apparently lacking sufficient ammunition, seldom used artillery on Mount Austen. The west side of the Gifu was weak, and the omission of Hill 27 from the perimeter of the strong point left the Gifu open to eventual envelopment. On 25 December General Sano, commanding the *38th Division*, tried to raise morale with an "Address of Instruction." He assured his men that the Americans had lost their fighting spirit and promised that patient endurance of starvation by the Japanese would soon be rewarded by air, ground, and naval reinforcements. Sano, urging his troops to resist with "desperate determination," referred slightingly to the American reliance on fire power and faith in "material substance."[33]

The attack of the 132d Infantry was renewed on Christmas Day. The three rifle companies of the 3d Battalion were to advance southward in line from Hill 31 toward Hill 27. M Company was in reserve. At 0930 the rifle companies,

[31] Amer Div Int Rpt, Tab A; 132d Inf S–2 Rpt, 7 Jan 43; Capt Gerald H. Shea, "Lessons from Guadalcanal," *Infantry Journal* (July 1943), pp. 9–10; interv with Col Larsen. Americal Division sources estimate 75 pillboxes in the Gifu, but Larsen says there were about 45.

[32] 132d Inf S–2 Rpt, 7 Jan 43. Amer Div Journal.

[33]. XIV Corps Trans. Amer Div G–2 Journal.

supported by 60-mm. mortar fire, began advancing from the open area into the jungle. As the men entered the jungle their movements were impeded by the rocky terrain.[34] The Japanese maintained rifle and machine-gun positions out beyond the pillbox line to prevent the attackers from drawing close. The Americans were forced to fight for each yard of ground against an invisible enemy.[35] By 1335, after moving a short distance, the American companies had been completely halted by machine-gun and rifle fire from their front and flanks. Patrols then attempted to locate the enemy's right and left flanks, but Japanese fire halted their movements. The battalion had by that time lost three officers and nine enlisted men killed and sixteen enlisted men wounded. The regimental commander ordered the troops to retire to their original positions while howitzers shelled the enemy.

As a result of the day's action, the regimental commander concluded that the Japanese had built a perimeter defense in the area. He decided to resume the attack on the next morning. The 3d Battalion was to deliver a frontal attack while the 1st Battalion covered the 3d Battalion's left flank, and moved 1,000 yards to the south to establish a position from which patrols could deploy to locate the enemy flanks.[36]

At 1030, 26 December, after an artillery and aerial bombardment, the 3d Battalion again tried to move forward. K Company advanced on the right (west), I Company on the left (east). L Company was held in reserve on Hill 31. The 1st Battalion (less C Company) covered the 3d Battalion's left flank, while C Company covered the 1st Battalion's rear from Hills 29 and 30. The 3d Battalion was able to advance only to the line reached on the previous day. Heavy machine-gun fire halted the assault companies again. Soldiers from K Company located one machine-gun position and killed nine Japanese with grenades. Meanwhile B Company, given the mission of finding the enemy's east flank, had been halted by machine-gun fire. At 1600 the troops dug in along the south edge of Hill 31. K Company held the right, I and B Companies the center, and A Company held the left flank. The day's attack cost the 3d Battalion five killed and twelve wounded. In addition twenty-one sick men were evacuated on 26 December.[37] Nine Japanese were known to have been killed.[38]

[34] Interv with Lt Col John Hill (former FO, 221st FA bn), 19 Jun 46.

[35] Interv with Col Gavan.

[36] Msg, CO 132d Inf to G-3 Amer Div, 0830, 26 Dec 42. Amer Div G-3 Journal; msg, CO 132d Inf to CO 1st Bn, 132d Inf, 0725, 26 Dec 42. 132d Inf Journal.

[37] 132d Inf Unit Rpt, 26 Dec 42.

[38] 132d Inf ExO Rpt, 2005, 26 Dec 42. Amer Div G-3 Journal

The Gifu was still intact, but the 132d now held a line between the Gifu and Hill 31, from which the enemy could no longer observe the Lunga area.

The regimental commander decided to use both battalions in the next day's attack. While the 3d Battalion delivered a holding attack, A, B, and C Companies were to swing south and east to find the enemy flanks.[39] The 3d Battalion moved forward at 0800 but was halted by machine-gun fire. The 1st Battalion meanwhile moved south in a column of companies. But it had become confused in the jungle. Ordered to assemble between Hills 29 and 30, the 1st Battalion actually assembled in the ravine between Hills 30 and 31, 400 yards too far to the west.[40] Its right flank closely crowded the left flank of the 3d Battalion, making free maneuver impossible. In the lead, B Company ran into the Gifu line instead of outflanking it. As B Company was quickly halted by machine guns, A Company then deployed to the left where it met less fire, for the Gifu's main eastern bulge did not extend east of Hill 30.

Patrols on 27 and 28 December could find no gaps in the enemy lines, nor any flanks, but on 29 December an 8-man patrol from the 1st Battalion brought in valuable information. It had found a clear route to Hill 27. Leaving Hill 29 and advancing south for 1,500 yards, it had turned west and advanced 200 yards before returning at 1330.[41] By advancing due south from Hill 29, the patrol had avoided the eastern bulge of the Gifu, and found the route by which Hill 27 could be economically assaulted.

By the end of December the battalions were dispirited[42] and in poor physical condition. Between 19 and 30 December the two battalions had lost 34 killed, 129 wounded, 19 missing, and 131 sick and evacuated, a total of 313 casualties.[43] Each battalion had been understrength at the outset, and by 28 December effective strength in both battalions totaled only 1,541.[44]

The Capture of Hill 27

The Plan

Although the attack of the 132d Infantry had bogged down, the American generals agreed that the Mount Austen operation should be continued. At a

[39] Msg, ExO 132d Inf to G–3 Amer Div, 26 Dec 42. Amer Div G–3 Journal.
[40] 132d Inf Hist, p. 7.
[41] 132d Inf Unit Rpt, 29 Dec 42.
[42] Msg, CO 132d Inf to G–3 Amer Div, 0830, 26 Dec 42.
[43] 132d Inf Unit Rpts, 19–30 Dec. 42.
[44] 132d Inf Unit Rpt, 28 Dec 42.

conference held at General Patch's command post on 29 December, Generals Harmon, Patch, Collins, and Sebree decided to attempt to complete the capture of Mount Austen because it was an essential preliminary to the corps offensive planned for January.[45]

The 132d's commander believed that a co-ordinated attack by the 1st and 3d Battalions from the north coupled with a wide envelopment by the 2d Battalion, would capture Hill 27.[46] The 132d Infantry's Field Order No. 1, issued on 30 December 1942, announced the plan for continuing the attack by taking Hill 27. The 3d Battalion was to continue attacking south from Hill 31 while the 1st Battalion pushed against the enemy's eastern line. To secure sufficient space for maneuver, the 1st Battalion was to jump off from assembly areas east of Hill 30, advance southward, then swing southwest to attack Hill 27.

The fresh 2d Battalion, commanded by Lt. Col. George F. Ferry, was to deliver the main attack. On 28 December the regimental commander was informed that this battalion would be released to him, and regimental headquarters immediately began to plan for its employment. The battalion executive officer and each company commander were ordered to reconnoiter the routes leading to Hill 27.

To capture Hill 27 from the south the 2d Battalion was to make a wide envelopment, starting from Hill 11 in a southwesterly direction. When the battalion reached a point southeast of Hill 27, it was to turn to the northwest and attack up the south slopes of Hill 27. Each battalion would be responsible for the security of its flanks.[47] H Hour was originally set for 0630, 1 January 1943, but was postponed to 0630, 2 January 1943, when the 2d Battalion's progress up Wright Road proved slow.[48] The 2d Battalion was to be in position southeast of Hill 27 on the night prior to the regimental attack.

While patrols from the 1st and 3d Battalions reconnoitered the enemy lines, the 2d Battalion left the perimeter defense on 30 December to march up Wright Road to Hill 11, where it bivouacked on the night of 31 December 1942–1 January 1943. At daybreak on New Year's Day the battalion left Hill 11. (*Map XII*) Hill 27 lies less than one air mile from Hill 11, but the enveloping march up and down almost vertical slopes covered 6,000 yards.[49] The terrain

---

[45] USAFISPA Guadalcanal ms No. 2, Ch. VIII, pp. a47–48.

[46] 132d Inf Unit Rpt, 29 Dec 42.

[47] 132d Inf FO No. 1, 30 Dec 42, in 132d Inf FO's and Msgs.

[48] Ltr, Col Arthur to Hist Sec, Hq, USMC, 11 Oct 45.

[49] Gavan, Personal account, p. 4.

THE MOUNT AUSTEN BATTLE AREA *viewed from the coast just east of the Matani-kau River (lower right). Light portions of the picture are open, grass-covered hills; dark areas are dense jungle.*

proved so difficult that on 2 January 175 litter bearers were to take five hours to evacuate 20 casualties over the same route.[50] Since the crest of Hill 27 was nearly invisible from the jungle, an airplane, gunning its engine at intervals, flew between Hill 11 and the objective every fifteen minutes to help orient the scouts. The 2d Battalion was fired on by a few enemy riflemen but did not delay its approach march, and the battalion arrived at the day's objective—the southeast slope of Hill 27—by 1600 without losing a man. Colonel Ferry was confirmed in his belief that the fire from the scattered Japanese riflemen usually called "snipers" was not dangerous when the troops kept moving.

Meanwhile the commander of the 132d Infantry, who was suffering from malaria and the debilitating effects of the tropics, had asked to be relieved.[51] Col. Alexander M. George took over command of the regiment and arrived at the 132d Infantry's forward command post at 0915, 1 January. One of his first acts was to stage a dramatic exhibition to demonstrate to the tired battalions facing the Gifu that Japanese small-arms fire was generally ineffective against a moving target. Clad in shorts and a fatigue cap, and armed with two .45-caliber automatic pistols and an M1 rifle, Colonel George inspected the front lines. He walked along erect in full view of the soldiers of the 1st and 3d Battalions. Some soldiers, unaware of his identity, shouted to him to take cover, but Colonel George finished his tour. Japanese soldiers in the jungle helped him to prove his point by shooting at him repeatedly but inaccurately.[52]

Artillery support for the regimental offensive of 2 January was heavier than on previous occasions. It included the 105-mm. howitzers of the 247th Field Artillery Battalion, the 75-mm. pack howitzers of the 3d Battalion, 10th Marines, and the 155-mm. howitzers of the recently landed B Battery, 90th Field Artillery Battalion, 25th Division.[53]

Operations of the 3d and 1st Battalions, 2 January

The 132d Infantry moved to the attack at 0630, 2 January. The 3d Battalion, pouring fire into the jungle in its zone, was able to advance in line from Hill 31 for a short distance into the jungle, although I Company on the left met heavy fire. At 1400 the battalion established positions just south of the tree

---

[50] Bunshaw Recon Rpt, pp. 14–15.

[51] 132d Inf Hist, p. 7; intervs with Gen Sebree and Cols Gavan, Long, and Hill; Amer Div Periodic Rpt, 15–31 Dec 42, in USAFISPA G–3 Periodic Rpt, 15–31 Dec 42.

[52] Interv with Col Hill.

[53] 247th FA Bn Journal, 2 Jan 43; 3d Bn, 10th Mar, Unit Rpt, 2 Jan 43; 90th FA Hist Bn, 1 Jan 43–30 Jun 43, p. 1. (The bulk of 25th Div records are in HRS DRB AGO). B Battery was the advanced echelon of the 90th Field Artillery Battalion.

line on Hill 31. In the day's fighting the battalion killed fifteen Japanese and lost four killed and eighteen wounded.

The 1st Battalion had moved in column to the southwest out of the ravine between Hills 29 and 30 simultaneously with the 3d Battalion's attack. When fire from Japanese patrols hit C Company which was leading, it deployed while A Company moved south and east to bypass the Japanese, and then turned southwest again, followed by B Company. By 1000 A Company had reached a point just east of the Gifu's eastern bulge. Before the end of the day C Company cleared out the enemy in its front and rejoined the main body. The 1st Battalion then dug in on a line east of the Gifu. The left flank lay near Hill 27, but a 200-yard gap remained between the 1st and 3d Battalions. During the day the 1st Battalion killed twenty-five Japanese, C Company accounting for most of them. Two 1st Battalion soldiers were killed and four were wounded.

Operations of the 2d Battalion

In a difficult zone of action, the 2d Battalion was able to take its objectives in one of the day's most successful operations. The battalion's roundabout march through the jungle on the previous day had not alerted the Japanese. At 0630 the battalion moved out of its bivouac area to attack; it advanced in column of companies with each company in single file. As the battalion began the climb up the southeast slopes about 0730, the troops deployed as much as the terrain would permit. E Company advanced on the left, F Company on the right, while G and H Companies were held in reserve. The climb was hard. Perspiration soaked the men's clothing and cut through the camouflage blacking on their faces. The slippery slopes delayed their advance, but no Japanese opened fire.

By 0907 the leading assault troops gained the summit without firing a shot, and by 1130 all assault troops had reached the top. The Japanese had been completely surprised. As E and F Companies reached the top they saw a 3-inch mountain howitzer in the open about 100 yards north of the crest. The enemy crew was sprawled at ease in the shade about thirty yards from the howitzer. The Japanese artillerymen ran for their weapon, but riflemen of the assault companies picked off each gunner before he could reach it.[54]

The 2d Battalion began to organize Hill 27 for defense, but digging in on the rocky crest was slow work. Like nearly all Army and Marine Corps units on Guadalcanal, the battalion was suffering from serious shortages, and did

---

[54] Interv with Col Long, 31 May 44.

not possess enough entrenching tools. Before the troops could complete their
foxholes and machine-gun emplacements, the Japanese north of Hill 27 recovered from their surprise and attempted to recapture the hill. Using mortars,
grenade dischargers, machine guns, rifles, and some artillery, they poured a
heavy fire on the exposed troops. An artillery forward observer on Hill 27
describes the fire fight:

> Then all hell broke loose. Machine guns and rifles pinged from all directions. Snipers
> fired from trees . . . Crossfire cut down our boys who were over the hill . . . Our Garands
> [M1 rifles] answered the fire and the battle was on. Enemy "Knee mortars" [grenade dis-
> chargers] popped on our lines with painful regularity. Our own 60's [mortars] opened and
> neutralized them only to have the shells start lobbing in from a different direction.[55]

In forty minutes, as the troops dug in under fire, the 2d Battalion lost eight
men killed and seventy wounded but they held the hill against the six successive infantry counterattacks launched by the Japanese in the afternoon.[56] After
mortar fire the Japanese infantry would rush southward against the American
lines, but the 2d Battalion beat off each assault.

In the late afternoon the 2d Battalion moved back off the exposed crest for
the night and dug in on the reverse slope, about 100 yards south of the military
crest where the hill was narrower. During the night of 2–3 January the battalion was almost surrounded, for the Japanese had penetrated to positions on
the north, northwest, and southwest of Hill 27. Heavy artillery concentrations
on the enemy's positions prevented him from getting close enough to the 2d
Battalion to break its lines. On one occasion, when enemy troops climbed the
north slopes to set up machine guns which could have covered the 2d Battalion's lines, the 3d Battalion, 10th Marines, placed one concentration directly
in front of the lines. The shells exploded between the Americans and the Japanese, who were unable to get even one gun into action. The Japanese employed
the standard ruse of firing mortar shells into the American lines while the
American artillery shells were bursting—a ruse designed to make the American
infantrymen think their own artillery fire was falling short. Some cried "cease
fire," but the forward observer kept the artillery firing.[57] By dawn the last
enemy soldier had been killed or driven off. The 2d Battalion moved back to
the military crest of Hill 27 to dig in securely, and H Company moved its
heavy weapons up to the hilltop.

[55] Capt John F. Casey, Jr., "An Artillery Forward Observer on Guadalcanal," *Field Artillery Journal,*
August 1943 (XXXIII, 8), 564.

[56] 132d Inf Unit Rpt, 2 Jan 43.

[57] Casey, *op. cit.,* p. 566.

On 3 January the 1st Battalion, attempting to push west to straighten the bulge in the line, established contact on its left with the 2d Battalion. By 1000, 4 January, patrols from companies of the 1st and 3d Battalions had met at a point about 500 yards south of the ravine between Hills 31 and 30.

The Results

The 132d Infantry was ordered to dig in and hold its gains and on 4 January it began to build a strong half-moon-shaped line around the eastern bulge of the Gifu between Hills 31 and 27. The troops built log-covered foxholes and wired in the lines. The addition of D Company, which was relieved from the Lunga perimeter defense, enabled Colonel George to place one machine gun platoon on the line in support of each rifle company. Every heavy weapons company sent one mortar platoon to form a provisional 81-mm. mortar battery on the reverse slope of Hill 29. The 132d Infantry's operations from 1 to 3 January had ringed the Gifu strong point on the north, east, and south with a strong line which was to prove impervious to enemy counterattacks.

Hard hit by battle fatigue, malaria, dysentery, and casualties, the 132d was incapable of further offensive action. It held the line until relieved by the 2d Battalion, 35th Infantry, of the 25th Division. During its twenty-two days on Mount Austen the 132d Infantry lost 112 men killed, 268 wounded, and 3 missing; it estimated that during the same period it had killed between 400 and 500 Japanese.[58] Part of Mount Austen was still in Japanese hands, but the 132d's accomplishments were of great value. Observation of the perimeter was denied to the Japanese, and the XIV Corps' troops could be safely deployed in the forthcoming southwesterly operations. The 132d Infantry had located and partly rolled up the Japanese east flank. With the arrival of the 25th Division, preparations could be made for more ambitious efforts.

[58] 132d Inf Hist, p. 9.

CHAPTER XI

XIV Corps' First January Offensive: The West Front

General Patch, it will be remembered, had ordered the attack against Mount Austen in December as a preliminary to a large offensive in January. Once the 132d Infantry had taken Hill 27 and encircled the east portion of the Gifu, it became possible for troops to operate over the hills west of Mount Austen in a drive, beginning on 10 January 1943, which was designed to destroy the Japanese or drive them from Guadalcanal.

Except for the attacks against Mount Austen, the American lines in the west sector had not changed substantially since November. The west line, running south from Point Cruz, was refused eastward at Hill 66, and joined the old perimeter defense line at the Matanikau River. South of the perimeter defense the 132d Infantry was facing the Gifu garrison between Hills 31 and 27 on Mount Austen.

In late December General Patch had ordered the west sector extended to provide more maneuver room for the projected January offensive, and to ensure the unhindered construction of a supply road west of the Matanikau.[1] The Americal Division's Reconnaissance Squadron had seized Hill 56—an isolated eminence about 600 yards southeast of Hill 66—against scattered opposition, while the 1st Battalion, 2d Marines, had taken Hills 55 and 54 west of the Matanikau. There are no ridges connecting Hills 56 and 66, or 56 with 55. The troops did not hold a continuous line, but patrols covered the deep canyons between the hills.

The supply road in question was an extension of Marine Trail, a track which led from the coast road southward along the east bank of the Matanikau to Hill 49. By 5 January Americal Division engineers had built a motor bridge across the Matanikau at the foot of Hill 65. Bulldozing the road, they had reached the 900-foot summit of Hill 55 by 9 January.

[1] Ltr, Col Arthur to Hist Sec, Hq, USMC, 11 Oct 45.

By the first week of January 1943, the divisions of the XIV Corps, it will be recalled, numbered over 40,000 men, as compared with less than 25,000 of the Japanese *17th Army* on Guadalcanal. All three combat teams of Maj. Gen. J. Lawton Collins' 25th Division had landed on Guadalcanal between 17 December 1942 and 4 January 1943, and bivouacked east of the Lunga River. Headquarters of the 2d Marine Division and the reinforced 6th Marines, Col. Gilder T. Jackson commanding, had reached Guadalcanal on 4 January to join the rest of the division. Brig. Gen. Alphonse De Carre, the assistant division commander, led the 2d Marine Division on Guadalcanal.[2]

Although the XIV Corps' troop strength and materiel sufficed for an offensive, the transportation of supplies to the front prior to and after 10 January was difficult. Poor roads and lack of sufficient motor transport slowed the movement of supplies to all units. Only the indispensable, rugged ¼-ton truck (jeep) could negotiate the rough corduroy trails and steep hills of the southern sector. The 25th Division's infantry units, operating in that area, were to depend almost entirely upon jeeps and hand-carriers for ammunition, food, water, and for evacuation. The supply of the 2d Marine Division was easier over the coast road and lateral trails.

At the start of the January offensives the Japanese positions west of the Matanikau were substantially the same as in December. The enemy had concentrated considerable strength between Point Cruz and Kokumbona. He did not hold a continuous line on the uphill flank but rather a series of strong points with patrols and riflemen covering the areas between. In the coastal sector the enemy continued to employ the north-south ravines to good advantage. By placing machine guns at the head of a draw the Japanese could enfilade with flanking fire any troops attempting to advance west. Thus a few Japanese could delay or halt hundreds of Americans. American headquarters believed that the Japanese held strongly the high ground south of Hill 66 and west of the Matanikau.[3] In the Gifu on Mount Austen soldiers from the *124th* and *228th Infantry Regiments* continued to resist and some elements of the same regiments, supported by artillery and mortars, were occupying areas to the west.

General Patch explained his plan for the first offensive in a letter to General Collins dated 5 January 1943. (Appendix B) He ordered the 25th Division,

---

[2] Maj Gen John Marston, USMC, CG, 2d Marine Division, remained in Wellington, N. Z. Since the Army furnished the majority of troops on Guadalcanal in January, General Patch was to command. General Marston, his senior in rank, remained in New Zealand. See USMC, Guadalcanal Campaign, p. 90.

[3] Ltr, Col Long to Col Buckley, 21 Mar 43.

then east of the Lunga River, to relieve the 132d Infantry on Mount Austen without delay and to seize and hold a line approximately 3,000 yards west of Mount Austen. (*Map XIII*) The 2d Marine Division was to maintain contact with the right flank of the 25th Division, which would provide for the security of its own left flank. General Patch gave General Collins the authority to deal directly with the 2d Marine Air Wing commander in securing close air support.

General Patch ordered the Americal Division Artillery and one recently arrived 155-mm. howitzer battery and one 155-mm. gun battery of the Corps Artillery to support the 2d Marine Division's advance along the coast and to be prepared to reinforce the 25th Division Artillery. The 75-mm. pack howitzers of the 2d Battalion, 10th Marines, were to support the 25th Division Artillery.[4] The Americal Division was to hold the perimeter defense from 9 to 26 January. Only its artillery, the Reconnaissance Squadron, the 182d Infantry, and the 2d Battalion of the 132d Infantry were to take part in the XIV Corps' January offensives.

Capture of the Galloping Horse

The 25th Division's Preparations

The offensive in January was to be General Collins' first combat experience. Graduated from the U. S. Military Academy in 1917 at the age of twenty, he had been sent to Germany to serve with the Army of Occupation in 1919. From 1921 to 1931 he attended and instructed in various Army schools, and was graduated from the Command and General Staff School in 1933. After a tour of duty in the Philippines, he was graduated from the Army Industrial and War Colleges. He taught at the War College for two years, served for several months with the War Department General Staff, and in 1941 became Chief of Staff of the VII corps, an organization which he was to command in the European Theater of Operations during 1944 and 1945. Immediately after the Japanese attack on Pearl Harbor in 1941, Collins became Chief of Staff of the Hawaiian Department and in May 1942 he was made a major general and given the command of the 25th Division.

Upon receipt of General Patch's orders, the 25th Division made prepara-

---

[4] 25th Div, Opns on Guadalcanal 17 Dec 42–5 Feb 43, App. II. The parts of this volume dealing with the 25th Division are largely based on 25th Div Opns. In his first radio messages General Patch, for security, referred to this operation as a reconnaissance in force, although it was actually a planned offensive. See memo, CG XIV Corps for COMGENSOPAC, 2145 of 16 Jan 43, in USAFISPA G–3 Worksheet File, 1–15 Jan 43.

THE FIRST JANUARY OFFENSIVE ZONE *was west of the Matanikau and Army fighting was concentrated in the area of Hills 54, 55, 56 (above). From Hill 42 on Mount Austen's northwest slopes, the sector could be seen clearly by 25th Division troops resting before the offensive started.*

tions for the attack. Patrols examined all ground which could be covered on foot. General Collins, Brig. Gen. John R. Hodge, the assistant division commander, Brig. Gen. Stanley E. Reinhart, the artillery commander, staff officers, all regimental commanders, and most battalion commanders flew over the division's zone of action. Air photographs and observation gave a good view of the open country, but jungle obscured the canyons, valleys, and ravines.

Intelligence officers of the 25th Division had little information on the enemy's strength and dispositions in the division's zone, but they did know that the Japanese were defending a series of strong points and that they held the Gifu and the high ground south of Hill 66 in strength.[5]

In the absence of complete information about the enemy's dispositions, terrain largely dictated the 25th Division's plan.[6] General Patch did not assign a southern boundary to the 25th Division, but the Lunga River would limit its movements south of Mount Austen. The northern divisional boundary ran along the northwest Matanikau fork. The Matanikau forks divided the 25th Division's zone into three almost separate areas: the area east of the Matanikau where the Gifu strong point was located; the open hills west of the Gifu between the south and southwest Matanikau forks; and the open hills south of the Hill 66 line between the northwest and southwest Matanikau forks.

General Collins issued Field Order No. 1 to the 25th Division on 8 January 1943.[7] With the 3d Battalion of the 182d Infantry, the Americal Division Reconnaissance Squadron, and the 1st Battalion of the 2d Marines attached,[8] the 25th Division was to attack at 0635, 10 January. It was to seize and hold the assigned line about 3,000 yards west of Mount Austen—a line running generally south from the Hill 66 positions taken in November 1942. To the 35th Infantry, a Regular Army regiment commanded by Col. Robert B. McClure, were attached the 25th Division Cavalry Reconnaissance Troop and the 3d Battalion, 182d Infantry. Colonel McClure's troops were to relieve the 132d Infantry at the Gifu, take the high ground west of the Gifu, and attack west to seize and hold the division objective in the 35th Infantry's zone, a line about 3,000 yards west of Mount Austen. The 27th Infantry, a Regular Army regiment commanded by Col. William A. McCulloch, was ordered to capture the high

---

[5] Annex 2, 25th Div FO No. 1, 8 Jan 43, in 25th Div Opns, App. VI.

[6] 25th Div Opns, p. 6.

[7] 25th Div FO No. 1.

[8] When the 27th Infantry had passed through the 1st Battalion, 2d Marines, the latter battalion was to revert to the 2d Marine Division.

ground between the northwest and southwest Matanikau forks. Col. Clarence A. Orndorff's 161st Infantry (less the 1st Battalion), formerly of the Washington State National Guard, was to be in division reserve.

Divisional artillery battalions were to fire a 30-minute preparation on 10 January, from 0550 to 0620, on the water hole near Hill 66 and the hills to the south in the 27th Infantry's zone. Artillery preparation and aerial bombardment were to be omitted in the 35th Infantry's zone to avoid warning the Japanese of the effort against their south flank.

The 8th Field Artillery Battalion (105-mm. howitzers) was to give direct support to the 27th Infantry. Directly supporting the 35th Infantry would be the 105-mm. howitzers of the 64th Field Artillery Battalion. The 89th (105-mm. howitzers) and the 90th (155-mm. howitzers) Field Artillery Battalions, and the 2d Battalion, 10th Marines, were originally assigned to general support. When General Collins later committed the 161st Infantry to mopping up actions, the 89th supported that regiment. The 75-mm. pack howitzers of the 2d Battalion, 10th Marines, were to support the fires of the 8th Field Artillery Battalion as a secondary mission, for the open terrain of the 27th Infantry's zone would permit profitable use of light artillery. On 10 January the 155-mm. howitzers of the Americal Division's 221st Field Artillery Battalion also supported the 25th Division's artillery.

The enemy's deficiency in artillery and air power simplified the problem of selecting forward artillery positions west of the Lunga River. Since defilade, camouflage, and concealment were not necessary, the artillerymen were able to emplace their guns on the forward slopes of hills with impunity.[9] All battalions prepared to move their howitzers from east of the Lunga to positions far enough west to be able to fire into Kokumbona. The 64th Field Artillery Battalion, supporting the 35th Infantry, selected positions on Mount Austen's foothills—the slopes of Hills 34 and 37, about 2,000 yards northeast of the Gifu and 9,000 yards southeast of Kokumbona. The 8th Field Artillery Battalion, supporting the 27th Infantry, selected positions on Hills 60, 61, and 62, south of the 64th and about 3,000 yards east of the easternmost hill in the 27th Infantry's zone. The 89th Field Artillery Battalion decided on Hill 49, a high bluff east of the Matanikau River. The 90th Field Artillery Battalion selected positions about 1,000 yards east of the junction of Wright and the coastal roads.[10]

Rough ground and insufficient motor transport complicated the movement

---

[9] 25th Div Arty Rpt Action Against Enemy (10 Jan–10 Feb 43), p. 1.

[10] 25th Div Opns, pp. 124–25; 90th FA Bn Hist, 1 Jan 43–Dec 44, p. 1.

CASUALTY MOVEMENT *taxed the facilities of medical units during the January offensive. The jeep, only vehicle able to negotiate the poor roads, was used as above to carry patients to hospitals after men were brought out of the front lines by hand-carry teams (below).*

of weapons, spare parts, ammunition, rations, and water. Every battalion initially hauled two units of fire from the ammunition dump near the Ilu River to
its battle position, a distance of over ten miles for each battalion. Two units of
fire for the 105's weigh 135 tons, or fifty-four 2½-ton truckloads. Each 105-mm.
battalion possessed but five 2½-ton trucks. The 90th's heavy transport originally
consisted of only ten 4-ton trucks. In addition each battalion had but five jeeps,
two ¾-ton weapons carriers, and four 1-ton trailers.[11] By borrowing six 2½-ton
trucks from the American Division and driving all vehicles day and night, the
artillery battalions were able to put their howitzers into their positions and haul
enough ammunition to support the projected offensive by 8 January.[12] With
their howitzers in place, the artillery battalions established check points and
registered fire on prospective targets.

Air officers worked directly with General Collins and the 25th Division
staff in planning air support. As some of the Japanese positions were defiladed
from artillery fire, dive bombers and fighter-bombers were needed. SBD's were
to drop 325-pound depth charges and P–39's; 500-pound demolition bombs, on
the defiladed positions.[13]

The 25th Medical Battalion solved the problem of evacuation from Mount
Austen and the hills to the west in the same manner as had the 101st in December 1942. Engineers and medical troops strung cableways across canyons, rigged
skids on light Navy litters so that they could slide, and later used a boat line on
the Matanikau to evacuate wounded. Carrying litters up and down steep slopes
exhausted litter-bearers so quickly that litter squads were enlarged from the
usual four to six, eight, and even twelve men.[14] Converted jeeps were used
as ambulances on the roads and trails.

H Hour for the 25th Division was set at 0635, 10 January 1943. This attack,
the most extensive American ground operation on Guadalcanal since the landing, was to open the final drive up the north coast. To make the offensive a
success, the 25th Division had to carry out two missions: reduce the Gifu strong
point, thus eliminating the last organized bodies of enemy troops east of the
Matanikau; and capture the high ground south of the Point Cruz–Hill 66 line,
thus beginning the envelopment of the Point Cruz–Kokumbona area and ex-

---

[11] 25th Div Opns, p. 134; see also FM 101–10, par. 121, p. 5.

[12] 25th Div Opns, p. 134. Throughout the January offensive 25th Division artillerymen hauled 53,344
rounds forward and fired 32,232 rounds.

[13] Memo, Col Dean C. Strother for CofS USAFISPA, 19 Jan 43, in USAFISPA G–3 Worksheet File, 1–15
Jan 43.

[14] Interv with Col George E. Bush (former CO, 3d Bn, 27th Inf), 5 Aug 46.

tending the western American lines far enough inland to make the forthcoming western advance a clean sweep.

27th Infantry's Preparations

In the 27th Infantry's zone, the 900-foot-high hill mass formed by Hills 55–54–50–51–52–57–53, called the Galloping Horse from its appearance in an aerial photograph, dominated the Point Cruz area to the north. (*Map XIV*) The distance from Hill 53, the "head" of the Galloping Horse, to Hill 66 is about 1,500 yards. Hill 50, the "tail," lies about 2,000 yards northeast of Hill 53. The Horse is isolated on three sides:[15] the Matanikau River's main stream separates it on the east from the high ground north of Mount Austen; the southwest fork of the Matanikau cuts it off from the hills on the south; and the northwest Matanikau fork flows between the Galloping Horse and the hills on the north. The heavy jungles lying along the river forks also help to isolate the hill mass. The southern slopes of the Horse's back and head—Hills 51, 52, and 53—are almost perpendicular, and Hills 50 and 55 are nearly as steep. The hills are open, with only a few scattered trees. The main vegetation consists of high, dense, tough grass and brush.

XIV Corps headquarters believed that the enemy's hold on the Galloping Horse was strong and that he would vigorously oppose the attack in this zone.[16] Throughout December 1942 and January 1943, patrols from the 2d Marines and the Americal Division's Mobile Combat Reconnaissance Squadron had met heavy enemy rifle, machine-gun, and mortar fire from the vicinity of Hill 52. The enemy troops, including elements of the *228th* and *230th Infantry Regiments* of the *38th Division*, also held a series of strong points along the banks of the southwest Matanikau fork south of the Galloping Horse.

Colonel McCulloch, commanding the 27th Infantry, determined to attack south across the 2,000-yard front of the Galloping Horse with two battalions supported by sections of the 27th Infantry's Cannon Company. Believing that the jeep trail from the Matanikau up to the summit of Hill 55 was not adequate for the delivery of supplies to two battalions attacking abreast, he decided to attack from two separate points. He ordered Lt. Col. Claude E. Jurney's 1st Battalion to attack on the right (west) against Hill 57 (the forelegs) from Hill 66 in the 2d Marine Division's zone. The battalion was to advance south of Hill 66 across the northwest Matanikau fork, to seize the water hole where the 182d Infantry's detail had been ambushed on 18 November, and to take the

---

[15] 25th Div Opns, p. 5.
[16] Ltr, Col Long to Col Buckley, 21 Mar 43.

Corps' objective in its zone, the north part of Hill 57. F Company of the 8th Marines and the Americal Division's Reconnaissance Squadron were to provide flank security for the 1st Battalion. Colonel Jurney's battalion was to be supplied over the more convenient Hill 66 route. Twenty-five men from each company of the 1st Battalion were to carry supplies forward from Hill 66.

The 3d Battalion, Lt. Col. George E. Bush commanding, was to advance on the left in a wide enveloping movement. Colonel Bush's troops were to assemble behind the 2d Marines' lines on Hill 55, and then advance south along the Galloping Horse's hind legs and attack generally southwest to take Hill 53, the Corps' objective in the 3d Battalion zone. Supplies for the 3d Battalion were to be brought from the coast road along Marine Trail, across the Matanikau, and up the jeep trail to Hill 55, from where they would be hand-carried by seventy-five natives escorted by soldiers of the Antitank Company. The assault battalions were to reach their lines of departure from the coast road.

Lt. Col. Herbert V. Mitchell's 2d Battalion was to be initially in regimental reserve in assembly areas at the base of Hill 55.[17] The 1st Battalion of the 161st Infantry, Lt. Col. Louie C. Aston commanding, was attached to the 27th Infantry for this action to block the southwest Matanikau fork between Hill 50 and the high ground to the south, and to assist in holding a defense line along Hills 50 and 51 after their capture. General Collins warned Colonel McCulloch that, if the 35th Infantry encountered difficulty in taking its objective to the south, the 27th might have to come to its assistance from the Hill 51–52 area before moving west to take Hill 53.

The First Day: 1st Battalion Operations

Artillery preparation for the attack on the Galloping Horse began at 0550, 10 January, when the 25th Division artillery fired a heavy concentration on the water hole near Hill 66 and on the Galloping Horse's forelegs. In thirty minutes 5,700 rounds were fired by six field artillery battalions—the 8th, 64th, 89th, and 90th from the 25th Division; the 2d Battalion, 10th Marines; and the 221st from the Americal Division. Fire was controlled by the 25th Division's fire direction center. The 105-mm. howitzers fired 3,308 rounds; 155's fired 518; 75's fired 1,874. The total weight of the projectiles was 99½ tons.[18]

To make all initial rounds hit their targets simultaneously, the artillery employed time-on-target fire. This technique, which the 25th Division had

---

[17] 27th Inf FO No. 2, 9 Jan 43, in 25th Div Unit FO's in misc docs from USAFISPA; 25th Div Opns, pp. 25–26.

[18] *Ibid.*, p. 136.

THE GALLOPING HORSE. *This vertical photograph was taken from about 12,000 feet.*

rehearsed in previous training, invariably caused carnage among troops caught in the open, for they were not warned to take cover by the shells from the nearest battery landing shortly before the main concentration. The artillery fired at irregular intervals, hoping that the enemy troops who had survived the first blasts would believe the shelling to be over and expose themselves during lulls to the next volleys.

This time-on-target (TOT) "shoot" was the first divisional TOT firing of the Guadalcanal campaign, and may have been the first divisional combat TOT firing by American artillerymen during World War II.[19] The fire devastated the vicinity of the water hole. It was so effective that when the 1st Battalion attacked south against its objective over a route known to have been formerly strongly held by the enemy, it encountered only minor opposition.

As steep cliffs masked some of the enemy positions on the Horse from artillery shells, aircraft from the 2d Marine Air Wing then struck at the positions on the reverse slopes. At 0620, when the artillery fire ceased, twelve P-39's and an equal number of dive bombers (SBD's) flew over to strike at the Japanese. Each P-39 carried one 500-pound bomb, and each dive bomber carried three 325-pound depth charges.[20] The artillery had laid a smoke line from the southwest tip of Hill 66 to the Horse's left (east) foreleg. No plane was to bomb east of the smoke line. But just before the attacking aircraft reached the target area, a quantity of ammunition blew up on Hill 56. It had been struck either by a short American shell or by an accurate round from the enemy's artillery. The leading bomber, apparently misled by the smoke from the exploding ammunition, dropped a depth charge on the 8th Marines on Hill 66, and the second bombed Hill 55 east of the smoke line. Fortunately no marines or soldiers were hurt.[21]

Success of the 1st Battalion's attack south from Hill 66 against Hill 57 on 10 January depended partly upon the security of its flanks while it crossed the northwest Matanikau fork in the ravine between Hills 66 and 57. After the bombardment F Company of the 8th Marines moved to the southwest corner of Hill 66 to be in position to tie the 2d Marine Division's left flank to the point where the 25th Division's right flank would be when it had reached its objec-

---

[19] Data on the "shoot" are taken from: 25th Div Opns, p. 128; 25th Div Arty Rpt, p. 3; Lt Col Robert Gildart, "Guadalcanal's Artillery," *Infantry Journal*, October 1943 (XXXIII, 10); and from intervs with Col William H. Allen, Lt Col Thomas J. Badger, Lt Col Dean Benson, and Col James J. Heriot.

[20] Guadalcanal and the Thirteenth Air Force, p. 153.

[21] 25th Div Opns, p. 45.

tive. By 0742 the Marine company was in place. B Company of Colonel Jurney's battalion left Hill 66 at 0735 to seize the water hole. F (8th Marines) and B Companies then joined their flanks, thus assuring the security of the 1st Battalion's right flank.

The Americal Division's Mobile Combat Reconnaissance Squadron had the mission of protecting the left flank of Colonel Jurney's battalion by blocking the ravine between Hill 56 and the Horse's left (east) foreleg. Soldiers of the squadron reached the ravine and set up a block by 0830. An hour and a half later B and A Companies of the 27th Infantry made contact with the squadron.[22]

While its flanks were being secured, the 1st Battalion moved off Hill 66 in column of companies, with A Company leading, followed by C and D. Progress was rapid; the terrain offered more resistance than the Japanese. The TOT concentration had prevented any vigorous enemy resistance, and only three machine guns fired at the 1st Battalion. By 1027 A Company had crossed the river fork, and by 1140 the entire battalion had reached its objective on Hill 57.[23] Colonel Jurney's men organized their positions on Hill 57 and fired in support of the 3d Battalion's advance against Hill 52. In the afternoon Colonel Jurney sent out a patrol which reached Hill 52 after dark to establish contact with the 3d Battalion.

The First Day: 3d Battalion Operations

In its zone the 3d Battalion was to have a harder and longer fight. There the terrain, though open, is extremely rough. The thick woods in the valleys extend along the north side of the zone for 1,500 yards between the Horse's hind legs and forelegs. The Horse's body, formed by an open area 600 yards across from north to south, is cut by hills and ravines. Waist-high grass and broken ground in this area provided cover for advancing troops. South along the Horse's body the precipitous, almost perpendicular slopes leading to the jungled gorge of the southwest Matanikau fork made troop movements in that direction almost impossible. Hill 52 in the middle dominates the neighboring hills. Between Hills 52 and 53 are two smaller hills, invisible from the ground east of Hill 52, which the 25th Division later called Exton and Sims Ridges after two 2d Battalion lieutenants who were killed on 12 January.

Because it dominated the surrounding area, Hill 52 was an intermediate objective for the 3d Battalion in its attack toward Hill 53. It was a naturally strong position that a few troops could easily hold. Its level crest dominated

---

[22] Mob Combat Recon Sq Hist, p. 17; Unit Rpt, 11 Jan 43, in XIV Corps G–3 Journal, 11 Jan 43.
[23] 25th Div Opns, p. 31; 27th Inf Journal, 10 Jan 43, in 27th Inf Combat Rpt, 10–27 Jan 43.

the approaches from the east and north, and the steep palisades on the south blocked any flanking movements from that side. Sheer drops on the west and south protected the defenders from American fire. Marine and Reconnaissance Squadron patrols had previously approached Hill 52 and reported it to be a "hornet's nest."[24] Although the area to the east had been scouted, no patrols had been able to push west of Hill 52 prior to 10 January. The 27th Infantry's information about the terrain west of Hill 52 had been derived from aerial reconnaissance and photographs.

Colonel Bush, commanding the 3d Battalion, planned to move south from Hill 55 to take Hills 50 and 51, and then to attack west to seize Hills 52 and 53. Since Hill 52 was too formidable to be taken by frontal assault, he hoped to take it by a double envelopment from the south and north, L Company on the left (south) and I on the right (north), and K in battalion reserve. To each assault company he attached a machine gun platoon from M Company. Two 37-mm. guns from the Antitank Platoon of Battalion Headquarters Company, plus M Company's 81-mm. mortar platoon, were to constitute the base of fire on Hill 54, which was also the site of the battalion command post. Hill 52 had not been a target for the preparatory aerial and artillery bombardments, although the artillery had registered on the crest. The 8th and other supporting battalions were to fire on call to support the 3d Battalion's attack.

The 3d Battalion left its assembly area at the foot of Hill 55 at 0300, 10 January. By 0610 the battalion had climbed Hill 55 and reached its line of departure on the north slopes. At H Hour, 0635, the battalion moved southward through the Marine lines in column of companies to deploy for the attack. By 0646 the troops were moving down the forward slopes of Hill 54 toward Hills 50 and 51. L Company captured Hill 51 without opposition and there established a base of fire. One platoon covered the company's left and rear; another platoon was held in support. Capt. Oliver A. Roholt, the company commander, sent the 1st Platoon to attack the southeast corner of Hill 52. Protected by the uneven ground and high grass, the platoon advanced rapidly and aggressively and by 0700 was halfway up the east slope.[25] As the soldiers prepared to assault the crest, Japanese machine-gun and mortar fire from their front and left flank forced them to halt. Captain Roholt, on Hill 51, did not believe that the platoon could outflank the enemy position, for mutually sup-

[24] 25th Div Opns, p. 32.

[25] 27th Inf Journal, 10 Jan 43; 3d Bn, 27th Inf, Activities 10–27 Jan 43, p. 1, in misc docs from USAFISPA.

porting Japanese riflemen and machine gunners could cover all approaches from the east and north, and the steep precipice on the south would prevent the platoon from approaching the Japanese right flank or rear. The platoon had actually attacked along the front of the enemy line, and had thus exposed its own left flank to the enemy.

Colonel Bush had planned to call for artillery fire to neutralize the crest of Hill 52 prior to the infantry attack, but L Company had moved too rapidly. The artillery could not fire on Hill 52's crest without endangering the platoon. While the 1st Platoon hugged the ground American artillery put fire on targets beyond Hill 52 but did not dare risk shelling the enemy strong point.[26] American 37-mm. guns and mortars put direct fire on and over the crest, but the 37's could not reach the Japanese troops, who were defiladed by the sheer drop. Mortar fire could have hit the enemy on Hill 52, but the 3d Battalion mortar crews did not know the exact location of the enemy weapons.

Captain Roholt ordered the platoon to withdraw 100 yards east to enable him to cover the whole crest with mortar fire. The message was relayed to the platoon leader, but, as the words "100 yards" had been inadvertently dropped from the message by the time he received it, he pulled his men all the way back to Hill 51.[27] L Company did not then renew the assault against Hill 52 but continued to fire at the crest. Captain Roholt informed Colonel Bush that the terrain created difficulties of control and communication which made a deep southern envelopment impracticable. He advised the colonel to abandon the idea of envelopment from the south.

Meanwhile Capt. H. H. Johnson, Jr. was leading I Company in its attempted northern envelopment on the battalion's right. At 0635 I Company had moved off Hill 54 in column of platoons to advance along the edge of the woods north of the Horse. The enemy fired at Captain Johnson's company from two directions, with the machine guns and mortars emplaced on Hill 52 on the left, and with rifles from the woods on the right. Captain Johnson was forced to deploy an entire platoon to cover his right flank. The company established a base of fire on a small ridge about 200 yards southwest of Hill 54 and prepared to attack Hill 52.[28] While mortars and antitank guns struck Hill 52,

[26] Colonel Bush later declared that an artillery concentration on Hill 52, on which fire had been previously registered, should have been made an integral part of the attack plan. See 25th Div Opns, p. 33.

[27] *Ibid.*, p. 34. Communication and control were otherwise fairly satisfactory on 10 January. The SCR 536 and the sound-powered telephone operated efficiently in the open terrain.

[28] Interv with Col Bush, 5 Aug 46.

I Company assaulted uphill, but the enemy machine guns and mortars stopped it 200 yards short of the objective. The attempted double envelopment thus failed on both flanks.

Captain Johnson requested help at 0930. In view of this request and the impracticability of a southern flanking movement, Colonel Bush decided to commit K Company, and to shift his attack to the north to envelop Hill 52 from the northeast and north. He ordered Capt. Ben F. Ferguson, commanding K Company, to advance west beyond I Company to make a deeper envelopment. Slowed by rifle and machine-gun fire, K Company covered the 900 yards between its reserve position on Hill 54 and the north slopes of Hill 52 by 1300. While K Company was advancing along the edge of the woods, the heavy weapons on Hill 54 and L Company's 60-mm. mortars on Hill 51 continued to fire on Hill 52.

Colonel Bush's final plan for the capture of the hill called for another envelopment. The holding force, I Company, was to attack from the northeast while K Company, with one rifle platoon from L and a machine gun platoon from M Company attached, enveloped the position from the north. L Company, holding Hill 51 with one platoon, was in reserve. The attack would be supported by field artillery fire, machine guns, mortars, and antitank guns. The assaulting units moved into position; by about 1400 Colonel Bush had determined the exact location of the assault companies, although the battalion command post on Hill 54 had been harassed by enemy rifle fire. The forward observer then called for artillery fire to be delivered on the crest of Hill 52, but a communication failure delayed the artillery until 1430.[29]

About noon, after the 3d Battalion's attack had bogged down, Colonel McCulloch had sent the air support commander forward to confer with Colonel Bush on Hill 54. The 3d Battalion commander had shown him the most likely targets on the Galloping Horse, and the air officer had agreed to bomb Hill 52 at 1500 unless the hill had been captured by that time. An artillery smoke shell was to mark the target and indicate to the pilots that they were to execute the planned bombing mission. Bush's plan called for K Company to assault Hill 52 before 1500, and had Hill 52 fallen before then, the planes were not to drop their bombs. By 1430, when the artillery was ready to fire the concentration on Hill 52, the planes were overhead. Colonel Bush decided to use the planes despite the fact that K Company would have to withdraw the right (western)

---

[29] Interv with Maj Mischa N. Kadick (former CO, Hq Co, 25th Div Arty), 9 Jan 47.

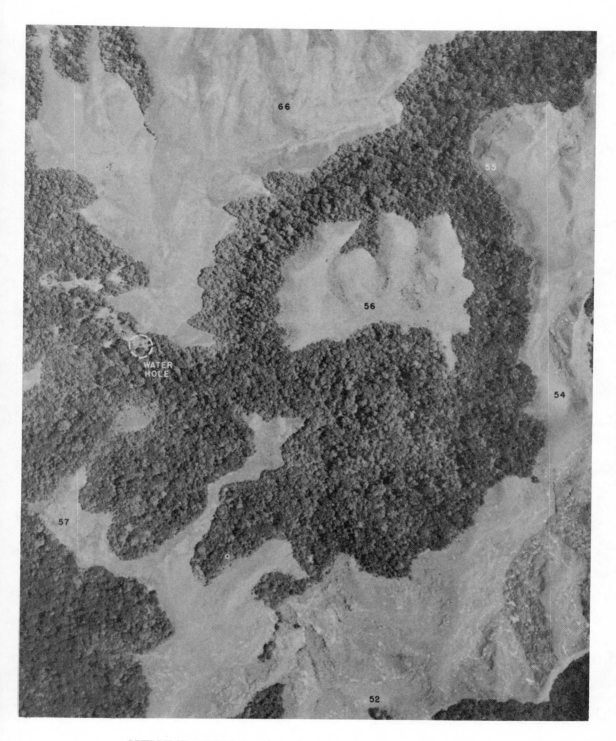

66

55

56

WATER
HOLE

54

57

52

27TH INFANTRY AREA, *10 January 1943, as seen from the air.*

part of its deployed front, which lay along a prolongation of the bombing line, which ran from north to south. Delayed bomb releases would have endangered the troops.

The planes bombed Hill 52 successfully; they spaced the depth charges well.[30] Not one fell on the east slope but all hit the reverse slope. Four charges exploded on the target, and two were duds. After the bombing four howitzer battalions put a 20-minute concentration on Hill 52. When the 105's ceased firing, the 37-mm. guns and mortars fired in support of the infantry.

Under cover of the 37-mm. and mortar fire, the infantrymen launched a co-ordinated attack. K Company had resumed its position on the north slopes of Hill 52. The platoon from L Company covered the gap between K and I. The soldiers crawled close to the crest under cover of the supporting fire, then, with bayonets fixed, rushed and captured it.[31] By 1635 the 3d Battalion had cleaned out the enemy's positions on the western slopes, captured six machine guns which had survived the bombardment, killed thirty Japanese, and secured the hill. The battalion did not attack again that day but organized a cordon defense on Hill 52 for the night.

The 25th Division, carrying out the most ambitious divisional offensive on Guadalcanal since the capture of the Lunga airfield, had made good progress in its first day of combat. The artillery fire had been especially effective. The 1st Battalion, 27th Infantry, had reached the division objective in its zone. The 3d Battalion, meeting heavier resistance, had advanced 1,600 yards toward its objective and captured Hills 50, 51, and 52. Over half the Galloping Horse was in American hands. Patrols from the 1st Battalion had reached Hill 52 to make contact with the 3d Battalion. Colonel Mitchell's 2d Battalion, 27th Infantry, in regimental reserve, occupied the Hill 50–51 area, and had established contact between the 3d Battalion, 27th Infantry, and the 3d Battalion, 182d Infantry, on the Matanikau. American casualties had been light.[32] It had not been necessary to commit the division reserve, the 161st Infantry.

The Second Day

The 3d Battalion of the 27th Infantry prepared to renew its attack toward Hill 53 on 11 January but was faced with a shortage of water. Very little drink-

---

[30] Colonel Bush had called for the artillery to fire a smoke shell to mark the crest of Hill 52 but the shell fell short just south of the battalion observation post, 200 yards south of the battalion command post on Hill 54. When the shell struck, Colonel Bush immediately ordered the 81-mm. mortars to mark the target with smoke. The pilots were not misled by the short shell, and all bombed the correct target. 25th Div Opns, p. 35.

[31] Interv with Col Bush, 5 Aug 46.

[32] 27th Infantry casualties for January 43 were 74 killed in action, 226 wounded.

ing water had been brought forward to the 3d Battalion during its fight on 10 January, which was a hot, sunny day. Springs and streams are usually plentiful in the Solomons, but there was then no running water on the Galloping Horse. Colonel Bush delayed his attack against Hill 53 on 11 January until after 0900 in the vain hope that water would reach his thirsty troops. The water point at the foot of Hill 55 was adequate and the supply officer had sent water up the trail but units in the rear had apparently diverted it before it could reach the soldiers in combat.[33] As most of the soldiers of the 3d Battalion had entered combat with but one canteen of water, they had to attack on 11 January carrying only the water which remained in their canteens from the previous day.

Colonel Bush's plan for 11 January called for two companies to attack abreast after artillery bombardment. On the left I Company was to deploy on the ridge along the top of the gorge and attack southwest over the first ridge (Exton Ridge) west of Hill 52, to the next ridge (Sims Ridge) 200 yards away, while it secured its rear and left flank with one platoon. K Company, following, was to pass through I on Sims Ridge to take Hill 53 which lay 850 yards beyond Hill 52. On the right, L Company was to advance northwest from Hill 52 to that part of Hill 57 which lay in the 3d Battalion zone, make contact with the 1st Battalion, drive south to clear the woods between Hills 57 and 53, and make contact with K and I Companies. One machine gun platoon from M Company was to accompany each assault company; the 81-mm. mortars were to remain on Hill 54. Colonel Bush assigned eleven men from Headquarters and M Companies to carry water to the advancing troops.

Both assault companies moved off the right (north) end of Hill 52 after the artillery preparation. The security platoon of I Company reached a narrow bottleneck west of Hill 52 between two ridges. The rest of the company followed. When fire from Japanese mortars, machine guns; and rifles began to hit them, the soldiers halted. I Company requested that mortars and artillery put fire on the enemy but did not move forward nor maneuver to the enemy flanks.[34] Squeezed in the narrow gap, the company was hit repeatedly by mortar fire. Many spent and thirsty men collapsed. In one platoon only ten

[33] Major Joseph Ryneska, 27th Inf S–4, later stated that water supply had not been thoroughly planned. 25th Div Opns, p. 43. Colonel Bush stated afterward that the attack should have been delayed until water had arrived. *Ibid.,* p. 35.

[34] 3d Bn, 27th Inf, Activities, p. 2, asserts that I Company tried to maneuver but that fire from concealed positions halted it. Colonel Bush stated that it did not attempt maneuver. 25th Div Opns, p. 36.

men were still conscious at noon.[35] Mortar fragments wounded Captain Johnson about 1300, and he was evacuated.

Also unsuccessful was L Company's attack. The lead platoon and one attached machine gun platoon cut through the ravine north of Hill 52 to secure the right flank. They turned west, and advanced to Hill 57, then turned left to climb the southeast slopes. When heavy machine-gun fire from the flanks and rear halted them, they dug in to await the main body, which did not arrive. When dusk fell the two platoons, out of communication with the battalion, returned to Hill 52.[36] The main body of L Company had not advanced, but had deployed behind I Company to hunt down scattered enemy riflemen.

By midafternoon Colonel Bush felt certain that the 3d Battalion could not take its objective that day. Since the position reached by I Company was untenable, I and L Companies returned to Hill 52 for the night. After dusk the force which had been halted on Hill 57 also returned. Between 1500 and 1600 accurate, heavy Japanese mortar fire forced the 3d Battalion to take cover, and delayed defensive preparations for the expected night attack. The enemy did make a slight effort to infiltrate the lines that night, but was repulsed by L Company.

Colonel McCulloch ordered the exhausted 3d Battalion to go back to Hills 55 and 54 into regimental reserve on the morning of 12 January, and Colonel Mitchell's 2d Battalion took over the assault against the ridges and Hill 53. Up to this time the 2d Battalion had held the rear areas taken by the 3d Battalion and had helped to carry supplies forward. The 1st Battalion of the 161st Infantry then took over the Hill 50–51 area.

The Third Day

Colonel Mitchell planned to attack on 12 January to capture Hill 53 and that part of Hill 57 which lay in his zone. (*Map XV*) The attack was to be delivered from Hill 52 with two companies abreast. F would be on the left, G on the right, and E in reserve. F Company was to capture Hill 53, while G Company moved to the right to join with the 1st Battalion on Hill 57. H Company was to emplace its heavy machine guns and 81-mm. mortars on Hill 52. Artillery and aerial bombardments were to support the infantry's attacks.

---

[35] 3d Bn, 27th Inf, Activities, p. 2.

[36] Colonel Bush said later that I Company should have attempted to move even without water; leaders had not exerted themselves sufficiently. 25th Div Opns, p. 36. On 5 August 1946, Colonel Bush stated that when I's advance was halted, L should have moved to the right behind its leading platoon. The leading platoon had lost communication; otherwise he would have ordered it to hold its ground.

After a preliminary bombardment both assault companies moved out of the cordon defense on Hill 52 at 0630, 12 January. On the right G Company advanced to the north and west. Some enemy riflemen in the woods north of Hill 52 opened fire but were hunted down by patrols from G Company. As the company moved west Japanese in the jungle north of Sims Ridge opened fire, but G Company continued its march and by noon had made contact with the 1st Battalion on Hill 57.

G Company was the only unit which reached its objective on 12 January. In general, vigorous Japanese resistance halted the 2d Battalion's advance. At the beginning of the day the Japanese were occupying Exton Ridge, and Sims Ridge 200 yards west of Exton; Hill 53 southwest of Hill 52; the jungle north of Sims; and the shallow dip between Exton and Sims Ridges. Enemy machine guns covered all approaches, and the steep precipice above the southwest Matanikau fork prevented F and E Companies from enveloping the enemy from the south.[37]

F Company attacked Exton Ridge but moved too far to the right and exposed the battalion's left flank. By then the Japanese had pulled off Exton Ridge and F Company took it quickly but could advance no farther toward Hill 53. Colonel Mitchell then committed his reserve, E Company, to F's left to cover the battalion's south (left) flank, but E Company also failed to advance beyond Exton Ridge.[38] Fire from Sims Ridge held both companies in place. Colonel Mitchell decided to envelop Sims Ridge. He withdrew F Company from Exton and ordered it to move to the right to attack Sims Ridge from the north. E Company continued its attack but failed to progress. When F Company attacked southward against Sims it was able to capture the north slopes, but about halfway to the crest it was halted by an enemy strong point that was dug in on the reverse (west) slope. At first the soldiers could not locate the position which machine guns were defending from all sides. Meanwhile E Company, trying to advance over Exton, in avoiding enemy fire had moved to the right and partly intermingled with F Company.

To give closer support to the assault companies, H Company then moved its heavy machine guns to Exton Ridge.[39] On Sims Ridge the infantry sought out the enemy strong point. Capt. Charles W. Davis, the battalion executive

---

[37] 25th Div. Opns, pp. 38 and 45.

[38] Interv with Col. Herbert V. Mitchell (former CO, 2d Bn, 27th Inf), 9 Aug 46.

[39] While Lt. Robert M. Exton was firing a machine gun on this ridge, an enemy mortar shell blew off his legs. Soldiers attempted to give him first aid, but, dying, he ordered them not to waste time. *Ibid.*

officer, with Capt. Paul K. Mellichamp and Lt. Weldon Sims crawled down the east side of the ridge behind a waist-high shelf, a natural approach. When Lieutenant Sims exposed himself above the shelf, a Japanese machine gunner shot him fatally through the chest. His companions then pulled his body down and returned to the 2d Battalion lines.[40]

When the strong point was thus approximately located, American machine guns and mortars opened fire while the infantry made one more effort to overcome the enemy. Captain Davis crawled behind the shelf close to the strong point and radioed firing data to H Company's 81-mm. mortar squads. As both he and the men of E and F Companies were then less than fifty yards from the enemy the exploding shells showered dirt, rock chips, and fragments among them, but failed to destroy the enemy position.[41] The enemy machine guns were still in action and kept the American infantry in place.

Meanwhile Colonel Mitchell had left the battalion command post on Hill 52 to join the assault companies on Sims Ridge. As the Japanese and Americans on Sims Ridge were within grenade-throwing distance of each other, he decided not to use 81-mm. mortars. The 1st Battalion mortar sections on the north end of Hill 57 offered to fire at troops visible to them on Sims, but Colonel Mitchell feared that the troops were his own and declined. By the time the last attacks by E and F Companies had been halted halfway to the objective, the day was nearly gone.

By late afternoon the two companies had exhausted their drinking water; the men were on the verge of collapsing. They organized an all-round defense on the north slopes of Sims Ridge in anticipation of a Japanese night counterattack. Colonel Mitchell decided to spend the night with the troops on Sims Ridge instead of returning to the battalion command post on Hill 52, for the regimental executive officer was then at the command post and could act in emergencies.[42]

During the day the 8th Field Artillery Battalion had fired the seventeen concentrations requested by Colonel Mitchell. Together with its supporting battalions, the 8th also adjusted fire on Hill 53 in preparation for the next day's assault.

The Japanese did not attack the 2d Battalion that night, but they did

[40] *Ibid.*

[41] 25th Div Opns, p. 46; note by Davis enclosed in personal ltr, Brig Gen W. P. Shepard to Col John M. Kemper, Hist Div, WDSS, 6 Dec 46. A copy of the note is in the files of the Hist Div, SSUSA.

[42] Interv with Col Mitchell, 9 Aug 46.

succeed in cutting the telephone line between Colonel Mitchell and Hill 52.[43] Some of the American soldiers, facing the Japanese for the first time at night, fired indiscriminately in the enemy's direction.

Fourth Day

The 2d Battalion's attack plan for 13 January called for E Company to continue the attack against Sims Ridge from the north. At the same time F Company was to withdraw from the ridge and advance along a covered route between the jungle and the Horse's neck to attack the north end of Hill 53. H Company was to maintain the base of fire on Hill 52 and Exton Ridge.

E Company attacked as ordered but was immediately halted by machine-gun fire from the strong point. Six volunteers from F Company then worked their way to within twenty-five yards of the strong point, but two were killed by machine-gun fire and the survivors withdrew.

The short distance separating the Japanese from the Americans on Sims Ridge protected the Japanese from 60-mm. mortar fire. E and F Companies fired their 60-mm. mortars from the north end of Sims Ridge but the range was too short and the enemy position too high up to make such firing effective. The 60-mm. squads moved back and fired repeatedly to hit the strong point. They shortened the range until the barrels pointed almost vertically, but they still could not hit the target. For safety's sake Mitchell ordered the 60-mm. mortars to cease firing.

Colonel Mitchell and the battalion executive officer then devised a plan to break the stalemate. The colonel took part of E Company down Sims Ridge behind the shelf on the east slope to a point directly east of the enemy. Meanwhile Captain Davis, the executive, and the four survivors of the party which had previously approached the strong point crawled and wriggled their way southward down the west slope close to the enemy position. They were to neutralize the strong point with grenades to prepare the way for Colonel Mitchell's unit to assault from the east on Davis' whistle signal.

The five men had crawled to within ten yards of the position when the Japanese hurled grenades at them. Although their aim was accurate, the grenades failed to explode. The Americans replied with eight grenades which did explode, then sprang up to rush the enemy, some of whom fled. Captain Davis' rifle jammed after one round. He threw it away, drew his pistol, and the five men leaped among the surviving Japanese and finished them with

[43] Colonel Mitchell had wished to effect a surprise night attack, but Regimental headquarters forbade it. *Ibid.*

rifles and pistols. E Company witnessed this bold rush and, in the words of General Collins who observed the day's fighting and helped to direct mortar fire from Hill 52, "came to life" and drove uphill to sweep the last Japanese from Sims Ridge.[44] For his gallant action, Captain Davis later received the Medal of Honor.[45]

Like the 3d Battalion on 11 January, the 2d Battalion had received almost no water after it attacked on 12 January, and thirst might well have caused the 13 January attack to stall. But shortly after E Company had cleared Sims Ridge a quick heavy cloudburst soaked the earth and cooled the soldiers who were able to obtain a little water from standing pools and by wringing their clothes. The amount they obtained, though scanty, proved sufficient to sustain them.[46]

While F Company was moving along its covered route, three field artillery battalions put fire on Hill 53. When the artillery fire ceased both companies (F and E) attacked Hill 53. E Company advanced south and west along Sims Ridge to seize the high ground on the top of the Horse's head, and F Company emerged from the jungle to attack the head from the north. The infantrymen capitalized on the shock effect of the artillery by attacking immediately after it stopped firing.[47] The 2d Battalion found that organized Japanese resistance had ceased.[48] By 1030 the 2d Battalion had captured all but the southwest tip of Hill 53; by noon it had taken the entire hill and reached the division's objective in its zone.[49]

E Company destroyed a Japanese 70-mm. gun on Hill 53, and captured a number of rifles, grenade dischargers, machine guns, and some ammunition. Colonel Mitchell's battalion, in two days of action, had lost two officers and twenty-nine enlisted men killed, and had killed an estimated 170 Japanese soldiers from the *228th* and *230th Infantry Regiments, 38th Division*. A few of the enemy dead wore good clothes and had been in good physical condition, but the remainder were ragged and half-starved.[50]

G Company, which had made contact with the 1st Battalion on Hill 57

---

[44] 25th Div Opns, pp. 38, 46; interv with Col Mitchell, 9 Aug 46.

[45] WD GO No. 40, 17 Jul 43.

[46] Interv with Col Mitchell, 9 Aug 46.

[47] 25th Div Opns, p. 41.

[48] Col H. V. Mitchell, Notes, 2d Bn, 27th Inf. Colonel Mitchell lent these notes to the author, who had them copied for the Hist Div, SSUSA files.

[49] 25th Div Journal, 13 Jan 43; 27th Inf Periodic Rpt, 14 Jan 43, in misc docs from USAFISPA.

[50] 25th Div G–2 Journal, 14 Jan 43; 27th Inf Periodic Rpt, 14 Jan 43.

FINAL ATTACKS ON THE GALLOPING HORSE *were supported by howitzers of the 2d Battalion, 10th Marines (above) as the 27th Infantry cleaned out the enemy from positions such as the one below, dug into the coral rock hillside and camouflaged with kunai grass laid over a stick framework.*

on 12 January, sent one platoon to cover the low-flying jungle area between Hills 57 and 53. The next day the 2d Battalion cut a trail from Hill 53 to Hill 57.

By nightfall of 13 January the western American lines on Guadalcanal extended 4,500 yards inland (south) from Point Cruz across Hill 66 to Hills 57 and 53. The 27th Infantry had taken all its objectives, pocketed the enemy in the river gorges, and was firmly seated on the Galloping Horse, waiting for the 35th Infantry to complete its longer advance to the division's objective in its zone to the south. From 15 to 22 January the 161st Infantry, in a series of sharp fights, cleaned out the Japanese positions south of the Galloping Horse in the gorge of the southwest Matanikau fork.[51] During this period the 27th Infantry fought no more major actions, but mopped up the Japanese remaining in the jungled gorge north of the Galloping Horse, built defense positions, constructed roads, and patrolled to the west to prepare for the next assault.

The Coastal Offensive

The 2d Marine Division, holding the Hill 66–Point Cruz line on the coast on the right of the 25th Division's zone of action, remained in place during the first three days of the Galloping Horse action. On 12 January the Marine division received orders from General Patch to begin its advance westward from the Hill 66–Point Cruz line.

This attack, which was to be supported by Americal and 2d Marine Division artillery and the 2d Marine Air Wing, was the 2d Division's first operation as a complete division. The only fresh infantry regiment in the division was the 6th Marines, which had landed on Guadalcanal on 4 January 1943. The 2d Marines, which had landed in the Guadalcanal–Tulagi area on 7 August 1942, by January was overdue for relief. The 8th Marines, which had arrived in November, had also taken part in several engagements. In December 1942 the 2d and 8th Marines had relieved the weary 164th and 182d Regiments west of the Matanikau, and in January the 6th Marines had begun relieving the 2d and 8th Marines while those units were in contact with the enemy. Two battalions of the 2d Marines participated in the attack of 13 January and withdrew to the Lunga perimeter defense the next day. The 8th Marines remained in action until 17 January.

---

[51] 161st Inf Hist, 30 Dec 42–1 Jul 43, p. 1; 25th Div Opns, p. 121.

Japanese soldiers from the *2d Division* were then holding the coast sector. In some areas, especially in the wooded ravine just west of the Point Cruz–Hill 66 line, their defenses were very strong. As in November and December enemy machine guns at the head (south end) of each draw were able to pour flanking fire into advancing American troops.

The enemy's ravine defenses determined the 2d Marine Division's plan of attack. The assault was to be delivered in successive echelons from left to right. The units on the left were to move forward to knock out the enemy weapons at the head of each draw, thus clearing space through which the units on the right could maneuver.[52]

The 2d Marines opened the attack at 0500, 13 January. (*Map XVI*) By 0730 the regiment had moved 800 yards west from Hill 66, at a cost of 6 killed and 61 wounded.[53] At noon the 6th Marines moved forward to relieve the 2d.

Ten minutes after the 2d Marines had jumped off, the leading units of the 8th Marines on the right of the 2d began the attack. They moved from the east slopes of Hills 80 and 81 toward the ravine to the west. The Japanese in the ravines stopped the move with machine-gun, mortar, and rifle fire. Thus at the end of the first day the left flank units of the 2d Marine Division had advanced, but the attack in the center had been halted. The 8th Marines tried again on 14 January but failed to gain.

The regiment brought up tanks on 15 January to crack the Japanese emplacements, but failed to achieve much success. In the afternoon the marines brought a flamethrower forward to use it in action for the first time. The flamethrower burned out one Japanese emplacement ten minutes after its two-man operating team reached the front, and burned out two more emplacements later in the day.[54]

By the end of 17 January the 8th Marines had cleared out the ravine to its front and had advanced its line forward beside the 6th Marines on the left. In five days of fighting the 2d Marine Division had gained about 1,500 yards. It reported that it had killed 643 Japanese and captured 2 prisoners, 41 grenade dischargers, 57 light and 14 heavy machine guns, 3 75-mm. field pieces, plus small arms, mines, and a quantity of artillery ammunition.[55]

---

[52] 2d Mar Div D–3 Periodic Rpt, 14 Jan 43. XIV Corps G–3 Journal.

[53] Ltr, Col Arthur to USMC Hist Sec, 11 Oct 45.

[54] 8th Mar Unit Rpt, 16 Jan 43. XIV Corp G–3 Journal. On 15 January 43 flame throwers were first used in action on the beach and at the Gifu. The marine operators had been instructed by Amer Div CWS section. See ltr, Lt Col John M. Coffman, USMC, to Editor, *Marine Corps Gazette*, July 1943 (XXIX, 7).

[55] XIV Corps G–2 Summary, 19 Jan 42.

By 18 January, when the 8th Marines were withdrawn, American troops were holding a continuous line from Hill 53 north to the coast. It reached the beach at a point some 1,500 yards west of Point Cruz. The XIV Corps had gained a position from which it could start its drive into Kokumbona, long a major objective. This drive was begun just before the 35th Infantry of the 25th Division completed its task on Mount Austen.

CHAPTER XII

XIV Corps' First January Offensive: The South Flank

While the 27th Infantry had been making spectacular gains over the open hills of the Galloping Horse, the 35th Infantry of the 25th Division was heavily engaged in its zone, which included Mount Austen and the hilly, jungled areas south of the southwest Matanikau fork. Except for the open hills previously taken by the 132d Infantry, there was only one extensive piece of open ground in the 35th's zone. This ground, formed by Hills 43 and 44, was named the Sea Horse from its appearance in an aerial photograph.

Lying about 1,500 yards northwest of Hill 27 and about 1,500 yards east of the objective line, the Sea Horse dominated the low ground along the Matanikau. As capture of the Sea Horse would bottle the Japanese along the Matanikau and its forks, the 35th Infantry decided to capture the Sea Horse first, and then to advance to the objective in its zone. Like the Galloping Horse, the Sea Horse is also isolated by river forks, deep canyons, and solid jungle. The best route to the Sea Horse lay over Mount Austen, south of the Gifu, and through the jungle to the south end of Hill 43.

The task of the 35th Infantry in the Corps offensive was fourfold: to relieve the 132d Infantry at the Gifu, to capture the Sea Horse, to cover the Corps' left flank, and to push west to seize and hold the objective in its zone, a line south of the head of the Galloping Horse about 3,000 yards west of Mount Austen. For this operation the 3d Battalion of the 182d Infantry, commanded by Lt. Col. Roy F. Goggin, and the 25th Division's Cavalry Reconnaissance Troop were attached to the 35th Infantry.

Colonel McClure, commanding the 35th Infantry, ordered the 2d Battalion and the Reconnaissance Troop to relieve the 132d Infantry at the Gifu and to press against that strong point and keep in touch with Goggin's battalion on the right. The 3d Battalion, commanded by Lt. Col. William J. Mullen, Jr., was to advance southwest from Hill 27 (south of the Gifu on Mount Austen),

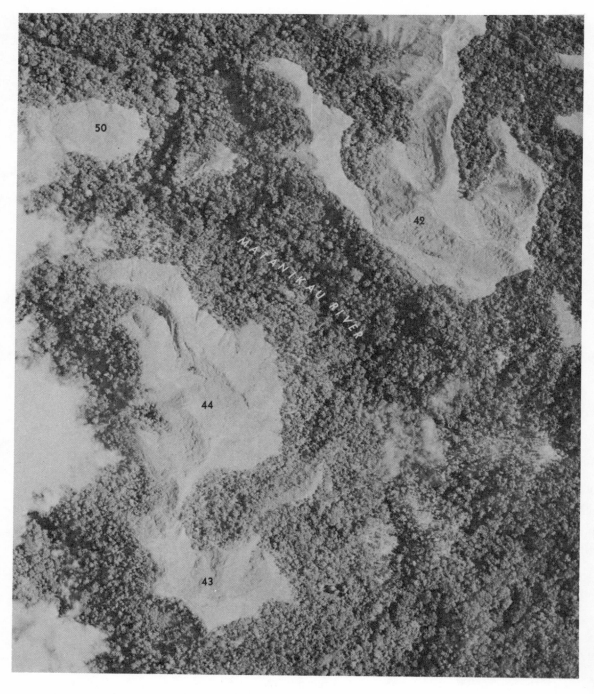

THE SEA HORSE, *Hills 43 and 44, lies just west of the Matanikau River from Mount Austen and southeast of the Galloping Horse, of which Hill 50 is a part. The head of the Sea Horse is Hill 43; the neck extends north to Hill 44, the body.*

and then swing north to seize Hills 43 and 44. Lt. Col. James B. Leer's 1st Battalion was to be initially in regimental reserve, following about a half day's march behind the 3d Battalion. The 3d Battalion, 182d Infantry, was to protect the 25th Division's artillery positions on the open ground north of Mount Austen and east of the Matanikau by advancing south from Hill 65 to block the river gorge and the ravine between Hills 31 and 42 against Japanese infiltration. The battalion was to maintain contact with the 27th and 35th Regiments on either flank.[1]

The 35th Infantry's attacks, if successful, would pocket the enemy in the Gifu and in the ravines and valleys of the Matanikau forks. The 3d Battalion, by attacking the Sea Horse from the south, would attempt to encircle the right flank of the Japanese and cut off their lines of supply and retreat. The final movement of the 35th Infantry west from Hill 43 to the objective, where the southeast Matanikau fork cuts southward, would complete the trap.

Wright Road, the jeep track from the coast road to Mount Austen, had been extended forward to a point just east of the 132d Infantry's line at the Gifu, but no lateral roads then connected Wright Road with Marine Trail on the Matanikau's east bank. In the initial operations, Wright Road was to supply the four battalions under Colonel McClure's command plus the supporting artillery. The absence of enemy tanks in the 35th Infantry's zone, coupled with the difficulty of moving infantry cannon over jungle ridges, obviated the immediate tactical employment of the 35th Infantry's Antitank and Cannon Companies. Soldiers from these companies were not to be committed to action for the present, but with 300 native bearers were to hand-carry supplies forward from the terminus of Wright Road. When the American lines were pushed south along the Matanikau after 10 January, soldiers floated supplies in and evacuees out on pole and motor barges and boats between Hill 50 and the mouth. The boat operators used some captured enemy assault boats, and engineers constructed two barges from gasoline drums. Although they used some outboard motors, they called the line the "Pusha Maru."

Taking of the Sea Horse

Advancing to their lines of departure was considerably more difficult for the battalions of the 35th Infantry than for those of the 27th. The 35th In-

---

[1] 25th Div Opns, p. 69.

THE "PUSHA MARU" *was a supplementary supply line, employing American (left) and some Japanese boats on the Matanikau River.*

THE ENVELOPMENT OF THE SEA HORSE *took troops of the 3d Battalion, 35th Infantry, through rugged jungle where no trails existed. The scene above is a typical example of the dense growth.*

fantry, having pulled out of the Lunga perimeter defense on 7 January, the next day marched up Wright Road to Mount Austen in column of battalions, with the 3d Battalion leading. While the 2d Battalion moved into line at the Gifu, the 3d Battalion, followed by the 1st, cut south and west through the jungle south of the Gifu to bivouac for the night of 8–9 January on a small ridge about 700 yards south of Hill 27. (*Map XVII*) The mortar sections of these battalions remained at the Gifu, but the light machine guns were carried along during the advance. The next day the 3d Battalion marched over slippery ravines and ridges to its line of departure, a small knoll about 1,500 yards southwest of Hill 27, and about 2,000 yards southeast of Hill 43. The 1st Battalion moved west to occupy the bivouac held by the 3d Battalion on the previous night. These movements were made in secret, for success of the 3d Battalion's attack depended upon surprise. To avoid warning the enemy of the impending attack, there were to be no preliminary artillery or aerial bombardments in the 35th Infantry's zone.

From the 3d Battalion's bivouac area Colonel Mullen was able to see a small wooded hill, a short distance south of Hill 43. From direct observation and photographic study he concluded that a narrow ridge connected the small hill with Hill 43. He decided to capture the small hill first since it would provide a good route to the grassy slopes of Hills 43 and 44.[2]

At H Hour, 0635 of 10 January 1943, while the 27th Infantry was beginning its attack, the 3d Battalion began its envelopment. Fearing that the enemy might have observed his troops, Colonel Mullen kept I Company, the battalion reserve, spread out over the bivouac area to deceive the Japanese while the assault companies, K and L, formed in the dense woods prior to attacking. By 0800 K and L Companies were ready to move.[3] Patrols on the previous night had reconnoitered in front of the bivouac area to feel out the Japanese. Relying on data from these patrols, the battalion pushed southwest through the jungle. Advancing in column of companies, the battalion then turned north toward the Sea Horse. K Company, leading, cut a trail for about 1,000 yards with machetes and bayonets, but its route led it down onto low ground along a branch of the Matanikau. At noon it reached a small knoll about 700 yards southeast of Hill 43. The company was then on ground that was dominated by ridges and bluffs on all sides.

The battalion had turned northward too soon, and it was now southeast

[2] *Ibid.*, p. 73.
[3] 0800 is the time shown in 25th Div Opn Overlays, 0600, 10 Jan–0600, 11 Jan. 43.

instead of southwest of Hill 43. The assault companies had to advance farther west before they could envelop the south flank of the Sea Horse.[4] As hills, deep ravines, and a branch of the Matanikau lay between K Company and Hill 43, patrols advanced to the west and northwest, and one found a faint trail that led westward.

The 35th Infantry then requested that artillery fire be placed on the Sea Horse. At 1300 the battalion commander ordered K Company to advance over the west trail. L Company, also following an old trail, was to advance on K's left. I Company, which had been relieved at the line of departure by the 1st Battalion, was to follow the assault company that found the best route. Colonel Mullen, who wished his battalion to reach the greater security of high ground before dark, ordered that the advance be pressed vigorously.

K Company turned west and, to cover its right flank while crossing a branch of the Matanikau, posted two light machine guns from M Company, plus some riflemen, on a knoll. The covering force faced to the northeast toward the gorge cut by the branch. As the company crossed the branch, a group of Japanese from the area of Colonel Oka's command post farther down the river attacked toward the southwest and nearly broke through to strike the company's right flank. They drove off the riflemen, knocked one machine gun out of action, and killed the gunner and wounded the assistant gunner of the second. They were prevented from hitting the flank of the vulnerable company by the heroism of two soldiers from M Company—Sgt. William G. Fournier, the machine gun section leader, and T/5 Lewis Hall. Although ordered to withdraw, the two men ran forward to the idle gun and opened fire on the Japanese, who were then in the low stream bottom in front of and below them. As the gun on the knoll would not bear, Fournier lifted it by its tripod to depress the muzzle sufficiently to fire on the Japanese while Hall operated the trigger. Both soldiers stayed at their exposed post, pouring fire at the Japanese, and were fatally wounded before other Americans could come forward.[5] But Fournier and Hall had broken the Japanese attack, and for their gallantry were posthumously awarded the Medal of Honor.[6]

As the assaulting American companies were advancing to the west, K Company surprised a Japanese supply party near a water hole at the junction

[4] 25th Div Opn Overlay 10–11 Jan 43, and General Collins' statement in 25th Div Opns, p. 100.
[5] Ltr, Lt Col William J. Mullen to author, (no sub), 24 Feb 48; intervs with Col Larsen and Lt Col James B. Leer, 20 Oct 47.
[6] WD GO No. 28, 5 Jan 43.

of two trails, killed seven, and dispersed the rest.[7] Having then reached a point about due south of Hill 43, the companies swung northward toward their preliminary objective, the wooded hill south of Hill 43. Only a few scattered Japanese were in front, and they failed to offer any effective opposition. By 1700 K and L Companies had reached high ground 400 yards south of the open slopes on Hill 43. As dusk was falling rapidly, the 3d Battalion, which to gain high ground had kept moving much later in the afternoon than was considered advisable in the jungle, halted and hastily dug in for the night.[8]

While the 3d Battalion was advancing toward the Sea Horse, Colonel Leer's 1st Battalion, in reserve, moved farther west. Patrols from A and C Companies covered the right and left flanks. Platoons of B and D Companies relieved I Company at the water hole in a gulch about 600 yards south of Hill 43.

Colonel Mullen's battalion resumed the attack against the Sea Horse at dawn on 11 January. K Company led the attack north along the ridge toward Hill 43, while L Company covered the left flank and I followed in reserve. The progress of K Company was slow against enemy machine gunners who fired to delay the attack, then fell back to new positions. In one hour it gained only 100 yards.[9] The advance gathered speed later in the afternoon, however, and the 3d Battalion emerged from the jungle, drove the enemy off Hill 43, and by 1831 had advanced to Hill 44.[10]

Meanwhile Colonel Leer's battalion had come forward to assist the 3d Battalion when its advance was retarded. But when K Company cleared Hill 43, and it became evident that the 3d Battalion would reach its objective unaided, Colonel McClure ordered the 1st Battalion to relieve I and L Companies on the south and southwest wooded parts of Hill 43. When relieved those companies joined the remainder of the 3d Battalion on the Sea Horse.[11] By nightfall on 11 January, the 35th Infantry had completed the encirclement of the Gifu on the east and west by seizing the Sea Horse, and had progressed halfway toward its objective, about 1,500 yards west of the Sea Horse.

In their southerly envelopment around the enemy's right flank the 3d and 1st Battalions had traveled more than 7,000 yards. Their route had taken them over Mount Austen's ravines and ridges, down its west slopes to the Matanikau,

---

[7] 35th Inf Journal, 10 Jan 43, in misc docs from USAFISPA.
[8] 25th Div Opns, p. 71; intervs with Cols Larsen and Leer.
[9] 35th Inf Journal, 11 Jan 43.
[10] 25th Div G–2 Journal, 11 Jan 43.
[11] 25th Div Opns, pp. 71, 76.

and up the Sea Horse. The trails they had followed were passable only for
men on foot; vehicles could not get through. The advancing battalions had
depended upon native carriers for supply pending the completion of dredging
for the Pusha Maru boat line on the Matanikau. The 7,000-yard advance of the
1st and 3d Battalions had outdistanced the native bearers who could not make
the round trip in one day, and thus created a serious problem of supply. Until
the native camp could be moved forward and the Pusha Maru boat line could
be completed, the regiment's advanced battalions were supplied by air drops
from B–17's. As cargo parachutes were not available for all gear, some supplies

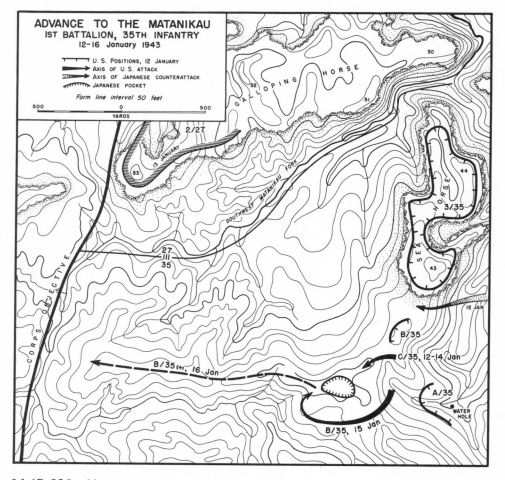

MAP NO. 11

were wrapped in burlap or canvas and thrown from the bombers. On 13 January one B–17 dropped 7,000 pounds in four flights, and two days later another dropped four tons. Rations stood the rough treatment fairly well; 85 percent of the food was usable, but only 15 percent of the ammunition could be used, and nearly all the 5-gallon water cans were ruined. Regular ground supply was not resumed until 17 January when the Pusha Maru reached the foot of Hill 50, and carriers began hauling supplies up the north slopes of Hill 44.[12]

Advance West from the Sea Horse

When L and I Companies had reached the Sea Horse Colonel Mullen organized a perimeter defense, with L Company holding Hill 44, I Company the narrow neck between 44 and 43, and K Company, Hill 43. On the morning of 12 January the 3d Battalion made contact with the forces which had just taken the eastern half of the Galloping Horse.[13]

Colonel Leer's 1st Battalion assumed the brunt of the attack west to the objective on 12 January. (*Map 11*) B Company defended the hill south of Hill 43, A Company the water hole, while C Company attacked along a narrow ridge southwest of Hill 43. Enemy fire from a ridge about 150 yards to the southwest halted the advance.[14]

While patrols from C Company were seeking the enemy flanks, an enemy force from east of Hill 43 struck just south of Hill 43 against the supply trail and isolated the 3d Battalion on the Sea Horse. At 1730 one B Company platoon counterattacked and by nightfall it had recaptured the trail.

Japanese rifle fire again stopped C Company on 13 January. The 64th Field Artillery Battalion meanwhile continued registration on enemy targets, and Colonel Leer asked regimental headquarters to send forward to Hill 43 the mortars which were then on Mount Austen under regimental control.

Operations on 14 January again failed to gain ground. C Company attacked the enemy ridge twice without success. The terrain slowed the movement of the mortars, which failed to reach Hill 43 until late afternoon. In the afternoon, however, one of Colonel Leer's patrols found a route around the enemy's right flank.

The next morning B Company relieved C Company. The 64th Field Artillery Battalion then fired 553 rounds on the Japanese on the ridge in a 30-minute concentration ending at 1005,[15] followed by fire from machine guns and mortars.

---

[12] Guadalcanal and the Thirteenth Air Force, p. 154.
[13] 25th Div Opn Overlay, 11–12 Jan 43.
[14] 25th Div Opns, p. 77.
[15] 64th FA Bn Hist, Jan–Jun 43, p. 3.

When the artillery ceased firing B Company, reinforced by one platoon from D, moved around the enemy's right flank and struck him in the rear. B Company killed thirteen Japanese and captured twelve prisoners; it also took two 70-mm. guns, three light machine guns, and a quantity of ammunition. B Company had penetrated an enemy bivouac area with room for an estimated 1,000 troops. It was then occupied by one platoon. The platoon had no rations; six of the prisoners were too weak to walk, and there were seventy-eight graves in the area.[16] Since daylight was ending, B Company halted for the night.

The defunct enemy platoon had been the only effective enemy force between the Sea Horse and the objective in the 35th Infantry's zone. The next day, 16 January, B Company and the reinforcing platoon from D Company moved west to the objective without fighting. About 1500 they reached a precipice overlooking the southwest fork of the Matanikau. So dense was the jungle that the troops could not determine their exact location until the next day, and on 18 January they built smoky fires and fired amber flares to reveal their location to the 25th Division observation posts.[17]

In capturing the Sea Horse and advancing to the Matanikau, the 1st Battalion reported that it had killed 144 of the enemy; the 3d Battalion, 414. Enemy prisoners totaled 17 for both battalions. The 3d Battalion had captured 35 light and heavy machine guns, the 1st Battalion, 9 light machine guns. The 1st Battalion had also captured 112 rifles and 18 pistols, while the 3d Battalion took 266 rifles and 26 pistols.[18] In the days following the capture of Hills 43 and 44 the 3d Battalion reduced a pocket of Japanese along the Matanikau just east of Hills 43 and 44.[19] The capture of the Sea Horse and the advance to the Matanikau had covered the XIV Corps' left (south) flank, and brought the 35th Infantry up to the objective on the left (south) of the 27th Infantry.

Reduction of the Gifu

Preliminary Operations

While the rest of the 25th Division was advancing, the 2d Battalion of the 35th Infantry on Mount Austen had the slow, grueling task of clearing the Japanese out of the Gifu which had halted the 132d Infantry in December.

[16] 25th Div Opns, pp. 72, 77.
[17] 35th Inf Journal, 18 Jan 43; 25th Div Opns, p. 77.
[18] Rpt, CO 35th Inf to CG 25th Div, 27 Jan 43, in 25th Div FO's in misc docs from USAFISPA.
[19] Interv with Lt Gen J. Lawton Collins (former CG, 25th Div), 5 Dec 46.

CAPTURE OF THE SEA HORSE *brought the 35th Infantry half way to its objective on the left flank of the American forces. With the exception of a small enemy force still holding out in the Gifu, all territory east of the Matanikau (center of picture above) was clear of Japanese.*

JAPANESE POSITIONS IN THE GIFU *were well camouflaged and difficult to locate in the dense jungle. Log-roofed, covered with earth and vegetation, the boulder-screened hole at left was a machine gun position, the one at lower right a foxhole. Picture taken after the fall of the Gifu.*

The 2d Battalion, commanded by Lt. Col. Ernest Peters, had left its positions east of the Lunga River on 7 January, and early the next morning had followed the 3d Battalion up Mount Austen to advance toward the 132d Infantry's lines. Battalion Headquarters, G, and H Companies were to infiltrate directly into the 132d's line while E and F Companies followed a back trail south of Hill 27 to get into line via the latter hill.[20] The main body, following Wright Road, reached the line without difficulty, but E and F Companies had to labor through thick jungle. The companies followed the 3d Battalion to a point about 800 yards southeast of Hill 27, then turned northwest toward Hill 27. Struggling over a rough, muddy trail, and using telephone wires to help pull themselves along, they reached Hill 27 by nightfall of 8 January and bivouacked on its southeast slopes.

The next day, 9 January, the 2d Battalion and the Cavalry Reconnaissance Troop completed the relief of the 132d Infantry, which returned to the Lunga perimeter. By nightfall the 2d Battalion of the 35th Infantry had occupied the line from Hill 31 to Hill 27, a front of over 2,000 yards. (*Map 12*) E Company, the 35th Infantry's Reconnaissance Platoon, and a platoon from the Reconnaissance Troop held Hill 27; F Company, plus platoons from H Company and the Reconnaissance Troop, held the center; G Company and platoons from H Company and the Reconnaissance Troop held Hill 31. The remainder of H Company emplaced mortars on Hill 29. Soldiers from Headquarters Company were to carry supplies from the jeep terminus on Wright Road to the companies in the line. There was no battalion reserve.[21] By the end of 9 January, a day characterized by random rifle fire and some mortar shelling, the 2d Battalion estimated that over 100 Japanese with 10 machine guns held the pocket.

When General Collins and Colonel McClure had first observed the Gifu from Hill 27, they had discussed the possibility of enveloping it from the west sides of Hills 27 and 31. Persuaded that the terrain was impassable, they agreed on a frontal assault to hold the Japanese while the 3d and 1st Battalions made their flanking movement. Time would have been saved had the double envelopment been attempted at once.[22]

On 10 January, when the 25th Division began its advance, the 2d Battalion made a reconnaissance in force. After an artillery and mortar preparation two combat patrols from each company tried to move forward but Japanese fire halted them all. The battalion commander then requested that tanks be sent up to

[20] 25th Div Opns, p. 79.
[21] *Ibid.*, p. 80.
[22] General Collins' statement in 25th Div Opns, p. 102.

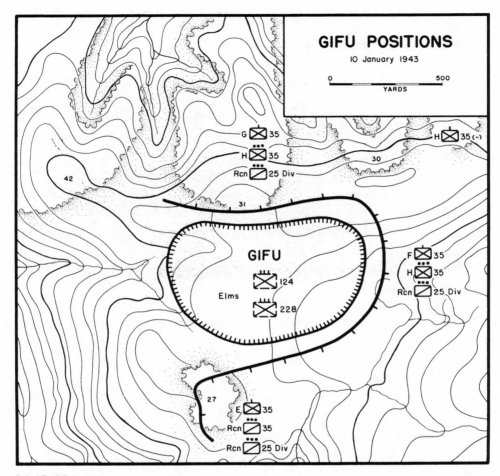

MAP NO. 12

Mount Austen to crack the pillbox line, but the only tanks on Guadalcanal were then under Marine control.[23] After the patrols were halted the 2d Battalion estimated that the enemy forces facing it consisted of 400 men and 20 machine guns. The battalion eventually captured 40 machine guns.

The next day, 11 January, patrols again met fire from the Gifu. The 3d Battalion of the 182d Infantry completed its southward move to close the gap between the right flank of the 2d Battalion, 35th, and the 27th and 161st Regiments on the Galloping Horse. By the end of 11 January the 3d Battalion of the 182d

[23] 25th Div Opns, pp. 80, 102; CO, 35th Inf, states that tanks were first requested on 12 January. See *ibid.*, p. 87.

Infantry, holding more than 1,500 yards of front, was blocking the valleys north-west of the Gifu, the portion of the Matanikau just east of Hill 50, and the south-west Matanikau fork.[24] This move, coupled with the capture of the Sea Horse, ringed the Gifu on all sides, but its pillbox line still remained to be broken. The situation of Colonel Oka's troops in the Gifu had become serious in December, yet the majority of the trapped Japanese, who were without food or reinforcements, were to fight to the death.

The 2d Battalion of the 35th Infantry again tried to advance on 12 January to straighten the line. In the morning 60- and 81-mm. mortars fired a three-quarter-hour preparation into the Gifu. When they ceased fire F and G Companies attacked, but again heavy enemy fire blocked the advance. By 1300 G Company had gained about 100 yards, but F Company, which was hit by intense machine-gun fire, had gained only 50 yards by 1815.[25]

American soldiers had discovered the exact locations of very few of the Gifu pillboxes. Poor visibility in the jungle, the high quality of the Japanese camouflage, and the heavy fire made scouting difficult. The 132d Infantry had shown the locations of two machine guns to the 35th Infantry; a patrol from F Company had located two pillboxes on 10 January but machine-gun fire drove the patrol back before it could destroy the positions. On the same day a patrol from E Company knocked out one machine gun before enemy grenades drove it back. The next afternoon when F Company ran into fire from a pillbox just twenty-five yards in front of the American lines, soldiers from Headquarters and F Companies killed some of the occupants with grenades. On 13 January, a quiet day, a patrol from F Company met fire from three emplacements, whereupon all battalion mortars fired into the area and knocked out one pillbox.

By 14 January, only 75 percent of the 2d Battalion was fit for duty.[26] Malaria and battle casualties had accounted for the remaining 25 percent. To reinforce the depleted battalion, the 35th Infantry's Antitank Company was attached as infantry to the battalion, and on 14 January moved into line between F and G Companies just northeast of Hill 27.

On the same day patrols from the 3d Battalion of the 182d Infantry attempted to find the Japanese left flank. At 1100 the battalion intelligence officer led two squads from I Company and three soldiers from M Company to reconnoiter the area south of Hill 42. Reaching a small knoll, they saw what appeared to be para-

[24] 3d Bn, 182d Inf, Opn Rpt, 9 Dec 42–7 Apr 43, p. 3; 182d Inf S–2 Journals, 9–11 Jan 43.
[25] 35th Inf Journal, 11 Jan 43.
[26] 25th Div Opns, p. 81.

chutes and ammunition lying on the ground. As the patrol circled back toward the American lines some entrenched Japanese soldiers opened fire and killed the intelligence officer and one sergeant. The patrol opened fire, but to avoid being trapped it withdrew. Later in the day a second patrol returned to the spot and engaged the enemy, but it could not find the bodies of the dead men.[27]

On 15 January the Gifu was still virtually intact. On the morning of that day the 2d Battalion of the 35th Infantry attempted to break through the Gifu to advance west to make contact with the 3d Battalion on the Sea Horse. The plan called for a 15-minute preparation by all battalion mortars, after which the Anti-tank, G, and F Companies were to assault the Gifu and converge after gaining 500 yards on their respective fronts. E Company, in reserve on Hill 27, was to help envelop the strongest points of enemy resistance developed by the attack.

The mortars fired from 0645 to 0700, whereupon the assault companies tried to advance. A few moved forward, but the majority of the 2d Battalion was halted almost immediately. G Company gained 100 yards, but by 0940 it had been halted by machine guns. The soldiers replied with grenades and a flame thrower operator from Division Headquarters Company tried unsuccessfully to burn out the enemy.[28] G Company was unable to advance after 0940 and returned in the afternoon with the rest of the battalion to its original lines.

Attacking northward from Hill 27, F Company could make no progress. The Antitank Company advanced west a few yards but halted when fire from the eastern pillboxes killed five and wounded ten soldiers. When the Antitank and F Companies lost contact in the morning, twelve soldiers from H Company moved in to fill the gap but were thrown back after losing two killed and one wounded.[29] The Pioneer Platoon from Battalion Headquarters Company then filled the gap. F Company was still attempting to advance north at 1510 when E Company moved off Hill 27 to try to envelop the enemy in front of F. This effort failed when a misunderstanding of orders caused the entire battalion to withdraw to its original line. About 1630 the battalion executive officer ordered one badly shaken platoon from G Company to withdraw, but as the order was passed

[27] 3d Bn, 182d Inf, Opn Rpt, p. 4; 182d Inf, S–2 Journal, 14 Jan 43. The S–2 Journal concludes that the Japanese left (northwest) flank extended to the Matanikau.

[28] 35th Inf Journal, 15 Jan 43. On 15 January, the 2d Marine Division also used flame throwers on the beach, but with greater success. The 35th Infantry ceased to use them because it was believed they needlessly exposed the operators. Interv with Col. Larsen.

[29] 35th Inf Journal, 15 Jan 43; 25th Div Opns, p. 81, states that the gap developed between the Antitank and G Companies. At the time neither company was moving, according to 35th Infantry Journal, and there is no record of an enemy counterattack on 15 January.

verbally along the line, the soldiers misinterpreted it as an order to the entire battalion to retire, and all fell back.[30]

Bombardment and Envelopment

Colonel McClure, the regimental commander, relieved the 2d Battalion commander on 16 January and placed the battalion under command of Lt. Col. Stanley R. Larsen.[31] After assuming command Colonel Larsen reconnoitered his front and correctly concluded that mutually supporting pillboxes ringed the easternmost three-fifths of the Gifu line. Individual combat groups of riflemen and machine gunners held the western areas. The enemy positions could not be bypassed, he decided; the Japanese in the Gifu apparently had no intention of escaping but preferred to hold out until death.[32]

The position of the defenders of the Gifu had been rapidly deteriorating. They ate their last rations sometime between 10 and 17 January. Colonel Oka, commanding the *124th Infantry,* is reported to have deserted his troops about 14 January. He and his staff left the command post on the Matanikau and made their way to safety, and later sent orders to the Gifu defenders to evacuate and infiltrate through the American lines to the coast.[33] But Major Inagaki's starving troops in the Gifu elected to stay at their posts and fight to the end rather than desert their sick and wounded comrades.[34]

Colonel McClure then decided to attempt the double envelopment which he and General Collins had originally decided against. To tighten the noose around the Gifu, he decided to extend the 2d Battalion's lines from Hill 27 to Hill 42, thus closely encircling the strong point. E Company was to march northward around the American lines from Hill 27 to Hill 42, and by 17 January be ready to attack the Gifu from the rear (northwest) while troops on Hill 27 pushed north.[35] As a deep, tangled ravine northwest of Hill 27 would make movement too difficult to employ a whole company in that area, E Company had completely to circle the American lines at the Gifu before attacking. Colonel McClure

[30] Interv with Col Larsen.

[31] Intervs with Gen Collins and Col Larsen.

[32] 25th Div Opns, p. 83; interv with Col Larsen. When interviewed Colonel Larsen volunteered the information that he had employed Colonel Peters' original plan in reducing the Gifu, i.e., heavy artillery bombardment and tank attack.

[33] Amer Div Int Rpt, Tab A; XIV Corps, Enemy Opns, p. 6. Ito, when interrogated by Sebree at Rabaul in 1946, claimed that Oka did not desert his post but was killed on Mount Austen. Interv with Gen Sebree. Ito may have been attempting to uphold the honor of the *Imperial Army* by trying to conceal Oka's defection. It will be noted that Oka's operations in October were sometimes hesitant and tardy.

[34] XIV Corps, Enemy Opns, *18th Div* Hist, p. 5; Amer Div Int Rpt, Tab A.

[35] 25th Div Opns, p. 83.

SURRENDER BROADCASTS TO THE GIFU *were made by Capt. John M. Burden from* *Hill 44. He is shown here (at microphone) during the late afternoon of 15 January with Lt.* *Col. Stuart F. Crawford, 25th Division G-2. No immediate surrender resulted.*

requested that every available artillery piece be used against Gifu.

Psychological warfare was also employed by XIV Corps headquarters in an attempt to persuade the Japanese to surrender. Capt. John M. Burden of the Corps intelligence section, accompanied by intelligence officers of the 25th Division, set up a loud speaker on Hill 44 on the northern part of the Sea Horse on the afternoon of 15 January. Burden had intended to broadcast in Japanese at 1600, but a fire fight broke out between a part of the 35th Infantry and some of Oka's troops to the east. The broadcast was delayed until 1715, when Burden told the Japanese to send an officer to Hill 44 to arrange for the surrender. But it was too close to nightfall to expect results, and at 1815 the Japanese were told not to try to surrender until the next day. At 0600 the next morning Burden repeated the first broadcast of the previous day. When two hours passed without a response from any Japanese officer, Burden broadcast again to urge the Japanese soldiers to ignore their leaders and save their lives before being annihilated. Five emaciated prisoners were obtained in this area. They asserted, perhaps untruthfully, that neither they nor their fellow soldiers had any stomach for more fighting, but continued to resist because they feared that the Americans killed their prisoners. On the basis of this testimony, Captain Burden decided to make one more broadcast.[36]

The artillery had meanwhile been preparing for a heavy bombardment. A heavy artillery concentration to smother the Gifu was an essential prelude to a successful attack, for light mortar shells left the pillboxes undamaged, and there were not enough 81-mm. mortars to cover the entire area. During the first days of the operation the 64th Field Artillery Battalion, directly supporting the 35th Infantry, had fired little at the Gifu but had fired a few missions in support of the 27th Infantry, and a few counterbattery and harassing missions into Kokumbona.[37]

Prior to 10 January soldiers of the 64th had emplaced their 105-mm. howitzers in the vicinity of Hill 34, about 2,000 yards northeast of the Gifu. The proximity of this position to Wright Road somewhat simplified the movement of supplies. Two of the batteries occupied sharp, exposed hill crests, advantageous positions made tenable by the enemy's deficiencies in artillery and air power. Artillery problems on Guadalcanal were always complicated by the lack of accurate maps, but since American soldiers had ringed the Gifu it was possible to

---

[36] Capt Burden's Rpt to ACofS G–2, XIV Corps, 19 Jan 43, sub: Rpt Broadcast Propaganda, in Amer Div G–2 Journal, 16–25 Jan 43.

[37] 64th FA Bn Hist, p. 2; 25th Div Opns, p. 90. (These accounts are identical.)

place observed fire in the pocket. Forward observers, who frequently encountered difficulty in locating their own positions in the jungles, often crawled so close to the enemy lines that their own fire fell within 100 yards of them.[38]

The artillery preparation requested by Colonel McClure was assigned by 25th Division artillery headquarters to the 105-mm. howitzers of the 89th Field Artillery Battalion, one 105-mm. howitzer of the 8th, and the 155-mm. howitzers of the 90th and 221st Field Artillery Battalions in addition to the 105-mm. howitzers of the 64th Field Artillery Battalion. Because the 64th was in a better position to control fire on the Gifu than division artillery headquarters, the 64th's fire direction center was to direct the fire. Direct wires from the 64th's fire direction center were to carry data to the fire direction centers of the 8th, 89th, and 90th Battalions. Data from the 64th would be transmitted to the 221st via the 25th Division Artillery fire direction center, where the 221st liaison officer was stationed.

On the morning of 17 January Captain Burden again attempted to persuade the Japanese to surrender. Broadcasting from G Company's line at the Gifu, he warned them of the impending bombardment and advised that they escape before the shelling began. The Japanese were assured that they would be permitted to enter the American lines even after the bombardment started. Burden then moved to Hill 27 to repeat the broadcast. But heavy rains fell during most of the period of the broadcast, and the volume of the loud-speaker was reduced. No one surrendered. One Japanese company is reported to have discussed the possibility of surrender but decided against it because most of the men were too ill to walk.

The artillery had planned to adjust its fire in the morning, but the broadcasts delayed the adjustment of the twenty-five 105-mm. and the twenty-four 155-mm. howitzers until noon. At 1130 infantrymen of the 2d Battalion, 35th, were pulled back 300 yards to the rear. The forward observers remained out in front. The 35th's main line on Hill 31 lay less than 250 yards north of the Gifu line. The 64th Field Artillery Battalion's 105-mm. howitzers lay only 2,000 yards from the Gifu. Two thousand, eight hundred yards was the minimum range for high-angle fire listed in the firing tables in use at that time. The 155-mm. howitzers could not fire at quadrant elevations greater than 800 mils (45 degrees). To hit the ravines inside the Gifu, all shells would have to be fired almost directly over Hill 31, with no margin of safety for clearing the hill. The known vertical probable error in the angle of fall of the howitzer shells made it obvious that some

[38] 64th FA Bn Hist, p. 2.

would hit Hill 31.[39] It was therefore necessary to pull the infantrymen back to the south from Hill 31.

The artillery battalions began adjusting their fire on the Gifu at 1200 after the broadcast had ceased, but were interrupted frequently by calls of "cease fire," especially from infantrymen on Hill 42 who believed that the shells were falling short. The artillery battalions then adjusted each howitzer individually on the target, a slow task which took over two hours to complete.

For ninety minutes, starting at 1430, the forty-nine howitzers fired for effect. They placed over 1,700 rounds in an area less than 1,000 yards square. The 2d Battalion's mortars fired into the most defiladed areas. The noise, concussion, and reverberation were tremendous, and the effect of the bombardment was doubtless great, for the Japanese prisoners captured during the next few days were nearly all shell-shocked.[40] But poor timing largely vitiated the effects of both the broadcasts and the shelling.

After the bombardment the infantrymen moved forward and by 1630 had reoccupied their lines. They did not then assault because the approaching dusk would have made an attack over such terrain very risky.[41] The shock effect of the artillery was thus partially lost.[42] Colonel McClure did not repeat the bombardment the next morning because he did not wish to withdraw the infantry again.[43]

The double envelopment began the next day, 18 January. I Company of the 182d Infantry advanced 450 yards south from Hill 42 to make contact about 1700 with a platoon detached from G Company. The platoon had advanced northwest from Hill 27 through the ravine.[44] While these two units were advancing, E Company, which had followed I Company of the 182d off Hill 42, swung to the left (east) to strike the Gifu from the west. The company knocked out three or four enemy machine guns and killed seven Japanese before wired-in machine guns halted it.[45] Meanwhile, to the right of E Company, the platoon from G

[39] *Ibid.*, pp. 4–5, asserts that the Cannon Company might have been profitably employed on Hill 42, and that the artillery battalion commander "missed a bet" by not placing some 105-mm. howitzers on Hill 42 for direct fire.

[40] 25th Div Opns, p. 84.

[41] *Ibid.*, p. 94.

[42] Colonel McClure disapproved of the broadcasts. 25th Div Opns, p. 87. General Collins pointed out (p. 103) the necessity for capturing prisoners. XIV Corps, Enemy Opns, *38th Div* Hist, p. 3, states that the broadcasts were effective, for of the 248 prisoners taken later, 118 came from the *124th* and *228th Infantry Regiments,* the units toward which the broadcasts were directed.

[43] Interv with Lt Col Thomas J. Badger (former S–3, 64th FA Bn), 6 Dec 46.

[44] 3d Bn, 182d Inf, Opn Rpt, p. 4; 25th Div Opns, p. 84.

[45] 35th Inf S–2 Rpt, 18 Jan 43. This was the first enemy barbed wire encountered in that area. XIV Corps G–2 Summary, 20 Jan 43.

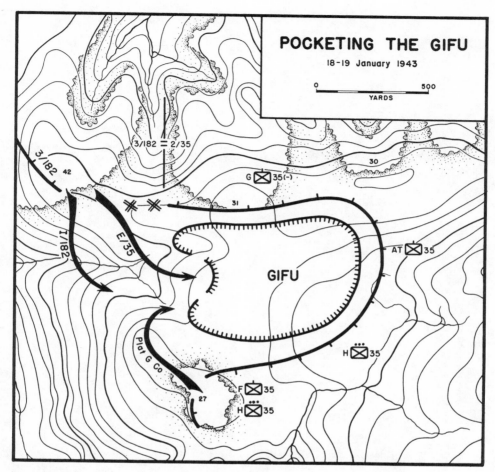

MAP NO. 13

Company had located two pillboxes on its front, one of which was knocked out after the platoon leader had given firing data to 81-mm. mortars.

The next day, 19 January, E Company resumed its attack, but a pillbox and machine-gun defense held it down. (*Map 13*) The Gifu, however, was beginning to crack. A 37-mm. antitank gun and an 81-mm. mortar hit one of the two pillboxes discovered in front of Hill 27 by an F Company patrol. G Company reported that it had definitely located twelve pillboxes on its front. E Company, which had begun its attack at 0800, reported at 1615 that it had killed six of the enemy, knocked out four machine guns, and located twelve machine-gun posi-

35TH INFANTRY TROOPS LEAVE THE LINE *after 21 days of fighting to capture the Gifu. Tense nerves and weariness are apparent in the first two men of the returning column.*

tions and pillboxes on a small ridge. One hour later the company reported that it had destroyed three more positions, but that nine wired-in pillboxes, from ten to twelve feet apart, held it back. Grenades failed to damage them, and E Company dug in for the night.[46]

Heavy rain, mud, and particularly poor visibility limited operations on 20 January and prevented the 2d Battalion from exploiting its successes immediately. One patrol penetrated 150 yards north from Hill 27, and another found three pillboxes northwest of Hill 27. Two were empty. The patrol leader and one automatic rifleman approached within ten feet of the occupied pillbox before they were observed. The patrol leader shot one Japanese, and the automatic rifleman shot two more who were trying to escape, but machine guns forced the two Americans to withdraw. That night several small groups of enemy soldiers failed in their efforts to escape from the pocket. Eleven Japanese were killed.[47]

The Cracking of the Line

Tanks were made available to the 2d Battalion on 21 January, and the task of breaking the enemy lines was greatly simplified. Three Marine Corps light tanks, manned by soldiers from the 25th Division's Cavalry Reconnaissance Troop, started up the jeep trail toward Mount Austen's 1,514-foot crest. Two broke down, but the third reached the top. As the tank drew near the Gifu infantrymen fired mortars and machine guns to drown its sound, then cut down trees to permit the tank to approach the Japanese front lines.

Supported by sixteen infantrymen, the tank drove into the northeast part of the Gifu line, on G Company's left flank, at 1040 on 22 January. (*Map 14*) It pulled close to three pillboxes and destroyed them with 37-mm. high explosive shells, and shot the Japanese soldiers with canister and machine guns. Turning left (south), the tank broke out through the east end of the Gifu. At 1500 it made one more attack against the north side of the Gifu and destroyed five more pillboxes. The infantrymen then moved forward before dark to occupy the gap. That same day E Company, on the west, was again held in place by the pillboxes on its front. One platoon attempted to outflank them in the afternoon, but darkness fell before it could complete its move. But the tank, in a few hours, had torn a 200-yard hole in the line which had withstood infantry assaults for a month.

The Gifu area remained quiet until 0230 on the night of 22–23 January, when about 100 Japanese soldiers led by Major Inagaki rushed the sector held by F Company and the Antitank Company. Inagaki's desperate men used grenades,

---

[46] 35th Inf Periodic Rpt, 20 Jan 43; 35th Inf Journal, 19 Jan 43.
[47] 25th Div Opns, p. 85.

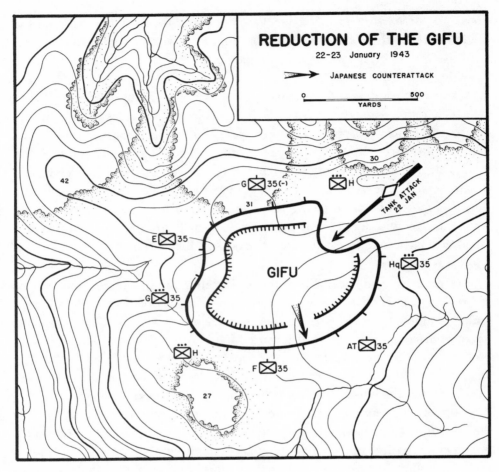

MAP NO. 14

small arms, and automatic weapons. The American companies immediately opened fire and easily broke up the attack. When day broke the Americans found 85 dead bodies in front of the two companies, including those of Inagaki, one other major, 8 captains, and 15 lieutenants.[48] Inagaki had directed his attack against pillboxes on the strongest part of the 2d Battalion's line. Had he attacked southwest against the G Company platoon northwest of Hill 27, his chances of success might have been greater, since each 15 yards of line was held by only two men.[49]

[48] Amer Div Int Rpt, Tab A; 25th Div Opns, p. 86.
[49] Interv with Col Larsen.

As the XIV Corps had already begun the second phase of the January offensives, Colonel McClure ordered the 2d Battalion to clear the remnants out of the Gifu on 23 January. The tank attacks, the success of the enveloping companies, the effect of the artillery, Inagaki's desperate attempt, and the demoralized state of the few prisoners captured had convinced Colonel Larsen that the Gifu could no longer offer serious resistance. He put his battalion in skirmish line and advanced. There was almost no fighting; the enemy survivors were trying to hide, not to fight. The only American injured was one private who was shot through the shoulder by a Japanese officer. By nightfall Colonel Larsen's battalion had cleared the Gifu.[50] Mount Austen was free of the enemy.

The reduction of the Gifu had cost the 2d Battalion 64 men killed and 42 wounded.[51] The battalion reported that it had killed 518 Japanese and had captured 40 machine guns, 12 mortars, 200 rifles, and 38 sabers. The Gifu garrison had been almost completely wiped out. Colonel McClure reported that the 35th Infantry in its operations on Mount Austen and the Sea Horse had killed almost 1,100 of the enemy, and had captured 29 prisoners, 88 light and heavy machine guns, 678 rifles, 79 pistols, plus a quantity of ammunition.[52]

The destruction of the determined defenders of the Gifu strong point had engaged five battalions of infantry, and lasted over one month. Finally the last effective enemy force east of the Matanikau River had been wiped out, and the 35th Infantry became the reserve of the 25th Division, which was then advancing rapidly to the west.

The first January offensive by the XIV Corps had gained about 3,000 yards of ground. (*Map XVIII*) The western line, running from the coast west of Point Cruz inland to the southwest Matanikau fork, had been firmly established. The south flank, extending east to Mount Austen, was now secure. In the opinion of the Corps commander, the 25th Division had performed brilliantly.[53]

---

[50] *Ibid*

[51] 25th Div Opns, p. 88.

[52] Rpt, CO, 35th Inf to CG, 25th Div. 25th Division Operations lists 431 Japanese killed. Colonel McClure's report includes those killed by artillery fire.

[53] Rad, CG Cactus to COMSOPAC, 0507 of 14 Jan 43, in USAFISPA G–3 Worksheet File 1–15 Jan 43. General Patch, in XIV Corps GO No. 52, 7 Mar 43, cited the 25th Division for "outstanding performance of duty" from 10 January to 9 February 1943. He recommended that the Division be cited in War Department General Orders, and COMGENSOPAC concurred, but the recommendation was not approved. See ltr, CG XIV Corps to TAG, 7 Mar 43, sub: Recommendation of Citation of 25th Inf. Div. WPD 210.54 (3–1–42) in HRS DRB AGO.

CHAPTER XIII

Fighting on Guadalcanal

By January 1943 all Army and Marine Corps units which were to take part in the campaign had landed and been committed to action. From hard experience the Americans had learned a great deal about jungle fighting, acquiring a knowledge which was to be advantageous to the forces which were to take part in the final offensive, as well as in later campaigns in the Pacific. The lessons of the Guadalcanal campaign, ably compiled by the men who fought there, reflect in concrete terms the nature of the fighting described above, as well as that which was still to come.[1]

The Americans

Tactics

Thus far the fighting on Guadalcanal was clearly showing that the offensive and defensive principles embodied in the American tactical manuals were basically sound and sufficiently flexible to be adapted to the terrain in the Solomons. The Americal Division, in its operations on the beach, advocated advancing on a broad front with units in column and echeloned to protect the flanks. Because the rough terrain and thick jungles prevented commanders from exercising close control over widely dispersed units, the columns deployed as late and as close to the enemy as possible.

The 25th Division, which operated over open hills and jungle country, found that squad columns and skirmish lines could operate effectively over open ground. For approach marches in deep jungles, where an entire battalion often moved over a single trail, a column of files, deploying as late as possible, was best.

---

[1] Unless otherwise indicated data in this chapter are generally derived from XIV Corps, Informal Rpt (to COMGENSOPAC) on Combat Opns, 3 Jun 43. For a clear statement of the opinions of individuals, see Close-Up of Guadalcanal, October–November 1942 (1943) which is a verbatim report of participants' statements by Lt. Col. R. P. Reeder, Jr. This study is also available under the title Fighting on Guadalcanal (OPD, WDGS, 1943).

All divisions and regiments agreed that the wisdom of enveloping one or more of the enemy's flanks, rather than attacking frontally, had been repeatedly demonstrated. When the Japanese resisted vigorously from a pocket or strong point, the best technique was to bypass the pocket, continue the advance, and reduce the pocket at leisure.

Except in rare instances, advancing units usually halted early enough in the afternoon to establish all-round defenses and permit defensive artillery and mortar concentrations to be registered before the fall of darkness. Halting in the afternoon gave the troops time to dig foxholes and emplacements, string barbed wire, emplace and site heavy weapons, and camouflage the position as much as possible. By halting in daylight, troops in the jungle could also determine the location of the units on their flanks. If this was not done, inexperienced troops were apt to fire on each other during the night. All movement within a defensive area ceased after nightfall.

Infantry fighting was close work, as most targets lay less than fifty yards from the infantrymen. The nature of the terrain broke most engagements into "small unit scraps" in which "success is dependent upon the individual soldiers, NCO's, and platoon leaders' ability to act promptly and intelligently when confronted with a situation." [2]

The soldiers and marines had seen repeatedly demonstrated the obvious truth that success in war demands skillful and vigorous leadership from all ranks charged with the responsibility of providing leadership. Those whose leadership faltered under the stress of combat had to be relieved of their commands.

Weapons

American weapons had generally proved to be both potent and practical. The U. S. Rifle, M1 (Garand) had shown itself to be superior to the M1903 (Springfield), with which many marines had been armed. Other small arms were less satisfactory. The .45-caliber automatic pistol found little use. The Marines' Reising Gun, a .45-caliber submachine gun, proved to be almost worthless.[3] The .45-caliber Thompson submachine gun, while efficient, sounded too much like Japanese .25-caliber weapons, and could not be safely employed at the front. Bayonets and knives were valuable in close combat at night, as were hand grenades, but rifle and antitank grenades lacked sufficiently sensitive fuzes.

The larger infantry weapons were extremely efficient, although most troops complained of their weight. The light air-cooled .30-caliber machine gun sup-

[2] Gavan, Personal Account, p. 4.
[3] 1st Mar Div Rpt, II, 16.

EMPLOYMENT OF TANKS *in Guadalcanal was hampered by the nature of the terrain. Light tanks were difficult to maneuver in the dense jungle and vulnerable to enemy mines and antitank guns.*

planted the heavy water-cooled .30-caliber machine gun in supporting infantry attacks, but the most valuable infantry weapon for an attack was the light, mobile .30-caliber Browning automatic rifle. Caliber .50 machine guns and 37-mm. antitank guns, while not generally used offensively, were excellent in defense positions, as were the heavy .30-caliber machine guns. The 60-mm. mortar, carried by hand, followed closely behind assaulting infantrymen, and its fire was effective in open terrain. The 81-mm. mortar could not follow closely behind an attack, but it was usually brought forward as soon as possible and was invaluable for close support of the infantry.

American troops, in accordance with standard tactical doctrines, were relying heavily upon artillery for both offense and defense despite inaccurate maps, limited observation, and the difficulties of hauling ammunition. Of the three calibers of howitzers generally used on Guadalcanal, the 75-mm. pack howitzer, though mobile, was too light; the 105-mm. howitzer was very good, and the 155-mm. howitzer was excellent. Neither the XIV Corps nor the divisions possessed any organic aviation, and adjustment of the artillery was usually effected through forward observers. Since infantrymen in their first battle were often apprehensive when their own artillery put fire over their heads to hit targets directly in front of them, forward observers usually laid the first registration shots deep in enemy territory, and then brought the fire back toward the American front lines.

Close support of ground troops by aircraft, used consistently by the 1st Marine Division, was being continued by the XIV Corps. Close air support was not always easy to employ, for complete radio facilities for air-to-ground communications were not always available, and the designation of the enemy targets and American front lines by panels and smoke was not always accurate in rough terrain. The best solution for these difficulties lay in careful planning, close liaison, and direct observation of the targets and front lines by the pilots before taking off.

Tank destroyers, in support of the infantry, were effective in defensive missions, and where there was space for maneuver they were useful offensively. Tanks were very good in the offensive but the jungle, by hampering their fields of vision and freedom to maneuver, limited their effectiveness by making them easy prey to mines and antitank guns. They were safe only when closely supported by infantrymen. Light tanks, the only kind employed on Guadalcanal, were vulnerable to enemy gunfire; medium tanks would have been better.[4]

---

[4] Ltr, CG 1st Mar Div to Comdt Mar Corps, 1 Jul 43, sub: Final Rpt Guadalcanal Opn.

Intelligence

In addition to the information it received from coastwatchers and higher headquarters, the XIV Corps, like the 1st Marine Division, was deriving knowledge of enemy strength, dispositions, and capabilities from all the units under its control. Motor torpedo boats, patrolling Sealark Channel and the coasts of the adjacent islands, reported regularly. Direct aerial observation and aerial photographs yielded valuable data. Corps headquarters, though hampered by lack of enough photographic interpreters, based its plan of attack in January largely upon conclusions derived from the study of photographs. The Corps depended on ground patrols, usually of reinforced platoon strength, for close-in combat intelligence—finding routes of approach, enemy front lines, soft spots, and strong points. The quality of patrolling had been improving since D Day. Reconnaissance patrols had learned to avoid battle but to gather information, and the men had become more confident of their ability to move and fight in the jungle. But until the end of the campaign reports from ground patrols were often erroneous. Misled by the difficulty of walking through dark, rough jungle, patrols frequently overestimated the distances they had traveled.

Captured documents were still a fruitful source of data on enemy units, for the Japanese carelessly carried diaries and orders into the front lines. Prisoners of war, if well treated, usually gave voluminous testimony on all subjects. Apparently the Japanese belief that it is dishonorable to surrender had led the *Imperial Army* to neglect to instruct soldiers on what to do if captured, for the enemy soldiers, once taken prisoner, talked freely. But very few Japanese soldiers ever gave themselves up voluntarily. The American troops, who were fearful of the widely publicized treacherousness of the enemy, were reluctant to take prisoners, and the Japanese soldiery usually fought until they were killed rather than capitulate.

The XIV Corps, besides the voice broadcasts at the Gifu, also employed leaflets to induce surrenders. On 10 January Allied planes dropped 18,000 copies of a War Department propaganda leaflet which compared the hardships of the front-line soldier with the ease of those behind the lines. Two days later 25,000 copies of Emperor Hirohito's poem on peace were dropped. The War Department had also furnished a surrender leaflet, but because it urged the Japanese to surrender at any time, it was altered. In the revised version the Japanese were instructed to surrender by entering the American lines through open areas in daylight, unarmed, their hands above their heads. These leaflets were dropped on 16 January. Their effectiveness is difficult to measure. Out of a group of eighty-four prisoners taken by the XIV Corps between 1 January and 15 February 1943, thirty-three were sick or wounded men who could not walk. Fifty-one gave up voluntarily, and only twelve of these had surrender leaflets in their possession.[5]

The Measure of the Enemy

American troops, none of whom had received the specialized jungle training that was later given to all units in the Pacific, were learning that the Japanese, though a brave, resolute, and often skillful soldier, could be soundly beaten. On the offensive his endurance, high morale, and soldierly ability made him dangerous. Yet there were grave weaknesses inherent in Japanese offensive tactics. His artillery was seldom present in sufficient strength, by American standards, to support an offensive, and his artillery techniques were not sufficiently developed to mass fire and change targets quickly. Although fairly efficient in night operations, the Japanese often ignored the dangers of assembling in or marching through areas on which American artillery fire had already been registered. The maneuver employed in the October counteroffensive—an attack against an axis of communication, coupled with an envelopment through "impassable" terrain culminating in a mass rush on a narrow front—employed dense concentrations of infantrymen, which were vulnerable targets for both artillery and infantry fires. The Japanese, in an offensive, was wont to follow a fixed plan rigidly; he apparently lacked either the flexibility of mind or enough military technique to alter his plans when they went askew. The Japanese, on the other hand, believed that American troops lacked initiative, that they would execute a given order and then stop rather than exploit their opportunities to move forward.[6]

Japanese military judgment appeared to err on the side of optimism, for in offensive action on Guadalcanal the enemy almost invariably committed forces smaller than those of the Americans. His intelligence techniques were apparently unsound; he consistently underestimated the size of the forces opposing him.[7] However, the Japanese had learned caution in one respect. Although continuing to stress infiltration and harassment, he had learned that American flanks and rear areas were not as vulnerable as he had once believed.[8] (Appendix D)

[5] Amer Div Int Rpt, Tab F.

[6] ATIS, SWPA, Enemy Pub No. 56, 21 Nov 43, Characteristics of American Combat Methods on Guadalcanal, trans of Japanese booklet of 4 Nov 43, p. 3.

[7] See ltr, CG 1st Mar Div to Comdt Mar Corps, 1 Jul 43, sub: Final Rpt Guadalcanal Opn.

[8] Cf ATIS, SWPA, Enemy Pub No. 56 with ATIS, SWPA, Enemy Pub No. 64, 1 Dec 43, U. S. Army Combat Methods, Trans of an *Oki Shudan* (*17th Army*) brochure issued in Sep 42.

TRANSPORTATION PROBLEMS *were a major factor in the progress of the Guadalcanal battle. Where roads could be constructed, the jeep and 2½-ton truck served well, as along Marine Trail (above) on the east bank of the Matanikau. Off the trails, troops had to hack their way through dense jungle with machetes, covering only a mile or two a day.*

In defense the Japanese soldier was more skillful, and hence more formidable, than in offense. His strong points were well located and well organized, his weapons well sited, and his camouflage superior. His tenacity, his willingness to starve or be shot rather than surrender, may be denounced as fanaticism, but such qualities gave vital strength to his defense. His weapons—.25-caliber rifles, mortars, grenade dischargers, and artillery—were well made and efficient although his technical proficiency in the use of weapons was lower than that of the Americans.

The Japanese was also learning much about American troops and methods, although he does not always appear to have applied his lessons in the Solomons campaigns. In general, he was impressed by American equipment and fire power. He admired the mechanized equipment and the abundance of ammunition, although claiming that many of the artillery shells fired on Guadalcanal failed to explode. He particularly admired the skill of American artillerymen in massing and shifting fire. While denying that American tactics were better than Japanese, he noted that the former, though somewhat cautious, were thorough, well planned, systematic, and sound. Co-operation between the Army and Navy, he believed, was good. He considered that American troops, though unduly prudent and apt to fire too high, were steady in the attack.[9] In the words of the *17th Army's* former chief of staff: "As a former soldier I must pay respect to the American infantrymen, artillerymen, and tank corpsmen who attacked the Japanese Army sustaining severe losses in each battle, while suffering the hardships of malaria and amoebic dysentery in the Guadalcanal and New Guinea campaigns."[10]

Logistics

Transportation

On the best motor roads of Guadalcanal, trucks could travel at twenty miles per hour if the roads were not muddy. Off the roads, they could scarcely move. On the jungle trails, the average march speed for troops was one mile per hour. Off the trails in the jungle, where troops had to hack their way through the undergrowth with machetes and bayonets, a half mile per hour was a rapid march speed. Under these conditions, supply and evacuation posed grave problems. Supply dumps were located as far forward as possible, and trucks carried

---

[9] Interrog of Hyakutake, Maruyama, Miyazaki, Sumiyoshi, Tamaki, Tajima, and Konuma.

[10] Miyazaki, Personal Account, p. 8.

supplies from the dumps to the termini of the roads. From the road-end forward, supplies were carried by hand, by boat, and by cableways. In the front lines, where men were forced to remain under cover, supplies were usually distributed by being thrown from foxhole to foxhole.

There were never enough trucks, but those which were available were giving excellent service. The powered front axles of American military trucks enabled them to traverse bogs, mud, and sand which would have stopped ordinary vehicles. The 2½-ton truck, although not always sufficiently powerful to pull a 105-mm. howitzer, worked well, as did the jeep.

One interesting experiment in transportation in jungle warfare was the use of mules. The 97th Field Artillery Battalion (75-mm. pack howitzers) which supported the advance up the north coast had mules. The presence of the animals complicated rather than simplified the logistical problem. Mules could not traverse all the types of terrain that a man on foot could negotiate. They could not get over boggy ground or cross muddy banks and stream beds. Although able to cover from four to five miles per hour over favorable terrain, the mules could cover only one mile per hour over Guadalcanal's roads and trails. As a result they caused traffic jams and impeded the trucks. Nor could the battalion easily supply itself. Each firing battery had 193 men and 117 mules. This entire strength was required to transport the four 75-mm. pack howitzers and 200 rounds of ammunition allotted to each battery. To assist in moving ammunition forward, one ammunition section from the Service Battery—including 43 pack mules and 23 riding mules—was attached to the firing battery, to increase its strength to 212 men and 182 mules. But each mule required eight pounds of oats and 14 pounds of hay per day for feed. Thus, keeping four guns in action required the services of 212 men and 182 mules. To feed the mules necessitated hauling 1,500 pounds of oats and 2,600 pounds of hay to the front daily by some agency other than the firing battery, for the mules could not haul feed as well as howitzers and ammunition. The experiment was unsuccessful.

Evacuation of the wounded was effected by the same general means by which supplies were brought forward. Cableways, hand-borne litters, jeeps, boats, ambulances, and trucks were all employed.

Engineering problems, like all others on the island, were difficult to solve. Roads through the jungle and over the steep hills were hard to build and maintain. Since the XIV Corps possessed no corps engineers, Americal and 25th Division engineer battalions functioned as both corps and divisional engineers. Each battalion had been able to transport only two bulldozers to Guadalcanal, and the

CONSTRUCTION EQUIPMENT *was scarce and inadequate. The light bulldozer above is shown improving the trail over "Windmill Hill" (Hill 35) on Wright Road. Runways were leveled by small Army Corps of Engineers earth movers which had been brought to Guadalcanal only when already-crowded transport space would permit.*

bulldozers were too old and too light for efficient service. Not until January was there a power shovel for the Army engineers, and at no time was there a sawmill.

Since flash floods on the rivers usually washed out temporary bridges, the 1st (Marine) Engineer Battalion in November ingeniously built its own pile driver with salvaged steel trusses, a ¾-inch steel cable, a gasoline-driven winch, and a 500-pound hammer. This contrivance, which could drive 8-inch piles from eight to ten feet into the river bottoms, enabled the marines to build bridges that would withstand the floods.[11]

Rations and Clothing

The rations usually served to troops in combat were the C and K rations. These were nutritious but somewhat greasy for use in the tropics. The C ration consisted of prepared meals—meat and beans, stew, or meat and vegetable hash in the dinner ration, and biscuits, candy, and a concentrated beverage powder for breakfast—packed in tin cans. One day's ration weighed over five pounds, and was bulky and heavy in a man's pack. The concentrated nonperishable K ration included a small can of cheese or meat paste, biscuits, candy, beverage powder, chewing gum, and two cigarettes. It was packed in waterproof paper packages, was lighter than the C and easier to pack. But most men found the cold K rations tiresome, and agreed that the C ration, whether hot or cold, was wearisome.

Men did not carry complete mess kits into action with them. A canteen cup and spoon sufficed each man. Both C and K rations could be eaten out of the containers with either hands or spoon. Means of washing mess kits thoroughly were not to be found at the front, and to eat from an improperly washed kit led to violent diarrhea.

In the rear areas, when kitchens and messes were established, hot meals were served. But they were little better than those at the front, for they were prepared from canned and dehydrated meats and vegetables. There were virtually no fresh foods—eggs, milk, butter, or meat—then available on Guadalcanal, and shipping and refrigerator space was too scarce to ship such commodities for anyone but hospital patients. The only fresh food most men tasted during the campaign came from a shipment of turkey, fresh potatoes, oranges, and celery brought in for their Christmas dinner.

For combat in the jungle, the light color of the cotton khaki uniform was too conspicuous. The uniform most suitable for combat was, for the soldier, the two-piece green twill fatigue uniform rather than the one-piece coverall, and for the

---

[11] 1st Mar Div Rpt, V, Logistics Annex Z, 6.

marine, the two-piece green utility suit. Shoes made of undressed leather, well covered with waterproofing grease and soled with rubber or a composition material, rendered the best service. Canvas leggings did not give good service. They held the damp and chafed the ankles, and the buckles, straps, and hooks caught in the underbrush. The steel helmet was invaluable; besides protecting the head it served as an entrenching tool, cooking pot, and wash basin.

Communications

Voice radio sets were not functioning at full efficiency on Guadalcanal. Moisture and corrosion affected the circuits and metallic contacts, altered frequencies, and occasionally drowned out sets completely. The heavy jungle and deep valleys blocked the waves from some of the lighter sets. Some sets assigned to the infantry divisions were too heavy to move conveniently by manpower when trucks and roads were not available. The SCR's 194 and 195 (the "Walkie Talkie"), powered by dry batteries, possessed a range of from one to two miles. They served well enough in open and high ground, but were ineffective in the jungle. The battery-powered 6-pound SCR 536 ("Handy Talkie"), with a range of 1½ miles, could be used only in open terrain and was very fragile.

The 20-pound battery-powered SCR 511, with a range of five miles, was dependable if kept dry, and could readily be carried by one man. The most reliable set for infantry use was the portable, hand-generated SCR 284. This set, with a range of seven miles, weighed 110 pounds, and required several men to carry it. The SCR 284 could be transported in a jeep, but jolting over the rough roads was apt to damage it. The bulky, long-range SCR 193 proved to be effective for ground-to-air communications, as well as for communication between division and corps headquarters.

In the absence of reliable radio communications the infantry regiments, battalions, and companies were relying most heavily on wire communications. They employed the EE–8 field and the sound-powered telephones for long and short distances, respectively. Wire communications, though reliable, required continuous maintenance. Wires had to be strung overhead for complete efficiency, since vehicles and men on foot were apt to break wire laid on the ground. One of the most effective circuits for field telephones was a ground return circuit superimposed upon a metallic circuit by the use of repeating coils. Ground return circuits gave more reliable service than completely metallic circuits, but were subject to interception by the Japanese.

The lessons of the first months of Guadalcanal had been well learned, were applied in the final stages of the campaign, and were to be embodied in future training programs. Training for jungle combat would need to be realistic and rigorous; it would need to employ difficult, extended maneuvers over long and arduous distances, intensive practice in scouting and patrolling, experience in undergoing overhead fire, close infantry-artillery teamwork, and wide envelopments, as well as thorough training in the use of weapons.

The morale and mental attitude of the troops had been and would continue to be an integral part of their preparation for combat. The exaggerated reputation which the Japanese fighting man enjoyed during the early part of 1942 had by now been deflated, but a few superstitions remained in men's minds. One of the great bugaboos of the Guadalcanal campaign which slowed nearly all advances by the infantry was the belief, firmly held by nearly all troops, that Japanese "snipers" operated from treetops. But this belief, which the Japanese curiously entertained about American "snipers," was seldom supported by facts. The Japanese rifleman was not especially equipped for sniping, nor did he usually climb into trees to shoot.[12]

Realistic training would also be needed to accustom troops to battle and jungle noises, for the average American unit, during its first night in the jungle on Guadalcanal, would nervously fire at the sounds made by birds, land crabs, creaking branches, and falling foliage. Rigid discipline and training in sanitation were likewise necessary. It was essential that soldiers be thoroughly indoctrinated in the need for disposal of all waste materials, and that malaria discipline, including the use of mosquito nets, complete clothing after dusk, killing of mosquito larvae, and the regular use of atabrine tablets, be strictly enforced.

---

[12] Statement made by Ito to Gen Sebree in 1946. Interv with Gen Sebree, 19–20 Jun 47. Equally false was the rumor that there were Japanese women on Guadalcanal. This belief may have been engendered by the quantities of contraceptive devices and women's underclothing that were found in Japanese bivouacs. Only three men—a field officer, a lieutenant, and a 1st Sergeant—claim to have *seen* a Japanese woman. The field officer and the sergeant found a female corpse on the southwest coast which they thought was that of a Japanese. Amer Div Int Rpt, p. 17; interv with Gen Sebree. The lieutenant asserted that he saw the dead body of the Japanese woman "sniper" that had been cut down from a tree on Mount Austen about 20–22 December 1942. Statement by the lieutenant, of K Co, 132d Inf, 18 Feb 43, in notes of G–2 Hist Sec, USAFISPA, in files of Hist Div, SSUSA.

CHAPTER XIV

XIV Corps' Second January Offensive

When the 25th Division completed the capture of the Galloping Horse on 13 January, it doubled the length of the Corps' west front. The front now extended far enough inland to enable the Corps to advance westward on a broad front without much danger of having its left flank enveloped. General Patch then prepared for a second co-ordinated attack designed to carry through Kokumbona to the Poha River, about 9,000 yards west of Point Cruz.

Such an attack had to wait until supplies could catch up with the troops. The 25th Division was forced to halt after capturing the Galloping Horse until the road net could be extended sufficiently to bring enough supplies forward to support the next drive.[1] Engineers immediately began to push the Hill 66 road to the southwest, but it was 22 January before the Corps could resume its advance on a two-division front. The units on the beach, on the right flank of the 25th Division, were not impeded in their forward movement by lack of supplies. These were brought to them over the coast road network, and they were able to move forward almost every day from 13 to 24 January.

General Patch hoped to trap and destroy the Japanese in Kokumbona. There were only two routes by which they could escape from that village. The easiest lay along the flat ground on the north coast between Kokumbona and Cape Esperance, and was then controlled by the Japanese. The second route lay over a 20-mile-long native trail which ran from Kokumbona southwestward through the mountains to Beaufort Bay on the south coast.

Allied patrols had explored most of the trail in December.[2] Beaufort Bay was friendly territory. The Japanese had never operated in strength on the south coast. Emery de Klerk, a Belgian missionary of the Roman Catholic Society of Mary who had maintained a station at Beaufort Bay before the war, had declined to be evacuated when the marines had come, but gave his services as a coastwatcher, recruiter of native labor, and authority on terrain.[3]

---

[1] Rad, CG Guadalcanal to COMSOPAC, 20 Jan 43. XIV Corps G–3 Journal.

[2] Amer Div G–3 Periodic Rpt, 15 Dec–31 Dec 42, in USAFISPA G–3 Periodic Rpts.

[3] 1st Mar Div Rpt V, Int Annex N, 9.

To prevent the Japanese from escaping via Beaufort Bay, General Patch had dispatched there a shore-to-shore expedition even before the opening of the first January offensive. The expedition was to land at Beaufort Bay and proceed over the trail to block the passes in the mountains near the village of Vurai, which lay southwest of Kokumbona. In the narrow mountain defiles, a small force might withstand entire battalions of infantry.[4] Troops for the expedition were provided by the 147th Infantry. Commanded by Capt. Charles E. Beach, the force consisted of I Company, one platoon from M Company, one platoon from the Antitank Company, and pioneer, medical, and communication troops.[5]

On 7 January Captain Beach's command boarded two tank landing craft (LCT) at Kukum to sail around Cape Esperance at night, and reached Klerk's mission at 1315 on 9 January. The force landed and one I Company platoon, plus the antitank and heavy weapons platoons and pioneers, established beach defenses.

Two days later, while the 27th Infantry was fighting on the Galloping Horse, the remainder of the expedition set out over the mountain trail and reached Vurai on 14 January. There the troops established a base camp, a defensive line, and outposts. When patrols failed to find any Japanese the main camp was moved farther north to Tapananja on the upper reaches of the Nueha River, about six miles south of Sealark Channel. Outposts guarded the upper Poha, but no Japanese attempted to make their way from Kokumbona along the blocked trail.

The blocking force subsisted on scanty rations. Natives were to have carried food over the mountains, but apparently little food actually reached I Company, which after trying to subsist on baked green bananas reported that they "taste like hell." Captain Beach requested that aircraft drop food to his force, but XIV Corps headquarters refused for fear of revealing the block to the enemy.[6]

The Japanese never attempted to make their way over the trail; the block by Beach's detachment, however, was an economical method of ensuring that the enemy did not escape southward from Kokumbona to hide in the mountains or on the south coast.

[4] Interv with Col Long, 26 Mar 46.

[5] 147th Inf Hist, 1940–1944, Annex No 1. (n. p.); 147th Inf FO No. 19, 7 Jan 43, in misc docs from USAFISPA. Practically all data on the Vurai Block are derived from the 147th Inf Hist.

[6] Rads between Capt Beach and XIV Corps G–3 in XIV Corps G–3 Journal, 20 Jan 43.

FIRE SUPPORT FOR THE SECOND JANUARY OFFENSIVE *was given by both Army and Navy units. Above, a 155-mm. gun is seen firing on targets in the Kokumbona area while below, a destroyer steams along the coast farther west to hit Japanese positions. Cape Esperance is on the horizon just above the gun blast.*

Plans and Preparations

XIV Corps' Offensive Plans

Two days after Captain Beach's force reached Vurai, General Patch directed the XIV Corps to resume its co-ordinated attacks. (Appendix C) Field Order No. 1, issued on 16 January, ordered the Corps to attack west to gain a line extending southwest from a point on the beach about 2,600 yards west of Point Cruz inland to a point about 3,000 yards west of the Galloping Horse. Since most of the regiments of both the 2d Marine and American Divisions were too badly worn out for further offensive action, the Corps commander formed the Composite Army–Marine (CAM) Division from the 6th Marines, the 182d and the 147th Infantry Regiments, and the 2d Marine and American Division artillery units. The CAM Division was to continue the coastal drive on the right of the 25th Division on a 3,000-yard front. It was also to keep contact on its left with the 25th Division and guard the shore line between the Matanikau River and the objective.[7] General Patch ordered the 25th Division to attack to the southwest to envelop the Japanese south (right) flank and cover the XIV Corps' left (south) flank. "Isolated points of enemy resistance" were to be contained, bypassed, and reduced later. After reaching its objective the Corps was to be prepared to continue the attack to the northwest.

Artillery support arrangements were the same as those made on 10 January. General Mulcahy's 2d Marine Air Wing was to give close air support. Destroyers of the U. S. Navy, assisted by fire control parties on shore, would bombard enemy coastal positions. During the attack the American Division (less the 182d Infantry) and the 2d and 8th Marines were to man the Lunga perimeter defense.[8]

The ground over which the XIV Corps was to fight is similar to that covered in the first January offensive. On the coast the rocky north-south ridges, with deep ravines between, furnished the enemy with strong natural positions from which to oppose the CAM Division. The 25th Division's zone covered higher ground than the CAM Division's. The outstanding feature of the inland zone is the hill mass formed by Hills 87–88–89, the highest ground on the

---

[7] By 20 January 2d Marine Division units in the front lines consisted of Headquarters, 2d Marine Division and the 6th Marines, with 182d Infantry (less 3d Battalion) and 147th Infantry attached. In subsequent field orders this unit was called CAM (Composite Army–Marine) Division, and for simplicity's sake will be so termed here.

[8] XIV Corps FO No. 1, in 25th Div Opns, App. VIII, and Amer Div G–3 Journal.

north coast between the Matanikau River and Cape Esperance. These hills dominate Kokumbona just as Mount Austen dominates Lunga Point.

25th Division's Preliminary Movements

To carry out General Patch's orders for the offensive, General Collins, on 20 January 1943, ordered the 25th Division to attack west from the Galloping Horse on 22 January. The 27th Infantry was to deliver a holding attack while the 161st Infantry, making the division's main effort, moved southwest to outflank the enemy. The 35th Infantry was to complete mopping up the Gifu, then pass to division reserve.[9]

In the 161st Infantry's zone, three small open hills lay southwest of the Hill 53. (*Map XIX*) Hill Z, the most distant, was 2,500 yards from Hill 53, and 6,900 yards south of Sealark Channel. The 161st Infantry was to seize these hills, then move northwest through the jungle to attack Hill 87, the division objective, from the rear. After the capture of Hill 87 the regiment was to seize the other two eminences (Hills 88 and 89) comprising the hill mass.

The road up to the Galloping Horse had been extended to Hill 53. Supplies for the 161st Infantry had been trucked to Hill 53, and native bearers were to hand-carry supplies forward from there to support the attack. The 161st Infantry assembled on the southern parts of the Galloping Horse. On 20 January the 2d Battalion advanced to Hill X, and the next day to Hill Y, but found no strong forces there. The battalion killed only one Japanese on 21 January.

In the northern half of the 25th Division's zone, the 27th Infantry prepared for its holding attack. A long, slender, open ridge runs from a point southwest of Hill 66 near the northwest Matanikau fork to a point east of Hill 87. This ridge, called the "Snake" from its appearance in an aerial photograph, provided a route of approach for the 27th Infantry. To supply the 27th's attack, the 57th and 65th Engineer Battalions extended the road from Hill 66 up to the Snake's back prior to 22 January, and when the infantry advanced the engineers were to push the road to Hill 87.

On 17 January Colonel Jurney's 1st Battalion, the assault unit, had outposted the Snake. C Company, with one light machine gun section attached, occupied the Snake's head. On 20 January a patrol from A Company—one rifle and one mortar squad—advanced west over the Snake toward Hill 87. As the patrol neared Hill 87C enemy machine-gun and mortar fire forced the soldiers to take cover. When the patrol radioed for assistance one rifle platoon

---

[9] 25th Div FO No. 2, in 25th Div Opns, App. IX.

THE AREA OF ADVANCE FROM THE SNAKE *was over Hills 87, 88, and 89, then northward over Hill 90 toward Kokumbona. At bottom of the photo is seen the west side of Hill 57 (part of the Galloping Horse).*

from the 1st Battalion started forward. Before the reinforcing platoon reached the scene an artillery forward observer with the beleaguered patrol radioed firing data to his battalion. The resulting artillery bombardment forced the enemy to cease fire and the 1st Battalion patrol returned safely.[10]

The enemy still held Hill 87; the mortars and machine guns emplaced there helped to confirm the American belief that the position would be strongly defended. Because Hill 87 dominated Hill 87C, the 1st Battalion did not try to hold the latter prior to 22 January.

A second 1st Battalion patrol marched without incident to Hill 87G, 1,000 yards northwest of 87C, on 20 January. Because the route led the patrol over such rough terrain that it took three hours to travel the distance, Colonel Jurney determined to attack only over the Snake on 22 January.

Colonel Mitchell's 2d Battalion of the 27th Infantry, in reserve, took over the 1st Battalion's old positions on Hill 57 on 21 January. The 3d Battalion, Colonel Bush commanding, moved to the Snake's head on the same day to be in position to follow closely behind the assaulting 1st Battalion.

The 25th Division's Advance to Kokumbona

First Day: The Change in Plan

Infantrymen of the 25th Division attacked at 0630, 22 January. (*Map XX*) The divisional field order had not specifically ordered a preparatory artillery bombardment, but at the requests of the regimental commanders the division artillery fired 12½ tons of 75-mm., 105-mm., and 155-mm. ammunition into the 161st Infantry's zone southwest of the Galloping Horse, and 55½ tons on Hill 87. Four battalions put fire on Hill 87; the 8th Field Artillery Battalion, for example, fired at an extremely rapid rate—fourteen and one-half rounds per gun per minute.[11]

While the 1st Battalion of the 161st Infantry covered the division's left flank, the 2d Battalion, which had been designated as the assault battalion, moved off Hill Y into the deep jungle. The 3d Battalion followed to Hills X and Y. The 2d Battalion began marching along an old trail toward Hill 87.[12]

The 27th Infantry launched its holding attack simultaneously with the 161st's attempted envelopment. At 0630 the 1st Battalion started over the nar-

---

[10] 25th Div G–2 Journal, 20 Jan 43; 25th Div Opns, p. 52.
[11] *Ibid.*, pp. 63 and 136.
[12] This battalion turned north too soon. Gen Collins' statement in 25th Div Opns, p. 122.

row Snake in a column of companies led by C Company. At 0700, when the artillery battalions ceased firing, the 27th Infantry's mortars and 37-mm. guns on the Snake opened fire at Hill 87. C Company started to climb Hill 87F but Japanese machine-gun fire from the top of Hill 87 forced it to halt. American mortars and antitank guns on the Snake silenced the enemy, and by 0745 the battalion had resumed the advance.[13] The battalion then deployed—A Company on the right, B in the center, and C on the left—and assaulted Hill 87. But the enemy had withdrawn; there was no opposition. By 0910, in less than three hours, the battalion had advanced almost 3,000 yards to the summit of Hill 87, the day's objective.

Fortunately the XIV Corps possessed officers who were flexible enough to change their plans to exploit this unexpectedly rapid advance. General Patch had orally instructed the 25th Division commander that if the attack progressed well, the 161st Infantry was to push past the day's objective to take Hills 88 and 89 without waiting for the 27th to reach Hill 87.[14] But the 27th had reached its objective while the assault battalion of the 161st was still deep in the jungle. Colonel Jurney's battalion therefore advanced past the objective. While A Company held Hill 87, B Company went forward 500 yards to seize Hill 88 and C Company advanced 1,000 yards west and north to take Hill 89 by 1035.[15] By 1100 all companies were in place and digging in.

General Collins witnessed this rapid advance from the division observation post on Hill 49 east of the Matanikau. In view of General Patch's instructions to go beyond the objective if possible, General Collins, who in Admiral Halsey's words was "quick on his feet and even quicker in his brain,"[16] left the observation post and started toward Hill 89 by jeep and on foot to make arrangements to continue the attack, for the 27th Infantry had outrun its wire communications. Reaching Hill 66, he met Brig. Gen. Robert L. Spragins, the Corps chief of staff, and obtained authority from him, in the name of the Corps commander, to continue the 25th Division's advance into Kokumbona as rapidly as possible. The boundary between the two divisions was immediately changed to place Hills 91, 98, 99, and Kokumbona in the 25th Division's zone. It then ran north to the beach in front of the CAM Division's zone of action.[17]

[13] 27th Inf Journal, 22 Jan 43.

[14] 25th Div Opns, p. 9.

[15] 27th Inf Journal, 22 Jan 43.

[16] *Admiral Halsey's Story*, p. 140.

[17] 25th Div Opns, pp. 9–10; interv with Gen Collins, 5 Dec 46.

General Collins reached Hill 89, where he conferred with the 27th Infantry's commander, Colonel McCulloch. As the 27th was obviously best situated to pursue the retreating Japanese, General Collins and Colonel McCulloch agreed that the 27th Infantry should resume the attack to capture Hills 90 and 97 just south of Kokumbona.[18] The 2d Battalion of the 161st, then deep in the jungle, continued toward Hill 87 against a few Japanese riflemen. It gained its objective in the afternoon. The 1st and 3d Battalions of the 161st were immediately withdrawn from the south flank and dispatched to the Galloping Horse and the Snake.

The main body of the 3d Battalion of the 27th Infantry had followed the 1st Battalion over the Snake to Hills 87 and 88. I Company, in covering the right flank, kept contact with the 182d Infantry in the CAM Division's zone. E Company of the 2d Battalion moved from the Galloping Horse to the Snake's head in the early morning, and later in the morning the rest of the battalion marched to the Snake to guard the regimental supply route.

The 1st Battalion, 27th Infantry, began its advance north to Hill 90 about 1400. With B Company in reserve, A and C attacked abreast. The 8th Field Artillery Battalion and D Company's heavy weapons on Hill 89 supported the infantry. Again the soldiers advanced rapidly and overran a few enemy riflemen in the deep valley between Hills 89 and 90. By 1700 Colonel Jurney's battalion, having covered nearly 2,000 more yards, had reached its objective, the high ground east and south of Kokumbona—Hills 90 and 98.[19]

The 27th's fast advance necessitated displacement of the artillery. The 64th Field Artillery Battalion, freed by the impending collapse of the Gifu, took over the missions of the 8th while that battalion moved across the Matanikau to Hill 66. On 22–23 January the 90th Field Artillery Battalion also moved its howitzers across the Matanikau to the Point Cruz area. During the displacement the 89th Field Artillery Battalion fired all general support missions, and on 23 January moved forward to Hill 49 east of the Matanikau. Only the 64th Field Artillery Battalion remained in its original position.

Second Day: The Capture of Kokumbona

The 27th Infantry's successful attack on 22 January carried it to the high ground immediately overlooking Kokumbona. In one day the 1st Battalion had gained over 4,500 yards and by nightfall the 2d and 3d Battalions were close behind. The supply route was protected, and the regiment was ready to exploit

[18] 25th Div Opns, pp. 9–10, 49, 67.
[19] XIV Corps G—3 Journal, 22 Jan 43.

U.S. LEADERS INSPECTING THE BATTLE ZONE *from a hill near the Matanikau (probably Hill 49). Left to right: Secretary of the Navy Frank Knox, General Patch, Admiral Nimitz, Admiral Halsey, and General Collins.*

A JAPANESE COASTAL POSITION *near Kokumbona, in the 6th Marines' zone, after it had been blasted open by artillery. The position apparently had housed a 75-mm. antiaircraft gun.*

its success by moving into Kokumbona. Plans to take Kokumbona on 23 January were completed on the night of 22–23 January. On the morning of 23 January the 3d Battalion, 27th, advanced north from its positions on Hills 89 and 91 to Hills 98 and 99. (*Map XX*) While the 1st Battalion's advance blocked the Japanese on the south, the 3d Battalion's move extended the regiment's right flank over the undefended hills to the beach to block the hills and the beach road and pocket the enemy facing the CAM Division in the ravines east of Hills 98 and 99.

Once the 3d Battalion was in position, the 1st Battalion, with E Company and one K Company platoon attached, sent two columns into Kokumbona from the east and south. The right flank column—B Company, the platoon from K, and one machine gun platoon and two mortar sections—attacked westward over the northern and western slopes of Hill 99. On the left A and E Companies plus one machine gun platoon and two mortar sections advanced north over Hill 90 into Kokumbona. By 1510 the two columns had each traveled over 1,000 yards to join forces in the village.

In the afternoon the 2d Battalion was ordered to hold the hills just south of Kokumbona (Hills 90 and 97), and to advance west through the jungle north of Hill 97 to complete the defense of the left flank by seizing Hill 100, about 500 yards beyond the west slopes of Hill 97. G Company assumed the defense of Hill 90, and Battalion Headquarters and H Companies extended their lines west to Hill 97. F Company moved west and killed about thirty Japanese in the jungled draw between Hills 97 and 100 cut by the Beaufort Bay trail and by the Kokumbona River, and took Hill 100 without suffering casualties.[20]

The nights were generally uneventful. The American troops built strong defenses each night, but the retreating Japanese attempted none of the night attacks which had previously characterized their operations on Guadalcanal. After the capture of Kokumbona, I Company of the 3d Battalion, 27th, blocked the road between Hill 99 and the beach. After nightfall on 23–24 January, a group of Japanese soldiers carelessly marched west along the road, talking, using flashlights, and wheeling a 37-mm. gun. Obviously unaware that the Americans had reached the beach, they walked right into I Company's block. The men in the company lay quiet until the Japanese were close, then opened fire with all weapons that would bear and killed about fifty of the enemy.

---

[20] 20th Div Opns, pp. 55–56: Mitchell. Notes. 2d Bn. 27th Inf.

CAM Division's Offensive

In the coast zone on the right of the 25th Division, marines and soldiers had been pressing forward prior to 22 January, supported by American and 2d Marine Division artillery and American destroyers firing from offshore. The 2d Marine Division's attacks from 13 and 17 January had advanced the line almost one mile beyond Point Cruz. When the battle-weary 2d and 8th Marines were relieved and returned to the perimeter defense, General Patch had attached the relatively fresh 1st and 2d Battalions of the 182d Infantry and the 1st and 3d Battalions of the 147th Infantry to the 2d Division to form the CAM Division.[21]

The 182d Infantry (less the 3d Battalion) moved into line on the left of the 6th Marines on 17 January.[22] By nightfall of 19 January the two regiments had advanced west slightly over 1,000 yards.[23] Progress was slow on the left on 19 January, although there was no heavy fighting. A gap developed between the 6th Marines and the 182d Infantry, and when the latter regiment halted short of the day's objective the 6th Marines also stopped. Only sixteen Japanese were killed during the advance on 19 January.[24] As a result of the halts and confusion on 19 January, some bitterness apparently arose between the two regiments.

By late afternoon of the same day the American Reconnaissance Squadron had relieved the 147th Infantry at Koli Point, and the 147th moved up to the Point Cruz area.[25] On 20 January the 3d Battalion, 147th (plus C Company and less I Company) began moving into the front line between the 6th Marines and the 182d Infantry. As the two battalions were not completely in position until 21 January, the CAM Division did not move forward.[26]

On 22 January the division opened a full-scale attack as part of the Corps offensive. Units from all three regiments participated; the 6th Marines attacked on the right along the beach, the 147th Infantry advanced in the center, and on the left the 182d Infantry maintained contact with the 25th Division. The

---

[21] XIV Corps Opn Memo No. 7, 16 Jan 43, in 182d Inf Journal, 16 Jan 43.

[22] 182d Inf Opn Rpt, p. 8.

[23] Rad, CG XIV Corps to COMSOPAC, 20 Jan 43. XIV Corps G–3 Journal.

[24] XIV Corps G–2 Summary, 20 Jan 43; USMC, Guadalcanal Campaign, p. 93; ltr, former D–3, 2d Mar Div to Comdt Mar Corps, sub: Completion Rpt Opn Sec 2d Mar Div, Jan 17–20, 1943. A copy is in the files of the Hist Div, SSUSA.

[25] Synopsis of tel and rad msgs, in XIV Corps G–3 Journal, 19 Jan 43.

[26] Synopsis of tel and rad msgs, D–3 2d Mar Div to G–3 XIV Corps; 2d Mar Div D–3 Log. XIV Corps G–3 Journal, 22 Jan 43.

KOKUMBONA

99

98

97

90

91

96

95

86

93

92

89

TERRAIN OF THE BATTLE FOR KOKUMBONA *as seen from an altitude of 7,500 feet. With the exception of the grassy, open hills and a narrow band of coconut palms along the coast, the area is covered by dense jungle (dark areas).*

attack, which opened at 0630, was supported by the artillery of the American and 2d Marine Divisions, and by aircraft and naval gunfire. In the zones of the 147th and 182d Infantry Regiments the terrain offered the only serious resistance to the advance. By 1600 G Company of the 182d had made contact with the 27th Infantry north of Hill 88.[27] The 147th Infantry seized Hill 95, and patrols from that regiment met some machine-gun fire in the ravine to the west.[28]

The beach was the scene of the day's hardest fighting. An estimated 250 Japanese who were occupying the ravine just west of Hill 94 stopped the advance of the 3d Battalion of the 6th Marines with machine and antitank guns. The 2d Battalion of the 6th, on the 3d Battalion's left, halted to protect its flank.[29] The CAM Division had advanced about 1,000 yards, but its front lines were still some 1,000 yards east of the high ground (Hills 98 and 99) east of Kokumbona.

The division resumed its attack the next morning, 23 January, the day on which the 27th Infantry captured Kokumbona. The 182d Infantry advanced 1,000 yards to its objective, Hill 91, keeping contact with the 25th Division on the left and the 147th Infantry on the right.[30] The 147th Infantry advanced slowly against enemy strong points on the north slopes of Hill 92 and on the coast road. All three battalions of the 6th Marines were committed to action. Though meeting small-arms and artillery fire, they captured Hill 92 and destroyed three 150-mm. guns, one light tank, two 37-mm. guns, and two machine guns.[31]

By the end of the fighting on 23 January, the XIV Corps had pocketed the main body of Japanese remaining east of the Poha in the ravine east of Hill 99. On 24 January the CAM Division resumed its advance. Soldiers of the 147th, attacking to the northwest, killed eighteen Japanese and reached Hill 98, where they made contact with the 27th Infantry by 0940.[32] The 6th Marines attacked and killed over 200 Japanese. By 1500 all three battalions had gained Hills 98 and 99 and had made contact with the 27th Infantry.[33]

---

[27] 2d Bn, 182d Inf, S–2 Journal, 22 Jan 43.

[28] 2d Mar Div D–2 Rpt, 22 Jan 43, in 182d Inf S–2 Rpts, 182d Inf Opn Rpt; XIV Corps G–2 Summary, 23 Jan 43.

[29] Opn Overlay in 25th Div Journal, 22 Jan 43; XIV Corps G–2 Summary, 23 Jun 43.

[30] Opn Overlay in 25th Div Journal, 24 Jan 43.

[31] XIV Corps G–3 Journal, 23 Jan 43.

[32] 147th Inf Journal, 25 Jan 43; 2d Mar Div D–2 Rpt, 24 Jan 43, in 182d Inf Opn Rpt.

[33] Synopsis of tel and rad msgs, D–3 2d Mar Div to G–3 XIV Corps, 24 Jan 43, in XIV Corps G–3 Journal; 2d Mar Div D–2 Rpt, 24 Jan 43, in 182d Inf Opn Rpt; XIV Corps G–2 Summary, 25 Jan 43.

Final Push to the Poha

With the CAM Division moving up to Hills 98 and 99 on 24 January, the 25th Division was able to continue the Corps plan to advance beyond Kokumbona. The 27th Infantry was again best situated to make the attack. Colonel Mitchell's 2d Battalion, 27th Infantry, took over the assault. E Company was released from service with the 1st Battalion and rejoined the 2d Battalion. Colonel McCulloch, the regimental commander, attached K Company of the 27th Infantry to the 2d Battalion when troops of the 147th Infantry took over K Company's position on Hill 98. The 27th Infantry's objective was the Poha River, whose mouth lies about 2,300 yards northwest of the west tip of Hill 100 and about 2,600 yards northwest of Kokumbona.

Supplies had run short, but the capture of the Kokumbona beaches made it possible for landing craft to bring supplies in by water. By noon enough supplies had reached the 2d Battalion to enable it to move out of Kokumbona.[34] Supported by H Company's machine guns and mortars on Hill 97, K and E Companies attacked west at 1300 on the right, with K Company's right flank on the beach. E Company, on K's left, attempted to drive over Hill 102, a bare hill just west of Kokumbona, but a vigorous Japanese defense held the company on the west tip. To avoid exposing its left flank, K Company halted, and both companies stayed in place for the rest of the day.

On the left G Company, with the antitank platoon of Battalion Headquarters Company and six machine guns from H Company attached, began its advance north from Hill 97; it turned northwest to attempt to seize Hill 103, about 250 yards beyond Hill 100. When G Company tried to cross one of the dry stream beds north of Hill 100, fire from the same well-hidden enemy positions that had halted E Company hit G Company from three sides. Colonel Mitchell ordered the company back. It withdrew and approached Hill 103 by moving safely around the south slopes of Hill 100, which protected G Company from the enemy fire. By nightfall it had reached Hill 103.

The 27th Infantry attacked in greater strength the next day, 25 January, again with orders to reach the Poha. Colonel Bush's 3d Battalion, which had been relieved on Hills 98 and 99 by the 6th Marines, was to attack along the beach west of Kokumbona, while the 2d Battalion on the left advanced to Hills 105 and 106 overlooking the Poha. K Company was detached from the 2d Battalion and ordered to clean out the Japanese between Hills 102 and 103.

[34] 25th Div Opns, p. 56.

The 3d Battalion left its lines on Hills 98 and 99, and passed through the 1st Battalion in Kokumbona about noon to advance northwest in columns of companies. L Company led, followed by I, Battalion Headquarters, and M Companies.[35] Deployed on a 400-yard front to comb the jungle, L Company advanced slowly. At 1600 Colonel Bush decided to narrow his front in order to speed the advance sufficiently to reach the Poha before dark. I Company passed through L Company, and moved northwest along the coast road. A few Japanese riflemen opposed the 3d Battalion, which killed about thirty-five of the enemy during the day.

Colonel Bush's battalion reached the Poha area in late afternoon. Colonel Bush, who had only a crayon map to guide him, had difficulty in finding the correct river. The Poha channel, like many other rivers on Guadalcanal, splits and wanders over alluvial bars as it nears the sea to form a small delta cut by several sluggish streams. Colonel Bush's troops, who were out of physical contact with the 2d Battalion, crossed six such streams, each one of which was part of the Poha, although the map represented the Poha to be a single stream. The battalion commander therefore requested the artillery to drop a round 1,000 yards offshore, opposite the Poha's mouth as shown on the map. When the shell fell into the channel behind him, Colonel Bush concluded that he had crossed the Poha and ordered his battalion to bivouac. The troops constructed a perimeter defense in a coconut grove, which is shown on aerial photographs as west of the river's main stream.[36]

Meanwhile the 2d Battalion was advancing to Hills 105 and 106. E Company passed through G on Hill 103 and advanced without fighting over steep hills and jungled ravines to reach Hills 105 and 106 by dusk. The battalion blocked the area extending from its front southeastward to the hill mass south of Kokumbona.[37] About fifty Japanese were killed on the night of 25–26 January at the stream and trail blocks.[38]

The two battalions regained contact at 0700, 26 January, when one platoon from L Company patrolled south along the Poha to meet F Company. The 2d and 3d Battalions held the Poha line until the 6th Marines and 182d Infantry passed through the lines about noon to pursue the Japanese up the north coast. To meet an apparent enemy threat to land once more on Guadalcanal in

---

[35] 3d Bn, 27th Inf, Activities, p. 4.
[36] Interv with Col Bush, 15 Aug 46.
[37] XIV Corps G–3 Journal, 25 Jan 43.
[38] Mitchell, Notes, 2d Bn, 27th Inf.

force, XIV Corps headquarters sent the 25th Division back to the perimeter defense to guard Henderson and Carney Fields.[39]

The 27th Infantry's successful January attacks had cost that regiment few casualties. Seven officers and 67 enlisted men had been killed in January and 226 were wounded, largely in the capture of the Galloping Horse.[40] Losses in Kokumbona had been light.

Kokumbona, formerly an important enemy landing beach, trail junction, and assembly area, was now in American hands. In addition the 27th Infantry had captured the highest ground dominating the landing beaches between Kokumbona and Cape Esperance, an enemy radar station, trucks, landing craft, ten field artillery pieces, two 37-mm. guns, three 40-mm. antiaircraft guns, flame throwers, and ammunition, besides killing over 400 of the enemy.[41] Had the Japanese attempted to land, they would have encountered greater difficulties in getting inland to envelop the perimeter defense than they did in October, for the XIV Corps held the important trail junctions in Kokumbona and dominated the landing beaches to the northwest. With the enemy retreating, the task facing the XIV Corps was to pursue and destroy the remnants of the *17th Army* before they could reach Cape Esperance to escape or dig in for a suicidal stand like that of the determined defenders of the Gifu.

[39] 25th Div Opns, p. 10.

[40] 27th Inf Combat Rpt.

[41] 3d Bn, 27th Inf, Activities, p. 4; rad, CG Guadalcanal to COMSOPAC, 0306 of 25 Jan 43, in USAFISPA G–3 Worksheet File, 16–31 Jan 43.

CHAPTER XV

Final Operations on Guadalcanal

By the first week of February 1943, the American forces in the South Pacific expected the Japanese to make another full-scale attempt to retake the Guadalcanal positions. The Japanese were known to be massing naval strength at Rabaul and Buin, and enemy air attacks were being intensified.

Admiral Halsey's naval strength had increased greatly since November 1942. Expecting a major Japanese attack, he deployed six naval task forces south of Guadalcanal by 7 and 8 February, including seven battleships, two aircraft carriers, and three escort carriers plus cruisers and destroyers.[1] The XIV Corps on Guadalcanal anticipated an attack by 2 aircraft carriers, 5 battleships, about 8 cruisers, 11 transports, 28 destroyers, 304 land-based aircraft, from 150 to 175 carrier-based aircraft, and one infantry division.[2] General Patch prepared to resist enemy attempts to land by deploying the large part of his corps between the Umasani and Metapona Rivers, and also decided to continue to pursue the retreating *17th Army* to Cape Esperance.[3] But Allied intelligence agencies had erred in their estimate of Japanese intentions.

Japanese Plans

After a long succession of failures, the Japanese high command had at last decided to abandon its efforts to drive the Americans from Guadalcanal. This decision harked back to October and November of 1942, when the defeats had caused concern in *Imperial General Headquarters* in Tokyo. The 1st Marine Division's successful defense of the Lunga airfields against the *17th Army* reduced the number of Japanese troops available for campaigning in New Guinea. The Japanese clearly realized that the Solomons and New Guinea

---

[1] Halsey, Narrative Account of the South Pacific Campaign, p. 5; ONI, USN, Combat Narratives: Solomon Islands Campaign, VIII, Japanese Evacuation of Guadalcanal, 29 January 1943–8 February 1943 (Washington, 1944), pp. 26, 45–50; rad, COMSOPAC to CG XIV Corps, 1 Feb 43, in XIV Corps G–3 Journal.

[2] XIV Corps FO No. 3, 5 Feb 43, (Annex No. 1, 6 Feb 43) in Amer Div G–3 Journal; 25th Div G–2 Rpts for 21, 24, 25, 28, and 29 Jan 43.

[3] XIV Corps FO No. 3.

campaigns were integral parts of one whole.[4] Attempting to reinforce Guadalcanal at the expense of New Guinea, the Japanese lost the campaign.[5]

Following the failure of General Hyakutake's *17th Army* in October, *Imperial General Headquarters* decided to use stronger additional forces to retake the Lunga area. The attempt to transport the *38th Division* in force to Guadalcanal, resulting in the naval and air actions of mid-November, had been decided on by the local Japanese commanders. It had not been the result of direct orders from *Imperial General Headquarters,* which had arrived at its decision for a third offensive on 15 November.[6]

Accordingly Gen. Hitoshi Imamura, commanding the *8th Area Army,* left Java to assume control of operations in the Solomons and Eastern New Guinea. He arrived at Rabaul on 2 December 1942. During the month following Imamura's arrival, 50,000 troops of the *8th Area Army,* including elements of the *4th Air Army,* reached Rabaul. Imamura's command operated directly under the command of *Imperial General Headquarters.* It included the Japanese Army forces in Rabaul, the Solomons, and Eastern New Guinea—the *17th Army* in the Solomons and the *18th Army* in eastern New Guinea.[7] Imamura planned to recapture the Lunga airfields by landing two more divisions on Guadalcanal. The air strip then under construction at Munda Point on New Georgia would have provided advanced air support. The date of the attack was to be about 1 February 1943.[8]

Problems of transportation and supply caused the projected counteroffensive to be canceled. Prior to December 1942 the Japanese lost about twenty troop transports in the Solomons.[9] After the November disaster the Japanese never again used transports to reinforce or supply Guadalcanal. Although Imamura had 50,000 men at his disposal at Rabaul in January 1943, he could not deploy them. General Miyazaki declared:

The superiority and continuous activity of the American air force was responsible for our inability to carry out our plans. The superiority of American Army [*sic*] planes made the seas safe for American movement in any direction and at the same time immobilized the Japanese Army as if it were bound hand and foot.[10]

---

[4] Miyazaki, Personal Account, p. 5.

[5] *Ibid.,* pp. 2–3; USSBS, *Interrogations,* II, 409; *Allied Campaign Against Rabaul,* p. 89.

[6] *17th Army* Opns, I; Miyazaki, Personal Account, p. 9, *Allied Campaign Against Rabaul,* pp. 9, 83–84.

[7] *Ibid.,* pp. 82–87.

[8] *17th Army* Opns, II; *Allied Campaign Against Rabaul,* pp. 82–87.

[9] *Ibid.,* p. 89.

[10] Miyazaki, p. 7. At peak strength in May 1943, Imamura's forces totaled 200,000 men, including 20,000 troops and 300 planes of the *4th Air Army—Allied Campaign Against Rabaul,* p. 84.

Japanese ship losses in the Solomons forced *Imperial General Headquarters,* on 31 December, to cancel the proposed counteroffensive; on 4 January Imamura and Vice Adm. Jinichi Kusaka, commanding the *Southeastern Fleet,* were ordered to evacuate the survivors from Guadalcanal and to hold final defensive positions in New Georgia.[11]

The American corps offensive which began on 10 January had torn great holes in the Japanese front lines. General Hyakutake recognized that he could no longer maintain troops in the Kokumbona area. In December the Japanese front line troops had been ordered to hold their positions until the last man was dead, but sometime after the XIV Corps attacked, Hyakutake changed his mind. He ordered his troops to withdraw west to Cape Esperance, where they were to offer "desperate resistance."[12]

The Japanese prepared to deceive the American forces in order to cover the rescue of a sizable body of troops from Guadalcanal. Massing strength at Rabaul, for a time they intensified their air attacks against Henderson Field to lead Allied forces to expect another major Japanese attempt at landing on Guadalcanal.

The Japanese put about 600 replacements ashore near Cape Esperance on 14 January to cover the withdrawal, while an additional covering force landed for a short time in the Russell Islands. The Japanese planned to remove their troops from Cape Esperance at night by destroyers, cramming 600 men aboard each vessel.[13] In the event that American air and naval forces drove the destroyers off, barges were to carry the troops to the Russells, where the destroyers would pick them up for the trip north.[14]

By 8 February General Patch was no longer convinced that the Japanese would attempt a landing to recapture the airfields. They were known to be withdrawing supplies from Doma Cove, and Patch expressed his belief that the Tokyo Express was evacuating the remaining Japanese.[15] Aerial photographs of the Cape Esperance area would have shown conclusively whether the enemy forces there were being evacuated or reinforced, but XIV Corps headquarters

---

[11] *Ibid.,* pp. 9, 45, 84, 89; *17th Army* Opns, II.

[12] Miyazaki, Personal Account, p. 10.

[13] *17th Army* Opns, I; *Allied Campaign Against Rabaul,* p. 45. The Americal Division Report calls the 14 January unit a battalion of rear guard specialists; XIV Corps Report lists it correctly as the *Yano* or *Yanno Battalion,* from its commander's name. Ito stated that this battalion came from the *6th Division.* Interv with Gen Sebree. *Allied Campaign Against Rabaul* calls the Guadalcanal force a regiment.

[14] *Allied Campaign Against Rabaul,* p. 45.

[15] 161st Inf Journal, 8 Feb 43; 2d Mar Div D–2 Rpt, 5 Feb 43, in Amer Div G–2 Journal; rad, CG Cactus to COMSOPAC, 1115 of 8 Feb 43, in USAFISPA G–3 Worksheet File, 1–15 Feb 43.

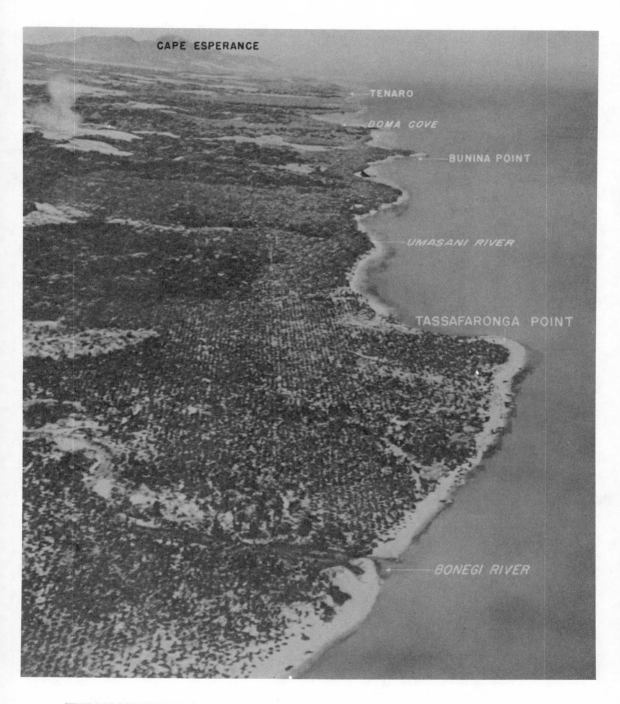

CAPE ESPERANCE

TENARO

DOMA COVE

BUNINA POINT

UMASANI RIVER

TASSAFARONGA POINT

BONEGI RIVER

THE NORTHWEST COAST OF GUADALCANAL, *scene of the final battle to trap and destroy the Japanese on the island. A large coconut plantation can be seen in the foreground and, toward the top left, a smoke burst marking the approximate front line at the time this picture was taken.*

could not obtain photographic coverage on 7 and 8 February. One squadron, flying P-38's, of the 17th Photographic Reconnaissance Group had just relieved the 2d Marine Air Wing of reconnaissance duties on Guadalcanal. The 17th had good planes and cameras but did not possess filters for the camera lenses, nor proper paper on which to print pictures.[16] Thus General Patch had no way of determining exactly what General Hyakutake's troops at Cape Esperance were doing.

Pursuit of the Enemy

The North Coast

When the XIV Corps reached the Poha River on 25 January, the American offensive was ready to enter its final phase—the pursuit of the retreating enemy. Enemy intentions and dispositions at this time were not clear. In general, the Americans did not expect to meet a formidable Japanese force but they did expect the Japanese to defend the beach road and the Bonegi River line.[17] While few Japanese prisoners had been taken in January, a study of captured documents led to the belief that the beach was defended by troops of the *2d Division*.[18]

West of the Poha River the terrain resembles that of the Point Cruz–Kokumbona area. The coastal corridor is generally narrow; the distance from the beach inland to the foothills varies from 300 to 600 yards. The coral ridges run north and south; the coastal flats are cut by a great many streams. There were no bridges. The lack of room for maneuver limited the size of the pursuing force, and allowed, in most areas, only enough space for the deployment of one regiment.[19]

XIV Corps' Field Order No. 2 of 25 January 1943 directed the CAM Division to pass through the 25th Division at the Poha line to attack west at 0630, 26 January. The 6th Marines on the beach and the 182d Infantry on the high ground inland were to attack abreast; the 147th Infantry was to be in division reserve. Americal and 25th Division artillery, and the 2d Marine Air Wing, would support the offensive.[20] Wishing to locate and destroy the remaining

[16] Interv with Col Long, 26 Mar 46.
[17] Compare 147th Inf Journal, 28 Jan 43, with 147th Inf FO No. 8, 29 Jan 43.
[18] Amer Div Int Rpt, Tab A; XIV Corps, Enemy Opns, p. 6.
[19] Ltr, Col Long to Col Buckley, 21 Mar 43.
[20] XIV Corps FO No. 2, 25 Jan 43, in Amer Div G-3 Journal; 147th Inf FO No. 7, 25 Jan 43. 25th Division (less detachments) was in Corps reserve; 3d Battalion, 182d Infantry, elements of 35th Infantry, and 161st Infantry were to cover the Corps left flank from the Sea Horse to the Poha.

Japanese forces, General Patch ordered his troops to "effect the kill through aggressive and untiring offensive action."[21]

The CAM Division attacked on 26 January and advanced 1,000 yards beyond the Poha.[22] (*Map XXI*) There was little fighting; the 182d Infantry met only stragglers and a few riflemen and machine gunners. The tempo of the advance increased the next day, and the CAM Division, gaining 2,000 yards, reached the Nueha River. Patrols met some enemy machine gunners west of the Nueha on 28 January, but reported that the Japanese were not aggressive.[23]

On 29 January General Patch detached the 147th Infantry from the CAM Division. To that regiment he attached the 75-mm. pack howitzers of the 2d Battalion, 10th Marines, and of A Battery of the 97th Field Artillery Battalion. This composite force, under General De Carre's command, was to pursue the enemy. American Division artillery was to give general support. The 6th Marines were to cover the 147th's rear. The 182d Infantry then reverted to control of the American Division in the Lunga perimeter.[24]

The 147th Infantry passed through the lines west of the Nueha to attack about 0700, 30 January. On the beach the 1st Battalion advanced against light opposition to the mouth of the Bonegi River, about 2,000 yards west of the Nueha. One patrol crossed the river about 1152. Inland on the left flank, Japanese machine guns stopped the 3d Battalion 1,000 yards east of the Bonegi. When Japanese on the west bank placed heavy fire on the 1st Battalion, the patrol withdrew from the west bank and the battalion pulled back from the river mouth.[25]

On 31 January the 147th Infantry again attacked with the intention of crossing the Bonegi to capture the high ground west of the river. Both battalions were assisted by artillery preparations and gunfire from an American destroyer standing offshore. In the inland zone the 3d Battalion crossed the Bonegi and captured part of the ridges on the west bank, about 2,500 yards inland from Tassafaronga Point. The enemy was defending the river mouth in strength and Japanese patrols infiltrated to the east bank to harass the 1st Bat-

---

[21] XIV Corps memo, 26 Jan 43, in Amer Div G-2 Journal.

[22] 182d Inf Opn Rpt, p. 9.

[23] XIV Corps G-2 Summary, 28–29 Jan 43. Reports written during the campaign erroneously called the Nueha the Mamara River.

[24] XIV Corps Opn Memo No. 11, 28 Jan 43, in Amer Div G-3 Journal. Soldiers and mules of A, B, Headquarters, and Service Batteries of 97th FA Battalion, a 75-mm. mule pack unit, had landed on Guadalcanal on 16, 27, and 30 January 1943 to serve as part of Corps artillery. See 97th FA Bn Hist, 1 Jan–30 Jun 43, pp. 2–3 in HRS DRB AGO.

[25] 147th Inf Journal, 30 Jan 43; XIV Corps G-3 Journal, 30 Jan 43.

talion. Despite the Destroyer's fire and two artillery barrages, the 1st Battalion could not get across but was held in place about 300 yards east of the Bonegi.

Between 10 and 31 January the XIV Corps' operations had been quite successful. The Corps had driven the Japanese back seven miles at a cost of 189 soldiers and marines killed and about 400 wounded. One hundred and five Japanese had been captured, and 4,000 were estimated to have been killed. The Corps had also captured 240 Japanese machine guns, 42 field pieces, 10 anti-aircraft guns, 9 antitank guns, 142 mortars, 323 rifles, 18 radios, 1 radar, 13 trucks, 6 tractors, and 1 staff car, besides a quantity of ammunition, land mines, flame throwers, and piles of documents.[26]

On 1 February command of the western pursuit passed from General De Carre to General Sebree.[27] The 1st Battalion of the 147th again vainly attempted to cross the river to join forces with the 3d Battalion on the west bank. The destroyer and the field artillery fired into the Bonegi River valley, and patrols, finding that the enemy had withdrawn from the east bank, reached the river mouth by 1525, but the battalion did not cross. The Japanese unit holding the west bank was a delaying force from the covering battalion which the Japanese had landed on 14 January.[28]

The 147th Infantry's attacks on 2 February were more successful. The 1st Battalion, supported by artillery, crossed the Bonegi at its mouth, and by 1710 the 1st and 3d Battalions had made contact south of Tassafaronga.[29] The river crossing cost the 147th two killed and sixty-seven wounded.[30] The 147th Infantry estimated that 700–800 Japanese troops had occupied the positions east and west of the Bonegi. They had executed an orderly withdrawal, but the Americans captured a mobile machine shop, a signal blinker, two 70-mm. guns, eight 75-mm. guns, and a radio station.[31]

On 3 February, while the main body of the pursuing force was establishing itself along a line running south from Tassafaronga Point, patrols reached the Umasani River, about 2,300 yards west of Tassafaronga.[32] The next day the main body advanced 1,000 yards farther on to a line about 1,000 yards southeast

---

[26] XIV Corps G–3 Periodic Rpt, 16–31 Jan 43, in USAFISPA G–3 Worksheet File, 16–31 Jan 43.

[27] Amer Div Narrative of Opns, p. 5.

[28] *17th Army* Opns, II; 147th Inf Journal, 1 Feb 43; 147th Inf Hist, Feb 43; 147th Inf Unit Rpt, 1 Feb 43, in XIV Corps G–3 Journal.

[29] 147th Inf Journal, 2 Feb 43.

[30] 147th Inf Hist, Feb 43.

[31] Rad, CG Cactus to COMSOPAC, 3 Feb 43, in USAFISPA G–3 Worksheet File, 1–15 Feb 43.

[32] XIV Corps G–2 Summary, 4 Feb 43.

of the Umasani River. A few Japanese fired on the 3d Battalion on the inland flank, but there was no heavy fighting.[33] On 5 February, operations on the western front were limited to patrolling. Patrols again reconnoitered to the Umasani River, but found no organized enemy forces.[34]

The South Coast

Meanwhile XIV Corps headquarters had completed plans to land a reinforced infantry battalion on the southwest coast in the enemy's rear. From there the battalion was to advance to Cape Esperance in an attempt to trap the remaining enemy forces. As early as October Admiral Turner and General Vandegrift had planned to land the 2d (Marine) Raider Battalion at Beaufort Bay on the south coast to operate against the enemy flanks and rear. The Japanese landings in October and November had led to the cancellation of these plans, and the raider battalion had been used instead to pursue some of the enemy troops who had landed at Koli Point.[35]

When General Patch assumed command on Guadalcanal, he desired to land an entire regimental combat team on the south coast to prevent further Japanese landings at Cape Esperance, Visale, and Kamimbo Bay, and to press against the enemy's rear. Naval forces were not then sufficient to transport and supply so large a body of men. During January 1943, however, six tank landing craft arrived at Tulagi to be based there permanently.[36] About 21 January it was decided that naval strength was adequate to make the landing with one reinforced infantry battalion. The reinforced 2d Battalion, 132d Infantry, was selected as the landing force, with Col. Alexander M. George in command.

The landing force would not be sufficiently strong to land against enemy opposition, but General Patch wished it to land as close to the enemy as possible. Troops from I Company of the 147th Infantry at Beaufort Bay were to outpost the area to cover the landing. Lt. Col. Paul A. Gavan, operations officer of the Americal Division and assistant operations officer of the XIV Corps, led a reconnaissance party along the south coast. It picked Titi, near Lavoro Passage, as the landing beach, and Nugu Point (Cape Nagle) as an alternate. Verahue, lying between the two, offered a good beach but Colonel Gavan feared that landing craft would not be able to reach the beach through the narrow

---

[33] 147th Inf Journal, 4 Feb 43; XIV Corps G-2 Summary, 5 Feb 43.

[34] CAM Div D-3 Rpt, 6 Feb 43, in XIV Corps G-3 Journal; XIV Corps G-2 Summary, 6 Feb 43.

[35] 1st Mar Div Rpt, V, Int Annex N, 8.

[36] O-in-C, LCT Flotilla 5, Nav Adv Base Ringbolt, Action Rpt, 3 Feb 43, Annex O to CINCPAC Ser 00712, in Office of Naval Records and Library.

channel lined with offshore reefs. An observation post, equipped with a radio, was established at Verahue.[87]

The covering force—eight riflemen and three gunners from I Company, plus machine gunners and automatic riflemen from M Company, 147th Infantry —boarded the island schooner *Kocorana* at Beaufort Bay at 0100, 31 January. The *Kocorana,* a local schooner which like others had been hidden from the Japanese and turned over to the Americans, sailed to Lavoro to discharge the force which was to outpost Titi. One officer and five riflemen from the schooner had pulled toward shore in a rowboat about 0600 when enemy troops on a ridge about 100 yards inland opened fire on the landing party and the *Kocorana* and mortally wounded one soldier on board the schooner. Some confusion resulted; the landing party reached shore and the rowboat went adrift. Since the *Kocorana* could not be beached, Maj. H. W. Butler, executive officer of the 2d Battalion, 132d Infantry, took the helm and put out to sea, leaving the six men on shore. The *Kocorana* reached Beaufort Bay about 1600 to take fifteen more riflemen, two automatic riflemen, and three native scouts aboard. Major Butler intended to land his force near Verahue and to march overland to Lavoro to reinforce the six men ashore.

In the meantime, the shore party at Titi had eluded the enemy and recommended to XIV Corps headquarters by radio that the 2d Battalion, 132d Infantry, land at Nugu Point instead of Titi. When Butler and the *Kocorana* reached Nugu Point the next morning they found the six men there, safe.[88]

Meanwhile the reinforced 2d Battalion of the 132d Infantry had assembled and loaded trucks, artillery, ammunition, and rations on board six tank landing craft at Kukum.[39] By 1800, 31 January, when the last craft had been loaded, the force, escorted by destroyers, left Kukum and sailed around Cape Esperance.[40] Arriving off Nugu Point at dawn on 1 February, an advance party went ashore in small craft and met Major Butler, who reported that Verahue was clear. When the naval beachmaster agreed that the landing craft could beach safely at Verahue, the expedition moved there and, covered by friendly fighter planes, began unloading.[41] About noon Japanese bombers flew over the beach

[87] Interv with Col Gavan.

[88] Capt W. D. Foster (of XIV Corps G–2), Rpt, 5 Feb 43, in XIV Corps G–3 Journal.

[39] The entire force consisted of 2d Battalion, 132d Infantry; Antitank Company, 132d; M Company (less one .50-caliber platoon), 132d; 1 rifle platoon, K Company, 132d; F Battery, 10th Marines (75-mm. pack howitzer), and engineer, medical, intelligence, and communication troops. 132d Inf Hist, p. 11.

[40] LCT Flotilla 5, Action Rpt, 3 Feb 43.

[41] Interv with Col Gavan, 14 Nov 46.

but did not attack. By 1500 all troops and supplies were safely ashore, and the unloaded craft departed for the Lunga area.[42]

The next morning, 2 February, Colonel George's force began its advance. The main body moved along the beach, while G Company and twenty native scouts covered the high ground on the right flank. The coast between Verahue and Titi was passable for vehicles, and the trucks brought up some of the supplies.[43] By 1415 the main body had marched 3½ miles to Titi. On 3 February tank landing craft moved more supplies to Titi, while ground patrols advanced as far as Kamimbo Bay. By 4 February, the whole expedition—troops, artillery, transport, and supplies—had reached Titi.[44] During the next two days the battalion remained in position, but continued patrolling to its front and its flanks.[45]

Beyond Titi, mud and jungle vegetation halted the trucks. Supplies then had to be carried by tank landing craft based at Kukum, one or two of which were usually available for Colonel George's men. The self-contained battalion combat team did not expect to be re-supplied or reinforced. The commanding officer therefore kept his supplies and main body of troops together to be prepared for an enemy counterattack or landing in strength. In the absence of accurate information about Japanese capabilities and intentions, Colonel George felt constrained to move cautiously.[46]

By 7 February the force was ready to move out of Titi. In column of companies, the battalion began the advance at 0730. When Colonel George was wounded in the leg on 7 February, Lt. Col. George F. Ferry, commanding the 2d Battalion, 132d, assumed command and Major Butler took over the 2d Battalion.[47] Shortly afterward Colonel Gavan, acting for General Patch, arrived by boat from XIV Corps headquarters "to speed things up." He found that the troops were ready to move rapidly and therefore did not alter the plans or dispositions. Colonel George was evacuated on the boat which had brought Colonel Gavan.[48] The battalion advanced to Marovovo and bivouacked there for the night.

[42] LCT Flotilla 5, Action Rpt, 3 Feb 43; 132d Inf Hist, p. 11. Since data in the 132d Infantry Journal on this operation are confusing, the 132d Infantry History is the best source.

[43] Interv with Col Gavan.

[44] Amer Div Int Rpt, Tab A.

[45] 132d Inf Hist, pp. 11–12.

[46] Interv with Col Gavan.

[47] 132d Inf Hist, p. 12.

[48] Interv with Col Gavan.

The Junction of Forces

General Patch, relieving the understrength 147th Infantry on the north coast on 6 February, ordered the 161st Infantry of the 25th Division to pass through the 147th's lines to continue the pursuit. The 2d Battalion of the 10th Marines, the 97th Field Artillery Battalion, and Americal Division artillery were to support the 161st. A supply dump which had been established at Kokumbona was to service the advancing force.[49] Command of the western pursuit was to have been given to General Collins on 6 February, but his division was assigned to defense positions in the Lunga–Metapona sector. General Sebree continued, therefore, to command the pursuit.[50]

The 161st Infantry, then commanded by Col. James L. Dalton, II,[51] passed through the 147th about 1000, 6 February. Preceded by patrols, the 3d Battalion moved along the beach; the 2d Battalion covered the foothills; and the 1st Battalion was in reserve. By 2020 the 161st Infantry had reached the Umasani River, and patrols had crossed the river. The day's only skirmish occurred when one patrol from L Company ran into a small Japanese force in a bivouac area on a ridge just west of the Umasani. The patrol killed at least seven of the enemy, and withdrew without losses.[52]

On 7 February the 161st crossed the Umasani and advanced to Bunina, while patrols penetrated to the Tambalego River, 1,200 yards farther on. The Japanese did not offer a resolute defense, but retired as soon as the American infantrymen attacked them.[53] The 161st Infantry encountered some Japanese at the Tambalego River on 8 February, but after a brief fight drove the enemy off and advanced to Doma Cove.[54]

Since coastwatchers had warned that about twenty enemy destroyers would reach the Cape Esperance area during the night of 7–8 February, Colonel Ferry's 2d Battalion of the 132d Infantry at Marovovo, about six miles southwest of Cape Esperance, expected action that night but saw no enemy. When the American soldiers left Marovovo on the morning of 8 February, they found

---

[49] XIV Corps Opn Memo No. 13, 4 Feb 43, USAFISPA G–3 Worksheet File, 1–15 Feb 43.

[50] XIV Corps Periodic Rpt, 1–18 Feb 43, in USAFISPA G–3 Worksheet File, 1–15 Feb 43.

[51] Following the 22 January attack General Collins had relieved Colonel Orndorff, who had fallen too ill from malaria to continue in command. Interv with Gen Collins, 5 Dec. 46.

[52] 25th Div Opns, p. 109; 161st Inf Journal, 6 Feb 43, in misc docs from USAFISPA; XIV Corps G–2 Summary, 7 Feb 43, lists 14 Japanese killed.

[53] 25th Div Opns, p. 109; XIV Corps G–2 Summary, 8 Feb 43. Reports written during the campaign erroneously called the Tambalego the Segilau River.

[54] 25th Div Opns, p. 110; 161st Inf Hist, p. 3; XIV Corps G–2 Summary, 9 Feb 43.

CAPE ESPERANCE. *Tenaro village (in a palm grove seen near left edge of upper photo) was the junction point where the two American forces linked at the end of the battle. Visale Peak (right) towers above a mission at the tip of the cape. Below: numerous weapons, in good condition, were abandoned along the way by enemy troops.*

several abandoned Japanese landing craft and a stock of supplies on the beach.[55] Realizing that the enemy was evacuating, the battalion narrowed its front and advanced to Kamimbo Bay.[56]

On 9 February the 2d Battalion, 161st Infantry, which had been traveling over the uphill north coast flank on scanty rations, went into regimental reserve. The 1st Battalion, 161st, passed through the 3d Battalion at Doma Cove to take over the assault, and was followed closely by the 3d Battalion and the antitank company. By afternoon the 1st Battalion had marched five miles, crossed the Tenamba River, and entered the village of Tenaro.

On the morning of 9 February, Colonel Ferry's force had started around Cape Esperance toward the same objective, the village of Tenaro, which was the point selected by Colonel Gavan for the forces to meet. Advancing in column of companies, the battalion met fire from some Japanese machine guns and mortars but did not halt. The infantrymen, who pushed on beyond the range of the 75-mm. pack howitzers of the supporting artillery, used their mortars for support.[57] Between 1600 and 1700 the 2d Battalion of the 132d Infantry marched into Tenaro and there met the 1st Battalion of the 161st Infantry, an event that marked the end of organized fighting on Guadalcanal.[58] Only scattered stragglers from the *17th Army* remained on the island.[59]

General Patch, after the juncture of forces, sent the following message to Admiral Halsey: "Total and complete defeat of Japanese forces on Guadalcanal effected 1625 today . . . Am happy to report this kind of compliance with your orders . . . because Tokyo Express no longer has terminus on Guadalcanal."[60] The reply from South Pacific Headquarters was characteristic: "When I sent a Patch to act as tailor for Guadalcanal, I did not expect him to remove the enemy's pants and sew it on so quickly . . . Thanks and congratulations."[61]

The Japanese Evacuation

While the American troops could feel justly elated over the end of Japanese resistance on Guadalcanal, they had let slip through their hands about 13,000 of the enemy—by Japanese count. The western pursuit and the shore-to-

---

[55] Interv with Col Gavan.

[56] 132d Inf Hist, p. 12.

[57] *Ibid.*; interv with Col Gavan, 14 Nov 46.

[58] Amer Div Narrative of Opns, p. 5; 132d Inf Hist, p. 13; 25th Div Opns, p. 110.

[59] XIV Corps GO No. 29, 9 Feb 43, in 25th Div FO's; Airmailgram, CG Guadalcanal to COMSOPAC, 10 Feb 43, in XIV Corps G-3 Journal.

[60] Rad, CG Cactus to COMSOPAC, 0718 of 9 Feb 43, in USAFISPA G-3 Worksheet File, 1–15 Feb 43.

[61] Quoted in *Admiral Halsey's Story*, p. 148.

shore envelopment had been boldly conceived but were executed too slowly to achieve their purpose—the complete destruction of the enemy.

On 12 January, General Imamura had directed some of his staff officers to board a destroyer and proceed to Guadalcanal, there to give the *17th Army* commander the instructions to evacuate. Hyakutake, receiving the order on 15 January, explained the prospective movement to his men as "a change in the disposition of troop[s] for future offense."[62]

The *17th Army* began its withdrawal to Cape Esperance on the night of 22–23 January. The rescuing destroyers ran down the Slot to Esperance three times and evacuated troops on the nights of 1–2, 4–5, 7–8 February.[63] The *38th Division,* some naval personnel, hospital patients, and others left first, followed by *17th Army* headquarters and the *2d Division* on 4–5 January, and by miscellaneous units on the last trip.[64] The Americans claimed that three of the destroyers were sunk and four were damaged.[65] About 13,000 Japanese—12,000 from the *17th Army* and the rest naval personnel—were evacuated to Buin and Rabaul.[66]

In post-war interviews the Japanese commanders ironically expressed their gratitude over their escape. The Americans, they felt, had moved toward Cape Esperance too slowly and stopped too long to consolidate positions. General Hyakutake stated that resolute attacks at Cape Esperance would have destroyed his army.[67]

Summary

The Japanese had displayed skill and cunning in evacuating the troops from Guadalcanal, but the essential significance of the Guadalcanal campaign

[62] *17th Army* Opns, II, which states elsewhere that the *17th Army* was ordered on 5–6 January to evacuate. Since the order had not then been issued by Imamura, it is obvious that "5–6 January" is either an error in the Japanese text or a mistranslation.

[63] *17th Army* Opns, II; Amer Div Int Rpt, Tab A. XIV Corps, Enemy Opns, lists only 2 trips. Figures in *Allied Campaign Against Rabaul* vary from 12 destroyers, p. 5, to 15, p. 45. *Interrogations,* I, 81, states that 20 were used.

[64] *17th Army* Opns, II.

[65] Compare interrog of Hyakutake, Miyazaki, Maruyama, and Sakai, and *Allied Campaign Against Rabaul,* p. 45, with Amer Div Int Rpt, Tab A.

[66] *17th Army* Opns, II; *Allied Campaign Against Rabaul,* pp. 45, 79; interrog of Hyakutake, Miyazaki, and Maruyama. USAFISPA, Japanese Campaign in the Guadalcanal Area, p. 35, lists 9,100 evacuated. Amer Div Int Rpt, Tab B, lists 4,000, and XIV Corps Enemy Opns, pp. 7–8, 3,000. It should be emphasized that the figure 13,000 was given by the Japanese after the conclusion of hostilities.

[67] Interrog of Hyakutake, Miyazaki, Maruyama, Sakai, and Obara.

was unchanged. American forces, in executing Task One as prescribed by the Joint Chiefs of Staff, by taking the first major step toward the eventual reduction of Rabaul had decisively defeated the Japanese.

The cost of victory, though dear, had not been prohibitive. A total of about 60,000 Army and Marine Corps ground forces had been deployed on Guadalcanal. Of these, about 1,600 were killed by enemy action and 4,245 wounded. The 1st Marine Division bore the heaviest burden of casualties, losing 774 men killed and 1,962 wounded. Three hundred and thirty-four of the Americal Division were killed, and 850 wounded. The 2d Marine Division suffered equally with the Americal, losing 268 killed and 932 wounded. The 25th Division, which was in action a shorter length of time than the others, suffered correspondingly fewer casualties—216 killed and 439 wounded.[68]

The Japanese suffered much more heavily. More than 36,000 Japanese from the *17th Army* and the *Special Naval Landing Forces* fought on Guadalcanal. Of these, over 14,800 were killed or missing, and 9,000 died of disease.[69] About 1,000 were taken prisoner.[70]

In other respects the Japanese were to feel the cost of defeat much more heavily than in manpower. Their ship losses had been heavy, and the loss of over 600 aircraft with their pilots was to hinder future operations.[71] The Allies had won a well-situated base from which to continue the offensive against Rabaul. The Allied offensive into the Solomons had halted the Japanese advance toward the U.S.–Australian line of communications, and also had taken the initiative away from the hitherto victorious Japanese.[72]

[68] Amer Div Casualty Rpt, 25 Jun 43, in Hist Data; 25th Div Opns, p. 162. Marine figures were furnished by the Hist Sec, Hq, USMC. Battle Casualties of the Army (prepared by Strength Accounting Br, AGO, WDGS, 1 Jul 46), is inaccurate. The figures listed in the text are the best available, but are subject to future correction, as are all casualty figures in this book.

[69] Interrog of Hyakutake, Miyazaki, Maruyama: *1st Demob Bureau's* Table I. Deaths from battle and disease in the *17th Army,* according to *17th Army* Opns, II, totaled 21,600. American intelligence reports prepared at the conclusion of the campaign have proved to be fairly accurate. USAFISPA's Japanese Campaign in the Guadalcanal Area estimated that 43,726 Japanese were dispatched to Guadalcanal, 4,346 were lost at sea, and 37,680 fought on Guadalcanal, suffering 28,580 casualties. Americal Division Intelligence Report, always conservative, estimated that 32,000 Japanese landed or attempted to land on Guadalcanal, losing 24,330.

[70] Amer Div Int Rpt, Tab B.

[71] Guadalcanal and the Thirteenth Air Force, p. 270; USSBS, *Interrogations, passim.*

[72] Miyazaki, Personal Account, p. 36; USSBS, *Interrogations,* II, 353, 423.

EPILOGUE

Occupation of the Russells

Prior to the final advances on Guadalcanal, the Allied command in the South Pacific had been considering additional measures to counter the Japanese infiltration down the Solomons. The Americans wished to attack New Georgia but in January 1943 lacked the forces for so large an undertaking. The occupation of the Russell Islands, a small group lying about 35 miles northwest of Cape Esperance and about 125 miles southeast of the New Georgia group, seemed feasible. Possession of the Russells would deny them to the Japanese, who had been using the islands as a staging area for shipping troops to Guadalcanal. In addition, airfields could be built in the Russells which would shorten the airline distance from Henderson Field to Munda by about sixty-five miles, and motor torpedo boat and landing craft bases could also be established. The Russells would not only strengthen the defenses of Guadalcanal but would serve as a useful advanced base and staging area to support the invasion of New Georgia.[1]

On 29 January Admiral Halsey received permission from Admiral Nimitz to proceed with the occupation.[2] Halsey's first plans for the attack called for an infiltration from Guadalcanal by one infantry battalion and antiaircraft units carried on two destroyer-transports.[3] On 30 January, however, General Patch reported that four hundred Japanese were in the Russells.[4] At that time the Americans were unaware that the Japanese were evacuating their troops from Guadalcanal, so could not know how the enemy would react to the loss of the island. South Pacific intelligence estimates in February assumed that between 33,000 and 41,000 enemy troops were stationed in the Solomons at Buka, Bougainville, the Shortlands, New Georgia, and Rekata Bay at Santa Isabel; 157 Japanese aircraft, besides 3 cruisers, 21 destroyers, and 9 submarines

---

[1] Russells Appreciation in Russell Islands Folder, USAFISPA Hist Sec files, in HRS DRB AGO.

[2] SOPAC War Diary, 29 Jan 43.

[3] Rad, COMSOPAC to CG CACTUS, 28 Jan 43, in Russell Islands Folder.

[4] Rad, CG Guadalcanal to COMSOPAC, 0111 of 30 Jan 43, in Russell Islands Folder.

were supposed to be distributed throughout the area. In addition 15 warships and 30 noncombatant craft were estimated to be in the Bismarck waters.[5] If the Japanese were determined to recapture Guadalcanal, they could be expected to react violently to the American occupation of the Russells. The Russells occupation force, it was decided, would have to be strong.[6]

Admiral Halsey gave orders for the occupation of the Russells on 7 February. He directed that the landing force consist of two infantry regimental combat teams, one Marine raider battalion, antiaircraft detachments from a Marine defense battalion, and naval base and construction units. Admiral Turner was to command the operation. Once the amphibious phase had ended and a 60-day level of supply had been established, command of the occupation troops would pass to the commanding general of the XIV Corps on Guadalcanal, who would then assume responsibility for the supply of the islands.

South Pacific land-based aircraft under Admiral Fitch would support Operation CLEANSLATE (the code name assigned) by covering the movement of the troops to the Russells and the landings there, and by executing long-range search and bombardment missions. South Pacific naval forces would also support and cover the invasion.

The CLEANSLATE Amphibious Force, under Turner, had no large warships, transports, or cargo ships. It consisted of four destroyers, four destroyer-transports, five high-speed minesweepers, twelve tank landing craft, a number of smaller landing craft, a 1,000-ton barge, and the Russells Occupation Force. The transports would be protected by eight motor torpedo boats, an integral part of the Amphibious Force, as well as by the South Pacific air and naval forces.

The Russells Occupation Force, commanded by Maj. Gen. John H. Hester (Commanding General, 43d Division), consisted of the 43d Division, less the 172d Regimental Combat Team which was then at Espiritu Santo. As Operation CLEANSLATE was to be mounted from Guadalcanal, seven ships moved the 103d and 169th Regimental Combat teams and thirty days' supply, five units of fire, and 40 percent of the division's vehicles from Noumea to Koli Point. Four thousand men of the first echelon landed at Koli Point from three

---

[5] CTF 61, Opn Plan No. A4–43, FE 25/A16–3(1), Ser 00113, Opn CLEANSLATE, 15 Feb 43, in 43d Div, Rpt Russells Opn, in HRS DRB AGO. Unless otherwise indicated this chapter is based upon the 43d Division Report which, however, contains some errors.

[6] Ltr, COMGENSOPAC to Pac Gp, OPD, WDGS, 1 May 43, sub: Summary Occupation Russells. OPD 381 PTO Sec. III (4–17–43).

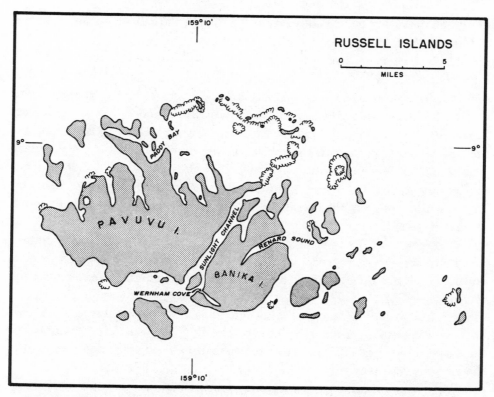

RUSSELL ISLANDS

159° 10'

9°

PADDY BAY

PAVUVU I.

SUNLIGHT CHANNEL

RENARD SOUND

BANIKA I.

WERNHAM COVE

159° 10'

0   5
MILES

MAP NO. 15

ships between 0900 and 1700 on 16 February. The second echelon, 4,500 men aboard four ships, was unsuccessfully attacked by Japanese bombers about 100 miles southeast of Guadalcanal on 17 February. It suffered no damage, and debarked at Koli Point the next day. The two combat teams thereupon sorted their supplies in preparation for loading the destroyers, minesweepers, destroyer-transports, and landing craft.

While the combat teams were moving to Guadalcanal, officers of the 43d Division and Navy and Marine officers reconnoitered the Russells to determine whether the Japanese were there and to select landing beaches and sites for airfields and torpedo boat bases. They sailed from Guadalcanal on the New Zealand corvette *Moa* and went ashore in a landing boat at Renard Sound at Banika, the easternmost main island, after dark on 17 February. (*Map 15*) Natives assured them that the Japanese had evacuated. The next day the patrol examined the area around Paddy Bay at Pavuvu, the largest island, and returned to Guadalcanal on the night of 18–19 February.

The 43d Division, which was to use two small echelons in the initial landings, continued its preparations at Koli Point. The first echelon consisted of division headquarters, the 1st and 2d Battalion teams of the 103d Regimental Combat Team, the 43d Cavalry Reconnaissance Troop, the 3d (Marine) Raider Battalion, a detachment of the 11th (Marine) Defense Battalion, and the 43d Signal Company. It assembled on the beach on 19 and 20 February. At 0530 on 20 February loading of the LCT's was begun, and by 1600, when the landing craft, destroyers, mine sweepers, and destroyer-transports were loaded with troops, supplies, weapons, and ammunition, the Amphibious Force was ready to sail.

CLEANSLATE was more a shore-to-shore than a ship-to-shore operation. The destroyers, mine sweepers, and destroyer-transports were loaded with men and materiel, but they also towed fully loaded landing craft. Ten of the ships towed one LCM (landing craft, mechanized), two LCP's (landing craft, personnel) and one LCV (landing craft, vehicle) each; two ships towed two LCV's and two LCP's each, and one ship towed one LCV and one LCP. A tug towed the barge, and the LCT's proceeded under their own power. The movement to the Russells was uneventful.

Early in the morning of 21 February, about ten miles east of the Russells, the Amphibious Force divided into three groups, each of which proceeded to a separate beach to land the troops in accordance with tactical plans previously prepared by Admiral Turner and General Hester. Plans for a preliminary bombardment by the destroyers, mine sweepers, and destroyer-transports had been prepared, but the absence of the Japanese made naval gunfire unnecessary.

By 0530 all landing craft had cast their tows loose and were closing in toward the assigned beaches, and at 0600 the assault waves went ashore unopposed. The plans were executed in accordance with the original schedules without hindrance from the Japanese. Headquarters and the 1st Battalion Team of the 103d Regimental Combat Team, the 43d Signal Company, the 11th Defense Battalion detachment, and 43d Division headquarters landed at Yellow Beach at Wernham Cove at the southern end of Banika. The 2d Battalion Team of the 103d and the 43d Cavalry Reconnaissance Troop landed on Blue Beach on the north and south coasts of Renard Sound on Banika. The 3d Raider Battalion landed from the destroyer-transports at Red Beach and Paddy Bay at Pavuvu. Patrols immediately pushed inland, but found no

Japanese. The engineers patrolled to find drinking water, a more pressing problem than the enemy. By 1800 all elements of the landing force could communicate by telephone; wire crews had put a telephone line across Sunlight Channel to connect Banika with Pavuvu. By 1900 the troops had dug themselves into defense positions, and outposts and observation posts had been established.

Logistical operations at the beaches were progressing in a satisfactory manner. The invasion had been effected under radio silence; the enemy air and naval forces had not interfered, and the unloading had not been interrupted. The commanders had emphasized the necessity for unloading rapidly and moving the supplies inland to keep the beaches clear. About one-third of the landing force had been assigned to unload the ships and landing craft. Ship unloading details numbered eighty men per reinforced battalion; forty-five men were assigned to each LCT. The beach parties, besides naval elements, consisted of 200 soldiers or marines per reinforced battalion. By 1000 all craft except the barge had been unloaded and fifteen days' supply of B rations, ten days' supply of C rations, five days' of D rations, five units of fire, and thirty days' supply of gasoline had been landed. The ships and landing craft withdrew to Guadalcanal to embark the second echelon.

The destroyers, mine sweepers, destroyer-transports, and landing craft returned the next morning (22 February) to land the 169th Regimental Combat Team at Paddy Bay and Beach Yellow. Throughout the rest of February LCT's transported the remainder of the 43d Division (less the 172d Regimental Combat Team) from Koli Point to the Russells. By the end of the month a force of 9,000 men had landed in the islands. By 16 March 15,669 troops of all services had reached the Russells. Beach and antiaircraft defenses, including long-range and fire-control radar, 155-mm. guns, 90-mm., 40-mm., and other antiaircraft guns had been established. The Japanese never attacked the Russells by sea, although they launched frequent air raids.

The first evidence that the Japanese were aware of the occupation was an air raid on 6 March. As the Russells had been under radio silence, radars had not alerted the islands, but the damage from the raid was slight. Thereafter the Japanese continued to bomb the Russells by day and night, but the radars alerted the troops in time, and fighters from Guadalcanal usually drove the enemy off until the airfields in the Russells were completed.

By 16 April supplies had reached the prescribed levels—sixty days of most types, ten units of fire for field and seacoast artillery, and fifteen units for antiaircraft artillery—and the command of the Russells passed from Admiral Turner to the commanding general of the XIV Corps.

Construction of roads, airfields, and boat bases had begun in February, and by 15 April the first of the two airfields on Banika was ready for operation. Surfaced with rolled coral, it was then 2,300 yards long and 100 yards wide. The torpedo boat base at Wernham Cove had gone into operation on 25 February and by 15 February three landing craft bases were operating. The Allied base in the Russells was ready to support further advances northward.

Appendix A

Letter from General Harmon to Admiral Ghormley, 6 October 1942[*]

HEADQUARTERS USAFISPA
(Forward Echelon)

Noumea, New Caledonia
6 October 1942

SUBJECT: Occupation of Ndini. [Ndeni]
TO   : Comsopac.

1. From a military viewpoint the occupation of Ndini at this time under the existing strategic situation has not appealed to me as a measure best utilizing the capabilities of our forces.

I regret that I have not previously more completely expressed myself on this subject. While fully prepared to support to the utmost your final decision it does not appear that it is even now too late to review the plan, as action for its accomplishment has but just been initiated.

Attention is therefore invited to the following considerations:

    a. It is understood that the primary reasons for the occupation of Ndini are:

        (1) To provide a base for airplane operation for: Anti-submarine patrol; extension of patrols to the North and Northeast and protection of east flank of Line of Communication to the Solomons.

        (2) To deny it to the enemy.

        (3) To afford an intermediate field between Button [Espiritu Santo] and Cactus [Guadalcanal] for staging short range aircraft.

    Reference *a.* (1) These are all admittedly important reasons in favor of this line of action but cannot afford our forces any benefit or influence enemy action for at least two and probably three months. In the final analysis they are not individually or cumulatively vital to the success of main offensive operation or accomplishment of primary mission of maintaining security of South Pacific bases and lines of communication.

    Reference *a.* (2) It is not probable that the enemy will develop Ndini or occupy it in force as long as we are able to conduct intensive bomber operations from Button.

[*] This letter, when written, was classified "Secret."

Reference *a*. (3) While desirable this is not a necessity as practically all air-craft can make the flight Button–Cactus direct.

b. (1) The occupation of Ndini at this time represents a diversion from the main effort and dispersion of force. The situation in Cactus–Ringbolt cannot be regarded as anything but "continuingly critical." Infiltration continues and recent additions probably give the enemy a force ashore in the neighbor-hood of 3,500. Pack or other mobile artillery in the hands of this force if skillfully employed could develop into a serious danger. With or without augmentation by infiltration, this force could well tip the scales in favor of an enemy victory if skillfully used against our Southern and Western front in conjunction with a determined night attack from the seaward ap-proaches. There is no effective defense against his support of such an attack by fire from warships.

If we do not succeed in holding Cactus–Ringbolt our effort in the Santa Cruz will be a total waste—and loss. The Solomons has to be our main effort. The loss of Cactus–Ringbolt would be a four way victory for the Jap—provide a vanguard for his strong Bismarck position, deny us a jumping off place against that position, give him a jumping off place against the New Hebrides, effectively cover his operations against New Guinea.

It is my personal conviction that the Jap is capable of retaking Cactus–Ringbolt and that he will do so in the near future unless it is materially strengthened. I further believe that appropriate increase in strength of garrison, rapid improvement of conditions for air operation and increased surface action, if accomplished in time, will make the operation so costly that he will not attempt it.

(2) The airdrome (including both fields) cannot be considered suitable for continuous operation. The durability of the mat, considering the character of the surface on which it is laid, for continuous operation of heavy ships is open to doubt. The mat is not completed on the runway, and there are no taxiways or standings. With any considerable degree of rain, air operations under present conditions will practically cease. The Jap has not shown him-self unskillful at forecasting meteorological conditions nor slow in taking advantage of them.

(3) There may be some plan behind his recent method of Fighter-Bomber ap-proach. Is there perhaps the idea that on the right day, at the appropriate time, after having exhausted our Fighters and *apparently* withdrawn his Bombers, he will return with them and strike heavily? Dispersion at Cactus is poor. Of concealment and protection there is relatively none. We do not have sufficient Fighters or facilities to operate them in two echelons of suffi-cient strength. Such an attack, well executed, would be a stunning blow.

(4) The availability of a suitable runway and adequate facilities to permit the full effective operation of B–17 squadron would go far toward the security

of our position by extending the range of daylight reconnaissance and by providing a ready striking force to be used against appropriate objectives as far northwest as Buka.

2. It is recommended that any reconsideration of plans take cognizance of the following proposed lines of action.

a. The abandonment of the Ndini operation until such time as a condition of reasonable stability and security is achieved in the Southern Solomons.

b. The immediate re-enforcement of Cactus by not less than the equivalent of one Infantry Regimental Combat Team.

c. The intensification, as means and conditions permit, of naval surface action in South Solomon waters.

d. The prompt dispatch to Cactus of all the airdrome construction personnel, equipment and construction supplies that can be effectively employed and used; with the initial mission of:

(1) Completing one all-weather runway with taxiways and dispersed standings.

(2) Completing a second all-weather runway with taxiways and dispersed standings.

(3) Improvement of fueling system, dispersal, camouflage and protection of aircraft.

e. Material augmentation of fuel supply to a minimum level of 250,000 gallons.

f. Conduct of intensive air operations from Cactus against Buin–Tonolei–Faisi and Buka.

g. Continuation of intensive short range air operations against air, land and sea objectives.

h. Occupation of tactical localities in the New Georgia group by infiltration.

3. Appreciating that I have not exhausted this subject and that you may have important considerations in mind that are not covered herein, I nevertheless feel obligated to present these views to you.

M. F. HARMON
Major General, U.S.A.
Commanding

Appendix B

General Patch's Letter of
Instructions to General Collins,
5 January 1943[1]

HEADQUARTERS XIV CORPS

A.P.O. #709

5 Jan. 43

SUBJECT: Letter of Instructions

TO : Commanding General, 25th Infantry Division.

MAP : Aerial Photomosaic, GUADALCANAL ISLAND, "3 of 8", 1:13,833.

   1.   *a*. See G–2 Estimate.

        b. See Operations Overlay.

   2. The 25th Infantry Division will relieve the 132d Infantry on MOUNT OESTON (AUSTEN) without delay, and, upon completion of this relief, will attack from that area and seize and hold the line approximately 3,000 yards to the west thereof. See Operations Overlay.

   3.   *a*. The 132d Infantry will pass to the control of the Commanding General, Perimeter Defense, when relieved by the 25th Infantry Division. The Commanding General, 25th Infantry Division, will notify the Commanding General, Perimeter Defense, when this relief has been effected.

        b. The 35th Infantry will become available to the Commanding General, 25th Infantry Division, upon relief from the Perimeter Defense.

        c. The 25th Infantry Division will execute a passage of lines through the 3d Battalion 182d Infantry, the 1st Battalion 2d Marines, and the Reconnaissance Squadron Americal Division, and these units will be placed under the command of the Commanding General, 25th Infantry Division, when he indicates that he is ready to operate in the area now held by these units. The 3d Battalion 182d Infantry and the Reconnaissance Squadron Americal Division will revert to the command of the Commanding General, Perimeter Defense, and the 1st Battalion 2d Marines will revert to the command of the Commanding General, 2d Marine Division, when passing [passed] through by the 25th Infantry Division and released by the Commanding General thereof.

        d. The 25th Infantry Division will be responsible for the security of its left (south) flank.

[1] This letter, when written, was classified "Secret." The distribution list has been omitted.

e. The 2d Marine Division will maintain contact with the right (north) flank of the 25th Infantry Division.

f. The Commanding General, 25th Infantry Division, is authorized to deal directly with the Commanding General, 2d Marine Air Wing, in regard to air-ground support.

g. Artillery employment:

(1) The Americal Division Artillery with Battery A 1st Amphibious Corps (155-mm How.), and Battery F 244th Coast Artillery (155-mm Gun), attached, generally from present positions, will continue to support the 2d Marine Division in its present position, but will be prepared to reinforce the 25th Infantry Division Artillery with fire in support of the advance of the 25th Infantry Division.

(2) The 2d Battalion 10th Marines (75-mm How.) from present positions will fire in support of the advance of the 25th Infantry Division; its fires will be controlled by the 25th Infantry Division.

(3) Battery H 244th Coast Artillery (5-inch Gun) will continue on present sea-coast defense missions.

(4) The 1st and 3d Battalions 10th Marines (75-mm How.) will revert to control of the Commanding General, Perimeter Defense, when replaced by the 2d Battalion 10th Marines (75-mm How.) and the 90th Field Artillery Battalion (155-mm How.), respectively.

4.   *a.* Distributing Point, Class I and Class III ONLY: (71.5–200.0).[2]

b. Distribution Point, all other supplies: ISLAND DUMP.[3]

c. Evacuation to Division Hospital, 25th Infantry Division; overflow to 101st Medical Regiment.

d. Road Maintenance:

(1) The 57th Engineer Battalion Americal Division will be attached to the 2d Marine Division for road maintenance.

(2) Maintenance of roads will be by divisions in own zones of action.

(3) Maintenance by the 25th Infantry Division will include the entire WRIGHT ROAD.

(4) In the zone of the 2d Marine Division, first priority will be given to the SKYLINE DRIVE.[4]

(5) The BEACH ROAD west to include the NORTH MATANIKAU BRIDGE will be maintained by the 26th Naval Construction Battalion.

5.   *a.* SOI, Hq Island Command, 26 Dec 42.

b. Command Post: to be reported when determined.

A. M. PATCH,
Major General, U.S. Army,
Commanding.

[2] The distributing point lay by the coast road on the west bank of the Matanikau.
[3] The Island Dump lay near the Ilu.
[4] Skyline Drive was the trail which led from the beach over Hills 75, 74, and 72 to Hill 66.

Appendix C

XIV Corps' Field Order No. 1,
16 January 1943

HQ XIV CORPS,
APO #709
1200 16 Jan 43.

FO No. 1.

MAP: Gridded 8-sheet photomap, 1:15,000.

   1.   *a*. See current Summary.

        b. See Operations Overlay.

   2. This Corps, from present positions, will attack to the west at a time and on a date to be announced later, seize the high ground in the vicinity of (68.0–201.8)–(67–200)–(65–198) to the south thereof, and be prepared to continue the attack to the northwest.[1] See Operations Overlay.

   3.   *a*. 2d Marine Division (less 2d and 8th Marine Regiments), one (1) Infantry regiment American Division attached, will attack to the west and seize that part of the Corps objective within its zone of action. It will maintain connection and contact with the 25th Infantry Division during the attack, will cover its left (south) flank, and will assist the 25th Infantry Division by fire in taking the high ground in the vicinity of (66.0–198.5).[2] It will protect the shore line from the MATANIKAU RIVER (excl) to the objective (incl) against any attempted enemy landing.

        b. 25th Infantry Division will attack to the west and seize that part of the Corps objective within its zone of action. It will envelop or turn the enemy's right (south) flank and will protect the left (south) flank of the Corps.

        c. The Perimeter Defense (less one (1) Infantry regiment American Division), with 2d and 8th Marine Regiments attached, will intensify patrolling to insure protection of air fields and rear installations of the Corps. It will extend beach protection to insure against possible enemy landings as far west as the MATANIKAU RIVER (incl). One (1) Infantry regiment will be kept immediately available for use by the Corps Commander in support of the attack or in defense of rear areas; it will be committed to action only on orders of the

---

[1] The objective line ran from Hill 87 northeast to the beach.

[2] Hill 87.

Corps Commander. A second regiment of Infantry will be so utilized that it can be assembled in two and one half (2½) hours for use by the Corps Commander.

    d. 147th Infantry (–) will prepare to cover KOLI POINT AIR FIELD with two (2) rifle companies reinforced. The remainder of the 147th Infantry at KOLI POINT will await orders there in Corps reserve and will be committed to action only on orders of the Corps Commander.

    e. Artillery.

        (1) Americal Division Artillery, with 10th Marines (less two (2) battalions) (75-mm. Pack How), Battery A 1st Marine Amphibious Corps (155-mm How), and Battery F 244th Coast Artillery (155-mm Gun) attached, will support the attack of the 2d Marine Division. It will be prepared to reinforce the fires in the zone of action of the 25th Infantry Division with two (2) battalions of light artillery and one (1) battalion of medium artillery.

        (2) Two (2) battalions 10th Marines (75-mm How) will remain on Perimeter Defense.

        (3) 25th Infantry Division Artillery will be prepared to reinforce the fires in the zone of action of the 2nd Marine Division with two (2) battalions of light artillery and one (1) battalion of medium artillery.

        (4) A fifteen (15) minute artillery, sea, and air preparation will precede the attack. Thereafter, artillery, without instructions from other headquarters, will promptly take under fire targets of opportunity.

    f. 2d Marine Air Wing will support the attack and will engage targets of opportunity as indicated by organic air surveillance and this headquarters, paying particular attention to enemy artillery and concentrations of enemy troops. Requests for air-ground support missions will be transmitted to the AC of S, G–3, this headquarters.

    g. Naval gunfire support, utilizing such naval vessels as are available, will be coordinated by the Corps Artillery Officer. This support will include an initial preparation of (15) minutes, commencing at H–15, in the areas (67.8–201.8)–(67.5–201.0) (66.8–200.2) and (67.8–201.8)–(66.2–200.0), followed by missions on targets of opportunity as far west as Visale Mission as indicated by air surveillance, shore surveillance, and this headquarters.[3]

    h. (1) An artillery, sea, and air preparation of fifteen (15) minutes will precede the attack. Thereafter, these units will fire on targets of opportunity.

        (2) Isolated points of enemy resistance will be contained and by-passed; they will be reduced later. Maximum use will be made of artillery and air support in effecting reductions.

        (3) All Infantry units will keep their supporting artillery and the AC of S, G–3, this headquarters, advised of their locations at all times in order that targets of opportunity may be fired upon promptly.

    4.   *a.* Rations, gasoline, oil, and ammunition will be drawn directly from the ISLAND DUMP as long as practicable, thereafter from ADVANCE DUMP in the vicinity of (71.7–

---

[3] The coordinates refer to points on the beach about 3,200 yards west of Point Cruz, to the ravine between Hills 93 and 92, and to the west slopes of Hill 92.

200.0). The 25th Infantry Division will exhaust the WRIGHT ROAD DUMP prior to drawing from the ADVANCE DUMP.

b. Evacuation will be by divisions to Division Collecting Stations, thence by Corps to Clearing Hospitals.

c. Burial will be by the Quartermaster in ISLAND CEMETERY.

d. Prisoners of War will be sent to the rear by Divisions to Division Collecting Points, thence by Corps to ISLAND STOCKADE.

e. Main Supply Road: BEACH ROAD. Priority of use: combat troops, evacuation, supply.

f. Traffic Control: Divisions will maintain Military Police control of traffic as follows:

2d Marine Division:	BEACH ROAD west of the command post 2d Marine Division (incl), and the MARINE TRAIL.[4]
25th Infantry Division:	BEACH ROAD east of the command post 2d Marine Division (excl) to the perimeter, WRIGHT ROAD, and RUST TRAIL.[5]
Americal Division:	All hard-surfaced roads within the Perimeter.

5.   *a*. Signal Operations Instructions, Hq Island Command, 26 Dec 42.

b. Command Posts: to be reported to this headquarters when determined.

c. Strict radio discipline and cryptographic security will be maintained at all times by all units.

PATCH

RIDINGS
   G–3

---

[4] Marine Trail ran from the coast road southward along the east bank of the Matanikau to Hill 67.

[5] Rust Trail ran from Marine Trail eastward over Hills 67 and 69.

Appendix D

A Japanese Analysis of American Combat Methods on Guadalcanal[1]

I. Offense

1. Preceding an attack by the American Army, there is always artillery bombardment for at least 12 hours. When this is begun at dawn or on the previous night, there are frequently an attack and an advance in the afternoon. At this time, we invariably open up a persistent checking fire....

2. Attack formation: ... They are quite brave, and use mainly automatic rifles. On rare occasions they send out ahead patrols of 2 or 3 men.

3. Outline of Infantry Attack: When they come 300 or 400 meters in front of the fortified positions, first of all, they always stop, construct fortified positions, and about 100–200 meters to their rear flank they put up tents (the tents, for the most part, are for one section each, and are not large). Moreover, in front of these positions they station pickets. While reconnoitering they push forward their ... [battalion howitzers], they continue their bombing, and concentrating their trench mortars on a certain sector, they advance and attack.... When they reach 100 or 150 meters in front of the position, they stop to bombard. They press on while sweeping with fire with their grenade rifles, light [machine] guns and automatic rifles. (In the last phase of combat they use flamethrowers and molotov cocktails). So long as even one of our men remains in a position and resists, they

---

[1] This document, which was captured by Allied forces in New Guinea, was reproduced by ATIS, SWPA, on 21 November 1943 as Enemy Pub No. 56. It is a translation of a 10-page, mimeographed booklet written by a Japanese divisional staff officer and originally distributed to the Japanese in the South and Southwest Pacific Areas on 4 March 1943. The ATIS translation employs several American colloquialisms. After the war a search for the original Japanese booklet was made, that the colloquialisms might be removed, but the booklet could not be found. In this appendix, English words are substituted for the Japanese map symbols which are occasionally used by ATIS. Three sketches in the ATIS publication, showing American attack formations, methods of penetration, and organization of defensive positions, employ Japanese map symbols and have been omitted here. The Japanese and Allied distribution lists have also been omitted. Some changes have been made in grammar, punctuation, and spelling. Col. Sidney F. Mashbir, Co-ordinator of ATIS during the war, checked the appendix and concurred in this version. Except for the alterations noted above, the text of the ATIS publication is reproduced almost in full, without change.

do not break through. Even though they realize that the position is completely demolished, they concentrate their trench mortars and then penetrate, yelling loudly.

4. Penetration: . . . If a strong reconnaissance force discovers an opening, after repeated bombardment they occupy it about evening. They build fortified positions until dawn, later adding to them and increasing the number of men. After that, they extend their penetration further to the front and flanks. Consequently, in Guadalcanal they never attempted to break through the depth of our position at one blow.

They penetrate little by little, most cautiously, but very steadily. They advance while successively destroying every fortified position.

5. Attack according to schedule: American troops conduct their attacks according to a planned table. Consequently, as a general rule, there is no such thing as taking advantage of an opportunity. Once they have executed an order which they were given at the outset, they seem to stop.

When their attack fails, they revise their plans on a larger scale. However, the signal unit follows up [establishes and maintains communication] with unexpected speed.

6. Night attack: Although they fire, infantry forces do not engage in night attacks.

II. Defense

1. Organization of an enemy position: It is a zone position without strong points which has as its nucleus special fire points and heavy fire arms. . . . The same class of troops is generally disposed in all sectors. The . . . [battalion howitzers] (they must be above medium) and the . . . [artillery] are moved by . . . [truck] according to the situation. . . .

2. Enemy close range defensive battle depends on . . . [machine guns and battalion howitzers]. As soon as they perceive (by their microphones, etc.[2]) that we are approaching, they repeatedly carry out a concentrated searching fire of 20 guns in the already prepared zone of fire.

If one breaks this zone or rushes through the pockets, it becomes unexpectedly easy. But breaking through the zone of fire by force, whether by day or night, requires a considerable degree of neutralization and tremendous spirit. One

[2] The Japanese apparently believed that American troops employed electric devices, such as microphones, at observation posts to warn them against approaching enemy infantrymen. A similar idea was expressed by Colonel Furumiya (CO, *29th Inf*), who was killed in October 1942. He suggested that the Americans were perhaps using machine guns which were operated by remote control, thus eliminating the need for a crew to man the gun. See extracts from his diary in 1st Mar Div Rpt, V, Annex I.

should not employ mass formations. The enemy is not clever in a certain sense, for when his positions are penetrated by one of our units he becomes panic-stricken. We should take full advantage of this and should lose no opportunity to penetrate his positions and drive him out of them.

3. Enemy fire is only on prepared points (sectors) and it is almost random fire. In the evening it is especially intense. For that reason we thoroughly reconnoiter the zones which they have prepared, and avoid them. At the same time, there is great value in drawing out enemy fire by a show of force and making the enemy expend recklessly. Moreover, a "feint" . . . attack by a small force is an effective method of attack against this type of enemy.

III. Camp Duties

The functioning of an American camp is extremely crude and imperfect. Although the American Army engages unexpectedly in 5th column activities, the functioning of its outposts is bad. Their security measures have many loop-holes and their night reconnaissance in particular is almost non-existent. There are sentry guards only in the daytime. At night they place pickets (between 15 and 20 men) very sparsely at important points so that infiltration by patrols and small forces is comparatively easy. In these openings, instead of sentry guards, they frequently place microphones. The division has never been able to discover these, but the wires have been noticed. Also direct security of positions is generally bad and extremely careless.

IV. Other Items.

1. American rear and flank susceptibility: The American Army is not susceptible on the flanks and rear. The American positions on Guadalcanal were probably all-out defense positions, and there were none with unprepared rear and flanks. Because of the deployment of their troop strength, which is thought to be sufficient . . ., they very seldom experience any hurt. As is clear from our own attack and a summary of the enemy's attack, the enemy never experiences any great anxiety over his deployment. This is indeed unfortunate. It seems the enemy will never experience any real suffering unless dealt a crushing blow. Therefore, rather than seeking excellence of deployment against the American Army, if we concentrate our entire strength on desirable points whether in the rear of flank, or in front, the enemy will come to be considered comparatively weak.

2. Susceptibility to fire power: The American Army has a weak point in its great susceptibility to artillery and bombing attacks. Several effective rounds alone always rout an attack force of 300–400 or 500–600 in a moment, stemming the attack. For that reason, subjugation by shelling is easy, no matter what the type

of enemy troops. However, the American Air Force takes off from runways during bombardments and frequently maneuvers bravely against rifles, machine guns, etc.

3. Use of machine power and material power: They are skillful in the use of abundant material power and machine power. Even though they are the work of the enemy, newly established automobile roads, the strengthening of positions, speedy construction of . . . [airfields], the setting up of a network of communications, etc., are beautiful things. It demands all the more attention to force them out.

4. Stress laid upon areas in the rear. In the American Army the stress laid upon rear areas is quite considerable, and the Japanese Forces (including the Navy) cannot compare with them. Not only do they form strong points in their rear, but they make persistent and utmost efforts to cut off our rear. This is to say, the enemy is constantly attacking our transport ships rather than our warships. In Guadalcanal they carried this out to an excessive degree, with untiring efforts. Consequently, if we can cut off the enemy's rear areas to half the extent that they do ours, their suffering will be beyond imagination.

5. Progressiveness of American combat methods: The American Army is constantly endeavoring to devise new strategy. In a delaying action of 70 days the American Army used a "non-tactical" attack and defense, but gradually became enlightened thanks to the Japanese Army. Their methods of attack improved, and they finally developed sound methods. Moreover, with the troop deployment which they have decided upon, they are carrying out attacks which have completely changed their first reputation. Therefore it should be said that it is a big mistake generally to disregard the general characteristics of the American Army and to consider their strategy as a fixed thing.

6. The American Army is slow and steady, and does not place all its stakes on one big engagement. Individually or in small forces, they have often taken risks as in sports. As a whole group, however, they are extremely cautious and steady, advancing step by step. If they are not absolutely confident of their positions and strength, they do not attack. Therefore, in accordance with this situation, it is judged that vigorous operations and daring maneuvers will not be carried out for the present by large forces. One reason for this probably is that their officers of middle rank and below possess little tactical ability. Furthermore, if the enemy once gains self-confidence he becomes overly bold, but if any one opposes him he becomes radically less agressive at once. This is seen to be the usual attitude of foreigners. . . .

Appendix E
U.S. Army Battle Participation List for Guadalcanal

The following list of Army and Air Force units are those that participated in the Guadalcanal Campaign as defined by General Order Number 24, 4 March 1947. Units are listed as they were designated during the campaign, with later changes and redesignations shown in parentheses following. General Order Number 12, 1 February 1946, lists the units entitled to battle credit for the Guadalcanal Campaign as they appear in parentheses. Differences between the listing below and General Order Number 12 are a result of later research.

XIV Corps

XIV Corps Headquarters
Service Command, Guadalcanal
Coast Artillery
  214th CA Regt (redesignated 214th AAA GP, Hq & Hq Btry; 250th AAA Searchlight Bn; 528th AAA Gun Bn; 950th AAA Bn, Automatic Weapons)
  Btry F, 244th CA Regt and Provisional Btry H, 244th CA Regt (redesignated 259th CA Bn, Harbor Defense, Separate)
Field Artillery
  97th FA Bn (75-mm Howitzer Pack)
Chemical
  151st Chem Co, Decontamination (inactivated and personnel assigned to 218th Chem Composite Co, Depot Section)
  887th Chem Co, Air Operations

Engineer
  472d Engr Maintenance Co, Contact Plat
Infantry
  147th Inf Regt, less Cannon Co
Medical
  1st Section, 7th Medical Supply Depot (Personnel and Equipment transferred to 1st Section, Advance Depot Plat, 21st Medical Supply Depot)
  17th Field Hospital
  52d Field Hosp, 2d and 3d Units and Hqs
  20th Station Hospital
Ordnance
  22d Ord Medium Maintenance Co
  51st Ord Medium Maintenance Co
  Co A, 82d Ord Bn (redesignated 3465th Ord Auto Maintenance Co, Medium)
  482d Ord Co, Aviation, Bomb

XIV Corps—Continued

Quartermaster
  1st Plat, 45th QM Grave Regis Co (re-
    designated 29th QM Grave Regis
    Det)
  2d Plat, Co C, 60th QM Laundry Bn
  3d Plat, 177th QM Bakery Co (redesig-
    nated 352d QM Plat, Bakery)

  494th QM Depot Co, Supply
Signal
  1st Sect, Sig Pigeon Co, 5944–A
  69th Sig Co (redesignated 1069th Sig
    Co, Service Gp)
  670th Sig Aircraft Warning Co
  831st Signal Service Co[1]

American Division

Special Troops
  Hq & Hq Co
  39th MP Co, less one plat (redesignated
    MP Plat, American Div)
  101st QM Regt (redesignated 125th QM
    Co)
  26th Signal Co
Artillery
  Hq & Hq Btry
  Americal Div Artillery Band
  221st FA Bn, 155-mm. Howitzer
  245th FA Bn, 105-mm. Howitzer
  246th FA Bn, 105-mm. Howitzer

  247th FA Bn, 105-mm. Howitzer
Cavalry
  Mobile Combat Rcn Sq (redesignated
    21st Cav Rcn Troop, Mcz)
Engineers
  57th Engineer Combat Bn
Infantry
  132d Inf Regt, less Cannon Co
  164th Inf Regt, less Cannon Co
  182d Inf Regt, less Cannon Co
Medical
  101st Medical Regt (redesignated 121st
    Med Bn)

25th Infantry Division

Special Troops
  Hq & Hq Company
  MP Platoon
  Band
  25th QM Co
Artillery
  Hq & Hq Btry
  25th Div Arty Band
  8th FA Bn, 105-mm. Howitzer
  64th FA Bn, 105-mm. Howitzer
  89th FA Bn, 105-mm. Howitzer
  90th FA Bn, 155-mm. Howitzer

Cavalry
  25th Cav Rcn Troop, Mcz
Engineers
  65th Engineer Combat Bn
Infantry
  27th Inf Regt
  35th Inf Regt
  161st Inf Regt
Medical
  25th Med Bn
Ordnance
  725th Ord Light Maintenance Co

---

[1] Does not appear in General Order Number 12, 1 February 1946.

43d Infantry Division

Special Troops
 Hq & Hq Co
 Mp Platoon
 Band
 43d Signal Co
Artillery[2]
 Hq & Hq Btry
 152d FA Bn, 105-mm. Howitzer
 169th FA Bn, 105-mm. Howitzer
Cavalry

43d Cavalry Rcn Troop, Mcz
Engineers
 118th Engineer Combat Bn
Infantry
 103d Inf Regt
 169th Inf Regt
Medical
 118th Medical Bn
Ordnance
 743d Ordnance Co

Air Corps Units

XIII Bomber Command
 Hq, XIII Bomber Command
  23d Bomb Sq, 5th Bomb Gp, Heavy
  31st Bomb Sq, 5th Bomb Gp, Heavy
  69th Bomb Sq, Medium
  70th Bomb Sq, Medium
  72d Bomb Sq, 5th Bomb Gp, Heavy
  394th Bomb Sq, 5th Bomb Gp, Heavy
 11th Bomb Gp, Heavy, Hqs
  26th Bomb Sq
  42d Bomb Sq
  98th Bomb Sq
  431st Bomb Sq
XIII Fighter Command
 Hq, XIII Fighter Command

 12th Fighter Sq
 13th Troop Carrier Sq
 14th Fighter Sq
347th Fighter Gp, Hqs
 67th Fighter Sq
 68th Fighter Sq
 70th Fighter Sq
 339th Fighter Sq
Miscellaneous
 3d Bomb Gp, Light
 4th Photo Rcn and Mapping Gp
 17th Photo Sq, Light, 4th Photo Rcn &
  Mapping Gp
 29th Service Gp
 82d Service Sq

---

[2] 192d FA Bn, 43d Inf Division, is given credit for the Guadalcanal Campaign in General Order Number 12, 1 February 1946; however, the unit did not leave New Caledonia until 24 February 1943, three days after the campaign was over.

Guide to Footnotes

There exists no generally accepted practice for citing Army and Navy documents. The method adopted in this and other Pacific volumes is designed to furnish to the reader necessary information on the source, character, date, subject matter, and present location of the documents, and to make each citation as brief as possible. The security classifications of the documents have been omitted.

The citations are for the most part self-explanatory, but a brief exposition may assist the reader in finding the entries in the South Pacific War Diary. They are listed in the Diary, by month, according to their date-time groups in Greenwich Civil Time, and show the originator and the addressee of each message. The first two figures in a date-time group give the day of the month; the last four indicate the time of day. Thus, in a group of entries for July 1942, a date-time group of 021226 means that the date of the message was 2 July, and 1226 was the time.

In general, abbreviations conform to the usages in TM 20–205, the Dictionary of United States Army Terms, published in 1944. To assist the civilian reader, unfamiliar official and unofficial military and naval abbreviations, short titles, and code words which are used in the footnotes are explained below.

AAA	Antiaircraft artillery
ACofS	Assistant Chief of Staff
Adj	Adjutant
Amph	Amphibious
Arty	Artillery
ASF	Army Service Forces
ATIS	Allied Translator and Interpreter Section
Avn	Aviation
Bn	Battalion
Bn–1, Bn–2, etc.	See under G.
CA	Coast Artillery
CACTUS	Guadalcanal
CINC SWPA	Supreme Commander [Commander in Chief], Southwest Pacific Area
CINCPAC	Commander in Chief, U.S. Pacific Fleet
CINCPOA	Commander in Chief, Pacific Ocean Area
CG	Commanding General
CM–IN	Cable Message In
CM–OUT	Cable Message Out

CNO	Chief of Naval Operations
CO	Commanding Officer
CofS	Chief of Staff
COMAIRSOPAC	Commander, [land-based] Aircraft, South Pacific Force
COMAIRWING I	Commanding General, 1st Marine Air Wing
COMAMPHIBFORSOPAC	Commander, Amphibious Force, South Pacific Force
Comdr	Commander
Comdt	Commandant
COMGENSOPAC	Commanding General, U.S. Army Forces in the South Pacific Area
COMINCH	Commander in Chief, U.S. Fleet
COMNAVBAS	Commander, Naval Base[s]
COMNAVEU	Commander, U.S. Naval Forces in Europe
COMSERONSOPAC	Commander, Service Squadron, South Pacific Force
COMSOPAC	Commander, South Pacific Area and South Pacific Force
COMSOWESPACFOR	Commander, Southwest Pacific Force (the U.S. Naval commander under MacArthur)
CTF	Commander, Task Force
CTG	Commander, Task Group
D–1, D–2, etc.	See under G.
ExO	Executive Officer
FA	Field Artillery
FM	Field Manual
FO	Field Order
G	A generic label for the staff sections of large Army units. G–1, for example, indicates either the personnel section of a headquarters or the assistant chief of staff for personnel; G–2, intelligence; G–3, operations; G–4, supply and evacuation. In units smaller than divisions, the staff sections are labeled S–1, S–2, etc. In 1942 Marine units employed the same staff organization as the Army, but D indicated a divisional staff section, R that of a regiment, and Bn that of a battalion.
GHQ	General Headquarters
GO	General Order
Gp	Group
GSUSA	General Staff, U.S. Army (used after the reorganization of the armed forces in 1947)
HD	Harbor Defense
HRS DRB AGO	Historical Records Section, Departmental Records Branch, Administrative Services Division, Office of The Adjutant General
Int	Intelligence

Interrog	Interrogation
JCS	Joint Chiefs of Staff
JPS	Joint Staff Planners
MAC	Marine Amphibious Corps
MIS	Military Intelligence Service
Mob	Mobile
Msg	Message
NR	Number (relating to a radiogram)
Ntg	No time group
OB	Order of Battle
Obs	Observer
O-in-C	Officer in Charge
ONI	Office of Naval Intelligence
OPD	Operations Division, War Department General Staff (now the Plans and Operations Division, General Staff, U.S. Army)
Opn	Operation
Ord	Order
Org Rec Br, AGO	Organization Records Branch, Records Administration Center, Administrative Services Division, Office of The Adjutant General
Pac	Pacific
POA	Pacific Ocean Area
PTO	Pacific Theater of Operations
Rad	Radiogram
Recon	Reconnaissance
R–1, R–2, etc.	See under G.
RINGBOLT	Tulagi
SCAP	Supreme Commander for the Allied Powers
SEC NAV	The Secretary of the Navy
SGO	Office of The Surgeon General
S–1, S–2, etc.	See under G.
SOPAC	South Pacific Area, South Pacific Force
SOWESPAC	Southwest Pacific Area
SSUSA	Special Staff, U.S. Army
Stf	Staff
SWPA	Southwest Pacific Area
TF	Task Force
TG	Task Group
Trans	Translation
USA	U.S. Army
USAFISPA	U.S. Army Forces in the South Pacific Area
USSBS	U.S. Strategic Bombing Survey

WD	War Department (now the Department of the Army)
WDCSA	Chief of Staff, U.S. Army (prior to the reorganization in 1947)
WDGS	War Department General Staff (now the General Staff, U. S. Army)
WIA	Wounded in Action

Bibliographical Note

Manuscript Histories

No historians accompanied the Army forces to Guadalcanal to observe operations, conduct interviews and critiques, and collect records for the preparation of a history of the campaign. As a result the extant manuscript histories, which were prepared long after the campaign, are not as detailed as those of later campaigns which were covered by historians. The following manuscripts are, however, useful.

Particularly helpful is the History of United States Army Forces in the South Pacific Area during World War II, 30 March 1942–1 August 1944. This four-part, typewritten work was written under the supervision first of Maj. Frederick P. Todd, USAFISPA Historical Section, and later, of Capt. Louis Morton, G–2 Historical Section, South Pacific Base Command. Prepared by competent historians, this comprehensive administrative and logistical history is invaluable for the student of South Pacific operations in general and of Army operations in particular. A copy of the history is in the files of the Historical Division, SSUSA.

Two manuscripts on the Guadalcanal campaign were prepared, beginning in 1944, by USAFISPA historians. The first of these, 147 typewritten pages in length, covers the entire campaign. It deals with Ghormley's general plans, the 1st Marine Division's plans and preparations, and operations on Guadalcanal and the Russells from August 1942 to February 1943. The second manuscript contains five typewritten chapters, and covers Ghormley's plans, 1st Marine Division's plans, and part of the operations on Guadalcanal; other chapters covering operations in November 1942, and January and February 1943, were not completed. These manuscripts were originally prepared for the *American Forces in Action* series. Based on the best sources available to USAFISPA historians, they are accurate but not thoroughly documented. The USAFISPA Historical Section also prepared a full set of maps relating to the campaign. These maps are the best of Guadalcanal available in the Department of the Army, and are much better than the operational maps used by the combat troops during the campaign. They have been extensively used in the preparation of maps for this volume. Both manuscripts and maps are in the files of the Historical Division, SSUSA.

A work based primarily upon Marine Corps records is The Guadalcanal Campaign (Historical Section, Hq. U. S. Marine Corps, June 1945), prepared by Capt. John L. Zimmerman, USMCR, and circulated within the Marine Corps. The Guadalcanal Campaign deals fully with operations of the 1st Marine Division up to 9 December 1942. The chapters dealing with operations following the 1st Marine Division's relief are less adequate, since 2d Marine Division records are sketchy. Now a civilian, Mr. Zimmerman is preparing a revised version of his monograph which will be published by the Marine Corps.

Pending the completion of final Air Force histories, the chief source for Army Air Force operations has been Guadalcanal and the Origins of the Thirteenth Air Force (July 1945), Army Air Forces Historical Studies, No. 35, by the Assistant Chief of Air Staff, Intelligence, Historical Division. This typewritten history, somewhat lacking in operational detail, is generally excellent. It clearly analyzes Air Force problems of administration, command, supply, and tactics in the South Pacific. It is in the Air Force Historical Office.

Official Records

This volume is based primarily upon official records. These records are of five general types: papers of the Joint Chiefs of Staff and the Joint Staff Planners, records of the U. S. Army, the U. S. Navy, and the U. S. Marine Corps, and Japanese documents.

Joint Papers

A study of the contents of these papers is essential to an understanding of the most important strategic considerations and decisions relating to the war in the Pacific. Those consulted, filed in Registered Documents, Plans and Policy Group, Plans and Operations Division, GSUSA, are as follows:

JCS Minutes of Meetings from the 1st Meeting to the 50th Meeting.

JPS Minutes of Meetings from the 1st Meeting to the 50th Meeting.

JCS Directive to Admiral Nimitz and General MacArthur, approved by the President on 30 March 1942.

JCS 21/2/D, and JPS 27/7, Defense of the Island Bases along the Line of Communication between Hawaii and Australia, 22 June 42 and 18 April 42. (JCS 48 bears the same title).

Army Records

Army records relevant to the campaign are voluminous, but are uneven in quality and content. They range from such documents as radiograms between the Chief of Staff and area commanders to the journals of battalions in combat. Some of the action reports and so-called histories of units in the field are inexact and sketchy; many are almost useless, but each one has been investigated because often an all but useless document explains a point which is covered nowhere else. Only the Army records which bear directly on the Guadalcanal campaign are mentioned below.

The Chief of Staff's Log, 1942–1943, filed in the Staff Communications Branch, Office, Chief of Staff, GSUSA, consists of the daily radiograms between General Marshall and the Army theater, area and task force commanders, and between General Marshall and such officers as General Harmon, who held a command subordinate to the Commander of the South Pacific Area. These radiograms give a succinct daily summary of the strategic situation throughout the world, throw light on joint and combined command, and summarize important plans and decisions.

Files of the Operations Division, WDGS (now Plans and Operations Division, GSUSA) on the Southwest Pacific Area and the Pacific Ocean Areas for 1942 and 1943 contain a large amount of data on the Operations Division's plans, opinions, and decisions regarding the conduct of the war in overseas theaters. Many of General Harmon's letters to the War Department are included in these files, as is an original, signed copy of the JCS directive of 2 July 1942.

Since USAFISPA did not come into existence until 26 July 1942, and Army ground forces were not committed to Guadalcanal until 13 October 1942, official USAFISPA records are valuable largely for the latter months of the campaign. A number of USAFISPA records were used.

Lt. Gen. Millard F. Harmon, The Army in the South Pacific (6 June 1944), is a brief narrative which was prepared by General Harmon as a guide to USAFISPA historians. It provides a useful summary of the Army's role in the planning and execution of the South Pacific Campaigns. A copy of General Harmon's report is in the files of the Historical Division, SSUSA.

Assistant Chief of Staff, G–2, Headquarters, USAFISPA, the Japanese Campaign in the Guadalcanal Area, 7 August 1943, is a sound study based on captured documents, reports from the XIV Corps, and interrogations of prisoners. Careful, conservative and accurate, the study is an excellent summary of Japanese operations during the early months of the campaign. It is filed in the Military Intelligence Library, Department of the Army.

Headquarters, USAFISPA, G–3 Worksheet Files and Periodic Reports for the latter months of the campaign yield some information on the Americal Division which is not to be found in that division's records. USAFISPA G–3 documents are filed in the Organizational Records Branch, AGO, St. Louis, Mo.

USAFISPA Historical Section's Russell Islands Folder contains valuable material on the planning for the Russells invasion. This folder is in the Historical Records Section, Departmental Records Branch, AGO.

Some miscellaneous documents, which were forwarded by USAFISPA to the Historical Division, SSUSA, contain some scattered reports from combat units on Guadalcanal. These will be forwarded to the Historical Records Section, Departmental Records Branch, AGO.

Most of the records of the XIV Corps and its assigned units are in Historical Records Section, Departmental Records Branch, AGO. Because the Corps headquarters was never numerically adequate during the campaign, its records are scanty. There is no comprehensive action report on file, nor have any G–1, G–3, or G–4 reports yet come to light. The most useful documents from the XIV Corps, besides G–2 translations, G–2 summaries, and G–3 Journals and periodic reports, are XIV Corps' Informal Report on Combat Operations, submitted to General Harmon on 3 June 1943, and the G–2's Enemy Operations on Guadalcanal, 24 April 1943. The Informal Report is not a complete record of the campaign. It is the result of a questionnaire on weapons, tactics, logistics, etc., sent by USAFISPA headquarters to the XIV Corps. The Corps headquarters and component units answered the questions in detail. The report furnishes the student with a summary of tactical and logistical problems and procedures. Enemy Operations on Guadalcanal presents a detailed analysis of enemy order of battle, strength, plans, and operations, but it exaggerates enemy strength and presents several contradictory conclusions.

There are at least 100 separate files, documents, reports, and histories from the Americal Division, but they vary greatly in usefulness. The division's action report provides only an outline. Historical Data, Task Force 6814 and Americal Division, is a valuable compendium of orders, troop lists, and reports. Lt. Col. Paul A. Gavan's Personal Experience Account of an Assistant Chief of Staff, G–3, includes helpful information on command decisions and operations. The G–2 and G–3 Journals and periodic reports are complete. The most valuable single Americal Division document is the Intelligence Annex to the Combat

Experience Report, Americal Division, Guadalcanal, 18 November 1942 to 9 February 1943. Prepared by Lt. Col. William D. Long, it presents a large amount of information on enemy order of battle, dates of landings, orders and operations. A cautious, conservative report, it has been proved to be generally accurate. Reports and histories from the Americal Division component units, though often inadequate, have had to be relied upon. The 132d Infantry's History is lengthy but not always accurate; the unit reports and journals are fairly complete, but occasionally err. The 164th Infantry's operation reports are generally reliable; some of the unit reports covering the Koli Point and Matanikau operations in early November are missing. The 182d Infantry's operations reports are fair, but the journal entries for the period 18–31 January 1943 are missing.

Records of the 25th Division, though less voluminous than those of the Americal, contain more information. There are no G–1, G–2, G–3, or G–4 reports as such. The 25th Division, however, prepared a report which is a model of its kind—Operations of the 25th Division on Guadalcanal, 17 December 1942 to 5 February 1943. After the campaign General Collins conducted a series of critiques on the action, which were attended by virtually all the division's officers and by key enlisted men from each unit. The record of these critiques, compiled as 25th Division Operations, is an excellent source. It includes data on the functioning of the engineer, quartermaster, medical, and signal troops as well as a detailed analysis of infantry and artillery operations. Held to establish and clarify the lessons learned in combat and to avoid future errors, the critiques are honest and frank. 25th Division Operations is the most valuable single Army divisional source relating to the Guadalcanal campaign. Most of the reports and histories of the 25th Division's component units are identical with the relevant sections of 25th Division Operations.

The main source for the Russells operation is the 43d Division's Report of the Occupation of the Russell Islands, 9 February–2 May 1943, which includes, besides a narrative account, task force and divisional plans, field orders, troop lists, and shipping schedules.

Navy Records

Several naval documents were consulted. Unless otherwise indicated, naval documents consulted are in the files of the Office of Naval Records and Library. The following records have been used:

Admiral William F. Halsey, Jr., Narrative Account of the South Pacific

Campaign, 20 April 1942–15 June 1944 (distributed 3 September 1944). This work serves the same function as General Harmon's Army in the South Pacific. A copy is filed in the Historical Division, SSUSA.

Commander in Chief, U. S. Fleet [COMINCH] (FF 1/A 3-1/A16-3 (5), Serial 00322, Basic Plan for the Establishment of the South Pacific Amphibious Force [Lone Wolf Plan], 29 April 1942. A copy of this plan is filed in Registered Documents, Plans and Policy Group, Plans and Operations Division, GSUSA.

Commander in Chief, U. S. Pacific Fleet [CINCPAC and CINCPOA] (A4-3/FF 12/A16 (6) Serial 01994), Basic Supporting Plan for Advanced Air Bases at Santa Cruz Island and Tulagi–Guadalcanal, 8 July 1942. A copy of this plan is filed in Registered Documents, Plans and Policy Group, Plans and Operations Division, GSUSA.

——(Serial 00749), Cruiser Action off Savo Island on the night of August 8–9, 1942, 26 April 1942.

——(Serial 00599), Solomon Islands Campaign from Fourth Battle of Savo, 30 November 1942, to Munda Bombardment, 4–5 January 1943, 9 March 1943 (The Fourth Battle of Savo has been renamed the "Battle of Tassafaronga.")

——(Serial 00618) Solomon Islands Campaign from 6 January 1943 Through Vila Bombardment, 23–24 January 1943, 19 March 1943.

——(Serial 00712), Solomon Islands Campaign, Fall of Guadalcanal, Period 25 January to 10 February 1943, 17 April 1943.

South Pacific Area and South Pacific Force, War Diary, 1 May 1942–30 June 1943. This diary contains the radios between COMSOPAC and his superiors and subordinates. Messages are, in general, reproduced in full, with their time groups in Greenwich Civil Time (Z time).

Commander, South Pacific Area and South Pacific Force (A4-3/A16-3, Serial 0017), Operation Plan No. 1-42, 16 July 1942.

——(Serial 0053), Preliminary Report on WATCHTOWER Operation, 16 August 1942.

Commander, Task Force 61 [Commander, Cruisers, Pacific Fleet] (Serial 0032), Operation Order No. 1-42 Operation WATCHTOWER, 28 July 1942.

Commander Aircraft South Pacific Force [Commander, Task Force 63] (A4-3/A16-3, Serial 0016), Operation Plan No. 1-42, 25 July 1942.

Commander, Amphibious Force, South Pacific Force [Commander, Task

Force 62], War Diary, 1 August 1942–28 February 1943. Admiral Turner's war diary contains, on the whole, brief entries rather than complete messages.

——(Serial 0010), Operation Plan No. A3–42, Operation WATCH-TOWER, 30 July 1942.

——(FE 25/A16–3, Serial 0055), Operation Plan No. A9–42, Task Organization, Ndeni Occupation Force, 20 August 1942. (This plan was never carried out.)

——(FE 25/4, Serial 00206), Instructions for Ships Furnishing Logistic Support to Cactus and Ringbolt, 29 September 1942.

——(Serial 00195), Report of Operation for the Reinforcement of Guadalcanal Island Forces by the 7th Marines, Reinforced, 27 September 1942.

——(Serial 00469), Report of Operations of Task Force 67 and Task Group 62.4, Reinforcement of Guadalcanal, November 8–15, 1942, and Summary of the Third Battle of Savo, 3 December 1942. (The Third Battle of Savo has been renamed the "Battle of Guadalcanal.")

——(Serial 00486), Action Report, Loss of U.S.S. *Colhoun* and the U.S.S. *Gregory,* 13 December 1942.

——(Serial 00231), Report of Rear Adm. V. A. C. Crutchley, RN [Commander, Task Group 62.6], 1st Battle of Savo Island, 8–9 August 1942, 6 April 1943.

Commander, Task Group 62.1 [Commander, Transport Divisions] South Pacific Force (Serial 0027) Report Action, Guadalcanal–Tulagi Area, Solomon Islands, August 7–8 and 9, 1942, 23 September 1942.

Marine Corps Records

General Vandegrift's Division Commander's Final Report on Guadalcanal Operation is an excellent divisional report, including a narrative report and a large number of annexes giving data on intelligence, artillery, pioneer, engineer, and medical activities, journal entries, orders, and sections from regimental histories. General Vandegrift's report is in five sections, and was issued during June, July, and August 1943. Copies of both Captain Zimmerman's monograph and General Vandegrift's report are filed in the Historical Division, SSUSA.* Complete Marine Corps records are filed in the Historical Section, Headquarters, U. S. Marine Corps.

---

* Capt. Herbert L. Merillat's popular work on the 1st Marine Division on Guadalcanal—*The Island* (Boston, 1944)—contains largely the same material as General Vandegrift's report and Captain Zimmerman's monograph, as do the Guadalcanal chapters of Maj. Frank Hough's *The Island War* (Philadelphia, 1947) and Fletcher Pratt's *The Marines' War* (New York, 1946).

Enemy Records

Besides using the enemy data in USAFISPA, XIV Corps, and Americal Division records, this volume relies heavily upon interrogations of *17th Army* officers, made in Tokyo in 1946 at the author's request by G–3 AFPAC historians and members of ATIS, SCAP. Those interrogated were as follows: Lt. Gen. Harukichi Hyakutake (former CG, *17th Army*); Lt. Gen. Masao Maruyama (former CG, *2d Division*); Maj. Gen. Shuicho Miyazaki (former C of S, *17 Army*); Maj. Gen. Harua Konuma (former staff officer, *17th Army*); Maj. Gen. Harukazu Tamaki (former CofS, *2d Division*); Maj. Gen. Tadashi Sumiyoshi (former CG, *17th Army* Artillery); Col. Shigetaka Obara (former CO, *29th Infantry*), and Col. Yoshitsugu Sakai (former CO, *16th Infantry*). General Miyazaki's Personal Account is useful, if somewhat biased. ATIS, SWPA's Enemy Publications and Current Translations, filed in the Military Intelligence Library, yield much information on enemy movements during the early days of the campaign. ATIS, SCAP's Historical Reports of Naval Operations furnish much data on naval battles.

The most comprehensive account available of Japanese operations on Guadalcanal is to be found in *17th Army* Operations (2 vols., typewritten, n.p., September, 1946), which is part of the Japanese Studies in World War II, a series now being prepared by former Japanese officers in Tokyo under the auspices of the G–2 Historical Section, U. S. Far Eastern Command, and translated by ATIS, SCAP. Volume I of *17th* Army Operations was originally begun in 1944 by Lt. Col. Norikuni Sadashima* of the War History Investigation Section of the Japanese Army General Staff, from private and official sources; Maj. Gen. Harua Konuma, a former *17th Army* staff officer, gave Sadashima his personal recollections. Those sections of Volume II, consisting of four parts of Chapter IV, which deal with Guadalcanal were begun by Lt. Col. Norikuni Tagima* (Tajima?) in 1944, using official records, personal memories, and the notes and recollections of Komuna. *17th Army* Operations, which deals with Guadalcanal, New Guinea, and the rest of the Solomons, consists largely of reproduced army and divisional orders, strung together on a thin thread of tactical narrative. It is badly organized and the accompanying maps are poor. The translation is uneven; for example, *"1st Demobilization Bureau"* is reproduced on the title page of Volume I as *"1st Mobilization Department."* Although

---

* It is possible that these names are garbled. The only Japanese list available at this writing, ATIS, SWPA's Alphabetical List of Japanese Army Officers (GHQ, SWPA, 1943), does not list a Norikuni Sadashima or a Norikuni Tagima.

Hyakutake, Miyazaki, Maruyama, and Sumiyoshi were available for interrogation, the authors of *17th Army* Operations do not appear to have consulted them. In consequence the counteroffensive in October 1942 is not clearly or fully explained. Many of the errors in tactical judgment and execution committed by the Japanese are glossed over. The study, however, possesses great value; it furnishes the student with specific data on command decisions, plans, orders, strength and casualty figures, names, and dates which are not available elsewhere. *17th Army* Operations was received by the Historical Division in late June 1948, just as this volume was about to go to press. Every one of the volume's important conclusions about the Japanese on Guadalcanal, which had been reached by studying all other available sources, was supported by *17th Army* Operations. The enemy account was therefore used to fill, wherever possible, the existing gaps and add greater precision to the narrative.

Interviews

Besides the interviews by USAFISPA historians, interviews of available American participants were conducted by the author after the war to clarify obscure or contradictory points in the official records. Generals Harmon and Patch were both dead at the inception of the author's work on this volume, but several other officers were interviewed. Those interviewed were: Lt. Gen. J. Lawton Collins (former CG, 25th Division); Maj. Gen. Pedro A. del Valle, USMC (former CO and CG, 11th Marines); Brig. Gen. Robert H. Pepper, USMC (former CO, 3d Defense Battalion); Brig. Gen. Edmund B. Sebree (former Asst Div Comdr and CG, Americal Division); Col. William W. Dick, Jr. (former CO, 8th Field Artillery Battalion); Col. William H. Allen, Jr. (former CO, 64th Field Artillery Battalion); Col. George E. Bush (former CO, 3d Battalion, 27th Infantry); Col. Paul A. Gavan (former G–3, Americal Division); Col. James J. Heriot (former CO, 90th Field Artillery Battalion); Col. Stanley R. Larsen (former CO, 2d Battalion, 35th Infantry); Col. William D. Long (former G–2, Americal Division); Col. Mervyn Magee (former ExO, Americal Division Artillery); Col. Herbert V. Mitchell (former CO, 2d Battalion, 27th Infantry); Lt. Col. Thomas J. Badger (former S–3, 64th Field Artillery Battalion); Lt. Col. Dean Benson (former S–2, 25th Division Artillery); Lt. Col. James B. Leer (former CO, 1st Battalion, 35th Infantry); Maj. Mischa N. Kadick (former CO, Headquarters Company, 25th Division Artillery); and Capt. Harry C. Schleh (former Adj, 164th Infantry). Records of these interviews are in the files of the Historical Division, SSUSA.

Published Works

[BRITISH] CENTRAL OFFICE OF INFORMATION, *Among Those Present: The Official Story of the Pacific Islands at War*. London: HM Stationery Office, 1946. This work is useful and entertaining but lacks precision.

FELDT, COMMANDER ERIC A., RAN. *The Coastwatchers*. Melbourne and New York: Oxford University Press, 1946. This exciting book, prepared by the wartime chief of the coastwatchers, contains information essential to an understanding of the South Pacific campaigns.

HALSEY, FLEET ADMIRAL WILLIAM F., and BRYAN, LT. COMDR. JULIAN. *Admiral Halsey's Story*. New York: Whittlesey House, 1947. Halsey's book is an interesting and generally accurate popular account, but the chapters on the Solomons add little new information.

KING, ADMIRAL ERNEST J. *Our Navy at War: A Report to the Secretary of the Navy Covering our Peacetime Navy and our Wartime Navy and Including Combat Operations up to March 1, 1944. U. S. News*, March 1944.

MARSHALL, GENERAL GEORGE C. *Biennial Report of the Chief of Staff of the United States Army, July 1, 1941 to June 30, 1943, to the Secretary of War*. Washington: Government Printing Office, 1943.

ROBSON, R. W. (ed.). *Pacific Islands Year Book*. Sydney: Pacific Publications, Ltd., 1942. The *Year Book* is valuable for data on geography, climate, terrain, and natives, as is the secret Survey of the Solomon Islands (2 vols) by MID, WDGS, 15 March 1943.

U. S. NAVY, OFFICE OF NAVAL INTELLIGENCE printed confidential Combat Narratives which give a good account of each naval battle, but they were prepared during the war before enemy sources became available, and are subject to future revision. Those consulted were Miscellaneous Actions in the South Pacific, 8 August 1942–22 January 1943 (1943), and the Solomon Islands Campaign, Vols. I through X.

UNITED STATES STRATEGIC BOMBING SURVEY, PACIFIC, NAVAL ANALYSIS DIVISION prepared three studies which the student of the Pacific War will find extremely valuable if he uses them with caution. *The Campaigns of Pacific War* (Washington, 1946) provides a helpful summary of naval engagements, showing Allied and Japanese forces involved and their losses, but contains some minor errors. *Interrogations of Japanese Officials* (2 vols., n.d.) is valuable, but must be taken with more than a grain of salt; it should be remembered that the Japanese officers who were interrogated were naturally anxious to make a good case for themselves. The Marshalls–Gilberts–New Britain Party of

USSBS' Naval Analysis Division prepared an excellent study in the *Allied Campaign Against Rabaul* (1946), which contains a narrative account of the Japanese side as well as the interrogations of responsible Japanese *Army* and *Navy* officers at Rabaul upon which the narrative is based. *Allied Campaign Against Rabaul* gives more information on the later phases of the Solomons campaigns than on Guadalcanal, for most of the Japanese officers who were interrogated were not at Rabaul during the first months of the Guadalcanal campaign.

The following articles, all written by men who fought on Guadalcanal, are helpful:

BAGLIEN, LT. COL. SAMUEL, "The Second Battle for Henderson Field," *Infantry Journal*, LIV, 5 (May 1944).

CASEY, CAPT. JOHN F., JR., "An Artillery Forward Observer on Guadalcanal," *Field Artillery Journal*, XXXIII, 8 (August 1943).

CATES, BRIG. GEN. CLIFTON B., (USMC), "Battle of the Tenaru [Ilu]," *Marine Corps Gazette*, XXVII, 6 (October 1943).

DEL VALLE, BRIG. GEN. PEDRO A., (USMC), "Marine Field Artillery on Guadalcanal," *Field Artillery Journal*, XXXIII, 10 (October 1943) and *Marine Corps Gazette*, XXVIII, 2 (February 1944).

GILDART, LT. COL. ROBERT F., "Guadalcanal's Artillery," *Field Artillery Journal*, XXXIII, 10 (October 1943).

UNITED STATES ARMY IN WORLD WAR II

The following volumes have been published or are in press:

The War Department
Chief of Staff: Prewar Plans and Preparations
Washington Command Post: The Operations Division
Strategic Planning for Coalition Warfare: 1941–1942
Strategic Planning for Coalition Warfare: 1943–1944
Global Logistics and Strategy: 1940–1943
Global Logistics and Strategy: 1943–1945
The Army and Economic Mobilization
The Army and Industrial Manpower

The Army Ground Forces
The Organization of Ground Combat Troops
The Procurement and Training of Ground Combat Troops

The Army Service Forces
The Organization and Role of the Army Service Forces

The Western Hemisphere
The Framework of Hemisphere Defense
Guarding the United States and Its Outposts

The War in the Pacific
The Fall of the Philippines
Guadalcanal: The First Offensive
Victory in Papua
CARTWHEEL: The Reduction of Rabaul
Seizure of the Gilberts and Marshalls
Campaign in the Marianas
The Approach to the Philippines
Leyte: The Return to the Philippines
Triumph in the Philippines
Okinawa: The Last Battle
Strategy and Command: The First Two Years

The Mediterranean Theater of Operations
Northwest Africa: Seizing the Initiative in the West
Sicily and the Surrender of Italy
Salerno to Cassino
Cassino to the Alps

The European Theater of Operations
Cross-Channel Attack
Breakout and Pursuit
The Lorraine Campaign
The Siegfried Line Campaign
The Ardennes: Battle of the Bulge
The Last Offensive

Index

☆ U.S. GOVERNMENT PRINTING OFFICE: 1988   222–406